# ESSAYS OF
# A RECLUSE

TRANSLATIONS FROM THE ASIAN CLASSICS

TRANSLATIONS FROM THE ASIAN CLASSICS

EDITORIAL BOARD:

PAUL ANDERER

DAVID LURIE

RACHEL MCDERMOTT

WEI SHANG

HARUO SHIRANE

For a complete list of books in the series,
please see the Columbia University Press website.

# ESSAYS OF A RECLUSE

## A COMPLETE TRANSLATION OF THE *QIANFULUN*

## WANG FU

TRANSLATED BY
ANNE BEHNKE KINNEY
AND JOHN S. MAJOR

Columbia University Press  *New York*

Columbia University Press
*Publishers Since 1893*
New York   Chichester, West Sussex

Translation copyright © 2025 Columbia University Press
All rights reserved

Library of Congress Cataloging-in-Publication Data

Names: Wang, Fu, approximately 76–approximately 157, author. | Kinney, Anne Behnke, translator. | Major, John S., translator.
Title: Essays of a recluse : a complete translation of the Qianfulun / Wang Fu ; translated by Anne Behnke Kinney and John S. Major.
Other titles: Qian fu lun. English
Description: New York : Columbia University Press, 2025. | Series: Translations from the Asian classics | Includes bibliographical references and index.
Identifiers: LCCN 2024043491 (print) | LCCN 2024043492 (ebook) | ISBN 9780231193603 (hardback) | ISBN 9780231220323 (trade paperback) | ISBN 9780231550413 (ebook)
Subjects: LCSH: China—History—Han dynasty, 202 B.C.–220 A.D. | LCGFT: Essays. Classification: LCC PL2663.W33 C4813 2025  (print) | LCC PL2663.W33  (ebook) | DDC 181/.11—dc23/eng/2025

Cover design: Chang Jae Lee
Cover image: Model (positive) for casting metal monster mask, late 3rd century BCE–early 3rd century CE. China. Earthenware with traces of vermillion. H x W: 5.8 x 6.6 cm (2 5/16 x 2 5/8 in). Sackler-Freer no. FS 7435-10, accession # F1916.12, EDAN ID danmdm:fsg_F1916.12. National Museum of Asian Art, Smithsonian Institution

GPSR Authorized Representative: Easy Access System Europe—Mustamäe tee 50, 10621 Tallinn, Estonia, gpsr.requests@easproject.com

# CONTENTS

*Chronology* ix
*Translators' Introduction* xi

## ESSAYS OF A RECLUSE

Preface 1

1 讚學 In Praise of Study 5

2 務本 Concentrating on the Root 17

3 遏利 Suppressing Profit 29

4 論榮 Appraising Eminence 39

5 賢難 The Difficulties of the Worthy 49

6 明闇 The Enlightened and the Unenlightened 61

7 考績 Evaluating Merit 71

8 思賢 Thinking About the Worthy 83

9 本政 The Fundamentals of Government 93

10 潛歎 The Sighs of a Recluse 105

11 忠貴 Loyalty and Nobility 117

12 浮侈 On Excessive Luxury 131

13 慎微 Taking Care Over Minutiae 147

14 實貢 Substance and Recommendation 155

15 班祿 Ranked Emoluments 165

16 述赦 On Amnesties 175

17 三式 The Three Models 191

18 愛日 Using [the People's] Time Sparingly 203

19 斷訟 Judging Legal Cases 213

20 衰制 Governing in an Age of Decline 225

21 勸將 Exhorting Generals 233

22 救邊 Securing the Frontier 243

23 邊議 Discussions of the Frontier 255

24 實邊 Populating the Frontier 265

25 卜列 Divination Set Forth 277

26 巫列 Spirit Mediums Set Forth 289

27 相列 Physiognomy Set Forth 297

28 夢列 Dreams Set Forth 305

29 釋難 Explicating Difficulties 317

30 交際 On Social Relations 327

31 明忠 Enlightenment and Loyalty 349

32 本訓 Teachings on the Root 361

33 德化 Transformation Through Virtue 369

34 五德志 Treatise on the Five Powers 381

35 志氏姓 A Record of Lineage and Clan Names 395

36 敘錄 Postface 419

*Notes* 433
*Bibliography* 549
*Index* 561

# CHRONOLOGY

| | | |
|---|---|---|
| **Shang (Yin) dynasty** | | ca. 1600–1046 BCE |
| **Zhou dynasty** | | |
| | Western Zhou | 1046–771 BCE |
| | Eastern Zhou | |
| | Spring and Autumn period | 771–479 BCE |
| | Warring States period | 479–221 BCE |
| **Qin dynasty** | | 221–206 BCE |
| **Han dynasty** | | |
| | Western Han | 206 BCE–7 CE |
| | Xin "dynasty" (Wang Mang interregnum) | 7–25 CE |
| | Eastern Han | 25–220 CE |
| **Wang Fu's lifetime** | | ca. 85–162 CE |

# TRANSLATORS' INTRODUCTION

Wang Fu's essays bring to mind the impassioned editorials penned by the elite journalists of our own age. His essays rail against the dynasty's massive cadre of salaried officials who enjoy their stipends but do little to address the difficulties and concerns of the common people. He calls out a legal system in which functionaries require large bribes to do their work and which places crushing burdens of time and travel on ordinary people embroiled in lawsuits. He fulminates about sycophants and yes-men who work to insulate their sovereigns from the true concerns of the dynasty while busying themselves with feathering their own nests. And he fumes about charlatans and grifters who hoodwink and cheat the ignorant masses with promises of blessings, wealth, and good fortune. To Wang Fu, the antidote to all of these evils lay in the individual's receptivity to the guidance of good teachers, virtuous friends, and the wisdom recorded in the Five Classics. The essays in this book thus lay bare in graphic detail the evils of the age but also propose a variety of ways to save a world that was spiraling out of control.

Wang Fu 王符 (ca. 85–162 CE) was born in Linjing 臨涇 in Anding 安定 commandery, which was located in what is now eastern Gansu and southern Ningxia Province. Anding, located well beyond the dynasty's capital, lay at the western edges of the empire and suffered constant threat from non-Chinese nomadic peoples who eventually reclaimed the area. The earliest reference to his book, the *Essays of a Recluse* (*Qianfulun* 潛夫論), is found in the *History of the Later Han Dynasty* of Fan Ye 范曄 (398–446 CE), which provides the following basic biographical information:

> Wang Fu (style name Jiexin) was a man of Linjing in Anding commandery. As a youth he loved to study and embraced high ideals. He maintained close friendships with Ma Rong 馬融, Dou Zhang 竇章, Zhang Heng 張衡, and Cui Yuan 崔瑗.[1] In Anding, as the low-ranking son of a concubine with no [significant] maternal relatives, he was looked down upon by the people in his district. From the reigns of Emperors He and An, each generation strove for official appointments, but the people of each locality only recommended those within their group.[2] Nevertheless, Fu remained upright and resolute in his resistance to vulgar customs and because of these obstacles, he never rose to hold office. Frustrated in his ambitions he lived in seclusion and wrote more than thirty essays in order to critique the failings of his age. Not wanting to reveal his name, he called his book *Essays of a Recluse*. His efforts to point out and expose the shortcomings of the age and his discussion of the affairs of the time are sufficient to provide a view of customs and politics of the time.[3]

The *Hou Hanshu* biography also includes excerpts from five of Wang Fu's essays, namely, "Luxury" (浮侈 Fuchi), "Substance and Recommendation" (實貢 Shigong), "Amnesties" (述赦 Shushe), "Using [the People's] Time Sparingly (愛日 Airi), and

TRANSLATORS' INTRODUCTION ଔ xiii

"Enlightenment and Loyalty" (明忠 Mingzhong). Wang Fu's *Hou Hanshu* biography concludes with the following anecdote:

> Later Huangfu Gui, General on the Liao, had retired and returned to Anding. A person from his district who had purchased the rank of Grand Administrator and who had also left office to return home, wrote a message asking to visit Gui.⁴ Gui was resting and did not receive him. But since he had already come in, Gui asked, "Did you enjoy the bribes you received during your tenure in the commandery?" A moment later, he was also told that Wang Fu was at the door. Gui, having long heard of Wang Fu's reputation, was very surprised. He got up, and without fastening his robe with a belt or putting on his shoes properly, went out to welcome him. He took Fu by the hand and brought him back. He sat with him and was extremely pleased. People of the period summarized the event, saying, "Seeing the prospect of a mere two-thousand cash does not compare to seeing one sleeve of a robe." This shows that it is the Way and Righteousness that scholars consider precious. Fu never served in office and died at home.⁵

Notably, the biography does not provide dates for Wang Fu's birth or death. Scholars are therefore forced to base their conjectures on the recorded birth and death dates of Wang Fu's friends or admirers, such as the literary coterie of Ma Rong, Dou Zhang, Zhang Heng, and Cui Yuan, and the general Huangfu Gui, as well as on independent historical accounts of the Qiang 羌 rebellions from 107 to 118 and 140 to 144 CE, which are also mentioned in the *Qianfulun*.⁶ Another early tribute to Wang Fu in his role as a social critic comes from the Tang-dynasty literatus, Han Yu, 韓愈 (768–824 CE), who described Wang Fu as one of the "Three Worthies" of the Eastern Han.⁷ In present times, historians writing in Western languages, such as Etienne Balazs, generally regard Wang Fu as one of "the most important eyewitness of his times, about which we would know very little if it were not for his account."⁸

## THE HISTORICAL CONTEXT

Wang Fu lived during an era of long-term and deep political decline. The Western Han dynasty (206 BCE–7 CE) ended when Wang Mang, the regent of an infant emperor, established his own short-lived dynasty, the Xin (ca. 7–25 CE). After a series of devastating floods in eastern China that caused widespread suffering and peasant rebellions, Wang Mang's many enemies raised armies that, despite the usual treachery and shifting alliances, overthrew the dynasty in 25 CE. Wang Mang died fighting for his life; his severed head was displayed on the city wall of the capital, Chang'an. In 25 CE Liu Xin, a distant relative of the Han imperial family who had joined the rebel forces, took the throne as Emperor Guangwu (r. 25–57). The Han dynasty was officially restored, though intermittent civil war persisted for another decade.

Emperor Guangwu turned out to be well suited to manage the restoration. He was a mature man, engaged in the duties of rulership and adept at managing the political maneuverings of the great families who sought to dominate both the throne and the administration of local government. His thirty-two-year reign brought much-needed stability to the dynasty. His son and successor acceded as Emperor Ming on Guangwu's death in 57 CE, with a minimum of fighting over the succession, and the transition to his successor, Emperor Zhang (r. 75–88 CE), was likewise without bloodshed. But that was where the dynasty's run of good fortune came to an end. Over the course of a century stretching to the long reign of the dynasty's last sovereign, Emperor Xian (r. 189–220 CE), a parade of young, weak, and short-lived emperors reigned as puppets of rivals for power. The struggle for control of the throne settled into a three-way contest among the great families, the professional civil-service bureaucracy, and the eunuchs of the inner palace. Cronyism and corruption infected the military, weakening the defense of the northern and western frontiers as non-Chinese pastoralists made incursions into the border regions. The dynasty was placed under further stress by the uprising circa 184 CE of a peasant army known as the Yellow Turbans. As the Song-dynasty historian Ouyang Xiu (1007–1072) wrote, "When the Yellow turbans arose, the House of Han was in great disarray," and "beyond help."[9] Wang Fu's personal account of conditions in the second half of the second century CE conveys in great detail the dynasty's mismanagement and corruption that eventually led to its collapse in 220 CE.

## CONTENTS

The essays of the *Qianfulun* focus on six broad topics: (1) the effects of corrupt and wealthy high-ranking individuals who manipulate the ruler, monopolize his attention, silence the worthy, neglect the common people, and poison the manner in which people at all levels interact with each other; (2) the deleterious effects of a litigious populace and a corrupt and decadent legal system; (3) the decline in agricultural activities prompted by excessive calls for corvee labor and increasing urbanization that drew the peasantry away from their tasks; (4) the dithering, ineffectual and timorous response of the military on the western frontier and the mismanagement of populations under attack; (5) the various forms, deficiencies, and misuses of divinatory practices that hoodwink gullible people, place them in the thrall of predatory spirit mediums, and divert their attention from self-cultivation; and (6) the consideration of cosmological forces, including the generation and circulation of qi, its connection to governance, and impact on human life. Kung-chuan Hsiao observed that "the central purpose of the entire work is to reaffirm the governmental principles of heaven's [cosmic] ordering, and of the basic importance of the people."[10] The essays of the *Qianfulun* also address the critical nature of placing worthy men in office, and the central role of the classics in education and as a touchstone for good government.

All of these topics converge in expressing Wang Fu's outrage at the corrupt government of his era and his earnest views on how to correct the situation. While other works also mention in general terms the suffering of the common people, a striking feature of the text is Wang Fu's graphic and detailed descriptions of their travails. For example, in his essay "Using the People's Time Sparingly" Wang Fu describes the obstacles ordinary people must negotiate when seeking legal action to address an injustice:

> When the common people abandon farming and sericulture and rush to an official's office, if the plaintiffs are not on time for the morning or late afternoon sessions, they are not able to report their cases; and if they do not offer some kind of gift they will not be seen. Whether there is a case or not, the process always goes on for days or months so that the entire household must abandon their work in order to watch over the case, and the litigant's family must always ask a neighbor to respond to [the

TRANSLATORS' INTRODUCTION ○꽤 xvii

officials' questions] or to send them food. When the case concludes, a year's labor has been lost, and in this world there are always those who have starved as a result.

The essays also provide a valuable account of the period that extends beyond the capital to the peripheral areas of the Eastern Han Empire, and which represents the perspective of a man who was deemed unsuitable to hold office because he was the son of a concubine. The views of a social and geographical outsider are bound to provide insights into experiences that escaped the capital elite. Wang Fu's outsider status may also explain the curious omission of any discussion of eunuchs—a social class credited with triggering the chaotic demise of the later Han.[11]

Looking at Wang Fu's own summary of the *Qianfulun* in his postface, he not only states his aim to "transmit the teachings of the Five Classics" but also significantly summarizes his work as an effort to "emulate the worthies of former times" and "transmit the teachings of Zuo Qiuming," namely, the *Zuozhuan* (Zuo commentary to the *Spring and Autumn Annals*), and the *Guoyu* (Conversations of the states)."[12] While Wang Fu refers to all of these sources, his approach to remedying the tide of misrule, corruption, and vicious factionalism in his own time most frequently draws upon the recurring themes, strategies, and concerns of the third century BCE texts, the *Zuozhuan* and the *Guoyu*, as guides for dealing with political disorder.[13]

## THE GENRE

Wang Fu's work is an example of the genre called *lun* (variously translated as "discourse" or "essay"), which figures as one of the major forms of literary expression from Han times through the fifth century CE. Two descriptions of the major categories of writing from this period are still extant. One is found in the *Lunheng* 論衡 of Wang Chong 王充 (27–97 CE) and the other, which comes a century later, is preserved in the *Dianlun* of 典論 of Cao Pi 曹丕 (ca. 187–226 CE).¹⁴ Both of these summaries mention *lun*. Cao describes the eight major literary forms as follows: "Though all writing is essentially the same, the specific forms differ. Thus, memorials (*zou*) and deliberations (*yi*) should be decorous; letters; (*shu*) and essays (*lun*) should be reasonable and well organized; inscriptions (*ming*) and dirges (*lei*) should stick to the facts; poetry (*shi*) and rhyme-prose (*fu*) should be ornate [夫文本同而末異. 蓋奏議宜雅, 書論宜理, 銘誄尚實, 詩賦欲麗]."¹⁵ This statement tells us little about *lun*, apart from its characterization as "reasonable and well organized." It nevertheless singles out *lun* as one of the major divisions of Chinese literary forms. Wang Chong also distinguishes *lun* as one of the major categories of literature: "The Five Canons and the Six Arts form one class of literature, the records of the various masters are another, essays [論] and treatises are one class, memorials and reports are one, and so are the descriptions of generous and virtuous actions. The writers of these five classes of literature should all be regarded as worthies."¹⁶ Wang Chong then continues, describing how *lun* is more challenging than the other categories due to its dual focus on analyzing present-day events and expressing one's deepest concerns: "The composition of essays and the writing of discourses [造論] requires the greatest efforts, for to give expression to the thoughts of one's heart and to discuss the events of life is a more arduous task than to comment upon old classics or to supplement old texts."¹⁷ Wang Chong's stated commitment to analyzing present-day concerns is likely linked to his distaste for a contemporary trend that favored the composition of long-winded commentaries on classical works known as *zhangju* 章句,

"commentaries in paragraphs and sentences." These tedious interlinear notes, which were appended to and often overwhelmed each line of the classics, were criticized for distracting readers and preventing them from absorbing the text itself.

Wang Chong was not alone in expressing a distaste for this academic trend. The biographies of the great luminaries of the day—Yang Xiong 揚雄 (53 BCE–18 CE), Huan Tan 桓譚 (ca. 43 BCE–28 CE), and Ban Gu (32–92 CE) 班固—all specifically state that they did not make "commentaries in sentences and paragraphs" but instead emphasized discussion of the central ideas and broad significance of the classics in independent, noninterlinear writing.[18] In 55 CE, even Emperor Guangwu issued an edict decrying the excessive length of expositions on the classics in paragraphs and sentences and ordered that deliberations should be held to reduce them.[19] Wang Fu's failure to mention *zhangju* scholarship may suggest that this practice was no longer a pressing issue.[20] Nevertheless, both Wang Fu and Wang Chong leveled contempt for another form of writing: the verbal fireworks of *fu* (rhyme-prose). Their disapproval followed that of Yang Xiong, who forsook the genre in which he excelled because he believed that it encouraged rather than restrained luxury and extravagance.[21] In the *Lunheng*, Wang Chong interprets the sumptuous and florid language of rhyme-prose as an inadequate attempt to present facts: "If those who are skilled in rhyme-prose and eulogies, writing in grand and highly polished style, are considered worthies, then this must indeed be the case for Sima Xiangru and Yang Ziyun. Their styles were refined, their scope was grand, their expressions were exquisite, and their meanings were deep. But they could not find out right and wrong or discriminate between truth and falsehood."[22] Wang Fu is slightly more measured in his view of rhyme-prose and suggests that, while there is nothing inherently suspect about the genre, contemporary rhyme-prose exerts a bad influence on ignorant people and children:

> *Shi* poetry and rhyme-prose are the means for expressing the forces of good and evil and for revealing the emotions of sorrow and joy. Therefore, geniality and elegance are used to expand compositions, and metaphors and illustrations are used to plumb the meaning. [But] nowadays, writers of rhyme-prose and eulogies carelessly create prolix, catchy, and infelicitous phrases, and competitively circulate deceptive and fantastical occurrences so as to be treated as extraordinary in their generation. Ignorant and naïve people follow along and marvel at them. This is a case of corrupting children's thoughts and perpetuating insincere words.[23]

Wang Fu's repudiation of lowbrow rhetoric and sensational subject matter thus ally him with other Han writers of book-length *lun*, such as Wang Chong. Still, the various usages of parallel prose in the *Qianfulun* as discussed below demonstrate that Wang Fu's own writing reflects his attention to both aesthetic flourishes as well as didactic concerns.

The importance of *lun* as a literary genre is also reflected in the *Hou Hanshu* "Collected Biographies of Writers."[24] Taking into account only those genres used by nine or more writers who are listed in this section of the *Hou Hanshu*, we are left with five forms: rhyme-prose, dirges (*lei* 誄), eulogies (*song*), essays (*lun*), and letters (*shu* 書). Approximately half of the writers composed rhyme-prose, while a third were noted for composing *lun*.[25] Elsewhere in the *Hou Hanshu*, among the twenty-six individuals whose biographies include a list of the literary genres they practiced, the three genres of letters, rhyme-prose, and essays predominate.[26] These figures help to reconstruct the importance of the essay as a Han literary genre that is still generally overlooked or overshadowed by the very form it sought to expose as trite and overblown: rhyme-prose.

## THE ORGANIZATION, LITERARY STYLE, AND LANGUAGE OF THE *QIANFULUN*

The *Qianfulun* contains thirty-five substantive chapters that fall into five general categories: philosophy, cosmology, social criticism, military affairs, and the role of the worthy. All of the chapters are in essay form apart from one dialogue, "Explicating Difficulties," and the postface. Wang Fu opens the postface with a rhymed account of what prompted him to write the text, followed by a table of contents that is also set in rhyme. Wang Fu, who never served in office, compared his written legacy to the words of obscure and uncultured "grass and fuel gatherers" who were nevertheless consulted by the sages of ancient times. He also saw his work as a means to transmit lessons on morality and rulership found in the classics and other works from former times.[27] Jin Fagen suggests that the bulk of the *Qianfulun* was written between 144 and 163 CE, the period in which Wang Fu had settled into retirement in his native Anding.[28]

Unlike the arrangement of chapters in texts such as the *Lüshi Chunqiu* 呂氏春秋, which reflects an overarching structure that determines the placement of each chapter, the ordering of chapters in the *Qianfulun* is significant only in its conformance to the convention of opening a book with an essay on study.[29] Nevertheless, a number of essays that address a common subject are organized in groups, such as the chapters on the frontier or those addressing divination and various religious practices.[30]

Stylistically, the text alternates between passages in parallel or "semantically patterned" prose, with its dense, lapidary (and often particle-free) units of equal length, which W. A. C. H. Dobson calls "Late Han Classical Chinese," in contrast to a looser style in lines of irregular length that utilize the full scope of particles found in written texts of this period, which Dobson calls "Late Han Literary Chinese."[31] The alternation between the two modes—semantically patterned parallel prose and a looser contemporary style—creates two distinct textures in Wang Fu's prose.

Parallel prose lends to certain passages what Dobson calls an "antique effect."[32] Wang Fu often uses it to formulate expressions that seem to convey unassailable, "in the beginning . . . ," eternal truths. For example, chapter 32 of the *Qianfulun*, "Teachings on the Root," begins with seventeen parallel phrases describing the transformation of qi in the cosmogonic process that ultimately generates human beings. Wang Fu uses this block of four-character phrases to posit a monolithic and seemingly unimpeachable basis for the development of his thesis on how the human generation of harmonious qi can be applied to elicit the Great Peace.[33]

Wang Fu also uses the shift between these two modes, that is, semantically patterned and contemporary styles, for the purpose of explication. Stylistic contrast of this sort often involves presenting a quotation from an early text followed by a rendering into contemporary language that is presumably easier to understand, as in the following example from chapter 13, "Taking Care Over Minutiae."

A passage in the *Odes* says,

"Heaven protects and establishes you,
With the greatest security;

TRANSLATORS' INTRODUCTION ❧ xxiii

> Makes you single-minded and stout-hearted,
> That you may enjoy every happiness;
> Grants you much increase,
> So that you have all in abundance."[34]

> How fine are these words! They state that Heaven protects and aids the king, determining that his character and fate is most firm and secure. [As Heaven] makes you trustworthy and generous, how can you not secure good order? It profusely benefits you [with great abundance] that extends to the common people.

Wang Fu also relies on parallel prose to emphasize what is essential, affirm what is true, or to correct what is wrong. For example, in chapter 19, "Judging Legal Cases," he first raises what seems to be a popular misapprehension of the facts surrounding the conduct of two emperors and then sets the record straight using the emphatic "boldface" tone of parallel prose [italics added here for emphasis]:

> Is it possible that these two emperors, because of their love of money, brought harm to eminent subjects? In fact, they sought to
> *extirpate* the beginnings of deceit and fraud,
> *enforce* the laws of state and family, and
> *preempt* the causes of disaster and discord,
> in order to benefit the people."

Parallel prose is also occasionally used to create interlinking structures that demonstrate sequences, hierarchies, and connections among various things. In the following example from chapter 1, "In Praise of Study," Wang Fu casts the object of each clause as the modified subject of the next, resulting in pronouncements such as the following:

What Heaven and earth value is human beings.
What the sages revere is righteousness.
What virtue and righteousness produce is wisdom.
What enlightened wisdom seeks is learning.

The parallel structure not only underscores the ways in which the four subjects—Heaven, human beings, righteousness, and wisdom—are connected, but it also stresses the ultimate product of that interlinkage: namely, learning, the topic of this essay. A similar structure is also employed in which parallel phrases trace the generation of chain reactions. In the following case from chapter 30, "On Social Relations," the cascading effects of mutually profitable relationships among cronies proceed in one direction that ultimately lead to undeserved praise. In contrast, the second part traces how the virtue of impartiality can lead to disapproval and slander:

In the mutual generosity of common people,

The existence of profit gives rise to intimacy
the accumulation of intimacy gives rise to love;
the accumulation of love gives rise to approval; and
the accumulation of approval gives rise to regarding them as worthy.

If the emotions deem a person to be worthy, then unwittingly,

the heart will love him, and
the mouth will praise him.

The absence of benefit produces distance;
the accumulation of distance produces hatred;

the accumulation of hatred produces disapproval;
the accumulation of disapproval produces loathing.

If the emotions deem a person loathsome, then, unwittingly,

the heart will reject him; and
the mouth will slander him.

One final expression of parallel phrases appears in chapter 27, "Physiognomy Set Forth," in which Wang Fu creates a list of paired names using little further information to allude to stories recounted in the *Guoyu* and *Zuozhuan*, with the assumption that the reader will be familiar with the details:

Wangsun Yue read the face of Qiaoru,
Zishang examined Shangchen,
Ziwen feared Yue Jiao,
Shuji detested Shiwo,
Lord Xiang of Shan observed Li of Jin,
Zigong observed Zhu and Lu,
Zangwen heard Yuyue, and
Chen Xian saw Zhang [lacuna].

The educated reader in Han times was likely familiar with all of the anecdotes connected with the people mentioned above. Nevertheless, in the *Huainanzi* (ca. 139 BCE) and the *Lunheng*, there is a tendency to recount the entire story or at least provide a synopsis. It is possible that Wang Fu chose this form of "shorthand" to provide a thorough coverage of pertinent exemplars that also avoided including the complex details of each of the stories, all of which ultimately illustrate the same essential point, namely, that a talented physiognomer can discern a person's fate by analyzing his face or comportment.

In addition to the alternation of tight parallel units and looser, modern prose, euphonic effects that are almost impossible to reproduce in English are used throughout the text. For example, in the following lines from chapter 1, the impact of rhyme and assonance disappears in the translation of the four lines following "But when he comes to study":

his acuity and discernment become unobscured [*bias*], and
his mind and knowledge become unhindered [*des*].
[He turns to] the past and draws together [the successes and
    failures] of emperors and kings [*wan*];
he looks ahead and predicts [events for] one hundred [future]
    generations [*sas*].[35]

This passage is cast in four-character phrases with rhymes occurring at the end of each clause. Because it is surrounded by unrhymed lines of irregular length, the stylistic shift to rhymed phrases highlights this portion of the text. Elsewhere, the phonetic values of entire lines create euphonic effects. In "In Praise of Study," for example, Wang Fu compares studying to the work of a lapidary, noting that human beings are improved by learning in the same way that inanimate objects are primed for use. He then cites the example of precious jades offered to the throne in unpolished form that were rejected because the rough-hewn gems, "unground and unpolished, ... could not be distinguished from rocks" [*putek, putsak, puliai, lekdzak*]. This phonetically striking phrase punctuates the introductory section of the paragraph, signaling a transition to a new set of metaphors that make a different point. Elsewhere, as in the example below from chapter 30, the repeated use of a velar stop rhyme (*-k) seems to hammer into the reader's mind the futility of a social situation in which everyone who lacks high position or aristocratic rank is a regarded as a loser:

> It is easy for the rich and noble to achieve gratification;
> it is difficult for the poor and low-born to achieve satisfaction. (sek)
>
> If you have nice clothes—you're called "extravagant and a climber";
> if you have bad clothes—you're called "destitute and distressed." (?ek)
>
> [If you] move slowly—you're labeled "starving and feeble";
> [if you] move quickly—you're labeled "evades responsibility." (tsrek)
>
> [If you] do not visit superiors—you're labeled "haughty and rude";
> [if you] come repeatedly—you're labeled "looking for food." (zik)
>
> [If you] arrive empty-handed—you're labeled "thoughtless";
> [if you] present a gift—you're labeled "wants a loan." (tek)
>
> [If you] are respectful and unassuming—you're considered worthless;
> [if you're] firm and assertive—you're considered unvirtuous. (tek)

These are

> the halters and restraints of unemployed scholars and;
> the difficulties and abuses of the poor and lowborn. (kouk)[36]

In summary, the incisive analysis of *Qianfulun* derives much of its power from the vivid language and the variety of forms Wang Fu used to describe and call attention to the broken world around him.

## TEXTUAL HISTORY

The *Qianfulun* is listed as a work in ten *juan* in the bibliographic sections of the *Suishu* 隋書, the *Jiu Tangshu* 舊唐書, the *Tangshu* 唐書, and the *Songshi* 宋史. The earliest attested edition, a Song-dynasty manuscript, is reproduced in the *Sibu congkan zhengbian* 四部叢刊, though the original manuscript of this edition has been lost.[37] Wang Jipei 汪繼培 (1775–?) mentions seeing a Yuan-dynasty edition (ca. 1297), but this manuscript has also been lost. Nevertheless, Wang used the Yuan-dynasty edition as a base for his 1814 *Qianfulun jian* 潛夫論箋.[38] Wang Jipei's collated work has been generally regarded as the standard edition of the text and was included in the 1819 *Huhailou congshu* 湖海樓叢書. It was also the edition used in the *Sibu beiyao* 四部備 compiled by the Zhonghua Publishing House 中華書局 in 1936.[39]

An updated version of Wang Jipei's *Qianfulun* with modern punctuation and numbered notes was published by Shanghai Ancient Texts Press (Shanghai guji chubanshe 上海古籍出版社) in 1978. Peng Duo 彭鐸 has supplemented Wang Jipei's work with valuable additional notes and emendations in his 1985 *Qianfulun jianjiaozheng* 潛夫論箋校正 published by Zhonghua shuju. This edition also includes an appendix that reproduces important comments, prefaces, and colophons related to the *Qianfulun*.

Important modern editions with extensive notes include: Hu Chusheng 胡楚生 *Qianfulun jishi* 潛夫論集釋 (Taipei: Dingwen chubanshe, 1979); Peng Duo 彭鐸, *Qianfulun jianjiaozheng* 潛夫論箋校正 (Beijing: Zhonghua shuju, 1985); The *Xinyi Qianfulun* 新譯夫論 by Chen Manming 陳滿銘 and Peng Bingcheng 彭丙成 (Taipei: Sanmin shuju, 1998); the *Wang Fu Qianfulun yizhu* 王符潛夫論 譯注 of Hu Dajun, 胡大浚, Li Zhongli 李仲立, and Li Deqing 李德奇 (Lanzhou: Gansu Renmin chubanshe,

1991), and the *Qianfulun quanyi* 潛夫論全譯 of Zhang Jue 張覺 (Guiyang: Guizhou Renmin chubanshe, 1991). Zhang Jue's work represents the edition with the most extensive annotations and analyses. The entire text of the present-day edition *Qianfulun* is approximately 51,582 characters in length.

## ABOUT THIS TRANSLATION

The text that has come down to the present is damaged and includes lacunae as well as scribal errors. Lacunae are indicated in our translation, as are all readings that deviate from the standard modern edition of Wang Jipei. When commentaries offer conflicting views of what is missing in the text or offer multiple interpretations of words that are clearly scribal errors, our notes identify which commentator we have followed. In the translation, we use a single indent for parallel prose and a double indent for verse such as quotations from the *Odes*. Endnotes cite the Chinese-language sources for early Chinese texts quoted in the *Qianfulun* as well as their English-language translations, including close equivalents that have been modified for incorporation into Wang Fu's prose.

As is often the case in early Chinese texts, the postface—which for the *Qianfulun* comprises the individual prefaces for chapters 1 through 35—appears at the end of the text as chapter 36. To assist modern readers of our translation, we also place each preface at the beginning of its respective chapter. For continuity, notes to the postface appear only in chapter 36.

We are grateful to Cynthia Col for her excellent work creating our index.

# PREFACE

Now, among those born in this age,
Honor is given to those who achieve great deeds.
"The very greatest establish virtue,
Beneath them are those who establish words."
Being useless and untalented,
Lacking the capacity that would enable me to hold office,
I have never even served in the humblest of positions,
And have no way to bring about this sort of contribution.
From the core of my heart I am often possessed by emotion,
And pick up my brush and jot down various compositions.
These words bring together my foolish sentiments,
And simply keep them from being forgotten.
Though the grass and fuel gatherers were obscure and uncultured,
Sages of ancient times still consulted them.
I have made a draft emulating former worthies,
In thirty-six chapters,
In order to transmit the lessons of former times,
The works of Zuo Qiuming, and the Five Classics.

# CHAPTER 1 PREFACE

In the transmitted legacy of the sages of former times,
Nothing is greater than their teachings.
Their learning was broad and their memories prodigious;
When in doubt they pondered and inquired.
Their knowledge and insight was thereby formed, and
Their virtue and righteousness was thereby established.
Confucius was fond of study, and
"In his instruction of others he was tireless."

Thus I have written "In Praise of Study," chapter 1.

# 1

# IN PRAISE OF STUDY

What Heaven and earth value is human beings.[1]
What the sages revere is righteousness.[2]
What virtue and righteousness produce is wisdom.
What enlightened wisdom seeks is learning.

Though [one may] possess consummate sagacity, one is not born knowing.
Though [one may] possess consummate skill, one is not born able.

An old chronicle says,

Huangdi was taught by Feng Hou;
Zhuan Xu was taught by Lao Peng;
Di Ku was taught by Zhu Rong;

Yao was taught by Wu Cheng;
Shun was taught by Ji Hou;
Yu was taught by Mo Ru;
Tang was taught by Yi Yin;

[Kings] Wen and Wu were taught by Jiang Shang;
the Duke of Zhou was taught by Shu Xiu, [and]
Confucius was taught by Lao Dan.³

If these statements are true, then people cannot but follow a teacher. Now these eleven rulers were all sages of the highest order. By attending to learning,

> their knowledge became extensive, and
> their virtue became great.

How much more is this the case for ordinary people? Therefore,

> The artisan who wants to excel at his work must first sharpen his tools.⁴
> The scholar who wishes to disseminate his righteousness must first recite his texts.⁵

The *Yi* says, "Superior persons familiarize themselves with the words and deeds of former times in order to enhance their virtue."⁶ Hence, for people there is learning, just as for things there is priming. Therefore, though Xia Hou's jade arc and He of Chu's jade disc were [both] jades that possessed the qualities of Bian He's rough-hewn gem, unground and unpolished, they could not be distinguished from rocks.⁷ Now, the raw materials of

> *fu* and *gui* vessels, and
> court and sacrificial clothing,

are merely

> the wood of mountain wilds, and
> the silk of worm's cocoons.⁸

[But] if you direct

> a Clever Chui to apply the marking-cord and work [the wood] with axe and hatchet,
> and women artisans to apply the five colors and work [the silk] with loom and shuttle,

then they become

> the vessels of the ancestral temple, and
> the emblazonry of robes and vestments,

that can be

> displayed before ghosts and spirits, and
> presented to princes and dukes.[9]

How much more does this apply to the superior man's

> honest and pure nature, [and his]
> discerning and perceptive capacities?

> Assist him with virtuous friends,
> instruct him with perceptive teachers,
> refine him with music and the rites,[10]
> guide him with the *Odes* and *Documents*,
> assist him with the *Zhou Changes*, and
> enlighten him with the *Spring and Autumn Annals*.

How can he not succeed?

> A passage in the *Book of Odes* says,

> Look at the wagtail,
> Flying and at the same time twittering.
> My days are advancing;
> Your months are going on.
> Rising early and retiring late,
> Do not disgrace those who gave you birth.[11]

For this reason, "the superior man's vigilance throughout the day," his progress in virtue, and his cultivation of learning do not simply broaden him personally.[12] Isn't it the case that it also prompts [him] to consider and transmit his ancestors' good name so that he may glorify his father and mother?

Confucius said, "Once I went the entire day without eating and did not go to sleep all night for the sake of contemplation. It was of no benefit. It does not measure up to studying."

> Even farming sometimes entails times of shortage; and
> even learning may incidentally lead to high salary.

But the superior man's anxieties concern the progress of the Way; he has no anxiety concerning poverty.[13]

> The Count of Ji set forth the "Six Limitations."[14]
> The "Airs of the States" sing of the "Northern Gate."[15]

Therefore, as for "not being anxious about poverty," how can one be fond of poverty and deny its anxieties? Is it not the case that when the will is concentrated, it illuminates what is most important? It is for this reason that the superior man's pursuit of abundance and plenty is not for [the pursuit of] sumptuous food, fine clothing, or depraved enjoyment of music or sensuality, but in fact, so that he can depend on it to realize the Way and proceed in virtue.

Now,

The Way is perfected through learning and is stored in writings; study progresses with effort and is ruined by neglect.

Hence,

Dong Zhongshu throughout his life did not inquire about the affairs of his family and
Jing Junming passed a year without leaving home.

They attained

subtlety in learning, and
distinction in their occupations,

because they were men of wealthy families.[16] Those who are wealthy and leisured in this way and yet capable of diligence and concentration are men of talent.

Ni Kuan sold his labor as a cook, and
Kuang Heng hired himself out as an indentured laborer

because of poverty.[17] Those who are poor and straitened such as these men, yet able to persist in study as they did, are accomplished scholars. Scholars of the present age generally number in the tens of thousands, but those who actually finish what they set out to accomplish number no more than ten. Why is this so?

If they are wealthy, then affluence impairs their concentration.
If they are poor, then deprivation interferes with their plans.

Some, because of mourning or disorder, delay [their education] for years.[18] This is why they turn away from what they had begun, sacrifice their attainments, and revert back to childish ignorance.[19] Hence, for those lacking

Dong or Jing's talent, or
Ni or Kuang's determination,

but who force themselves to abandon their families and devote themselves to squandering their days at the gates of teachers, there is surely no hope. Now, these four men, [who were endowed with] keen ears, perceptive eyes, loyalty, trustworthiness, incorruptibility, and bravery, were not necessarily without equal. But having established their reputations and accomplished good deeds, their virtuous acclaim and high regard are imperishable; and there is a basis for this state of affairs. What is the reason? It is simply that they were able to

entrust themselves to the laws and canons of the sages of ancient times, and
concentrate their minds on the teachings transmitted by Confucius.

It is for this reason that

[If] Zao Fu ran swiftly, after a hundred paces, he would have to stop. [But] entrusting himself to a chariot, he could sit and be conveyed a thousand *li*.[20]

If a sailor drifting behind the rear of a ship became detached from the hawser, he would drown. [But] with boat and oar, he could sit and cross the Yangzi and Yellow Rivers.[21]

Hence, the superior man does not surpass others in his generation because of innate qualities but because he is skilled at entrusting himself to things.[22]

The [variety of] human temperaments and natures number less than one hundred, but [the differences in] discernment and wisdom range in the ten-thousands. This is not due to the quality of a person's true nature; it is often rather the utilization of things that brings it about. The superior person's inborn disposition is never completely enlightened. But when he comes to study,

> his acuity and discernment become unobscured, and
> his mind and knowledge become unhindered.

> [He turns to] the past and draws together [the successes and failures] of emperors and kings;
> he looks ahead and predicts [events for] one hundred [future] generations.

This, then, is the Dao's light, but the superior person is simply able to make use of it to illuminate himself.

Therefore, the Way is present in the heart in the same way that fire is present in a person's eyes. In a pit or cellar, all is pitch-dark; nothing can be seen. But once it is decked with numerous oil lamps, a hundred things will become clear. This, then, is the fire's brilliance, not the eyes' brightness. But if the eyes utilize it, then they will become perceptive.

The Way of Heaven and Earth, and
the workings of spirit illumination

cannot be seen. But if one

studies the canons of the sages, and
considers the principles of the Way,

then all things will come to be perceived. This, then, is

the substance of the Way, and not
the brilliance of the mind.

But if people utilize it, then they will make themselves knowledgeable.

Therefore,

for one who searches for something in a dark room, nothing is superior to fire.
For one who searches for the Way in this generation, nothing is superior to the canons.

The "canons" are the classics, the body of writings formulated by the sages of former times. The sages of former times who grasped the essence of the Way put it into practice themselves, hoping that worthy people would strive to enter the Way. Thus, the sages formulated the canon to be passed down to later worthies, just as Clever Chui created the compass, the square, the level, and the marking-cord to be passed down to craftsmen of later times.

In former times, Chui's craft was such that

his eye [alone allowed him to form] perfect circles and squares, and
his mind could determine what was level or straight.

Furthermore, he made the compass, the marking-cord, the square, and inked [lines] in order to instruct men of later ages. If one tried to make the disciples of Xi Zhong and Gong Ban discard these four gauges and imitate Chui's [ability to] determine [measurements] on their own, they would surely fail.[23] But if an ordinary craftsman or carpenter [grasps] a compass, holds a square, applies a level, and draws out a marking-cord, his craft can be the same as Chui's. Hence, Chui used his mind to devise the compass and square, and later craftsmen, using the compass and square, from then on could match the [measuring abilities of] Chui's mind. Therefore, craftsmen who use these measuring tools come close to Chui's [genius].

The wisdom of the sages of former times was such that

their hearts were in communication with spirit illumination, and
their natures were in direct contact with the Way and Moral Potency.

Moreover, they created the canon and laws to pass on to men of future times. If a worthy or a superior man was divested of learning and made to rely only upon his own resources, the effort would prove insufficient. But if they are made to follow a teacher, attend to learning, and rely upon the canon,

their perspicacious and penetrating brilliance,
their virtuous and righteous principles,

will be great indeed.

It is for this reason that

the sages used their own wisdom to create the canons and laws;
and
later men use these canons and laws to proceed in agreement with the sages.

Thus, the virtue of worthies who study the canon is close to that of the sage.
A passage in the *Book of Odes* says,

The high mountains, I look up at them,
The great road, I travel it.[24]

But by daily progress and monthly advance;
I will learn from those who are continuously bright in their enlightenment.[25]

Therefore, for all who desire to

manifest merit and accomplishments, and
display honor and eminence,

nothing is superior to learning.

# CHAPTER 2 PREFACE

Officers engaging in study,
Value the root and scorn the branch.
Great men are not flamboyant;
Gentlemen concentrate on substance.
Although ritual propriety facilitates social interactions, and
One must begin by presenting gifts,
Current customs rush toward the inessential,
Which I fear will destroy the practices [of the sage].

Thus I have written "Concentrating on the Root," chapter 2.

# 2
# CONCENTRATING ON THE ROOT

Among the greatest principles of ruling, none is better than suppressing the branch and concentrating on the root; none could be more harmful than neglecting the root and refining the branch.¹

Now, in ruling a country,

> enriching the people is considered the root, and
> rectifying learning is considered the foundation.²

> Only when the people are enriched can they be taught.³
> Only when learning is orthodox will they attain righteousness.⁴
> If people are poor, they will turn their backs on goodness;
> if learning is unorthodox, they will become deceitful and false.⁵
> If people enter into study, they will not be unruly;
> if they attain to righteousness, they will be loyal and filial.

Therefore, the method of the enlightened ruler concentrates on these two to form a foundation for the Great Peace and to summon propitious and felicitous signs.

Now, to enrich the people,

> farming and sericulture are considered the root;
> itinerant occupations are considered the branch.

For the various crafts,

> maximum utility is considered the root;
> clever ornamentation is considered the branch.

In trade,

> putting goods into circulation is considered the root;
> selling curiosities is considered the branch.

In these three areas,

> if one protects the root and abandons the branch, the people will be enriched;
> if one abandons root and protects the branch, the people will be impoverished.
>
> Impoverished, they will be distressed and forget virtue.
> Enriched, they will be content and may be educated.

In educational instruction,

> the Way and righteousness are considered the root,
> clever debate is considered the branch.

In forms of speech and expression,

truthfulness and integrity are considered the root,
artifice and ornamentation are considered the branch.

For eminent officers,

filial devotion and fraternal submission are considered the root;
making friends and forming contacts is considered the branch.[6]

For the filial and fraternal,

devoted care is considered the root;
ostentatious display is considered the branch.

For officials,

loyalty and uprightness are considered the root;
fawning love is considered the branch.

With respect to these five,

if one protects the root and abandons the branch, then benevolence and righteousness will flourish.[7]
If one abandons the root and protects the branch, then the Way and its Power will collapse.

To be careful about the root and to neglect the branch is permissible.
But to set aside the root and concentrate on the branch is despicable.

Now,

employing the Way of Heaven,
distinguishing the advantages of earth,

the six domestic animals bearing young in due season,
the myriad things accumulating in the wilds—

these are the root of enriching the country.[8] Itinerant and "branch" occupations that take profits from the people are the sources of impoverishment of the state.

Loyalty, truth, care, and caution—these are the foundation of virtue and righteousness.
Emptiness, nothingness, falsity, and deception—these are the roots that disorder the Way.

Therefore, working the land is the way to enrich the nation. But nowadays, the people eschew farming and sericulture, taking up itinerant occupations instead. They spread out to gouge the populace at large for profit and accumulate it in one household. Although in some private families there is wealth, public resources nevertheless become increasingly impoverished.[9]

The hundred craftsmen are the means by which utensils are supplied. A utensil is considered

good if it is serviceable, and
superior if it is sturdy.

Nowadays, craftsmen like to create carved and polished wares, cunningly and artfully decorating them in order to beguile people and take their money. Although the conniving craftsmen profit, national resources grow increasingly debilitated.

Trade is the means by which goods are circulated.[10] Goods

are necessary if they are useful, and
valuable if they are durable.

But merchants nowadays compete to sell useless items and extravagantly luxurious goods in order to bewitch the people into acquiring such property. Although the unscrupulous merchant makes a gain, the nation's economy in this way faces increasing losses.

On the surface, though these three groups have their personal reputations for strenuous effort and wealthy households, nevertheless, beneath it all is the public reality that the people are injured and the nation's economy is impoverished.[11] Therefore, if those who wield the government

> wisely supervise craftsmen and merchants and do not enable their indecent guile,
> hinder and shame those of itinerant occupations and do not allow the monopolization of profits,
>
> relax restrictions on essential agriculture, and
> favor and promote learned men,

then the people will be enriched and the nation will be at peace.

Now, education is the means by which one can put into practice the methods of the Way and exalt virtue and righteousness. Nowadays, scholars

> like to discuss matters of emptiness and nothingness, and
> compete to compose writings of intricacies and allure

so as to be treated as unique in their generation.¹² Ordinary people of little knowledge follow after them in veneration. This is a case of

> injuring the substance of the Way and the virtue, and
> befuddling large numbers of ignorant people.

*Shi* poetry and rhyme-prose are the means for

> expressing the forces of good and evil, and
> revealing the emotions of sorrow and joy.

Therefore,

> delicacy and elegance are used to expand the composition, and
> metaphors and illustrations are used to plumb the meaning.¹³

[But] nowadays, writers of rhyme-prose and eulogies

> carelessly create prolix, catchy, and infelicitous phrases, and
> competitively circulate deceptive, false, and fantastical occurrences

so as to be treated as extraordinary in their generation.¹⁴ Ignorant and naive people follow along and marvel at them. This is a case of

> corrupting children's thoughts, and
> perpetuating insincere words.

> Offering devotion toward one's father and mother,
> maintaining proper deportment in the family residence

are the means by which one becomes an exemplary officer. [But] nowadays, most concentrate on making friends in order to receive the patronage of cliques, deceiving the world and misappropriating fame in order to get ahead. Those who praise the superficial follow and revere them. This behavior

> threatens the integrity of the pure official, and
> bedazzles the minds of the common people.

Sustaining life and complying [with the wishes of parents] are the measures by which one is deemed filial.[15] But nowadays, many disregard their parent's wishes and are stingy in their care. They are frugal while their parents are alive as they await their demise. And it is only upon a parent's death that they

> lavishly prepare funerary arrangements to express their filiality; and
> sumptuously entertain guests to seek fame.

Flatterers follow and praise them. These circumstances, which confound true deeds of filiality and interfere with the younger generation's feelings of mourning, are distressing.

> To be loyal and correct in serving one's ruler, and
> to be honest and law-abiding in keeping order among one's inferiors

is the means by which one executes the duties of office. But nowadays, the majority

> deceive and flatter to win favor; and
> twist the law with their glib talk.

Opportunists follow their lead and think them worthy. This state of affairs works to

> obliterate acts of true purity and goodness, and
> opens wellsprings of confusion and danger.

Although these five groups

> outwardly possess empty reputations for promoting awesome sagacity and talent,
> within they have the full capacity to injure the Way and virtue.[16]

All eight of these [behaviors] are fundamental to a weakened age and are what an unenlightened ruler conceals.[17] Although none of these approaches the enormity of usurpation or regicide, they still in fact constitute a gradual encroachment that throws the Way into confusion.

Now, managing the growing or diminishing of the root and branch is all in the hands of the ruler. It is not something that can be changed by the common people. Indeed it is the case that people, of a certainty, accord with their ruler's desires and follow after advantage to survive. Therefore,

> if [the ruler] concentrates on the root, then even fraudulent and unscrupulous people will return to the root;
> if [the ruler] is occupied with the branch, then even magnanimous and respectful people will follow after the branch.

Moreover,

> people will always leave an area of cold and famine; and
> people will always occupy a place of warmth and plenty.

Thus, in a declining and dark age, people who concentrate on either root or branch are not necessarily good or bad. It is simply the case that the presence of bad or good fortune cannot help but cause the situation to be like this.[18] Therefore, the enlightened ruler's governance of a country must honor the root and suppress the branch in order to repress the sprouts of disorder and danger. The earnest management of the gradual onset of disorder cannot be neglected.[19]

# CHAPTER 3 PREFACE

People are all endowed with wisdom and virtue;
But they come to grief through the stupefying powers of profit.
To do evil in pursuit of glory,
Is like putting a basin on one's head to view the heavens.
Those who practice benevolence do not become wealthy,
Those who are wealthy are not benevolent.
If [a person] is about to cultivate virtuous behavior,
He must be careful about the basis [of his motivation].

Thus I have written "Suppressing Profit," chapter 3.

# 3

## SUPPRESSING PROFIT

In discussions among people of this generation, there are none that do not value incorruptibility and humility and denigrate wealth and profit. [But] when it comes to their actions, most reject incorruptibility and relish profit. These people only know that a particular thing will profit them, but don't know that when they obtain something, it could also work to profit others.[1] They know that tallow can illuminate a lamp, but don't know that if it is in excess then it can darken it. They know that profit can make them happy; they don't know that its accumulation will necessarily bring about disaster.[2] That

> people of the past considered it an impediment, [yet]
> later people consider it a goal

is indicative of the ignorance of the common people and the extremity of decline and darkness [of the age]. Thus, I sigh and say, "Why not examine this matter? One should

> look in the mirror of the Way,
> and not in the mirror of water.[3]

The elephant is destroyed for his tusks;
the oyster is split for its pearl.

An ordinary person may be blameless, until "cherishing his jade disc becomes his crime."[4] Alas, I have heard, "For those who are without virtue yet wealthy and noble, one may indeed begin making mourning preparations."

Furthermore, as for profitable goods, there is not one that is not the wealth of Heaven. Heaven's management of this wealth is like a state ruler's possession of a treasury: collecting, rewarding, taking away and bestowing, in each case involving a little or a lot. How then can the common people seize more than their share? Thus, the people who lack morals but who possess wealth and honor are the vicious people who steal official positions and rob the treasury. Ultimately, [their crimes] will be discovered, and when discovered, they will certainly be punished. If stealing from the people results in certain punishment, then how much more is it the case for stealing from Heaven? Would it be possible to avoid calamity?

Deng Tong died without a hairpin.[5]
[Yang] Sheng and [Gongsun] Gui killed themselves.[6]

Thus,

> the Son of Heaven is [ultimately] unable to oppose Heaven by enriching those without merit, and
> the various lords are [ultimately] unable to oppose the emperor by richly supporting their personal favorites.

This is a not matter of opposing Heaven.
This is not a matter of opposing the emperor.

The emperor uses Heaven to establish his rule;
Heaven uses the people to establish [its] desires.

What the people want is what Heaven must be in accord with. For this reason,

> those who have not strived to bring benefit to the people yet seek abundance [for themselves] have never avoided being forcefully toppled;
> those who are humble and modest in their service and kindness to the common people have never failed to be glorified.

From ancient times to the present,
from the emperor on high to the common people below,

there has never been

> one who loved profit and was not destroyed, or
> one who loved righteousness and was not glorified.

Formerly, Zhou King Li was fond of monopolizing profit.[7] Rui Liang admonished him but [his advice] was not taken.[8] He thereupon withdrew and presented the ode "Sang Rou" as a criticism. It describes how a great wind will make its path and how the covetous will subvert their peers. The king still did not come to his senses and therefore was banished to Zhi where he died. [Likewise] the Duke of Yu, because of his incessant demands, lost his state.[9] Gongsun Shu's worship of wealth was regarded as a crime.[10] Huan Tui was immoderate in drink and because of this was put to death.[11] They all

destroyed themselves because of precious items, and
annihilated themselves because of wealth.

Dou Ziwen of Chu was offered the position of chief minister three times, yet he had the look of one who was starving and a wife who had suffered cold and hunger, and who, each morning, never knew if he would make to the night.[12] Ji Wenzi served as minister to four rulers, yet

> his horses were not given grain, and
> his concubines never wore silk.[13]

Zihan refused an offering of jade;
Yanzi returned to his [humble] home.[14]

All of them were able to cast off profit and restrain themselves, thus they did not [provoke] the resentment of others, and for generations received in great measure Heaven's favor so that their fine reputations continued unceasingly.

Boyi and Shuqi starved at Shouyang Mountain.[15] The "White Colt" and Jie Zhitui fled to the mountains and valleys.[16] Yan [Hui], Yuan [Xian] and Gongxi [Ai], in response to a famine in the area outside the city,

> guarded their aspirations with firm resolve,
> held fast to their principles without stinting;

> while favored or salaried they could not be compromised,
> before might and power they could not be swayed.

Though in possession of the ruler's respect or holding the position of duke or marquis,

their virtue and righteousness being imperiled,
their propriety and sense of duty being indiscernible,

twisting their aspirations that are like sweet flowers,
disregarding their hearts that are like fragrant plants,

are things they certainly would not allow. Thus, even

> the ruler of all within the four seas would be unable to outweigh their reputation, and
> the lord of all the states would be unable to equal their importance.

> Maintaining their aspirations within one thatched hut, their righteousness overflows beyond the nine continents;
> their integrity established a thousand years in the past, and
> their names will be transmitted for the duration of one hundred generations.

Thus, the superior person says that

> wealth and riches being few,
> clothing and food being insufficient,
> music and women being unremarkable, and
> might and power being unexploited,

are not the concerns of the superior person. That

> one's acts of kindness are few,
> one's explanations of the Way are unclear,
> one's will is not firm, and
> one's virtue and righteousness are not obvious

—the superior person is ashamed of these.

That is why worthies and wise officers, in their relations with their sons and grandsons,

> motivate them toward high aspirations and do not motivate them toward artfulness;
> inspire them with rectitude and do not inspire them with evil;
> instruct them in frugality and do not instruct them in wastefulness;
> endow them words and do not endow them with wealth.

It is for this reason that Dong Zhongshu, over the course of his life, never asked about the affairs of his household, and Shu Guang did not leave behind a bequest of gold.[17] If sons and grandsons are worthy, they will not have to rely on wealth; if they are not worthy, then wealth will elicit resentment. Thus, it is said, "To lack virtue but be abundant in wealth is the incipient stage of disaster."

Formerly, Ji of Cao had a saying: "One who holds a rich conferral from Heaven must dispense virtue and righteousness. If he does not dispense virtue and righteousness, then what he possesses will be subject to loss."[18] If someone's household is wealthy and they lend to the poor,

> bestow wealth on the indigent and distressed, and
> take pity on the sick and suffering,

then that person will be able to occupy a position of wealth for a long time.[19] The *Book of Changes* says, "The Way of Heaven is to diminish the surplus in order to augment the insufficient."[20] Therefore, if one who uses benevolence and righteousness suffers losses in one sphere, then Heaven will reward him in another.

If one has treacherously acquired something in the past, he will lose it in the future. Therefore, since the way to stay full is to reduce and deplete, then one can also avoid

> the regret of the "overbearing dragon," and
> the imbalance of Qian and Kun.[21]

# CHAPTER 4 PREFACE

The world does not understand how to make appraisals,
Taking into account only [a person's] clan and rank,
While failing to inquire about his goals and behavior.
His official position and aristocratic title are the only standards.
To be unrighteousness yet wealthy and eminent,
Was what Confucius considered shameful.
[He was] pained by the gradual decline of customs,
And the growing distance from the arts of the sages.

Thus I have written "Appraising Eminence," chapter 4.

# 4

## APPRAISING EMINENCE

One who is called a worthy or superior person does not necessarily refer to their high position, generous emolument, wealth, nobility, eminence, or renown.¹ While these attributes are what a superior person may appropriately possess, they are not what make the superior person.

One who is called an inferior person does not necessarily refer to their poverty, low station, exposure to the elements, hunger, distress, disgrace, or desperation. While these conditions are those an inferior person may appropriately dwell in, they are not what make the inferior person.

How can this be made clear? Now, Jie and Djou were the rulers of the Xia and Yin dynasties; Chong Hou and E Lai were among the Three Excellencies of the Son of Heaven.² Yet, their being unable to avoid being called inferior was due to their evil actions.

Bo Yi and Shu Qi were men who starved to death [rather than compromise their principles].³ Fu Yue was a convict laborer, while Jing Bo and Yu were taken as prisoners.⁴ Yet the world still regarded them as superior persons because their ambitions were principled and admirable.

Therefore, in assessing an officer, if a determination is made on the basis of his ambitions and actions and not through his brushes with fate, then

> if he possesses all under Heaven, it is not enough to make him important;
> if there are none who will employ him, it is not enough to make him inconsequential;
> if he occupies the position of slave or groom, it is not enough to make him a disgrace;
> if he controls all within the four seas, it is not enough to make him an eminence.

Then how much more is this true for cases in which the contrasts are not as great? Thus it is said,

> a position of favor is insufficient to bring me honor;
> a position of abject subordination is insufficient to make me inferior.

Now, a good reputation arises in keeping with my [actions], while the two kinds of fate come down from Heaven.[5] A passage in the *Book of Odes* says, "Heaven has done it; / What then shall I say?"[6] Therefore,

> the superior person is not necessarily wealthy or noble;
> the inferior person is not necessarily poor and of low station.

> Some might be hidden dragons who have not yet been utilized;
> some may be overbearing dragons in the heavens.[7]

ESSAYS OF A RECLUSE ☙ 41

From antiquity it has always been so.

> Currently, upon observing the assessment of vulgar officers,
> it is by means of clan affiliation that [someone] is recommended as virtuous,
> it is by means of position that [someone] is recommended as worthy.

This can be described as obtaining one aspect of an appraisal but not capturing the most essential truths.

> Yao was a sage father, but Dan was wicked and arrogant.[8]
> Shun was a saintly son, but Sou was obstinate and evil.[9]
> Shuxiang was a worthy elder brother, but Fu was greedy and violent.[10]
> Jiyou was a worthy younger brother, but Qingfu was excessive and chaotic.[11]

If one's assessments demand using clan affiliation, then

> Dan should have been made successor, and Shun should have been executed.
> [Qing]fu should have been rewarded, and [Ji]you should have been killed.

That assessments must not require taking clan affiliation into consideration is demonstrated by these cases.

Formerly, Xi Qi had a saying, "Gun was put to death but Yu was raised to office. Guan Shu and Cai Shu were executed but [their brother], the Duke of Zhou, was the king's chief helper."[12] Thus, a passage in the *Book of Documents* says "Fathers, sons, elder brothers, and younger brothers do not suffer for one another's crimes."[13]

> The great eminence of [Kings] You and Li was that of Son of Heaven; they were moreover enriched with all within the four seas.[14]
> The low station of Yan Hui and Yuan Xian was that of commoners; they were moreover subject to freezing, hunger, and frequently in want."[15]

If assessments must be determined in terms of status, then the two kings should be considered great men of their generation, while the two who remained unemployed should be considered ignorant boors. Assessing others must not be in terms of social rank, yet it continues to be like this.

Therefore it is said,

> benevolence is valued while position is inconsequential;
> position is scorned while righteousness is honored.

In present-day discussions, since many reverse these [two principles], and moreover, base [their decisions] on the [identity of the candidates'] "nine generations [of ancestors]" or on where they come from, they are in fact moving even further from obtaining the true worthy!

Formerly, the Duke of Zhou refrained from seeking all things in one man. How much more should this be the criterion for those who, having been raised up for their virtue and righteousness, might for some other reason fail to be selected?[16]

You Yu was born among the Five Di;
Yue Meng was born among the Eight Man.[17]

Yet

their merit was spread throughout Qi and Qin, and
their virtue was established throughout the land.

Their good names and fine reputations have been recorded in imagery and books and to the present day have not perished.

Zhang Yi was a man of the Middle Kingdom;
Wei Yang was a descendant of Kang Shu.[18]

Yet they were both slanderous, flattering opportunists who delivered all within the four seas into chaos.[19] From this it can be observed that

a persons' good or evil [nature] is not necessarily due to
   generations of ancestors;
a disposition for being worthy or debased is not necessarily due to
   generations of lowliness.

[Just as]

fibrous weeds grow in the middle of temple paths; and
orchids and irises grow in the midst of the mountain wilds.[20]

Now,

the jade of Mr. He came from an unpolished stone; and
the pearl of the Marquis of Sui came from an oyster.[21]

A passage in the *Book of Odes* says,

> "Gathering mustard plants gathering radishes,
> we don't reject them because of their roots."[22]

Therefore, if there is something greatly praiseworthy and lauded in its age, though in its small details it might have minor flaws, how is that sufficient to reject it?

> For this reason, in the employment of officers,
>
> one should not be troubled because they are not [native to] our country, but concerned that they might be disloyal.
> One should not be troubled that there are no men from [office-holding] families, but troubled that they might be unworthy.

There should be no other considerations. Chen Ping and Hann Xin were men of Chu who surrendered to the Han, but Gaozu used them as guards and assistants, realizing peace for all within the four seas and stability in the house of Han.[23] Wei Qing and Huo Qubing were the [mere] henchmen of [the marquis of] Pingyang, yet Emperor Wu made them Commanders-in-Chief; they effectively drove out the Northern Di and created a commandery in Hexi.[24] Considering their performances, how could there have been any [occasion for] treating them disrespectfully or snubbing them? Thus, the difficulty [in promoting officials] is not based on where a person comes from, or if they descend from a family of generals or ministers, but rather

> whether or not they have the abilities [necessary for] the offices they occupy,

whether or not their morals [are commensurate with] their honored position,

or whether they might fail to support the ruler but avail themselves of the ruler's power.

# CHAPTER 5 PREFACE

Considering what worthies suffer, and
Examining the disasters that jealousy engenders,
[It can be seen that] all envy arises from one's being surpassed
    by others,
And evolves into deep resentment.
Some focus on fault-finding,
Some fabricate pretexts.
I am pained that my ruler does not examine this point,
But believes slanderous words.

Thus I have written "The Difficulties of the Worthy," chapter 5.

# 5

# THE DIFFICULTIES OF THE WORTHY

The reason the world is ungoverned stems from the difficulty of worthies. That which is called "the difficulty of worthies" is not simply a question of whether they embody wisdom and lucidity or pursue virtue and righteousness. It is, in fact, the difficulty of *obtaining* worthies, and nothing more; it is not a matter of what worthies themselves find difficult. Thus, what is called the difficulty of worthies actually refers to

> their cultivating goodness but being subjected to envy,
> their behaving in a worthy manner but being subjected to jealousy,

and their inevitable encounters with disaster and difficulty.

Shun of Yu's banishment and [Wu] Zixu's execution demonstrate that if even the loftiest sages and greatest worthies were unable to avoid jealousy and envy, then how much more is this the case for ordinary people of the present age?[1] This is why a refined officer, while possessing the worthy's capability and a fine natural endowment, will nevertheless still fail to be accorded a straight path to follow in the realization of his ambitions.

That

> the retired officer has no way to be upright in his actions, and
> the court minister has no way to be straightforward in his words

is due to

> the corruption of customs and culture, and
> the isolation of a benighted ruler.
>
> The Marquis of Qi, through the seizure of his state, and
> the Duke of Lu, through his expulsion and banishment,

were both definitively defeated, overturned, and crushed precipitously.[2] How could they have ever managed to rule? Thus,

> those deficient in virtue hate to hear about admirable actions, and
> those whose governments are in a state of chaos hate to hear discussion of order.

This is why the destroyed state of Qin punished discussion and buried the scholars.[3]

Now, among the ordinary people of the age,

> those who are rude to their relatives and hate those who respect them, and
> those who treat their relatives shabbily and hate those who love them

are not few in number. But surely it is not only ordinary people [who are like this]; worthies also occasionally fall in this [category]. Deng Tong, who was favored by Emperor Wen, was totally devoted and obedient. He licked [the emperor's] piles without any sign of disgust.[4] [Once, when] the emperor was ill and unhappy, in a languorous manner, he said "Under Heaven, who is the one who loves me most?" Deng Tong wanted to praise the crown prince's filiality and therefore replied, "No one loves you more than the crown prince." When the prince came to inquire about [his father's] illness, the emperor ordered him to lick his piles, [but the prince's] face showed his reluctance. The emperor was displeased and sent him away. When [the crown prince] heard that Deng Tong frequently licked his piles, he was mortified and came to hate him. When [the crown prince] came to the throne, he found Deng Tong guilty of an offense and caused him to starve to death. Thus, in considering Deng Tong,

> his actions were the means by which he expressed deep devotion and caused no one harm,
> while his words were the means by which he praised the crown prince and displayed the prince's filial love.

When the crown prince himself was unable to live up to this praise, he perversely nursed his anger and laid blame on [Deng Tong]. If praising a person's strengths in an effort to glorify their filiality is considered a crime, how much more is this the case when bringing to light others' shortcomings to reform current practices?

Moreover, the reason officers are considered worthy is, in fact, because of their words and actions.

> Loyal and correct words are not simply a matter of praise pure and simple; it must also involve some censure.
> The behavior of the filial son is not simply a matter of licking piles and nothing more; there must be some [points of] disagreement.

This being the case, an ethical and outspoken officer's ability to

avoid the allegations of the envious, and
escape the bad fortune of capital punishment,

is likely due to his luck.[5] This is

the reason Bi Gan's heart was cut open,
the reason Jizi was made a slave,

why Bo Zong died, and
why Xi Wan was destroyed.[6]

Now,

a country not lacking in jealous men is
like a family not lacking in jealous women.

From the past to the present,
from the public sphere to the private,

is it possible that those

who contend over merit and renown, and
who are jealous of those who surpass them

are few in number? I should think that two worthies would deem it fitting to not harm each other.

Yet Fan Ju impeded Bai Qi, and Gongsun Hong hindered Dong Zhongshu.[7] Was this competition the result of both men [serving in] the same court [and enjoying] the same ruler's favor?

Is it only officers of different states, who take different paths, and who are not involved in [the conferral of] benefits or harm who can avoid such things?
Yet,

> when Sun Bin began to hone his skills in Chu, Pang Juan, [far away] in the state of Wei, paled [at the thought], and lured him [to Wei] in order to subject him to the punishment of foot-amputation.[8]

> When Han Fei showed his legal brilliance in Han, Li Si, [far away] in the state of Qin, began to brood, brought him to Qin, and killed him.[9]

Alas, how can jealousy between officers reach such proportions? In these cases, was it that [the truth] had not reached the ruler and therefore [these two men] suffered misfortune? Or is it that only when one is already known that he will be trusted?

Yet Jing Fang on numerous occasions talked with Emperor Yuan about problems in hope of regulating the assessment and achievement [of officials].[10] Chao Cuo, who had long been a confidante of Emperor Jing, was charged by the emperor to regulate Han laws and make them less disorderly.[11] Now, these two men's relations with their rulers can be described as one in which they were deeply understood and truly favored and loved. Yet Jing Fang died unjustly and the ruler had no knowledge of it; Chao Cuo was beheaded and the emperor only then felt regret. Was it because their abilities and intellects were insufficient to protect their lives that they met with difficulties? Is it only the greatest sage who is able to avoid being implicated?

Yet

> Di Yi, because of his righteousness, was imprisoned.[12]
> King Wen [of Zhou], because of his benevolence, was seized.[13]

They embodied the practice of benevolence and righteousness, facing south with their various officials, yet they were still unable to avoid difficulties. Thus,

> Confucius was dispossessed,[14]
> Shu Xiang was bound and fettered;
> Qu Yuan was driven to the deep;
> Jia Yi was dismissed;
> Zhong Li was cast aside;
> He Chang was constrained;
> Wang Zhang was convicted of crimes;
> the Ping'a [marquis] was expelled—

all no doubt, due to their being regarded as unimportant.[15]

A passage in the *Book of Odes* says, "Without crime or offense of any kind / Slanderers' mouths are loud against me"; and "The heart of that man, / To what will it not proceed?"[16] Viewed from this perspective,

> attacks fueled by jealousy are truly devious;
> worthies and sages living in the world are indeed dangerous.

Thus, that which is called the difficulty of the worthy is not the difficulty of being worthy; it is avoiding [disaster] that is difficult. Considering the great sages and multitudes of worthies whose merit was complete and names were established,

some held the rank of marquis or earl,
some occupied positions as dukes or ministers, and

took charge of Heavenly offices,
having been selected at the emperor's discretion,

from the early [hours] till late, they shared meals [with him],[17] their names are prominent, yet if they were still [subject to danger] in this way, how much more is this the case of

people in fields and ditches, and
hermits of the mountains and valleys,

who can only rely on others to make their reputations known and await the appraisals that will allow them to finally be trusted? This is the reason these knowledgeable officers have

their mouths pinched shut,
their tongues bound, and
their "sacks" tied up,

[so that] they salute in silence and attempt nothing more.[18]

Furthermore, how can the common crowd within the village gates gain an independent understanding of the situation? It is merely a case of hoping to "grab dust and grasp sounds" and nothing more.[19] Considering their appraisal [of officers], it is not a matter of their being able to rely on their private actions and dealings as a basis to determine the presence or absence of right and wrong. It is simply a matter of regarding

those who praise us as being wise,
those who craftily promote themselves as being benevolent,

those who scheme for advantages as being competent, and
those who usurp positions as being worthy.

Furthermore, how can they understand

the foundation of filial piety and fraternal devotion,
the true nature of loyalty and correctness,
the transformative [power of] of laws and principles, and
the fundamentals of the true path?

This is why

Bao Jiao stationed himself by the side of the road, and
Xu Yan drowned himself in the ocean.[20]

There is a saying:

one dog barks at a shape, and
one hundred dogs bark at the sound.

The world's weakness for this sort of thing has gone on for a very long time indeed. I am vexed by the failure to examine the truth or falsity of circumstances, thus, I will set forth a parable to illustrate this sentiment. Nowadays, observing high ministers' selection of officers, it bears a similarity to a forester hunting. Formerly, there was a gamekeeper who went out hunting by torchlight in the wilds. The deer fled to the east and the gamekeeper followed, shouting at it.[21] A group of people in the west who were pursuing a boar heard the gamekeeper's calls, and joining together, raised a din. When the gamekeeper heard the sound of the people, he turned around, stopped his pursuit, and proceeded to wait in ambush, whereupon he encountered the boar, which had been wallowing in white mud. The gamekeeper was delighted and, thinking he had captured an auspicious and precious white beast, got a large amount of grass and grain, and filled up a trough to feed it. The pig looked up and down and grunted and squealed, making sounds of contentment. This made the gamekeeper prize it even more. Not long afterward, a fierce wind arose followed by a soaking rain. It drenched the great pig and the white mud was washed away. The pig was startled and voiced its ordinary *oink*. It was then that the gamekeeper realized it was nothing but a domestic pig. This was an error of following sounds and pursuing echoes. Ordinary people who encounter such things do not put their faith in them.

Rulers of this age, in their consideration of officers,

> see worthies with their own eyes but do not dare to employ them;
> hear of worthies with their own ears but regret not meeting them.

Even though they themselves are discerning, they are still unable to select someone for service and will wait for one who is recommended by the whole crowd of officials. At the same time, they are also afraid of losing a doe and end up capturing a domestic pig. Why is it that they are unable to make these distinctions? It is because they have not yet met with "the changes wrought by wind and rain." Let there be one day of governmental crisis for "the rain to collect," then

> those who follow dangerous routes, and
> those of little worth

will also become distinguishable.

Now, groups of small-minded friends form cliques and consolidate their positions; throngs of the slanderous and jealous bark and snap at the worthy—can the disaster and decline they create be considered insignificant?

> The overturning of the three epochs, and
> the annihilation of the various states

is something that people of a later age are still unable to change [in their own time]. This is the reason the ten thousand officials repeatedly lose their positions and why the mandate of Heaven so often proved inconstant. A passage in the *Book of Odes* says, "Since the kingdom is on the verge of destruction, how is it that you do not observe the state of things?[22] Alas, this is something that the mediocre rulers of our time fail to look into.

# CHAPTER 6 PREFACE

Searching for the origin of enlightenment,
Tracing the emergence of ignorance,
It is resisting good counsel that corrupts,
And how disaster and chaos are formed.
Those holding power,
Uniformly desire to control the ruler,
To thwart and conceal worthy officers,
And thereby monopolize the ruler's power.

Thus I have written "The Enlightened and the Unenlightened," chapter 6.

# 6

# THE ENLIGHTENED AND THE UNENLIGHTENED

What makes a state well-ordered is an enlightened ruler; what makes it chaotic is an unenlightened ruler.
What makes a ruler enlightened is listening to everyone; what makes him unenlightened is trusting one side.

For this reason,

if a ruler is aware of his prejudices and concentrates on listening to everyone, then his sagacity will broaden daily;
if he is dependent on favorites and partial in those he trusts, then his ignorance will worsen daily.[1]

A passage in the *Book of Odes* says, "The ancients had a saying: 'consult the grass and firewood carriers.'"[2]

Now, under the rule of Yao and Shun, they

opened the four gates,
observed the four [quarters'] perspectives, and
heard the four [quarters'] reports.[3]

This is how all under Heaven was assembled like the spokes [on a wheel] so that there was no place the sages' brilliance did not illuminate. Therefore

> among Gong and Gun's followers, none had the ability to interfere, and
> among their empty promises that were never delivered upon, none had the power to sway.[4]

The Second Emperor of Qin, working to conceal himself, cut himself off from the hundred officials; abandoning and rejecting the distant and humble, he placed his faith in Zhao Gao.

In this way

> his ears were closed by high-ranking and important servitors, and
> his vision was obscured by arrogant and jealous people.

Therefore, when all under Heaven rose in rebellion, he obtained no report of it. Of all those Zhao Gao killed, no one dared to speak of them.[5]

> It was not until Zhou Zhang arrived in Xi that he became afraid.[6]
> It was not until Yan Le offered counsel that he later felt regret.[7]

But it was, indeed, too late.
Thus, if the ruler of humankind listens to [all perspectives] and receives [the views of] all beneath him, then

> elite servitors will not be able to falsify, and
> those far removed will not be able to deceive.

ESSAYS OF A RECLUSE ☙ 63

If he offends the humble and trusts the nobles, then the good counsels of the court will not be received, and pure officers will preserve [their integrity] and accept guilt [and remove themselves to] obscure places.⁸

Now,

> court officers [exist] for the purpose of unifying and regulating, but if they befriend cliques and groups, the law will be thrown into confusion.
> Worthies [exist] for the purpose of offering their services, but if they hide away concealing themselves in the wilds, the ruler will be left on his own.

When the law is thrown into confusion and the ruler is alone, the possibility of his survival is nonexistent. For this reason, when the enlightened ruler governs people, he

> elicits the views of inferiors to illuminate the situation beyond [the court], and respects the lowly in order to entice worthies.

> His not rejecting advice is not necessarily because the advice is completely useful, but because he fears that by rejecting the useless, he will drive away the useful.
> His not despising the vulgar is not necessarily because a person is completely worthy, but because he fears that despising the wrongdoer will dash the hopes of the worthy.

For this reason, when the sage king

> commends small [achievements] in order to encourage the great, and rewards the humble in order to attract the worthy,

later on

excellent officers will gather at his court, and
conditions under [their jurisdiction] will be conveyed to the ruler.

Therefore

the ruler will avoid misguided strategies, and
the officials will avoid renegade officers.

This is

what the ruler and the people regard as beneficial, and
what the wicked and deceitful regard as disastrous.

Formerly,

Zhang Lu received one audience and Marquis Rang was dismissed.[9]
Yuan Si offered clever arguments and Zhou Bo was dismissed.[10]

Therefore, people who "occupy the roads" are always jealous of proper and upright officers and grasp opportunities to insert their opinions before the ruler in order to lie about the wrongdoing [of proper and upright officers].[11] Thus,

above, they gloss things over with false words to cloud the ruler's mind;
below, they establish awesome power to control the officials and people.

Zhao Gao threw the government into chaos. Fearing that his misdeeds would be made known to the ruler, he met the Second

Emperor in advance, saying, "If you frequently hold an audience with all of your officials to discuss state affairs, you will appear undignified. Being undignified will moreover reveal your shortcomings. This is not as good as concealing yourself and making decisions alone, [in a manner that is] spirit-like and imposing. The Son of Heaven refers to himself as "subtle" because only his voice is heard."[12] [Thereafter], the Second Emperor did indeed hide himself in deep seclusion, only admitting Zhao Gao. Zhao Gao would

> enter with laudatory words to please his master, and
> leave, relying upon the imperial mandate to bring honor to himself.

All under Heaven was like a rotten fish, and one state after another rebelled against Qin.[13] Zhao Gao was afraid. He laid the blame on his ruler and then ordered Yan Le to accuse and execute him.[14] [The emperor] wished to see Gao [one last time] but was not allowed, and so he died.

Now,

> Tian Chang imprisoned Duke Jian, and
> Zhuo Chui hanged King Min.[15]

The Second Emperor had in fact already heard about these [incidents]. Yet he still followed in these paths of destruction. Why? His error lay in

> the refusal to accept the exhortations of his ministers and officers, and
> the failure to take into account rumors circulated by the common people.

He thought that

> he himself was more worthy than Duke Jian and King Min, and that
> Zhao Gao was more worthy than the ministers of those two rulers.

Thus,

> the state had already become chaotic but the ruler was unaware; disaster was already upon him but his underlings did not come to the rescue.

This was not due to the masses coming together to oust a ruler but rather to the ruler taking the people's mandate and giving it to Zhao Gao. The ruler's failure arose from his detachment from the people. As for later rulers of doomed states, how can they understand this danger? Shun said, "When I am doing wrong, it is yours to correct me—do not agree with me to my face, and when you withdraw, have other remarks to make."[16] Thus, the way of governing a state is

> to urge people to express criticism, and
> to direct them to offer their views.

Only then will rulers discern the situation with clarity and their governing address the actual situation.

Furthermore, as for arrogant officers who like thwarting the worthy, not only do they fear that the [worthy] will utilize righteousness to constrain them,

> [they] also feel shame for occupying high positions while their wisdom is inferior to those below, and

for taking charge of official posts but failing to come up with their own policies.

Thus,

Xi Wan obtained [the confidence of] the people, but Zichang killed him;
Qu Yuan gained [the trust] of the ruler, but Zijiao and Zilan implicated him through slander.[17]

Geng Shou established the Ever-Normal Granary, but Yan Yan envied his plan;
Chen Tang killed Zhi Zhi, but Kuang Heng criticized his achievement.[18]

From these cases it can be seen that, if one occupies a low position and desires to bring about good for the ruler, then one must first become the enemy of his favorites. If [favorites] rely on long-standing favor to obstruct you from within, and you yourself rely on lowly connections to display your potential from beyond the court, then

rulers who yearn for virtuous officials, and
worthies who wish to be loyal,

though living in the same era, will fervently seek but ultimately fail to encounter each other.

# CHAPTER 7 PREFACE

Looking back upon the former kings,
The ways in which they elicited the Great Peace,
Was to examine achievements for dismissal or advancement,
As written in the Five Classics.
Punishments and reward should reflect the actual case,
And not be based on an empty reputation.
Clearly demonstrate a preference for those with virtuous reputations,
And look into [the records of] those promoted [for service at] court.

Thus I have written "Evaluating Merit," chapter 7.

# 7

## EVALUATING MERIT

Of all the great responsibilities of the One Who Faces South,[1] none is more urgent than recognizing worthies.
Of all the most efficient pathways to recognizing the worthy, none is more urgent than evaluating accomplishments.

If accomplishments are honestly investigated, then the difference between governing [well] and misgoverning will be revealed and made clear. If the distinction between good and evil is verified, then true worthies cannot be suppressed and obscured, and flatterers and crooked persuaders will no longer be able to conceal their villainy.

Now,

if a sword is not tested, its sharpness is unknown;
if a bow is not tested, its tensile strength is unverified;
if a falcon is not tested, its cleverness is questionable;
if a horse is not tested, its fitness is suspect.

The reason these four [qualities] are unknown is due to not examining and testing [them], thus yielding this sort [of result].

Now because the multitude of officials are not tested, the harm is not simply limited to [their qualities being] unknown, unverified, questionable and suspect—it also becomes manifest in incidents of negligence and arrogance.

Suppose a family has five sons and ten grandsons. If the parents do not monitor whether they are industrious or diffident, then

> [even] those who are diligent and industrious will become shiftless and lax, while
> those who are lazy and indolent will go on to utter profligacy.

This is the pathway to squandering one's patrimony and destroying one's family. If this is how fathers and sons and elder and younger brothers who live within the same gate are appraised, then how much more can it be applied to the general lot of various officials who have charge of public affairs? The [*Zuo*] *Tradition* says: "If [the distinction between] good and evil is unclear, how [can one tell] what to suppress and what to encourage?"[2] Therefore,

> when elders do not keep track of the merits [of their progeny], their sons and grandsons will be lazy, and the family will become impoverished and hard-pressed.

> When high officials do not keep track of the merits [of their subordinates], the functionaries will become indolent and arrogant, and debauchery and treachery will arise.

> When emperors and kings do not keep track of the merits [of their advisors], then the upright and worthy will be suppressed, and deceit and falsehood will triumph.

Thus, a passage in the *Book of Documents* says: "Every three years there was an examination of merits, and [after three examinations][3] the undeserving were degraded, and the deserving were promoted."[4] Surely that is the way to

> shed light upon the worthy and the worthless, and
> encourage the capable and the mediocre.

The sage-kings [of old], in setting up [the system of] the hundred officials, all took [as their model] the way Heaven rules Earth and shepherds and nurtures the myriad people. For this reason,

> A person's title must be proportionate to his duties, and
> A person's appointment must be realized through results.

Thus

> officialdom included none who were remiss in their duties, and
> those in office included no one who was unsuitable.

Now,

> the achievements of administrators and chancellors, prefects and chiefs [lay in] governing the people;[5]
>
> [the achievements of] provincial shepherds, inspectors and clerks [lay in] exhausting their intelligence and acuity.
>
> The Nine Superintendents[6] each assumed different responsibilities in order to assist the Three Excellencies.[7]
> The Three Excellencies together held comprehensive responsibility for harmonizing yin and yang.

All of them were examined to see if the accomplishments [expected of them] were realized so as to determine their promotion or retirement.[8]

Palace Intendants,[9] Dignitaries, Academicians, and Gentleman Consultants considered

> verbal communications as their responsibility, and
> critical admonitions as an official duty.

They also [nominated] for selection [men designated as]

> Flourishing Talents; Filially Pious and Incorrupt;
> Worthy, Virtuous, and Foursquare;
> Honest and Unspoiled; Possessing the Way;
> Understanding the Classics; Broadly and Extensively [learned];
> Martial and Courageous; and Quelling the Troublesome.[10]

These are all cases of

> letting names appoint themselves to tasks and
> letting titles determine themselves,[11]

and are the means by which all officials can devote their attention to the fullest and exhaust all effort to accord with the ruler's command.

Nowadays things are not like that. The subprefects, prefects, governors, and grand councilors

> do not think of making worthy contributions, but are greedy,
>     violent, dictatorial, and self-indulgent;
> [they] do not uphold the laws and commands, but abuse and
>     oppress the common people.

The territorial governors do not govern, causing those from afar to travel to the court to memorialize their complaints to court officials.

> The Grand Secretary does not take up [these concerns] and calls to account the Three Excellencies;
> The Three Excellencies do not take up [these concerns] and punish the [heads of] the provinces and commanderies;
> The [heads of] the provinces and commanderies do not take up [these concerns] and denounce the [heads of] the districts and townships.

For this reason, the cruel, evil, crafty, and treacherous can easily perpetrate injustice on [the common people]. Officials such as the Privy Councilors, Broad and Extensive Savants, and Censors sometimes stay in their posts for years, and to the very end do not breathe a word about

> advancing the worthy or rejecting the evil,
> fixing defects or rectifying deficiencies,

but worry about being criticized or dismissed.

As for the multitude of officials and elevated scholars, some

> [when asked to nominate] Flourishing Talent, they respond with the stupid and boorish;
> [when asked to nominate] the Filially Pious, they respond with the cruel and disobedient;
> [when asked to nominate] those of scrupulous conduct, they respond with the greedy and covetous;
> [when asked to nominate] the foursquare and upright, they respond with the cunning and cruel;

[when asked to nominate] the honest and straightforward, they
respond with flatterers and toadies;
[when asked to nominate] the serious and weighty, they respond
with the frivolous and careless;
[when asked to nominate] those who possess the Way, they
respond with the vacuous and empty;
[when asked to nominate] those who understand the classics,
they respond with the dull and ignorant;
[when asked to nominate] those who are lenient and
broad-minded, they respond with the cruel and
oppressive;
[when asked to nominate] the martial and courageous, they
respond with the timid and cowardly; or
[when asked to nominate] those who could manage
the troublesome, they respond with the stupid and
corrupt.

Names and realities do not match each other;
requests and contributions do not correspond to each
other.

The rich make use of their financial power;[12]
the noble rely on their positional advantage.

Lots of money is taken as worthiness;
obdurate strength is taken as superiority.

This is the reason

those in office are unsuitable, and
administrative affairs are usually chaotic and neglected.

In former times, when the feudal lords recommended scholars, if they recommended someone suitable once, they were called "lovers of virtue."

If they recommended someone suitable again, they were called "honoring the worthy."

If they recommended someone suitable a third time, they were called "having achievements,"

and were then given a reward. But for those who failed to recommend scholars,

on the first [occasion], they were punished by demotion;
on the second, they were punished by loss of land.[13]

The third time, they were punished by forfeiting the entirety of their territory and noble rank.

Those who relied on underlings to swindle their superiors suffered execution;

Those who relied on superiors to swindle underlings suffered mutilating punishments.

Those who were entrusted with the government of the state but failed to use it for the benefit of the people were reprimanded. Those who occupied high positions but were incapable of advancing the worthy were exiled.

[In the case of] those entrusted with the affairs of state, their emphasis on selecting and promoting [others], investigating [whether or not] the titles [of those they selected] matched reality, and administering reward or punishments—was observed to this extent.[14] Thus they were able to

distinguish the worthy from the worthless, and
obtain [the services of] the many knights,

> establish [the practice of] transformation through instruction
> and
> bring tranquility to [both] the populace and the refugees [from the borderlands].

The Three Eras,[15] each in its own time, established Great Peace. That the sage-like Han ascended the throne, performed the [imperial] sacrifices forty-eight [times?],[16] but has still not established Great Peace is because

> education was not cultivated, and accomplishments were not examined;
> reward and punishments were tardy, and amnesties and exemptions were numerous.[17]

As a proverb says,

> "Crooked timber hates the marking-cord's straightness;
> Heavy punishments hate clear testimony."

This is the reason the numerous officials love to be muddled together and hate the investigation of merit.
    Now,

> the sage is the mouth of Heaven;
> the worthy is the sage's interpreter.

That is why

> The sage's utterances
> [express] Heaven's heart; and

the worthy's speech
[expresses] the sage's intentions.

A teacher from a previous generation, the Honorable Jing,[18] formulated rules for assessing the merits of officials in order to bequeath them to worthies and eminent officials.

The foundation of the Great Peace must begin with them;
the transformations of nonaction must arise from them.

That is why the rulers of today who fail to carry out the investigation of merit but still have thoughts about [achieving an era of] Great Peace are like

[one who] discards compass and square but who wishes [to inscribe] circles and squares; or
[one who] without boat or oar wishes to cross a large body of water.

Although they might succeed sometimes, it is still not as good as following [Jing Fang's] straightforward and expeditious [plans and methods].

If the numerous officials and the royal preceptors all have their assignments, each one taking charge in their appropriate offices, and each, according to his duties, has his accomplishments assessed,[19] then the hundred commanderies and the thousand counties can, on the basis of past conditions, the plan for the future.

If each of [the officials'] utterances and responses are evaluated according to their written memorials in order to evaluate their actual realization, then office-holders will no longer be negligent, and the officials' reports will no longer contain falsehoods.

A passage in the *Book of Documents* says:

> They will set forth, and you will receive, their reports; you will make proof of them severally by their merits; you will confer chariots and robes according to their services. Who will then dare not to cultivate a humble virtue? Who will dare not to respond to you with reverence?[20]

This [declaration] demonstrates how Yao and Shun nurtured the black-haired people and brought tranquility to their age.

# CHAPTER 8 PREFACE

When rulers choose officers,
They all seek the worthy and able.
When officials make recommendations,
They all compete to promote inferior talents.
I detest these craven grifters,
What official business are they capable of managing?
When you purchase medicine and receive a fake,
It's difficult to use it as a cure.

Thus I have written "Thinking About the Worthy," chapter 8.

# 8

# THINKING ABOUT THE WORTHY

What preserves states is order.
What destroys them is disorder.

[Among] the rulers of humankind, there are none who do not

love good government and hate disorder, or
rejoice in survival and fear extinction.

But having looked at the chronicles of the past, [one sees that] in more recent antiquity, three dynasties have been destroyed, and innumerable states have been extinguished. What is the reason for this? Investigating these failures, [one finds that] all of them are due to rulers who consistently

prefer that which brings about disorder, and
hate that which brings about good government; and [who]
detest that which brings about preservation, and
love that which brings about destruction.[1]

Thus, although

separated by a hundred generations,
disconnected in time by [an entire] cycle,[2]
divided into nine provinces, and
[observing] distinctive customs every thousand *li*,

the traces of defeat and the evidence of extinction are still [as clear as if] one had repeatedly applied the compass or the square, or time and again fitted together [the two halves of] a credential or a tally.[3] Therefore it is said:

> even if one has the perfection of Yao and Shun, it is necessary to consult the "Hymns of Zhou";[4]
> although one has the wickedness of Jie and Djou, it is necessary to scrutinize "Reversal" and "Vast."[5]

"The mirror of Yin is not distant; it is found in the sovereigns of Xia."[6]

Now,

> a person who has the same illness as one who is dying cannot continue living;
> a person who acts in the same way as a state that is perishing cannot preserve himself.

Can these be [merely] empty words?

> How do you know that a person is going to be ill? It is because he shows no interest in food.
> How do you know when a state is about to lapse into disorder? It is because [its ruler] shows no interest in worthies.

Therefore,

> in the kitchen of a household where [someone] is ill, it is not because of the absence of delicious foods, but rather that the [sick] person is unable to eat them that he goes on to die.
> Among the officials of a state that has fallen into disorder, it is not because of the absence of worthy men, but rather that their ruler is incapable of relying on them that it heads toward extinction.

Now,

> fresh rice and good millet,
> excellent ale and sweet liquor

are the means for nurturing life. But the sick person finds them disgusting, and thinks them inferior to beans, barley, bran, dregs, and cold drinks.[7] This is a sign of immanent death.

> Respecting worthies and employing the able, and
> trusting the loyal and accepting criticism,

are the means for establishing security [of the state]. But the benighted ruler hates [these practices] and considers them inferior to the words of those who are deceitful, unworthy, and slanderous. This is a sign of immanent destruction.

The *Laozi* says: "[The sage] recognizes illness as illness; that is why he is not ill."[8] The *Yijing* says: "'Shall I perish? Shall I perish?' (so shall this state be firm, as if) bound to a clump of bushy mulberry trees."[9] That is why

> a gentleman of service[10] who wants to nurture his longevity[11]
>> anticipates illness by taking (prophylactic doses of) medicine; and
>
> a ruler who wants to nurture his era anticipates disorder by
>> employing worthies.

In this way, he himself will enjoy constant tranquility and his state will be forever preserved.[12]

The best doctor heals the state; the next best heals diseases.[13] Now when a person governs a state, it [in fact] resembles [the process of] governing himself.

> Disease is an illness of the body;
> disorder is an illness of the state.

> The illness of the body relies on the healer to be cured;
> the disorder of the state relies on worthies to be well governed. For governing the body there are the arts of the Yellow Emperor; for governing the era there are the Classics of Confucius.[14]

> But if the disease fails to be cured
> and the disorder fails to [yield to] good government,

>> it is not that the methods of acupuncture and moxibustion are wrong,
>> or that the words of the Five Classics are false,

but rather that the person applying them is not right [for the task]. If the person is not right [for the task],

> a compass will not make circles;
> a square will not make right angles;

a marking cord will not make straight lines;
a level will not make things level;
a kindling tool will not produce fire;
a bellows stone will not produce metal;[15]
a whip will not make a horse run faster;
a boat will not allow one to traverse water.

These eight all manifest Heaven's Grand Way; [they] are things that have [tangible] forms and can be [clearly] seen. [But] if it is not the right person [managing them], they will still be of no use. Isn't this all the more true of one

> who embraces the techniques of the Way to pacify the people, and who mounts the Six Dragons[16] to manage Heaven's heart?

Now, governing the world but not obtaining authentic worthies is comparable to treating an illness without obtaining authentic medicine,[17] and in treating an illness, when

> one ought to obtain genuine ginseng, [but instead] gets radish roots; or
> when one ought to obtain dwarf lilyturf tubers[18] [but instead] gets steamed barley.

Though ignorant of what is genuine, [the afflicted person] combines and swallows these [items]. When the illness gradually worsens, the patient does not know that he has been deceived but claims that the prescriptions are fraudulent, and that all of the medicines are useless in treating the disease. Thus he discards the remaining medicine, not daring to consume it, and then seeks out shamans, and even though he might die, it is fitting.

[Likewise], when a ruler of men seeks worthies, his subordinates might respond by offering him a boor. If he recommends an upright [person], his subordinates will respond with a crooked [candidate].[19] If he himself cannot distinguish true worthies, he will accept a vulgarian and appoint him. His state will gradually fall into disorder, and he will not know that he has been taken advantage of by his subordinates. He will then perversely say that the classics are not to believed, and that worthies are useless in rescuing a state from disorder. As a result, he will expel true worthies and will no longer recommend them. Instead, he appoints crass fellows as officials, and though he will face destruction, it is fitting. From the time of the Three Dynasties onward, all [rulers] because of their "radish and steamed barley medicinal concoction" saw their "illness" worsen daily until they finally perished.

A passage in the *Book of Documents* says: "When men have ability, urge them to engage in self-improvement, and the state will benefit."[20] That is why the Former Kings, in choosing men to be officials, were certain to obtain men with the appropriate talents, whose merits benefitted the people, and whose virtues matched their official posts. Both humans and spirits were consulted, and the common people were able to recommend the able.[21] Their devoted obedience thereby moved Heaven and earth and enabled the Three Dynasties to establish states, institute noble ranks and transmit them for hundreds of generations in succession over the course of thousands of years.

[But] after the Spring and Autumn period, during the regimes of the Warring States period, generals and powerful officials invariably relied on maternal relatives.

> The elder and younger brothers of the empress;
> the sons-in-law of princesses and the ruler's distaff grandsons,

no matter how young—[some] hardly out of swaddling clothes—
relied on these connections to step into official positions.

> Their achievements did not extend to the people, and
> their benefits did not trickle downward.

Most of the chosen marquises received "rush[-wrapped] clods"[22] without making any attempt at governing the populace in a way that would give recompense to the common people. They ate without performing any service and enjoyed generous emoluments, freeloading as if receiving sacrificial offerings,[23] merely concerning themselves with wasteful extravagance. Whether sitting or standing [they behaved with] prideful arrogance. Ruined and bereft, they had nothing to bequeath to later generations.

Zichan once said: "If you ask someone who has not yet learned how to handle a knife to cut something up, he will certainly suffer numerous wounds."[24] Thus, if the ruler of the age in his relations with elite relatives is fond of the easy countenance of his flattering favorites, fails to weigh their qualifications yet installs them as officials, and does not require them to establish merit or involve themselves with the people, but improperly attends to raising their noble ranks and increasing their reward, thereby consolidating the hatred of the lower orders,

> accumulating blame in the heart of Heaven,[25] and
> heaping up transgressions on top of those already committed,

how can this not end in their downfall? This is as the saying goes, "When one is fond of someone, one merely ends up injuring him."[26]

According to the procedure of the Former Rulers in [appointing] an official, it was essential to discuss his qualifications.

When the discussion was settled, he could be ennobled.

When his position was settled, he could [receive] his emoluments.

[But today's] rulers do not investigate [potential appointees][27] but merely select their maternal relatives or attractive [favorites] for appointment.[28] This is like

> asking a beloved son to stand in for a skilled charioteer, or substituting a roofing-tile for a lustrous pearl.

Although some feelings of love [for the recipients] are involved, it also carries the certainty that it will overturn the great chariot [i.e., the state] and kill the sick person. The *Book of Documents* declares, "The work is Heaven's—it is men's to act for it."[29] A commentary says, "Of those who have completed the accomplishments of Heaven and earth, there has never been one who has not [left] a flourishing and glorious [legacy]."[30] Considering it from this perspective, if rulers of the [current] age want [to appoint] men who have no accomplishments and grant them power and wealth, they are picking a fight with Heaven. To send a person without virtue to quarrel with August Heaven while wishing to hold one's position [as ruler] for a long time is something that has not been heard of from ancient times onward.[31]

# CHAPTER 9 PREFACE

Examining the fundamental principles of the heavenly and human realms,
The interdependence of the three [spheres of Heaven, earth, and humankind],
And the triggers for bringing about peace—
These techniques all reside with the ruler.
Esteeming law and selecting worthies,
The state's [stability] derives from him.
If the evil usurp positions,
Then who will there be to keep watch?

Thus I have written "The Fundamentals of Government," chapter 9.

# 9

# THE FUNDAMENTALS OF GOVERNMENT

In a ruler's administration of the government, nothing is more important than harmonizing yin and yang. Yin and yang take Heaven as their root.

>When according with Heaven's heart[1] yin and yang are harmonious.
>When transgressing against Heaven's heart, yin and yang are at odds.

Heaven takes the people as its heart.

>If the people are secure and happy, then there is an accord with Heaven's heart.
>If the people are despondent and bitter, then there is a transgression against Heaven's heart.

The people take the ruler as their leader.

>If the ruler's administration is good, the people will be harmonious and orderly.

If the ruler's administration is bad, the people will be resentful and chaotic.

The ruler takes sympathy with the people as fundamental.[2]

If the officials are loyal and virtuous, the ruler's administration will be good.
If the officials are debauched and crooked, the ruler's administration will be bad.

[The ruler] takes the selection [of officials] as fundamental.

If the selection process is complete and forthright, then loyal worthies will be advanced;
if the selection process is empty and deceitful, then immoral factionalists will be favored.

The selection process takes laws and ordinances as its root.

If laws and ordinances are foursquare, then the process of selection and promotion will be based on substance;
if the laws and commandments are fraudulent, the selection process will be unsound.

The law takes the ruler as its foundation.

If the ruler trusts in the law, then laws will be carried out smoothly;
if the ruler makes a mockery of the law, then laws will be disregarded.

The achievements of rulers and officials, laws and commandments, must be of service to the people. Thus,

if the ruler, officials, laws and commandments are good, then the
people will be secure and happy.
If the people are secure and happy, then Heaven's heart will be
accorded with.[3]
If Heaven's heart is accorded with, then yin and yang will be
harmonious.
If yin and yang are harmonious, then the five grains will be
abundant.

When the five grains are abundant, the people will be long-lived.
If the people are long-lived, they will be fond of righteousness.[4]
Being fond of righteousness, they will be free of depraved
conduct.

If they are free of depraved conduct, then the era will be peaceful, and

state and family will be tranquil,
the Altar of Earth and Grain will be secure, and
the ruler will be respected and glorified.

Thus, Heaven's heart, yin and yang, rulers and officials, the masses and commoners, good and evil, assist and elicit each other and replace and summon each other.

Now,

Heaven is the foundation of the state.
The ruler is the unifier of the people.
Officials are the resources of good government.

"If an artisan wishes to perfect his work, he must first sharpen his tools."[5] For the same reason, to usher in [an age of] Great Peace one must first harmonize yin and yang;

to harmonize yin and yang one must first accord with Heaven's heart;

to accord with Heaven's heart one must first appoint appropriate people;

to appoint appropriate people one must first examine and select appropriate people.

For this reason, a state's or ruling family's

basis for preservation or destruction, and
trigger for order or chaos,

lay in the enlightened selection [of officials] and nothing else. The ancient sages knew this, and so they gave priority to demotions and promotions. A passage in the *Book of Documents* says: "Now it is yours to give repose to the people: What choice should you be most concerned about? Should it not be proper men?"[6] That is how the Former Kings achieved [an era of] Great Peace and brought forth songs of praise.

"Obstruction" and "Greatness"[7] dissipate and grow [in turn]; yin and yang are not [dominant] simultaneously. Observing those whom [a ruler] gathers about him, the sprouts of his ascent or decline become visible.

When Hou [Ji], Xie, and Gaoyao[8] were assembled [by Shun], they brought about concord and happiness;

When Huangfu, Kui, and Ju[9] were assembled [by King You] they brought about disasters and portents.

These manifestations of good and evil are

matched by omens [even at] a distance of 1,000 *li*, and
their traces accumulate for a hundred generations.

"By nature we are alike; practice makes us different."[10] For that reason,

> worthiness and ignorance are located in the heart, not in noble or mean birth;
> trustworthiness and perfidy are found in one's nature, not in close or distant kinship.

> Those who contributed to the Second Emperor [of Qin's] losing the empire, were his prime minister and his imperial grand secretary.[11]
> Those who contributed to Gaozu's possessing All Under Heaven,[12] were a silk merchant and a dog butcher.[13]

> A ruffian from Mt. Li,
> a bandit from the Juye Marsh

both became famous generals.[14] Seen from this point of view,

> if you want to obtain the right person [for a task] don't fret about poverty or humble status;
> if you want to obtain the right talent, don't worry about fame or reputation.

Tracing a long way back to the beginning of the Han, whenever overbearing aristocratic officials were charged with capital offenses and when those who belonged to the same clique held official positions, [those] who were found guilty often amounted to two or three out of ten. From this perspective, [we see that] high-born and favored officials never demurred from empowering their personal followers or advancing the interests of perfidious cliques. That is why Wang Mang, together with Han-dynasty dukes, nobles, ministers, shepherds, and administrators, were able to overthrow the Han. [Emperor] Guangwu,[15] together with a loyal populace and disenfranchised gentlemen of service, punished [the usurper]. If it were the case that nobles are invariably worthy and loyal, while paupers are invariably stupid and untrustworthy, how could these events have occurred?

From [the time of] [Emperor] Cheng on down to [Wang] Mang, the dukes, nobles, marquises, magistrates, commandants, and officials high and low numbered roughly 100,000.[16] They were all [selected] from the ranks of what the Han dynasty considered worthy, brilliant, loyal, upright, noble, and favored officials. But when Wang Mang usurped the throne, only Liu Chong, Marquis of Anzhong, and Zhai Yi, governor of Dongjun, thought to take seriously the rituals [appropriate for] a ruler, and with righteous courage extended every effort in their desire to execute Wang Mang.[17] Although their objective did not meet with success, their steadfastness is worthy of being recorded. Thus of the 100,000 officials, those who were able to place country before self and requite the favor they had received [from the late emperor] were just two people, and that is all. From this perspective, [we may say that] in an era in decline, among all the officials there really were only a few worthies. Of the [other] officials,

> the more important the official, the weightier their transgressions;
> the higher the position, the deeper their crimes.

Thus it is said:

the virtues of a well-governed age, and
the evils of an age in decline,

frequently conform to the [actions of] the nobility and high officials.

Confucius said:

"In a country that has the Way, to be poor and obscure is shameful; in a country that does not have the Way, to be rich and prominent is shameful."[18]

The *Odes* laments:

"The brilliant white colt,
is there in that empty valley."[19]
"The artful speech flows like a stream,
and the speakers dwell at ease in prosperity."[20]

Essentially, these [passages] state that in an era of decline,

The purer the ambition, the more disparaged the person;
the craftier their flattery, the loftier their positions.

Affairs are arranged together according to kind;
things are divided by groups.[21]

Those with similar [powers of] vision recognize one another;
those with similar [powers of] hearing listen to one another.

It takes a sage to know a sage;
it takes a worthy to know a worthy.

At present, since those who occupy the road of [political power] are incapable of distinguishing the worthy from the base, they are nevertheless also forced to capitulate to the whims of eminent persons. Coerced by the demands of the powerful,

> petitioners clog their doorways,
> "courtesy gifts" [amass like] spokes on a wheel.

Overwhelmed by the urgent pleas of those right before their eyes, they give those [petitioners] priority. This is

> how upright gentlemen become isolated and ignored; and
> how the wicked form cliques and advance.

> The Duke of Zhou managed [his role as] prime minister by humbling himself before the lesser knights; thus he was able to obtain true worthies.
> Qi Xi managed [his role as] a grandee by promoting his enemy and [own] son; thus he was able to obtain upright men.[22]

In the present era, those who occupy [official] positions

> rely on their daughters' and sisters' [imperial] favor to lord it over the [honest] gentlemen of service; and
> avail themselves of the inherent power of the dragon [i.e., the emperor] to insult worthies,

while desiring to make the steadfast and virtuous gentlemen of service abase themselves by creeping and crawling and bowing and scraping, to do their bidding. [The corrupt officials] adopt false demeanors and engage in flattery to bind [them] ever more closely to themselves, and only then will they deign to support them. What then can an honest gentleman of service possibly do but "pick ferns," freeze and starve, hiding and dying in some mountain grotto?[23] How could there be anyone willing to cross *their* thresholds and befriend *them*?

# CHAPTER 10 PREFACE

Surveying ancient times to the present,
And events in books and commentaries,
[We see that] rulers all want order, while
Ministers perpetually delight in disorder.
The loyal and the toadies are jumbled together,
Each promoting its own ilk.
[I] am often pained by [the ruler's] failure to perceive [things] clearly,
And by his faith in the words of schemers.

Thus I have written "The Sighs of a Recluse," chapter 10.

# 10

## THE SIGHS OF A RECLUSE

Among all rulers who have possessed states, there has never been a case of one who did not desire [their states] to be well governed. But the reason good government is not seen in each era is because those who are appointed are not worthies. In every era there has never been an absence of worthies, but the reason worthies fail to find employment is because of the envy of the officials.

> The sovereign has the intention to recruit worthies but lacks the method to obtain them;
> The officials have the reputation of advancing worthies but lack the record of advancing them.

Because of this[1]

> above, the ruler is solitary and endangered, and
> below, [practitioners of] the Way[2] are isolated and oppressed.

As a rule,

> the means by which the ruler of a state achieves good government is public-spiritedness. When public-spirited

laws are put into practice, then treasonous disorders are cut short.³

The means by which deceitful officials advance their private interests is selfishness. When methods for [protecting] self-interest are employed, public-spirited laws are abrogated.

The means by which the exemplary officers establish integrity is righteousness. When upright conduct and integrity are established, disgraceful behavior is rooted out.

This is why licentious officials, disorderly functionaries, and lawless groups act night and day to impede any contact between the worthy ruler and the righteous gentlemen of service, and constantly try to prevent them from meeting with each other.

Now when worthies act as officials, they

> do not harm the ruler in order to cater to toadies;
> do not truckle to the masses in order to gain their approval;
> do not neglect the public in order to attend to the private;
> do not bend the laws in order to exonerate the powerful.⁴

Their

> brilliance is able to cast light on the evil, while
> their righteousness is not bound to cabals.

This was the case

> when Fan Wu returned to Jin, and the wicked persons of that state fled;⁵
> and when Hua Yuan returned to court, and Yu Shi absconded.⁶

Thus, an upright and righteous officer and a person who is crooked and depraved cannot both occupy the same place. But when rulers of the people choose gentlemen of service, they [prove themselves] incapable of simultaneously listening to the voice of the people and judging according to what they [themselves] hear and what they see. [But] on the contrary, they

> believe only the arguments of untrustworthy officials, and make sole use of the words of corrupt functionaries.

This can be called

> "partnering with enemies to select officials, and allowing convicts to appoint [prison] wardens."

A passage in the *Book of Documents* says:

> "Consult with your own heart;
> consult with the masses of the people."[7]

Confucius said,

> "When the masses like someone, it must be looked into. When the masses hate someone, it must be looked into."[8]

That is why the sage, in conferring or withholding [official appointments]

> does not necessarily trust [the opinion of] the masses, but also does not necessarily trust his [own views].

He must examine other people's as well as his own perspectives and consider them in terms of what is right, perhaps setting aside [the views of] others and choosing his own. Therefore,

> in his appointments there will be no omissions or errors, and
> in his government there will be no corruption or destruction.

A deluded prince does not proceed in this way. If he has his own favorites, then he relies on them to make decisions.

> He does not consult with the masses;
> he does not peer into his own heart.

If he is dazzled by a favorite, only their words are followed. This is how

> governments fall into destruction and chaos, and
> gentlemen of service are cast off and not employed.

In ancient times, [King] Djou [of Shang][9] loved beautiful women. Hearing this, the Marquis of Jiu offered [the king] his daughter. Djou was greatly pleased and believed that among the beauties of the whole world, there was no one [else] like her. He then told Daji[10] about her. Daji feared that [Jiu's daughter] would be selected for service and rob her of the king's love. So she deceitfully prostrated herself and wept, saying [to the king], "Has Your Majesty suddenly grown old? Has Your Majesty's eyesight already begun to fail? How can it be that when someone is as ugly as this, Your Majesty perversely claims that she is beautiful?" King Djou thereupon changed his mind and regarded [the marquis's daughter] as ugly. Daji, fearing that more people in the world would offer beautiful women [to the king], then said,

"The Marquis of Jiu's evil ploy was in fact an effort to use his daughter to befuddle Your Majesty. If Your Majesty doesn't execute him now, how will it be possible to prevent [such acts] in the future?" King Djou then flew into a rage. He had the daughter minced and boiled the Marquis of Jiu. After that, everyone kept their daughters closely confined in rooms protected by many layers of walls that remained locked all day for fear that Djou would hear about them.

Zhao Gao[11] monopolized power in Qin. He planned to kill the Second Generation Emperor,[12] but first he wanted to display his might to the masses. He gave the emperor a deer, saying that it was a horse. The Second Generation Emperor looked at it and said, "It is a deer." Zhao Gao said, "It's a horse." The emperor rubbed his eyes, scrutinized it carefully and said, "You, Prime Minister, are mistaken. It's a deer." Zhao Gao [persisted to] the end in calling it a horse. He then queried the court officials. Some of the court officials supported the emperor's [view] and rejected Zhao Gao's. Zhao Gao then explained to the emperor, "These are all flatterers who intend to do harm to Your Majesty. Their disloyalty could not be greater." He then executed all of them. From then on, no one dared to remonstrate with him, and Zhao Gao murdered the emperor in [the palace of] Wangyi. Ultimately, because of this, [the Qin dynasty] was destroyed.

Now beauty and ugliness[13] are revealed by one's eyes, and the difference between a deer and a horse is inherent in their form. [The two rulers] were also certain about this. But as soon as they were faced with a slanderous minister and a jealous concubine who fabricated words and falsified statements, it caused

> a ruler and a king to lose their own convictions, and
> people and things to be denied their physical forms.[14]

How much more is this the case when encountering someone living in seclusion or confined in prison and having to wait while their bona fides are being looked into, which is not like the impression made after looking at a bewitching woman. Making distinctions among worthies is not like that; it is not like the certainty of distinguishing between a deer and a horse. These two [i.e., ministers and concubines][15] can both be seen at court displaying their qualities for the eyes [of the ruler and the officials]. When it comes to bewitching the ruler through amorous pleasures, illicit sensuality, flattery, and crooked cunning,

> it is like bedazzling the ruler's vision, and
> altering the ruler's mind,

and thus deluding him into believing

> that the beautiful is ugly, or
> that a deer is a horse.

It is no wonder, then, that

> worthies who have retired to the distant countryside, and
> gentlemen of service who are far from the court

never come before the prince's sight?

> Now, some who hold office

> enjoy impeding worthies and
> endeavor to advance cabals.

This has been so since ancient times. Formerly, considering

> Yao of Tang's great sagacity—the brilliance of his understanding illuminated [the world];
> Shun of Yu's great sagacity—the report of his virtue was heard everywhere.

When Yao was Son of Heaven, he sought true worthies and consulted the Lords of the Lands.[16] The Lords of the Lands were not willing to recommend Shun, but on the contrary, touted people like Gong Gong and Gun. [But] by virtue of Yao's sagacity, they subsequently elevated Shun and banished the Four [Disobedient] Ones.[17]

Indeed, through

> the substance of the ancient sages—
> the illumination of Yao's comprehension;
> the clarity of Shun's virtue;

> the rulers' brilliance could not be exploited;
> their radiant virtue could not be concealed—

their dispositions were such that flatterers were few, and those who had [official] posts [lacuna] were exclusively like them as well.[18]

[But] nowadays the conduct of the gentlemen of service departs[19] greatly from that of Yao and Shun. Their customs are dissipated, and the laws they enact proliferate.[20] This being the case, the chance of

> a prince who searches for worthies, and
> gentlemen of service who pity the people

coming together is inevitably hopeless.

King Wen once was out hunting. Encountering Jiang Shang[21] by the banks of the Wei River, [the king] scrutinized his spoken words, observed his determination, and studied his heart.

>Without consulting [his ministers] of the left and right,
>Without querying his [entourage of] officials,

he [loaded Jiang Shang into his carriage] and brought him back with him [to the royal court]. Thereupon he entrusted him with the government, employing his skills to establish the Zhou [dynasty].

Thus, Yao scoured the countryside to get Shun; King Wen drew on his own resources to obtain Lü Shang. How do they compare with [Di] Xin of Yin or Zheng of Qin,[22] who, having obtained worthies, on the contrary abandoned them to their enemies, maimed and slaughtered the upright and honest, while advancing a cabal of corrupt and licentious officials?

This is why the upright Way of enlightened and sagacious princes [consists of] not

>being exclusively goaded by aristocrats and favorites, or deluded by favorites and flatterers,

>not casting off those with whom they have no close connections,
>not neglecting the young and impoverished,

and moreover consulting and employing such people.

Thus, in the Zhou dynasty's system of ruling, when the Son of Heaven administered state affairs, he ordered [all officials] from the Three Dukes through the ranks of the gentlemen of service to present documents and the good scribes to present writings [to the throne]. [He ordered]

> the officers to admonish,
> blind musicians to compose,
> poets to recite,

the various artisans to advise, [he ordered]

> ordinary people to relay their stories,
> [palace] servants to offer advice,
> his relatives to remedy flaws,
> the Music Master and the Grand Historian to impart their teachings, and
> the elderly to perfect him.[23]

After this the king would deliberate on their advice. In this way the affairs of state were all carried out without mishap.

In the end times, the situation is not like this.[24] [The ruler of such a time]

> only trusts the imperious and envious counsel of nobles, and
> exclusively adopts the poisonous and deluded propositions of the negligent and obsequious.

> Those who conduct themselves according to the rites suffer criticism and blame;
> those who discuss virtue and righteousness experience scorn and hatred.

Thus, sycophantic ministers even

> double down with laws against disparagement and calumny, supplemented by punishment for judging the emperor.[25]

This is the initial difficulty of worthy men of service. Now, disparagement and calumny laws are axes that cleave the worthy, and arrogant and envious ministers are dogs that bite worthies. When a ruler of the people privately

> wields the ax that cuts down worthies, and
> empowers the dogs that bite them,

while outwardly summons worthies in the hope that they will come, is this not truly distressing?

# CHAPTER 11 PREFACE

Official ranks depend on virtue to flourish;
Virtue values loyalty to stand firm.
This is what the altars of soil and grain rely upon.
Security and danger are bound to these.
If [a person] is not upright, straightforward, or sincere;
Benevolent, kind, gracious, or congenial,
Or [if he does not] serve the ruler as if he were Heaven,
Or [if he does not] treat the people as if they were his children,
Then he will be unable to preserve his status,
Or to protect his good name.

Thus I have written "Loyalty and Nobility," chapter 11.

# 11

## LOYALTY AND NOBILITY

A generation that

> has unsurpassed great good fortune,
> will also have unbearably painful bad fortune.

Those who occupy the highest of all positions cannot lack unsurpassed achievements. Those who usurp the highest of all ranks have never avoided ruin and extinction. Those whose achievements comply with Heaven and Earth have never failed to flourish and prosper.[1]

What emperors and kings venerate and honor and what Heaven deeply loves is the people. If an official receives from his ruler some weighty position shepherding those whom Heaven deeply loves, how can he not

> settle and benefit them, or
> nurture and assist them?

Thus, when

> a gentleman is entrusted with responsibility, he thinks about how to benefit the people; if

he succeeds to a higher position, then he thinks about advancing worthies.

What achievement could be greater than this? Thus,

> if he occupies a high position, his subordinates will not feel oppressed;
> if he is positioned in front, those behind him will not be endangered.[2]

A passage in the *Book of Documents* says: "The work is Heaven's—it is men's to act for it."[3] The [ancient] kings, patterning themselves on Heaven, established offices. From dukes and high ministers down to petty functionaries, in each case which of them is not Heaven's official? For that reason,

> an enlightened ruler does not dare to [appoint officials to advance his] private interests;
> a loyal minister does not dare to falsify his abilities.

Now to steal someone's goods is called robbery. How much the worse is it to plunder a Heaven[-endowed] office in order to gratify one's personal desires? Persons who commit crimes against others necessarily must suffer punishment; how much more is this the case for those who offend Heaven—can they escape blame?

The [lords of] the Five Eras[4] established the Lords of the Lands; created states and formed hereditary [fiefs],

> transmitted to posterity for a hundred generations,
> spanning years over a millennia.

All this was because

> their abilities matched their Heaven-appointed offices, and
> their efforts were applied to the common people.
>
> The Duke of Zhou led an expedition to the east, and later
>     generations savored the memory.[5]
> The Duke of Shao [rested beneath] a sweet pear tree, and people
>     could not bear for it to be cut down.[6]

Having been so beloved, how could anyone have selfishly wished to harm them? The enfeoffed lords who came after them have proliferated greatly.

> Some do not live out their [fated] span;
> others do not even last a month;

and there are none whose [hereditary offices and land holdings] are not obliterated within their times, their span never filling out a century. Why did this happen?[7]

The officials of the Five Sovereigns

> employed the Way in dealing with the ruler's affairs, and
> employed humaneness in attending to the age.
>
> Their beneficence extended to the grasses and trees;
> their bounty [was felt by all] both outside and inside
>     [the realm];

Everywhere under Heaven, to the edges of the Earth; there was no one who did not receive kindness. Their bringing of tranquility and safety was due to their being equal to [the task of] Heaven's work.[8] Thus,

> their happiness and blessings flowed and diffused, and root and branch [lineages were extended] for a hundred generations.[9]

But officials in an era of decline give no thought to being in accord with Heaven, and whoever is in power at the time is who they flatter.

> Those who defeat enemies are termed "loyal";
> [those who] kill the most are considered "worthies."

[Consider] Bo Qi and Meng Tian:[10]

> [The ruler of] Qin regarded them as meritorious, [but] Heaven regarded them as bandits.

[Likewise, in the case of] Xifu [Gong] and Dong Xian,[11]

> the ruler regarded them as loyal, [but]
> Heaven regarded them as robbers.

Although persons of this sort were seen as honorable by the rulers of the day, the outcome was that

> above, they did not accord with Heaven's heart, [while] below, they did not satisfy the people's expectations.

Ultimately, shedding tears of blood and crying out, [their lives] ended in disgrace. The *Book of Changes* says:

Virtue small and office high;
wisdom small and plans great;
strength small and burden heavy

—rarely do [such conditions] not end [in evil].[12]
That is why,

when [an official's] virtue does not correspond to his responsibilities, his misfortune must be brutal;
when his abilities do not correspond to his position, his calamity must be great.

Furthermore, [in the case of] a person illegitimately occupying an official position, Heaven will withdraw his enlightened understanding,[13] and spirits will trouble his heart. That is why when he is [still] impoverished, though he might possess enlightened understanding and adhere to benevolence and righteousness, if one day he becomes wealthy, he will turn his back on his family and spurn his old familiars, discarding his originally endowed nature.

He will reject all of his blood relations and draw near to his hangers-on;
he will be stingy to his closest friends but generous to his dogs and horses.

His wealth and property will be heaped on his servants and concubines,
and his emoluments will be reserved for his nefarious slaves.

He'd rather see the strings of ten million cash decay than give someone one coin;

he'd rather let rotting grain accumulate in his granary than lend someone one peck.

[Such a] person [will become] increasingly haughty and unrestrained, incurring debts that are never repaid.

His blood relatives resent him within his own home,
while commoners curse him in the street.

People from his past have been ruined because of him, [yet] before him are those who compete to succeed them. This is truly lamentable.

Surveying previous generations of eminent statesmen applying their minds is like [observing] infants.

Infants have the usual [childhood] diseases;
statesmen suffer the usual crises.
Fathers and mothers make the usual mistakes;
the rulers of men commit the usual transgressions.

When infants have the usual illnesses, it is because they are harmed by overeating;
when honored officials commit the usual transgressions, it is because they are harmed by indulgence.

The usual mistakes of fathers and mothers lay in their not being able to stop themselves from doting [on the child];
the usual transgressions of rulers of men lay in their not being able to stop themselves from indulging officials.
If an infant nurses too much, it will certainly convulse and develop epilepsy;
if the wealth of an honored person becomes too plentiful, he will certainly behave arrogantly and make mistakes.

Thus,

> those who spoil children to the point of harming their bodies are not found in just one household;
> those who indulge officials to the point of destroying their families do not appear in just one era.

[In the past],

> some [were destroyed because they] rebelled and acted contrary to the Way;
> some [were destroyed because their] virtue was slight and they did not merit the honors bestowed on them.

> [The spirit of the constellation] Cultured Brilliance[14] governed their achievements;
> [the spirit of the constellation] Arbiter of Fate[15] exposed their transgressions,

noting whether the evil was deep-seated or superficial, and weighing their crimes to hand down punishments.

> Some [malefactors] were executed by beheading.
> Some had their shoulders drawn back to tear open their chests.

> Some died in deep dungeons, or were
> decapitated in the city marketplace.

Their stiffened corpses, ruined families, annihilated kin groups, and obliterated clans were [all] due to their failure to provide meritorious service to the common people. [Still], those who come after them aspire to power and are greedy for favors, which they amass without limit.

Thinking to climb towers of perilous height,
content to follow the tracks of a cart that overturned,

hoping for good fortune and blessings to increase the holdings of those who are already overflowing [with wealth]—is any era without such people?

When the Lü clan had become eminent,

the Empress Dowager assumed power and gained sole control of the government.[16]
[Lü] Lu and [Lü] Chan[17] took control of affairs and consolidated power.
[The Lü family]

unilaterally set up four kings,[18]
enfeoffed many of their sons and younger brothers, and
controlled appointments of generals and ministers.

Inside and outside [the court] they forged tight alliances. They thought that like the

rise of Tang and Wu,[19] or
the reigns of the five hegemons,[20]

no one could endanger them. Thereupon

they did away with humaneness and righteousness and esteemed intimidation and oppression;
they obliterated ritual and honesty and concentrated on deceit and falsehood.

All within the four seas were [filled with] hatred and pain, and there was no one who did not wish for their destruction. Thus in a single morning their extermination was complete, and no one felt pity for them.

When the Huo clan became eminent, [Huo Guang] exclusively assisted the under-age monarch.[21] He executed [individuals] and exterminated [the clans] of his fellow aristocrats, dismissing one emperor and setting up another, so that no one dared to oppose him.[22] [Huo] Yu inherited his father's place, and [Huo] Shan and [Huo] Yun seized control [of the government].[23] Sons-in-law of Huo clan members took charge of the Imperial Guard and married only members of the imperial family.

When the Wang family became eminent, [their ranks included] nine marquises, five generals, and twenty-three persons with [the high privilege of having] vermilion wheels on their chariots. The Empresses Dowager[24] took control of the government and held power for three generations. [Wang] Mang became prime minister and was enfeoffed as "Lord Who Brings Tranquility to the Han." He served as regent and then usurped the title of emperor.[25] Occupying the position of "facing south," he ultimately usurped the position of the ruler. This went on for more than ten years. He felt that he had already been in that position for a long time, and since his authority had been established and his beneficence enacted, there would in perpetuity be no disasters or failures. Therefore, with an unscrupulous heart and unrestrained intentions, he favored the near and forgot the distant, assembled a coterie of the small-minded, heavily taxing and exhausting the common people to support those who made no contributions. He enacted treacherous and deceitful schemes, justifying them with [references to] canonical texts,

> casting a net of deceit over the populace, and
> cheating Heaven and Earth.

He thought his actions were secret, and [that] no one else knew them. [But]

> sovereign Heaven from on high caught the reflection of his falsehood,
> spirit-like illumination from the gloom shined a light on his behavior.

How deluded he was!
Now,

> birds consider mountains to be low, so they build their nests on their summits;
> fish consider abysses to be shallow, so they scrape out hollows in their midst.

Yet in the end, the way they are captured is by the use of bait. The empress,

> fearing her family's inauspiciousness, cultivated a good reputation, and
> fearing the palace gates' weakness, made iron hinges.

Yet in the end the reason they suffered, defeated not

> because they were encumbered by the prohibitions being too few, or
> because their palace gate hinges were rusty, but
> because they worshipped material wealth, and
> because they comported themselves with arrogance and excess,

tyrannizing the populace,
losing the hearts of the people,

and nothing more.

Confucius said, "Do not be concerned that you have no [official] place; be concerned with how you may fit yourself for one."[26] For that reason, officials who do not

promote and follow the rites and the laws;
exhaust all efforts thinking about their duties;
offer sincere assistance to the ruler;
make every effort to benefit the populace;

take care of the people below, or
conform to Heaven's will above,

in fact want to

rely on their own personal views and
usurp the ruler's awesome potency

in order to oppress the common folk. They

contravene Heaven and Earth, and
cheat and deceive spiritual powers.

Through improper measures they scheme for advancement and ill-gotten gain, and look to acquire even greater emoluments.

Their position is as dangerous as standing on a heap of eggs, but
they imagine it is as stable as Mount Tai.

Their acts are as ephemeral as morning dew, but they think their success will last for generations.

They are like the First Emperor of Qin, who eschewed virtue and [tried to rule through] mutilating punishments. Their chance of getting what they want is one in ten thousand. Are they not deluded?

# CHAPTER 12 PREFACE

When the kings of former times administered [the nation's] wealth;
They prohibited the people from wrongdoing.
The "Great Plan" expressed concern for the people.
The *Odes* criticized exhausting their resources.
When unscrupulous drifters become numerous,
The essential task of agriculture will decline.
There must be systemic regulation,
But why is there no discussion of this issue?

Thus I have written "On Excessive Luxury," chapter 12.

# 12

## ON EXCESSIVE LUXURY

The [true] king
considers all within the four seas as one family, and
takes the multitudinous population into full account.

If one man does not till, the world must accept its victims of hunger,
If one woman does not weave, the world must accept its victims
of cold.

Nowadays everyone casts aside agriculture and sericulture and pursues commerce and business. Oxen and horses, carts and wagons crowd the highways and roads; shiftless people working cunning schemes fill the capital and the cities.

Those who attend to the fundamental are few,[1]
while those who survive on frivolous pursuits are legion.

"The capital of Shang was neat and orderly;
a standard to the Four Quarters."[2]

But if we examine Luoyang, those who engage in nonessential trades outnumber farmers ten to one, while con men and idlers outnumber those engaged in nonessential trades by [a further ratio of] ten to one.³ So it turns out that

> one farmer tills to feed a hundred, and
> one woman raises silkworms to clothe a hundred.

One person supporting a hundred—who is able to provide such a quantity? In the world's hundreds of commanderies and thousands of counties, and its market towns and cities that number in the tens of thousands, everywhere the situation is like this. How can the supplies of essentials and nonessentials be adjusted to the demand? And then how can the people avoid hunger and cold? If hunger and cold arrive, how can they avoid wrongdoing? If they commit wrongdoings, how can they avoid [falling into] treachery and villainy?⁴

> If treachery and villainy become widespread, how can officials avoid responding with strictness and severity?
> If strictness and severity increase, how can the people under these [officials] avoid [feeling] anxious and resentful?

If anxiety and resentment abound, then inauspicious portents and phenomena will both appear. If

> below, the people lack what they need to sustain themselves, and
> above, Heaven sends down disasters,

then the state will become endangered.

Now,

> poverty is born of wealth;
> weakness is born of strength;

chaos is born of good governance;
danger is born of safety.

Therefore, in nurturing the people, the enlightened king

grieves with them, encourages them,
teaches them, and admonishes them,

taking pains with small matters and warding off sprouts [of discontent], thereby cutting short their evildoing. Therefore the *Book of Changes* praises "regulations that bring about order

without infringing on property, and
without injuring the people."[5]

And the ode "The Seventh Month" shows how [the ruler] instructs the people in matters great and small, [from the beginning of the year] to the end and then how it resumes again.[6] Seen from this perspective, it is certain that the people cannot be left to their own devices.

Nowadays people

indulge in [fine] clothing,
waste food and drink,
cultivate facile talk, and
practice deceit and deception,

working their schemes on one another. They are everywhere.

Some organize groups of malefactors as their occupation;
    while
some wander about as professional gamblers.

Some adult men have not touched a plow or a hoe in their entire lives. Grasping a supply of pellets and a crossbow they stroll about, hand in hand with their fellow drifters. Others use good soil to make pellets, which they sell, though

> outside they are useless for fending off bandits, and
> inside are inadequate for stopping rats.

[Duke] Ling of Jin[7] liked [shooting crossbows], which only added to his faults. It is unheard of for honest and righteous knights to delight in such amusements. Only mindless people, in their infantile packs, obtain and carry them about, randomly shooting at sparrows and [other kinds of] birds. In a hundred shots they fail to make even one hit, but instead cause injury to the face and eyes of [others]. Not only is this activity utterly useless, it is actually harmful.[8] Some sit and make bamboo reeds. They sharpen their tips to a point, giving them a dangerous appearance, and smear them with honey to make them seem sweet, just like "sweet talkers," none of whom [produce] good fortune or auspicious auguries.[9] Others make clay chariots, ceramic dogs, horses with riders, and singers and dancers, but these are merely toys for children, used to charm and cheat them.

The *Odes* admonishes: "She does not twist her hemp / but in the market place she dances."[10] At present, many women do not "attend to [the preparation of] food within [the home],"[11] and "abandon [their] silk worms and weaving."[12] Instead they take up the study of shamanistic prayers, drum and dance in service to the spirits, in order to

> deceive simple people, and
> hoodwink the populace.

Women, the infirm, and households where someone is ill, or where people are distraught with worry, distressed and troubled, all can easily be made fearful and anxious to the point of compelling them to

> flee at auspicious times, and
> leave behind their rightful homes

for rugged roadsides where they [encounter] drizzle above and dampness below. [In such places they are]

> injured by wind and cold,
> taken advantage of by evil men,
> made the targets of robbers and thieves

so that their misfortune increases and disaster grows to an unimaginable degree of severity. Some reject [appropriate] medicine but increase their service to the spirits. Thus, up to the point of death, they themselves do not recognize that it is the shamankas who are deluding them, but instead blame themselves for having served the shamankas too late. This [sort of occurrence] shows the degree to which the common people are hoodwinked.

Some cut up fine silk to make strips [for writing out] prayers, hiring artisans to [decorate them with] distinctive patterns and employing others to write out invocations, in trite and facile language expressing wishes for great good fortune. Others tear up colored silks, reducing them [to long, narrow strips] five inches in length, which are multicolored and embroidered to use as sashes. Others spin multicolored strands of silk to make cords, cutting them into pieces to make arm bands. These things will never affect good or ill fortune, but pointlessly destroy silk cloth and bedazzle the common folk. Others destructively cut up silk gauze, inch by inch, clipping the eight-colored [cloth] [into pieces the size and shape of] elm leaves, producing endless numbers [decorated] with stripes like watery waves, and covered with finely executed embroidery that are made into cases for bamboo utensils, as well as skirts and jackets, wasting hundreds of bolts of double-thread silk that require ten times the usual labor [for such garments]. People of this sort certainly do nothing to assist honest farmers and female artisans, nor do they do anything to add to the material well-being of the age. They sit and eat their fill of fine grain, wasting the light of day. They destroy [goods] that have been made, considering

> the perfect to be broken,
> the firm to be unstable,
> the large to be small,
> and the easy to be difficult.

All of these are things that must be prohibited.

> Mountains and forests cannot fuel a prairie fire;
> rivers and seas cannot fill a broken cup.

The filial emperor Wen[13] clothed himself in coarse black material. He wore leather shoes on his feet and a leather sword-belt at his waist. He collected the bags that had been used to submit memorials in order to make them into curtains.[14] In the height of summer, suffering from the heat, he wanted to erect a terrace. He calculated that it would cost a million cash, and deciding it was wasteful, did not build it.[15]

Nowadays, the upper nobility in the capital and the imperial kin [enjoy] clothing, food, drink, carriages, decor, and residences that all exceed royal regulations and egregiously usurp the emperor's privileges. Furthermore, their entourages of slaves, servants, and concubines all are clothed in finely woven silks —"Bamboo Tube" and "Damsel's Cloth" textiles,[16] fine plain weave, crepe silk, "icy white" silk, brocaded, and multicolored. There are [decorations of] rhino horn, elephants' ivory tusk, pearl, jade, amber, tortoiseshell, and minutely patterned agate. [Their interiors are decorated with] miniature mountain ranges, [objects with] gold and silver inlay, and various items all painted and carved.[17] [They wear] shoes of doeskin or buckskin with patterned laces and embroidered linings. In their arrogance and extravagances, they usurp the privileges of their superiors while boasting to each other. [The behavior] that made Jizu weep[18] is enacted by servants and concubines today. At weddings of the rich and high-born, carriages and curtained coaches by the dozens are surrounded by mounted grooms and slaves who guide them through the crush. Thus do the wealthy compete with one another, each trying to outdo the others, while the poor feel ashamed at not being able to match [such extravagance]. The expense wasted on such feasts would be enough to sustain an [ordinary] person for a lifetime.

In ancient times there were certainly people who were ennobled, but it was only after (an elevation in rank) that they could wear patterned-silk clothing, ride in chariots or on horseback.[19] Now, although it is impossible to bring back the past, ordinary people in fact should not be permitted [such luxuries] or to transgress the norms of the former Filial Emperor Wen, [demanding that]

clothing must be of the finest silk;
hunting shoes must be made from roe deer and muntjacs;
laces must be patterned and colored;
sashes must be of the finest fabric.

They decorate their chariots and horses and maintain countless numbers of slaves. Since everyone enabled in this way does not produce grain, they sink to the status of parasitic vermin.

Confucius said: "When the ancients buried their dead, they covered the body thickly with pieces of wood, after placing it in the wilds. They raised no mound over it, nor planted trees around it; nor had they any fixed period for mourning. In subsequent ages the sages substituted for these practices the inner and outer coffins."[20] They used

[wood of the] tung-oil tree to make the coffins, and
vines to bind them tightly together, so that

below [the corpse] would not pollute the underground springs, and
above it would not emit odors.

In later times, people used mallotus, catalpa, sophora, cedar, acacia, and ailanthus, depending on what was produced locally. They applied glue and lacquer, and fashioned "dovetail" mortises and tenon joints; they scraped away places that protruded so that joints and seams were invisible.

Their robustness was sufficient to make them last, and
their functionality was sufficient to serve their purpose,

and this was considered quite enough.

Lately, the imperial relatives in the capital compulsively crave [timber] from south of the Yangzi River, [such as] paper mulberry, catalpa, camphor, thorn-elm, and nanmu. These trees are native to distant border regions, and [the aristocrats] compete with one another to follow [the fashion]. Now paper mulberry, catalpa, and camphor and thorn-elm come from distant regions, and furthermore, grow on steep mountains or in deep valleys. [The foresters] must traverse

> lofty peaks that are thousands of feet high,
> gorges that are a hundred fathoms deep,

> [face] dangers in narrow declivities, and
> [challenges] along rugged paths.

> Searching for days on end, until they catch sight of [a suitable tree];
> hacking at it for months on end, until [the task] is finally complete;
> assembling a crowd [of workers], till they finally dislodge it, and
> harnessing teams of oxen, till they finally drag it to the river.

[On barges] they enter the sea via the You River. Then they ascend the Huai River to join the Yellow River. After [a journey of] several thousand li, they finally arrive at Luoyang. There, carpenters spend days and months carving [the wood]. Altogether, for one coffin to be finished requires the labor of thousands or tens of thousands of workers. When finally it is ready for use, it weighs ten thousand pounds, and

> without the [combined] effort of a great crowd [of workers] it cannot be lifted;

without [the use of] a great cart it cannot be shifted.

East as far as Lelang,
west as far as Dunhuang,[21]

amid this span of ten thousand li [the elite] compete with one another to use [such coffins]. This waste of effort harms agriculture; it is heartbreaking.

The ancients [made] tombs but not tumuli. When Confucius buried his mother, he made a tomb mound four feet high. When it rained, it eroded. His disciples asked permission to repair it. Confucius, weeping, said "It is a violation of ritual to repair a tomb." When [his son] Li died, he had a single coffin but no outer coffin.

Emperor Wen was entombed at Zhiyang, and
Emperor Ming was entombed south of Luoyang.[22]

In both cases [the tombs were not supplied with] pearls [or other] treasures. They did not build mortuary temples or raise tomb-mounds [like artificial] mountains. Though their tomb-mounds and graves were simple, their sagehood was lofty.

Nowadays, among

> the imperial relatives and nobility in the capital, and
> the great families in the commanderies and districts,

> when parents are alive they do not nurture them to the utmost, but
> when they die, they make elaborate arrangements for their funerals.

Some go the extreme of [draping the corpse with] a worked gold and engraved jade [suit], and using [rare wood such as] paper mulberry, catalpa, thorn-elm, and nanmu [to make coffins]. They

> take good farmland to make cemeteries, and
> deposit grave goods in the yellow earth.

They fill the tomb with precious gems and treasure, figurines of people, chariots, and horses. They

> raise up great tumuli,
> and plant the broad expanse with pine and cedar.

For the mourners' hut and ancestral temple, they employ the most extreme extravagance and exhibit the highest form of overstepping their ranks. As for favored officials and imperial relatives, eminent families and hereditary officials in the provinces and commanderies, whenever there is a burial, whether in the capital or in [rural] district, each requires [a staff of] lesser officials to make offerings. Their chariots and horses, banners and curtains, and various borrowed items for entertaining guests, compete in a sumptuous display. These things

> offer no benefit to paying final respects, and
> add nothing to filial expression.

On the contrary, they are troublesome, disruptive, destructive, and harmful to minor functionaries and the common people.
    Now, examining that

> the suburban districts of Hao and Bi have no tombs for [Kings] Wen and Wu;

the burial mound at Nancheng has no tomb for Zeng Xi;[23]

it is not the case

that the Duke of Zhou was disloyal, or
that Zengzi was unfilial.[24]

Rather, they considered that

honoring rulers and esteeming fathers does not lay in providing numerous burial goods, and that
lauding their names and glorifying ancestors does not lay in providing chariots and horses [to be buried in the tomb].

Confucius said: "Great wealth injures virtue; money obstructs the Rites."[25]

Lord Ling of Jin levied heavy taxation to decorate his [palace] walls, but the *Spring and Autumn* did not consider him to be a [true] ruler.[26]
Hua Yuan and Yue Lü gave Duke Wen [of Song] an extravagant funeral, but the *Spring and Autumn* did not consider them to be true ministers.[27]

How much more so the many office holders, gentlemen of service, and commoners [of today]. Can they [dare to] exceed the excesses of their superiors in violation of Heaven's Way?

In the time of Han Emperor Jing,[28] Wei Buhai, Marquis of Wuyuan, made arrangements for [his own] funeral in ways that violated regulations and was forced to surrender his fief.

In the time of Emperor Ming,[29] Sang Min, Marquis of Zongyang, erected a tomb mound that was higher than regulations permitted, and his head was shaved.[30]

Now All-Under-Heaven is awash in licentiousness and excess and ignores the fundamentals [i.e., agriculture and sericulture]. Such arrogance and insubordination has already become very serious indeed.

Now all that is criticized here does not represent the true nature of the people. Instead, it is those who compete for and foster these [unworthy goals] who bring chaos to the government and those who neglect [the importance of educational] transformation that makes them this way. Only a true king who brings order to the world, who watches over the people, and who establishes education can change customs and alter manners in order to bring about the great peace.

# CHAPTER 13 PREFACE

The accumulation of minute [errors] harms [virtuous] action,
Lust and ease destroy reputations.
Day and night indulging one's desires,
But lacking any expression of remorse.
Deserving but stubbornly resisting advice;
Hearing about virtuous [examples] but not following them:
Minute indulgences invite disgrace,
And in the end insure disaster.

Thus I have written "Taking Care Over Minutiae," chapter 13.

# 13

## TAKING CARE OVER MINUTIAE

I n all cases,

the height of a mountain peak is not sharpened to reach great heights; it must step by step increase and gradually reach upward.

The depth of a river valley is not cut asunder to make it collapse and sink; it must wear away, erode, and gradually sink downward.[1]

Thus,

by accumulating height without ceasing, [a mountain] will reach the height of Mt. Song;

by accumulating depth without halting, [a river] will plumb the depths of the Yellow Springs.[2]

Not only mountains and rivers, but human endeavors are also like this. A plain-clad [commoner] who

accumulates goodness without ceasing will achieve the worthiness of a Yan or a Min;[3] but one who accumulates evil without respite will acquire the reputation of a Jie or a Zhi.[4]

Not only are plain-clad [commoners] like this, but officials also behave like this.

> Tirelessly accumulating rectitude will produce a principled and righteous will.
> Unceasingly accumulating evil will produce a violent and regicidal heart.

Not only officials, but also rulers of states are also like this.

> In governing and educating, accumulating virtue will elicit the good fortune of tranquility and peace.
> In taking precautionary measures, multiple failures will elicit the bad fortune of danger and extinction.

Therefore Zhongni said,

> "Tang and Wu did not become kings by dint of one act of goodness;
> Jie and Djou did not perish by dint of one act of wickedness.

The rise and fall of the Three Ages lay in what they accumulated."[5]

> Even if one who has accumulated much goodness were to commit one evil act, it would be regarded as a transgression insufficient to bring about ruin.
> Even if one who has accumulated much evil were to perform one act of goodness, it would be regarded as an accidental success insufficient to preserve (the state).

Rulers hear this and can be made to tremble with fear;
plain-clad (commoners) hear it and can be made to improve their comportment.

Hence, the person of discernment is "fearful and apprehensive, cautious day by day," "aspires to self-mastery," "reflects on the three points," and "plans for things before they become manifest."[6] Confucius said:

> If goodness is not accumulated, it will be insufficient to bring oneself renown.
> If wickedness is not accumulated, it will be insufficient to destroy one's life.

The petty person

> regards small kindnesses as being of no benefit and does not perform them, and
> thinks of small evils as harmless and does not eschew them.

> Thus, evil accumulates and cannot be concealed, and when transgressions become great, there is no escape.[7]

This is how

> Gui and Yu sowed confusion in the kingdom and did not turn back, and why
> the three epochs followed their inclinations and were not restored.[8]

Now,

> the accumulation of the minute becomes visible,
> the accumulation of what is manifest forms [an image].[9]

Honesty and flattery elicit survival or destruction; the sage is thus ever cautious over these subtle signs.[10]

"King Wen was watchful and so reverent;
King Cheng was day and night so respectful,"[11]

considering and taking care over the minute and obscure, early on preventing what had not yet taken root. They were therefore able to solicit the Great Peace and pass it on to sons and grandsons.

Moreover, depravity and rectitude are like water and fire; they emerge from different sources and cannot flourish simultaneously.

"If people's upright nature prevails, they will value themselves and be unwilling to see themselves diminished in any way. Hence, Boyi starved to death with no bitterness."[12]

If people's depraved nature prevails, it will become habitual and they will be unwilling to cast it aside. Hence, Wang Mang usurped the throne without a sense of shame.

[The latter case] was the consequence of his accumulation of evil habits.[13]

Now, the accumulation of evil habits [lacuna][14] does not take long; and death and destruction do not result from a single [error].[15]

Now, if sages and worthies are humble and respectful, they will obtain suitable blessings. Qing Feng and Boyou gave themselves over to drink, indulging without restraint to the distress of their families.[16] Lord Ping of Jin neglected the government. He became infatuated [with a concubine] and thus weakened his will. Good ministers did not correct him, all of them therefore suffered misfortune.[17] At first, King Zhuang of Chu and King Wei of Qi were reckless and debauched and became victims of [territorial] encroachment and weakness.[18] They faced chaos and destruction, but in its midst, they came to their senses. They became earnest in their concern for the people's affairs, exerted their vital essence, overtaxed their thoughts, and were diligent and tireless. Thus, Chen Ying was expelled, Guan Su was ennobled, Jimo was summoned, and the minister E was boiled.[19] Their [rulers] were able to bring about a restoration [of their states] and forcefully lead the Lords of the Lands.

> At the time, they were honored and illustrious;
> in later ages, they were objects of veneration,

transmitting their illustrious reputations, recording them in images and books. From this it can be said that the conduct of commoners and lords is the same:

> to know oneself is called enlightenment;
> to conquer oneself is called strength.[20]

If a people have faults they are not yet aware of, once they are aware of them they will not repeat them. This is the reason Yanzi was praised for coming close to attaining [perfection.][21] A passage in the *Book of Odes* says:

> "Heaven protects and establishes you,
> With the greatest security;
> Makes you single-minded and stout-hearted,
> That you may enjoy every happiness;
> Grants you much increase,
> So that you have all in abundance."[22]

How fine are these words! They state that Heaven protects and aids the king, determining that his character and fate is most firm and secure. [As Heaven] makes you trustworthy and generous, how can you not secure good order? It profusely benefits you [with great abundance] that extends to the common people. How could one not follow the path of the five constancies, or [fail to] to heed and nourish one's character and fate, thereby insuring

> longevity like the southern mountains, and
> vigor like the pine and the cypress?[23]

"Virtue is as light as a feather."[24] "The practice of benevolence depends upon oneself."[25]

> "Have nothing to do with wasps,
>  or you will be looking for a painful sting."[26]

"Disaster and good fortune have no special gate; they are precisely what people bring upon themselves."[27]

> "Heaven assists those who are obedient;
> people honor those who are trustworthy.
> Treading the path of trustworthiness, considering how to be obedient, and honoring the worthy, one will enjoy good fortune; and nothing will be disadvantageous."[28]

How true are these words. Can we afford not to consider them?

# CHAPTER 14 PREFACE

The enlightened ruler longs for good servitors,
Belaboring his vital energies to find the worthy and intelligent,
   but
The One Hundred officials are partial and cliquish,
And do not investigate which [talents] are real and which are
   feigned,
Carelessly elevating those with empty reputations, and
Lavishing false praise on each other.
When they assume office and take on official duties,
They are utterly lacking in contributions or accomplishments.

Thus I have written "Substance and Recommendation," chapter 14.

# 14

## SUBSTANCE AND RECOMMENDATION

States

    flourish because of worthy servitors, and
    decline because of flatterers.

Rulers

    are secure because of loyal servitors, and
    imperiled because of jealousy.

This has been a constant principle from ancient times to the present, and is what everyone in our age knows. Yet declining states and endangered rulers endlessly succeed one another. Can it be that our era lacks gentlemen of service who are loyal and true, foursquare and upright? In fact, what bedevils the path of the loyal, true, foursquare, and upright is that it is obstructed and nothing more.

Now,

    within a span of ten paces there will surely be some flourishing grass;

in a village of ten families there will surely be some outstanding gentleman of service.¹

The birth of the worthy and talented, like the continuing succession of days and months, has never come to a halt. Thus [even] in the chaos of the Yin [dynasty] there were the Three Humane Ones.² Wey, though small, had many princely men.³ While taking into account the Han [dynasty's] broad and extensive [territory],

> its numerous throngs of officers and commoners;
> its clear-sighted and enlightened court; and
> its disciplined and orderly superiors and subordinates,

its

> offices lack upright functionaries, and its
> posts lack excellent officers.

This is not because our era lacks worthies. Rather it is because worthies are dismissed or blocked and have no access to the sage ruler's court, and nothing more.

Now

> those who are committed to the Way have few friends, while those who pursue the vulgar have plenty of company.

So throughout the world, friends form cliques and use them to pursue private [advantages], vying to turn their backs on the substantive and pursue the meretricious. Those who recommend officers no longer

address [the candidate's] character and abilities, or
assess their talents and accomplishments,

but merely make up empty achievements and imaginary excellences, all entirely unfounded, picking out their [supposed] abilities and committing them to writing. Dukes, ministers, and inspectors annually recommend about two hundred [designated as] "Flourishing Talents" or "Filially Pious and Incorruptible."[4] Looking at their recommendations, it is as if they were all like Yan, Bu, and Ran.[5] But ultimately, their actual capacities mostly do not [even] approach mediocrity. [If they] were all truly as good as their recommendations claim, then this would mean obtaining two hundred "great worthies" every year. If this were the case, then why does [Heaven] respond with catastrophes and portents as a reprimand? Isn't this its actual response?[6]

Now

> talking about [fine] millet and rice and eating meat brings delight to one's heart, but it is not as good as boiled millet or steamed vegetables that can be savored in your mouth.[7]
> A picture of Xi Shi or Mao Qiang[8] brings pleasure to one's eyes, but it is not as good as the homely wife or rustic concubine that can be of service right in front of you.

Empty exaggeration and vaunting recommendations that forcefully conceal a [candidate's] faults and shortcomings in order to be falsely judged as brilliant is agreeable to [the listeners'] ears, but it is not as good as faithfully choosing officials who, on the basis of substance and actions, can be entrusted with positions [in the government].

> King Xian of Zhou adhered to current [opinion] and thus
> distanced himself from Su Qin.⁹
> [King Kuai of] Yan coveted empty praise and thus abdicated his
> throne in favor of Zizhi.¹⁰

Both [rulers] are examples of rejecting reality, heeding rumors, and making vomit-inducing errors.¹¹

In general,

> Sages are pure; while
> Worthies are a mixture [of qualities].

> The Duke of Zhou did not require perfection.¹²
> The Four Friends were not complete in their individual
> endowments.¹³

How much more pertinent [are these examples] in an era of decline? Thus

> Gaozu's supporters and helpers, and
> Guangwu's generals and ministers

> did not go through a sham selection process, and
> were not required to possess all skills.

> Those who were abandoned with the collapse of the Qin
> dynasty, and
> those who were cast aside [with the fall of] Wang Mang,

were put to good use by the two founders to do away with violence and disorder to establish a reign of peace. But in an era of Great Peace, to say that there are no [true] gentlemen of service, or to make multiple broad searches without finding any genuine [worthies] is infuriating.

Generally speaking, the commands of an enlightened ruler are like a sound; the harmonious response of a loyal minister should be like an echo.

> Long or short, large or small,
> clear or turbid, urgent or calm,

[the ministers' response] must be in accord [with the ruler's wishes]. Therefore,

> if [the ruler] wants a horse, [the ministers] make inquiries about a horse;
> if [the ruler] wants a donkey, [the ministers] make inquiries about a donkey;
> if [the ruler] wants a falcon, [the ministers] make inquiries about a falcon;
> if [the ruler] wants a spotted dog, [the ministers] make inquiries about a spotted dog.[14]

If he issues orders accordingly, then rewards and punishments will definitely be carried out without fail.

Now, high-flown discourse that deceives others is not as good as loyal discourse that is sincere and truthful. Likewise we use

> stone to work jade,
> salt to polish gold,
> fish oil to waterproof silk, and
> ashes to wash cloth.

Thus, in [dealing with] things, assuredly

> we use what is cheap to perfect the valuable, and
> employ the ugly to perfect the desirable.

The wise set aside their shortcomings and muster their strength in order to bring about their achievements. Enlightened rulers, in employing gentlemen of service, also follow this principle. If every material object has its suitable properties; and [one should] not waste its [useful] properties, how much more so [is this true] of humans?

Now, cultivating oneself and taking care in one's actions, being

> generous, foursquare, proper, straightforward,
> transparent, incorruptible, pristine, irreproachable,

calm, mild, and inactive forms the root of transformation.[15] Demonstrating concern for the ruler and sympathy for the people, showing exceptional insight into the origins of disorder, esteeming the good, deploring the evil, rewarding and punishing with severity and insight, all represent the skills of governing. The enlightened ruler is pleased with [those who possess these] two [sets of skills] and avails himself of them both. [The first] is an implement for [stopping] evil actions and is like a vessel of gold or jade. [The second] is talent in government and is as useful as steel and iron.[16] Without these two treasures, if one were to attempt something

> unconventional to gain renown, or to
> feign a tranquil [lack of ambition] in order to fool the masses,

it would destroy customs and damage norms. In the world today, those who admire emptiness are called [proponents of] the "hard and white."[17] The behavior of [proponents] "hard and white" [rhetoric] is hated by the enlightened ruler and is something that the rule of a true king will never accept.

For that reason, those who recommend worthies and officers must examine the quality of their dispositions and rely on facts in their comments. If the candidate has minor defects, the recommender must not blatantly cover them up as a means to strengthen an empty reputation. Officers who have a single talent can each contribute with their one strength, be they out in the world or retired, silent or loquacious.[18] If one does not insist that they must all be endowed with all good qualities, then thinking in terms of men like Xiao, Cao, Zhou, and Han,[19] would it be difficult to obtain these kinds of people? Or in the case of Wu, Deng, Liang, and Dou,[20] dozens could be summoned. If each [recommended person] is appointed to a position that is consistent with his qualities, then among the officials none will be negligent and

> vitalizing projects can be achieved,
> the [era of] Great Peace can be attained, and
> *qilin* can be expected to gather [at court].[21]

Furthermore, the [state of] Yan was small and of modest rank, [but] King Zhao[22] was still able to attract and gather brilliant and promising [servitors] from other states [to his court]

> to punish the violent and disorderly, and
> to bring about good order and strength.

In our own time the territory of the Han [Empire] is broad and extensive, the Son of Heaven is virtuous and enlightened, but even so, he lacks even one worthy minister. This, in fact, is nothing more than

a failure to take pity on the suffering masses, and
a failure to urgently [seek] worthies to aid the government.

Confucius said: "It is only that we have not thought of them. It is not that they are distant.[23] It is easy to attract loyal and accomplished officials. It is simply a matter of whether the sage ruler wants them or not and nothing more.

# CHAPTER 15 PREFACE

Sages sustain the worthy,
In order assist to the myriad people.
In the system of the kings of former times,
All [deemed emoluments] a sufficient substitute for plowing.
Increasing a rank but lowering the salary,
Bi Cheng was thereby toppled.
First increase officials' salaries,
And only then can the Great Peace be realized.

Thus I have written "Ranked Emoluments," chapter 15.

# 15

## RANKED EMOLUMENTS

In remote antiquity, at humanity's inception, before the existence of the elevated or the humble, natural order prevailed.[1]

> Heaven had not yet taken charge of [the people], and rulers had not yet been established for them.

Later, when people gradually became unruly, some were cruel toward one another, plundering and robbing ceaselessly, causing the people great harm. Thereafter, Heaven appointed a sage to shepherd them, prompting them not to lose their natural endowment [for goodness]. All within the four seas received this benefit; there was no one who was not covered by his virtue. All venerated and supported him and called him the Son of Heaven. Therefore, Heaven's establishing a ruler was not because it was partial to that person. It was, without a doubt, in order to punish the violent, to remove harm, and to benefit the multitudes. Therefore, when the people are consulted and the spirits are consulted, one with ability will be enthroned.[2]

A passage in the *Book of Odes* says:

> Great is the Lord on High,
> beholding this lower world in majesty.
> He surveyed the Four Quarters,[3]
> seeking out the suffering of the people.
> Those two [earlier] dynasties
> had failed to satisfy Him with their government;
> So throughout the various States,
> he sought and considered
> those who were at fault.
> Hating their evil ways,
> he turned His kind regard on the west,
> and there gave a settlement.[4]

Indeed, these words relate how the government of the two states of Xia and Yin proved incapable. And because of their lavish extravagance, the Lord on High hated them and sought a sage to respond to the people's distress. Consulting the Four Quarters under Heaven, [the Lord on High] commissioned one to occupy [the throne].

Wise and virtuous people of former times despised the flaunting of wealth and luxury without restrictions of any kind.[5] Consequently they considered how to derive principles from images [of the heavens]. [They] clarified a ritual order, making good rules and standards, and displayed them permanently. Thus, the [*Zuo*] *Commentary* says, "Establishing rituals, the number of items[6] ranked as superior never exceeded twelve, which was Heaven's Way."[7] Thus, for the sages of former times,

> plowing the sacred fields was regulated;[8]
> offerings to the spirits were assessed;
> provisions for personal use were limited; and

rituals for honoring worthies were gradated.

Superior and inferior,
large and small,
worthy and base,
near [relations] and distant,

all have levels of decorum. As for the gradation of ranks from high to low, each is accorded what is due to its own rank; public and private [privileges] are consistent with rank and, in accordance with the rites, with the pursuit of virtue and righteousness.

In this age, all within the nine provinces altogether accounted for an area three thousand li square, comprising 1,800 states. As for the ranked salaries, they were based on the standard of a superior farmer's [output]. Beginning with ordinary people who served officials, their salaries were sufficient to take the place of farming and likely provided for nine people, as was also the case for the lower officials of the territorial lords.[9] Middle-ranked officials received twice as much as lower-ranked officials, which supported 18 people. Upper-level officials received twice as much as middle-level officers, which supported 36 people. Grandees received twice as much, which supported 72 people. Ministers of small states received twice as much as grandees. Ministers of great states received four times as much as grandees, which supported 288 people. Rulers of states all received ten times as much as their ministers.

The fiefs given to the Son of Heaven's Three Excellencies were the same as that of dukes and marquises, measuring one hundred li square. Fiefs given to the ministers of the Son of Heaven were about the same as those given to earls, measuring seventy li square. Grandees received the same as counts and barons, amounting to fifty li square. Head Scholars of the Son of Heaven received the same as the Attached Meritorious, amounting to thirty li square.[10] All with great accomplishments were given fiefs.

For this reason,

> senior officials holding office concentrated on the public [good] and did not consider private family [concerns].
> Sons and younger brothers concentrated on study and did not involve themselves with wealth or profit.

They closed their doors and guarded themselves, refraining from wrangling with the people, and thus the roads were not [filled with people suffering from] hunger and cold.

> When [the ruler] takes this path and does not stumble,[11]
> when the great officers provide abundantly and do not stint,
> when the officials cherish their positions and refrain from greed, and
> when the people are at peace and robust,

then this is indeed the foundation of the Great Peace.

Now, when one carefully considers recommendations and selections [of officials], if the situation is clear, [one must make a move to either] dismiss or advance [them], so that official positions will be filled with the right person, and the right person will occupy the appropriate position.

> "Reverently according with the wide heavens,
> respectfully delivering the people's seasons."

"Accompanying me—the wife and children;
Feeding them—the south acres folk."[12]

Superiors thus concentrated on rules and rituals, correcting themselves as an example to those beneath them, while those beneath them were pleased with [their way of governing], and all were happy to exert themselves in allegiance to their ruler. It was by this means that

Heaven and earth communicated and connected,[13]
Yin and Yang were harmonious and stable,

the people were without debauchery and evil,
the Jade Mechanism and Jade Transept were not overturned,[14]
virtuous qi flowed and spread, and

sounds of praise issued forth.
After this,

failing to support the worthy gave rise to the sentiments of the "Crying Deer";[15]
neglecting the ancestral clan gave rise to the resentment of the "Gathering Southernwood,"[16]
enacting land taxation gave rise to the composition of "Big Rats",[17]
heavy taxation gave rise to the communications of Tan's report;[18]
irregularities in ranked emoluments gave rise to the critique of "Minister of War";[19]
poor treatment of officers gave rise to the complaints of "Little Oriole."[20]

Thus, there was gradual chaos and decline.

When the House of Zhou declined and the Five Hegemons became active, and when the six states fell and the violent Qin emerged, it[21]

> turned its back on righteousness and reason while elevating awesome power,
> destroyed the canons and ritual while practicing insatiable greed,
> instated heavy land taxes and levies in order to enrich itself, and strengthened ministers in order to weaken the branch lineages.[22]

> The cultured and virtuous did not obtain titles and fiefs, and the marquises did not obtain [lacuna].

Because of this,

> worthies were unable to observe ritual in pursuit of the Way, and officials were unable to resist corruption in pursuit of gain.

The ruler furthermore issued multiple amnesties to release felons, while the people were without shame and frequently committed crimes. Why? When

> Perverse qi is dispersed and alters the behavior of [those] above;
> Disastrous difficulties worsen and beleaguer the people with hunger and cold.[23]

This is why Zang He was unable to restrain brigands.[24] A passage in the *Book of Odes* says, "Great winds have a path; / the covetous men try to subvert their peers"; and "What you teach / The people all imitate."[25]

For this reason when the kings of former times were about to issue a decree, they did so with great care, only fearing that they might not hit the mark and lead the people into evil. Therefore they created the canon to serve as the people's standard. Those above and below all [observed] it, and there was no selfishness or deviousness. The Three Excellencies established the laws but had never heard of amnestying those who commit crimes or of redemption fees being treated as treasure.[26]

For this reason, the enlightened ruler's supervision of the people must be in accordance with correct standards and entirely lacking in insatiable greed.[27] He must concentrate on principles and ritual and treat generously those beneath him, restoring the path of virtue and elevating transformative [teachings], enabling all to be

> generous in nurturing the living, and
> fierce in cultivating honesty and a sense of shame.[28]

In this way,

> officials will be upright and the hundred surnames will be transformed;
> evil minds will be eliminated and duplicitous and evil [dealings] will be eradicated.

Only then will it be possible to

> accord with harmonious qi, and
> bring about the Great Peace.

The *Zhou Yi* posits the view that, "The sage nourishes the worthy who extend this nourishing to the countless common folk"[29] as a fundamental concern, and the ruler considers his officials to be its foundation. [Only when this foundation is sturdy] will those of great abilities be esteemed.[30] Only when a horse is plump can it reach a distant [destination.] The lord of men who does not concentrate on this principle, but who nevertheless desires to attain the Great Peace, is like one

> who builds a flimsy foundation, hoping to use it for a tall and imposing wall, or
> who takes an emaciated horse and demands that it travel to distant roads.

The impossibility of such things is certain.

# CHAPTER 16 PREFACE

When the ruler worries, his servitors must toil—
This is a common principle of antiquity and present times.
The ruler is concerned with bringing about peace, so
His servitors should exhaust their wisdom in this pursuit.
Steadfast, good, and trustworthy officers,
All lament numerous amnesties.
Evildoers and miscreants in great numbers arise,
And it is simply because of amnesties.

Thus I have written "Amnesties," chapter 16.

# 16

## ON AMNESTIES

When treating one who is ill, one first must know the emptiness and fullness of the pulse and what is blocking the qi; only then can one make a prescription for him.[1] Only then can the disease be alleviated and lifespan be extended. When managing a state, one first must know what is afflicting the people and what is precipitating calamity. Only then can one devise [a plan] on their behalf to suppress it. Thus, wrongdoing can be stopped and the state will be secure.

In the present time, among the most serious situations that harm good people, none is greater than the repeated [granting of] amnesties. When amnesties and commutations [of physical punishment] are frequent, evil people run rampant and good people are harmed.[2] How can this be made clear? It is said that in families characterized by their filial piety and fraternal submission, [the members] cultivate themselves and act cautiously. They do not rebel against prohibitions [handed down] from above; and from birth to death they are free of even the smallest offenses.[3] But when amnesties and commutations of sentences are frequent, they never experience mercy; on the contrary, they often face disaster.

Why is this so? In the case of the conduct of upright officers who serve as officials, they

do not hide from the ruthless, and
do not curry favor with their superiors.

When assistant clerks and investigators harbor deep displeasure [over a crime], cliques of slanderous and malicious [persons] will likewise pile on scurrilous lies. They all know that there will be an amnesty before long, so in the meantime, they collude [with each other], brazenly and unjustly attacking [the officials], making false accusations and memorializing the ruler about their illegal activities, and urging the ruler to erroneously apply punishments: execution or banishment for the highest-level crimes and forfeiture of one's official position for lesser offences. But when the families that suffered injustice begin to demand redress of the injustice and offer explanations, it is of no use to the deceased.

Let us turn to

recluses, employed officers,
good people, or princely men,

who calumniators and slanderers, using vituperative language, have falsely accused, crushed, and persecuted. The unjustly accused from distant places who are able to go to court number in countless tens of thousands. But those who get a hearing number only one in a hundred. Among those who get a hearing before the chief scribe, six or seven out of ten leave empty-handed. Although the case might be reexamined, provincial and commandery officials will review it bit by bit and create obstacles to the process. Spring and summer turn into autumn and winter, and again are succeeded by [a new] spring and summer, and [as time goes by] the amnesties granted are innumerable.

Furthermore, prudent and cautious persons, availing themselves of Heaven's Way, divide up the bounty of the soil.[4] They pull out the weeds and hoe the soil.[5] They scrutinize themselves and live moderately, [knowing that] the gradual accumulation of minutiae will bring about small transgressions.[6] These are all excellent commoners;[7] they are the foundation of the state.

[But] reckless, worthless evil youths, and malicious people who are without the Way, think only of fornication and depravity, rise up to rob and pillage [in pursuit of] wealth and women,

> killing people's fathers and mothers, and
> slaughtering their sons;
> demolishing the gates of [people's houses], and
> plundering their treasures.

When it comes to rapacious, cruel, crooked, violent, evil, worthless officials who

> encroach on and violate the innocent, and
> oppress and aggrieve the common people,

everyone longs for a sage emperor to punish the wicked and control the oppressors to relieve the built-up anger [of the victims]. But on the contrary, everyone is granted an amnesty. This prompts evil men to hold lavish banquets and bluster and brag.

> Habitual thieves wear stolen clothing and valuables and saunter past the gates [of their victims].

Filial sons see the wrong-doers but are unable to have them punished.

The burgled see their [former] possessions but are unable to recover them.

Nothing is more distressing than these sorts of things. Therefore, when an amnesty is expected, the weather will suddenly turn cold, which is because of the many people who have suffered oppression, grief, and anger.[8]

Now,

one who cultivates weeds and invasives harms the grain;[9]
one who indulges malcontents and brigands steals from the good people.[10]

A passage in the *Documents* says: "King Wen made penal laws to punish [offenders] and not pardon [them]."[11] For this reason the kings of former times established punishments, not because they enjoyed inflicting physical harm and shortening people's lives, but rather to intimidate malcontents and punish the evil to prevent them from harming the people. The world is rooted in the basic principle that the people are incapable of governing each other. For that reason, kings were established to unify and govern them. Sons of Heaven in their service to Heaven's awesome mandate, carry out both reward and punishment. A classic text says:

"Heaven rewards the virtuous with the five garments [of rank] and the five ornaments;[12]
Heaven chastises wrongdoers with the five [mutilating] punishments and the five applications.[13]

And the *Odes* admonishes:

> There is one who ought to be held guilty,
> But you let him escape [from the net].[14]

In antiquity, it was only the rulers

> who had received the [dynasty's] inaugural mandate,
> who had inherited extreme chaos,
> who had suffered the evils of a prior administration, and

whose people, regarding each other foes, one and all plundered, murdered, and destroyed public order, while the malcontents and brigands ravaged and stole. By way of the change of the [Heavenly] mandate, these [inaugural] rulers received blessings and became the father and mother of the people. Therefore, they allowed for one amnesty. When their successors followed them, none went against this [policy].[15] Why was this the case? It was because the lord of men matches [the character and efficacy of the hexagram] Qian and is benevolent, accords with and nurtures the ten thousand things, and thereby brings about great achievements.[16] It was not a matter of

> allowing the evil to be regarded as if they were benevolent, or of releasing offenders against Heaven as if they were worthies.

Nowadays there are people with evil natures who,

> when at home, disregard filial behavior and fraternal submission, and
> when abroad, show no deference or respect [toward elders and superiors].

Careless, stingy, dilatory, haughty, cruel, and violent without variation, invariably it is clear that [they openly take]

> pride, scorn, predation, and personal profit as their [standard of] conduct, and
> brigandage, destruction, cruelty, and oppression as their [standard of] worthiness.

Thus the numerous [officials] who contravene the king's law are in fact oppressors of the people and persons of the most abysmal ignorance and wickedness. Even if one were to remove their shackles and spring them from prison, in the end they would have no sense of remorse, confident in being granted an amnesty and commutation of punishment.[17] When they are released from prison they are anxious and careful, but they will break the law again. How could it be otherwise?

Luoyang[18] has reached the point of having bosses who manage the recruitment of hired killers. They are called "brokers," and for each victim they receive tens of thousands in cash, while the assassins receive thousands. They also send large gifts to local officials and the officials join them in lewd entertainments. Their influence penetrates deeply and powerfully; their many henchmen are intricately connected.[19] Their pleas reach the imperial relatives and the emperor's ministers,

> their requests are heard by those on high,
> their wishes are executed by those below.

Therefore despite the efforts of a stern Prefect and Intendant, ultimately, it is impossible to assail and annihilate them.[20] How so? It is because those who dare to commit great wrongs are certain

> to have the aptitude to surpass the masses, and
> the ability to win the favor of their superiors.

They liberally distribute their ill-gotten spoils and offer flattering words to indirectly maneuver others. Unless one had the rectitude and integrity of Di Wulun,[21] who would be able to refuse to act at their behest?

If we look into the handling of [ongoing] murder cases in Loyang, then at most there are several dozens and at least there are four or five. If the murderers are not executed, the killing will not stop. This is all brought about by numerous amnesties. Viewed from this perspective, those endowed with an extremely evil nature can never be reformed; and since on a yearly basis they amnestied, this [policy] merely encourages vice.

There are some who say,

> "When the Three Regulators[22] manifest signs,
> the qi of Heaven is indicating the need for amnesties.

Therefore the ruler of humankind conforms to these signs and dispenses mercy to all." But there is no need for this. The king is the most highly honored of men. He is connected to Heaven through refined essence.

> The thoughts that arise in his heart, and
> the anxious care that arises in his mind

emit neither color nor sound.[23] Heaven on his behalf manifests these transformations, which are all like the various manifestations of good and bad fortune, or the moon's movement through the stars.[24] These are in fact things that ought to occur. Thus, the manifestation of good or bad omens is [construed as] a form of sympathetic resonance meant to warn the ruler. If he disregards them and makes no [further] examination, when in fact, they are what he himself has generated, and on the contrary, he regards them as Heaven's desiring them to be so, then this is not correct.

Vulgar people also say, "In former times, when [the ruler] wished to proclaim an amnesty, he always began by sending out riders divided into groups visiting the marketplace and the villages to listen to [what was being said] in the lanes and on the street corners. If all [the people] said that there ought to be an amnesty, it was by this means that he ascertained that it was Heaven's instruction, and on this basis he extended his mercy." If these words are regarded as credible, then it is almost certainly an error. The people are, by nature, strongly inclined toward conjecture.

> If they perceive yin dominating for a long time, they will say there will be floods.
> If they perceive yang dominating for a long time, they will say there will be drought.
> If they perceive prices increasing slightly, they will say there will be famine.
> If they perceive prices decreasing slightly, they will say there will be abundance.

Nevertheless, sometimes their [views] are reliable and sometimes they are not. Looking at it from this perspective, what the people say [will happen] in not necessarily what Heaven sends down.

In previous times, [the instances of granting] commutations and amnesties were few and far between, so the people had no expectations. In recent times, amnesties and commutations have been numerous. Thus, every spring and summer they unfailingly hope for another amnesty. Families whose members include criminals gamble on being amnestied. Therefore, they spread this sort of talk for their own gratification. If, in fact, a benevolent ruler hears of it, regards it as Heaven's instruction, and immediately complies with it, there could not be a greater error.

Critics often say, "If, over the course of a long period of time there are no amnesties, malefactors will proliferate, and officials will be unable to control them. Amnesties and commutations are therefore the means to remedy the situation." This is not the root of the chaos and represents the explanation of someone who has not examined how bad or good fortune arise. The reason

> people readily become bandits, and
> officials calmly engage in evil deeds,

is because amnesties and commutations are frequent, and [the people and officials] are willing to trust their luck. If a person who breaks the law and who becomes a wanted criminal his entire life is caught and made to face punishment, then

> his plans for further crime will be destroyed, and
> his evil schemes will be ended for good.

Now, the enactment of amnesties and redemptions can lead little boys to delinquency and average people can be led to behave like scoundrels. Thus, there is a proverb that says: "When amnesties come twice a year, youths crow and bluster." This means that when the king's punishments are not enacted, then even weak and ailing youths will think nothing of committing a crime. How much more would this be the case for the cunning? If one truly fears the proliferation of criminals and thinks malefactors cannot be vanquished and therefore declares an amnesty, then this is a case of ruling the country by allowing miscreants to make decisions. Now, the Way of Heaven rewards the good and punishes the bad. [It is said that] "the works of Heaven: it is human beings who carry them out on its behalf."[25] Thus, whenever a king is established, he must go on to punish the wicked and support the good. But if he rules by giving license to the evil and rebellious, there is nothing worse than this.

Furthermore, a country has no constant state of being well ruled, but it also has no constant state of being chaotic.

> When the ordinances of the law are applied, the country is well ordered.
> When the ordinances of the law are loosened, the country is chaotic.[26]

The law has no constancy in its application, and it has no constancy in its loosening.

> When the ruler respects laws, then laws will be applied.
> When the ruler neglects laws, then laws will be loosened.

Previously, in the time of Emperor Ming, Jing province recommended a man as an "Abundant Talent."[27] When he came to the imperial palace to give thanks for this beneficence, he was given a meal, and when it was concluded, the emperor asked him if he had [heard] anything interesting recently. The man responded, "In Wu there was a powerful band of nine bandits. Our Inspector came to our commandery several times to look into it. Ultimately, he was unable to apprehend them." The emperor said, "Aren't you the Attendant Clerk in charge of the southern commanderies?"[28] "That is correct," he replied. The emperor became extremely angry and said, "Bandits have emerged in your region, yet you are unable to apprehend them. In that case, exactly how is it that your 'talent' is considered 'abundant?'" He ordered a punishment of several hundred lashes, stripped the Attendant Clerk of his title, and severely censured the provincial and regional officials. In the space of ten days, the bandits were all executed. From this it can be observed that apprehending and annihilating criminals can be achieved with enlightened laws and not through multiple amnesties.

At present, there is no evident effort to enact rewards and punishments in order to clarify good and evil. Stern heads of provinces and commanderies, who have already apprehended malefactors but perversely go on to issue multiple amnesties, thereby encourage them. Their announcements often say: "All those guilty of plotting rebellion or committing crimes of great refractoriness and impiety who are exempt from amnesties should all be pardoned so that alongside their fellow officials they will reform and make a new start."[29] Every year they are empowered to reform, yet no one has ever seen miscreants or crooked officials who are willing to reform, repent, and conform to imperial orders. Officials who manage these cases are furthermore not willing to use minor offenses committed by people before an amnesty to damage their current bids for promotion. This being the case, edicts that uphold reforming past faults and cultivating future [good behavior] to make a fresh start are unrealistic.

The *Odes* warn: "Our sovereign makes frequent covenants, and the disorders are hereby increased."[30] Thus, rather than issuing fewer edicts, be true to your word. If one is unable to completely do without amnesties, then [issuing] fewer would be better. If, in the space of thirty years, one imitates antiquity and issues an amnesty once, then malefactors will be reduced by 80 or 90 percent—this is something that can definitely be accomplished. Formerly, when Grand Marshal Wu Han was ill and about to die, Founding Emperor [Guangwu] asked him for his final words of advice. Wu Han replied, "I am ignorant, unwise, and not qualified to know anything about governing. You should be careful not to declare any more amnesties—just that and nothing more!"[31]

Now, "Those [matters] with regular tendencies gather according to kind, and things divide up according to group."[32] People's sentiments can all be discerned in their words. Thus, if all those who say there should be no amnesties are not people who cultivate themselves or act cautiously, then they must be people who are distressed, saddened, apprehensive, and resentful of those who are evil. As for all those who [see] benefits in multiple amnesties, if they are not people who are unfamiliar with governmental affairs, then they must be those who harbor within themselves deep and hidden concerns and who have the desire to do something about [the situation]. When a ruler is about to issue an order [for an amnesty], he will confer with his ministers. The unprincipled ministers have inevitably committed crimes, and even though ethical and upright officials have in the course of public duties committed errors, unless one is a Yu Quan or a Li Li, who is willing to undergo punishment in order to maintain the proper functioning of the government?[33] This being the case, they all had their own concerns when discussing governmental affairs. As in the case of a fox talking about making a [fox] fur coat, at no time will it ever happen!

The [*Zuo*] *Commentary* says:

> "When the majority trust in good luck,

It is bad fortune for the domain"[34]

Now,

> one who commits a crime should admit guilt,
> one who suffers injustice should be exonerated,

this is Heaven's standard and the Kingly way. Thus it is said, "Let us give no indulgence to the wily and obsequious, / In order to make the unconscientious careful."[35] If one treats a good person unjustly in order to benefit an evildoer, this is called "Considering the gathering of enmities a proof of virtue."[36] The rulers of former times discussed those who concealed knives in their robes.[37] Why was this the case? Because such people harbored evil hearts and murderous thoughts.

> The sage ruler has feelings of loving kindness, while
> these people have thoughts of murder and harm.

Thus, how can executing them be constructed as a crime?

> The "Kang Gao" chapter of the *Book of Documents* says,

> The king says, 'Oh! Feng, deal reverently and intelligently in your infliction of punishments. When men commit small crimes, which are not mischances, but purposed, they of themselves doing what is contrary to the laws intentionally, though their crimes be but small, you may not but put them to death."[38]

This means that if evildoers commit crimes, even if they are minor, and if they do not commit them unwittingly, but in fact with a desire to continue perpetrating them for the rest of their lives, even if the offense is minor, they cannot be spared execution. Why is this the case? It is because they are people, who by nature, are obstinate and vicious and whose thoughts focus on evil and how to perpetrate it. "But in the case of great crimes, which were not purposed, but from mischance and misfortune, accidental, if the transgressors confess their guilt without reserve, you must not put them to death."[39] This passage states that although killing a person is a major crime, if the perpetrator has no desire to commit evil for his entire life, and if [the crime] was merely committed accidentally, then such a case does not call for putting him to death. For people like this, although they can be amnestied, this is also an acceptable [outcome]. "Money could be received for redeemable offences, and inadvertent offences and those which could be ascribed to misfortune were to be pardoned."[40] These words apply to good people and worthies who occasionally err and unfortunately become entangled in a criminal offense.

The kings of former times discussed [the details of] a crime in order to make a judgment.[41] They sought out motivation and discussed intent in order to rescue good and honest persons, and at the same time, it was definitely not because the wanted to allow the release of all depraved and wicked people who could harm others. For this reason, the *Institutes of Zhou* ranked and discussed eight categories [of penal] law. This was the means by which kings of former times

> brought order to the myriad people, and
> elicited an age of peace.

The *Book of Changes* thus speaks of viewing the people and establishing teachings [for them] and discussing the principles of according with changes across different periods of time.[42] To save the world in present times, nothing is more urgent than this.

# CHAPTER 17 PREFACE

When the kings of former times ruled the world,
They wielded both might and kindness.
Their rewards were the enfeoffment of nobles,
Their penalties were the punishments of great severity.
Only when rewards were substantial and punishments severe,
Did subjects respect their positions.
When cultivating the Great Peace,
One must follow this model.

Thus I have written "The Three Models," chapter 17.

# 17

## THE THREE MODELS

When Gaozu established the Han, he made a pact with his ministers, determining that anyone who was not a member of the Liu lineage could not hold the rank of king, and anyone without military achievement could not hold the rank of marquis.[1] Filial Emperor Wen was the first to enfeoff his maternal relatives, and [this policy] thereby became a standard practice that has been carried out to the present.[2] Filial Emperor Wu enfeoffed his prime ministers as a way to honor their virtue.[3] Afterward, this practice continued until the Jianwu period, when it was discontinued.[4]

According to accounts in transmitted records, Ji, Xie, Boyi, Gao Yao, and Bo Yih all received landed [fiefs].[5] During the time of King Xuan of the Zhou dynasty, prime ministers and senior ministers who assisted in governing by dint of their virtue also received states.[6] Thus, Yin Jifu wrote two pieces celebrating their enfeoffment that say:

> Full of activity is the chief of Shen,
> And the king would employ him to continue [his ancestors'] services,
> With his capital in Xie,
> Where he should be a pattern to the southern states.[7]

He also declared:

> With his four steeds, so strong,
> And their eight bells, all tinkling,
> The king had given charge to Zhong Shanfu,
> To fortify the city there in the east.[8]

These odes describe how the earl of Shen and Zhong Shanfu's civility and virtue brought about abundant peace, and how the king enfeoffed them with fine land and gifted him with plentiful equipage.

The *Changes* says, "A cauldron with a broken leg overturning the lord's viands: its form is sullied. There will be misfortune."[9] This means that when a lord is not equal to his responsibilities, he will suffer heavy punishment.[10] Thus, after the Three Excellencies are in office for three years, there should be a clear evaluation of their achievements that leads to dismissal of the undeserving or promotion of the talented.[11] Those who are as effective as [Hou] Ji, Xie, Boyi, the Earl of Shen, and Zhong Shanfu in bringing about good order should be enfeoffed as marquises and receive by decree southern lands and eight bells [for his horses].[12] Those who receive salaries and food but do no work, and those

> who do not promote effective governance, and
> who do not offer loyal or goodness advice

should be made to undergo severe punishment. This is what is known as the technique of exemplary virtue and punctilious punishment and the art of distinguishing those with ability from those without it.[13] If [these techniques] could truly be realized, then

> the Three Excellencies would compete to be mindful of their duties, and
> the hundred officials would strive to exhaust all efforts to demonstrate their loyalty.

Under the rule of the former kings [the system of] hereditary succession established the territorial lords as a means of representing the worthiness [of the deceased].[14] Although sons and grandsons enjoy privileges stemming from the virtue of former generations, nevertheless,

> constructing borders and establishing states was not done for the sake of the territorial lords.[15]
> Establishing offices and commissioning officials was not done for the sake of the grandees.

It was for the benefit of the people, and only then could their positions be safeguarded. Thus, there is the duty of evaluating achievements [resulting in] dismissal or promotion and [enacting] the Nine Rewards and the Three Demotions.[16] A passage in the *Book of Odes* says, "O that superior man! / would not fail to earn his fare."[17] From this it can be observed that [in antiquity] there had never been a case of one who received a salary while contributing nothing.

As for the nobles of present times, for the most part, all of them have

> inherited their ranks from their forebears,
> assumed the positions of their deceased ancestors.

They themselves

have made no contributions to the Han, and
have done nothing to bring virtue to the people.

Occupying their states, they face south [like kings];
reclining, they consume ample emoluments,

enfeebling the hundred surnames beneath them, while they are enriched through the possession of states and manors. This is an extreme case of "failing to earn their fare." Filial Emperor Wu was distressed that it had come to this and thus demanded gold [offerings] in order to remove them [when they were unable to pay]. [This policy caused them to become] even more resentful.[18]

At present some marquises are virtuous and suited to serving as a parent to the people, yet they still cannot implement the Way. Some are wicked, ignorant, and shameless, and not suited to possessing a state, yet their wickedness is unknown to the emperor. Nevertheless, as far as human nature is concerned, there is no one who does not consider himself worthy and willing to offer his talents. The Duke of Zhou warned [his son]: "Do not cause great ministers to be resentful over not being employed."[19] A passage in the *Book of Odes* says, "I yoke my four steeds, / my four steeds long-necked . . ."[20]

At present, marquises who are thirty years old or more should all be examined to assume the senior position of Black-Seal Cord and above, and Marquises of the Interior ought to fill positions at the rank of Yellow-Seal Cord

in order to exercise their ambitions, and
in order to display their abilities.

If they possess the virtue of Marquis Han and Shao Hu,

on high, offering assistance to the Son of Heaven, and
below, bearing benefits for the hundred surnames,

then elevate their positions and increase their lands in order to make manifest their possession of virtue.[21] If they harbor wickedness and conceal evil, and their iniquities lay beyond all description, diminish their lands and seize their states in order to distinguish the praiseworthy from the despicable.

Furthermore, all the nobles, having been issued split tallies and having received their orders, are the great officers of the state. "Though their persons be distant, / their hearts are with the royal house."[22] They should help the intelligent and worthy as a means to assisting the Son of Heaven.[23] How is it that at rest or in action, they are extravagant and live above their stations; they are arrogant, self-satisfied, and burdened with debt,

dissembling and abusive to the common people,
depraved and debauched with wine and women,

instigators in scaling the steps to chaos, and thereby do nothing more than damage the cultural influences?[24] Imperial orders for irregular appointments and even special promotions [are issued], but they do not order the nobles to recommend [officers]. This situation, in terms of

the great influence of the ruler's virtue, and
the great prosperity of the nobles,

is not the way to take charge of strategies, delegate responsibilities, and oversee with independent authority those beneath them.[25] At present, although the nobles are not made to take charge of ruling the people, since there are "irregular appointments," royal regulations should be followed and [the nobles] should be required to recommend officers and not be allowed any dereliction of this duty.[26]

If one sincerely

> enfeoffed the Three Excellencies in order to display their accumulated virtue, and tested the nobles in order to eliminate those who "failed to earn their fare,"
>
> above, they would be in accord with the principles of establishing the nobles, and
> below, they would be in accord with the laws on dismissal and punishment.

If the worthy and talented hold office, then superiors and inferiors will meet with good fortune, parasites will be made to relinquish their states, and positions will not be held by evil people. If it is truly like this, then the marquises will indeed concentrate on self-discipline and assist their states. At present the situation is not like this.

> Those with merit are not rewarded,
> Those without virtue are not made to forfeit [their territory].

This is not at all the way to encourage the virtuous, punish the evil, attract and promote the loyal and worthy, or change manners and customs.

In the past, the former kings pacified the world, selecting the enlightened and virtuous to unite and bring order to the people. They established standard fiefs that did not exceed one hundred [li square],[27] drawing their example from [the hexagram]

"Quake," and considering that a worthy's intelligence and virtue should not be stretched beyond the extent of this [area].[28] They also hoped that if his virtue and ability were excellent and [the size of] what he governed was small, then his office would be well managed and the people would be blessed. At present, governors or chancellors rule territories of a thousand li square. Their authority and power are greater than that of the marquises, but their talents, powers of insight, virtue, and sense of duty do not surpass the ancients, yet what they govern is greater than one hundred li square. This is why what they govern is largely desolate and turbulent. For this reason, administrators and chancellors cannot fail to be scrutinized.

Formerly, Emperor Xuan rose from the midst of the common people and had a profound understanding of them.[29] Thus, he often sighed, saying, "The reason the myriad people are secure in their fields and villages and do not fear calamity is because the government is just and lawsuits are handled properly. Those who are able to help me bring about this situation are the superior [commandery governors and chancellors of state] earning two thousand *shi*."[30] He thereupon wisely selected governors and chancellors. Those appointed for the first time he required to see in person to observe their predilections and understand their abilities. He discerningly examined their governing, placing special emphasis on punishments and reward. [The officials of] places where wrongdoing declined and population increased were rewarded with gold and silk and were promoted to the rank of marquis. The dim-witted and lawless were executed, and their blood flowed in the marketplace.

> Rewards were generous and dependable;
> punishments were painful and enforced.

Officers feared admonishing and competed to focus on their duties. Thus, they were able to

> bring about a peaceful rule and a generation of burgeoning peace, and
> elicit the descent of the phoenix and draw forth the *qilin*.[31]

> Heaven and humankind were pleased and joyful,
> omens and signs appeared together,
> achievements and virtues flourished and burgeoned,

establishing [Emperor Xuan's temple name] as "Ancestor of the Restoration." From this it can be seen that

> the shepherds and administrators and great officers are indeed the source of flourishing or decline and cannot fail to be [carefully] selected.
> Laws and regulations, rewards and punishments are indeed the pivot of order and disorder and cannot but be applied rigorously.

In the past Confucius once said, "When the government is lenient, the people are presumptuous, and when they are presumptuous, one corrects them with harshness. When the government is harsh, the people are harmed, and when they are harmed, one indulges them with leniency. Leniency tempers harshness, harshness tempers leniency, and in this way the policies are harmoniously adjusted."[32]

At present, inspectors, governors, and chancellors, for the most part, are scornful, disregarding laws and statutes and disdaining imperial decrees. They think only of making a profit, not caring about public concerns. The people are treated unjustly "with no place to turn for appeal."³³ Those from remote border areas who are able to come to the capital amount to several [possible plaintiffs] among ten thousand, and those whose cases are actually examined and dealt with do not even amount to one in a hundred. Commanderies and districts count on this. In such a situation, [officials] brazenly delay [work] though people arrive daily to present petitions. All of these things are what excessive indifference brings about.³⁴

The hexagram "Biting Together" represents movement below and brilliance above. Its "Image" [exegesis] says, "The kings of former times [used this hexagram to] clarify punishments with intelligence and to adjust laws."³⁵ Now, in terms of the long-term habit of indifference,

> when rewards are not generous, then goodness is not encouraged;
> when penalties are not severe, then evil is not punished.

Thus, for all who wish to change customs and alter practices, the rewards and punishments put into effect must be sufficient to terrify [people] to the core and destroy their fearlessness. The people will then change their perspectives. If the sage ruler is truly willing to clearly scrutinize his officials, then in the case of those who exert themselves to the fullest extent of their competence to achieve meritorious results, [the ruler] will not be miserly in terms of the expenditures in gold, silk, and marquisates. As for those who are inclined toward debauchery and conceal evils that are beyond description, a verdict must be made to pursue the axe and [executioner's] block. Then, virtuous officers such as Wang Cheng, Huang Ba, Gong Sui, and Shao Xinchen will be secured in every commandery, and divine auspicious omens will arrive on a yearly basis.³⁶

# CHAPTER 18 PREFACE

The people form the foundation of the state,
Grain is the lifeblood of the people.
If there is no time to do their daily work,
How can the grain be plentiful?
Dukes, ministers, intendants, and officers,
All draw on the labor of the hundred surnames.
Their thoughtless appropriation of the people's time,
Truly makes one protest in fury.

Thus I have written "Using [the People's] Time Sparingly," chapter 18.

# 18

# USING [THE PEOPLE'S] TIME SPARINGLY

What makes a state a [functioning] state is its people.
What makes a people a [secure] populace is its grain.
What makes grain yield copiously is human effort.
What makes [their] efforts efficacious is [their] daily toil.

A day in a well-ordered state is easy because it is long; therefore its people are leisurely and have a surplus of strength.
A day in a chaotic state is rushed because it is short; therefore its people are overburdened and their strength is insufficient.

What is meant by "a day in a well-ordered state is easy because it is long" is not a matter of requesting Xi and He to order [the solar chariot] to slow its pace.[1] It is also not a matter of being able to augment the span of a degree[2] or to add markings [on the indicator rod of the clepsydra].[3] In fact, when the ruler is enlightened and discerning, when the hundred officials are well ordered, and when those beneath them follow what is correct and obtain their proper places, then the people will be settled and tranquil, and their strength will be more than enough. Therefore, they will look upon their days as long.

What is meant by "a day in a chaotic state is rushed because it is short" is not a matter of Xi and He ordering [the solar chariot] to quicken its pace. It is also not a matter of being able to reduce units of time or decrease the marks [on the indicator rod of the clepsydra]. In fact, if the ruler is not enlightened and discerning, then the hundred officials will be in disarray, and treachery and deceit will flourish. If laws and ordinances are corrupted by bribery, and corvee and tax levies are numerous, the common people will be afflicted by corrupt officials, and officers will be beggared by perverse rites,

> commoners suffering injustice must offer bribes and only then obtain justice; and
> ambitious officers must make private arrangements and only then receive protection.

> Evil ministers do as they please when they are in charge, and disorderly customs become rampant below.

> Lords carrying gifts [to give to their superiors] rush past in their carriages, and
> the common people clutching cash scurry about.

Thus, they regard the days as short. A passage in the *Book of Odes* says, "But the king's business was not to be slackly performed, / And I had no leisure to nourish my father."[4] The ode expresses the idea that in antiquity there was leisure time to perform filial duties; but in present times the people are pressed and unable to offer [filial] care.

Confucius said that if the people are numerous, then enrich them, and once they have been enriched then educate them.[5] Thus,

propriety and duty arise from wealth and sufficiency;
theft and robbery arise from poverty and desperation.
Wealth and sufficiency arise from ample leisure;
poverty and desperation arise from a lack of days.[6]

The sages were deeply aware that labor is in fact fundamental to the people and is the foundation of the state. Thus, they concentrated on being abstemious in the use of corvee [labor] and for the people's sake used their time sparingly. This is how Yao ordered Xi and He, "in reverent accordance with [their observation] of the wide heavens, to deliver respectfully to the people the seasons."[7] When the Earl of Shao heard lawsuits, he could not bear to inconvenience the people and listened to their cases beneath a pear tree. [He was thereby] able to initiate an era of harmony and bring about the elimination of punishments.[8]

At present this is no longer the case.

The myriad officials vex the people, while
the prefects and chiefs put on airs.

As for the common people who must abandon their farming and sericulture and rush to [the officials'] offices,

if [they] do not arrive for the morning or late afternoon [sessions],
   they will not be able to report their cases;
if they do not offer some kind of gift they will not be seen.
Whether there is a case or not, [the process] always goes on for
   days or months.

The entire household must abandon their work in order to watch over the case. The litigant's family must always ask a neighbor to respond to [officials' questions] or to send them food. When the case concludes, a year's labor has been lost, and in this world there are always those who have starved as a result.

But the vulgar and ignorant officials in charge have never sensed this. In commanderies and counties injustices and grievances have increased, but the provincial officials do not regulate the situation, bringing ruin to families who must travel great distances to consult with ducal ministers. Since the ducal ministers are unable to clearly investigate whether a case is true or false, they can only tire out plaintiffs, using delays to overtax their resources. Thus, they uncaringly make rules, ordering that [plaintiffs] must wait a full one hundred days before the documentation can move forward. Before the full one hundred days has elapsed, they suddenly change that number, egregiously violating the message of the Earl of Shao's court [beneath the] pear tree. This is what is meant by the saying, "Though a man might be able to recite the Three Hundred Odes, if he is entrusted with a governmental charge, he knows not how to act [. . .] though his learning is extensive, of what practical use is it?"[9]

Confucius said, "In hearing litigation, I am just like anyone else."[10] From this point of view, anyone of mediocre talent or better can

> discuss the distinction between right and wrong, and
> the management of punishments and laws.

Officials at the county, canton, and regional level are competent to render decisions so that there are no complaints. But there is a reason this is not the case.

The [*Zuo*]*zhuan* says, "Many are those who hate the upright and vilify the correct."[11] Now, the upright are pure and correct; they do not bend their wills and have no affection for officials.

But families with grievances seek favor from officials, binding them with money and valuables. Thus, the village and district [officials] help them and oppose upstanding families. Later [if the case] is overturned, and the official is charged, the [family with grievances] will [join forces and] oppose the [upright] in the [county] court.

When disadvantaged people face formidable officials in a lawsuit, their power is insufficient. Thus, the county and the region join forces, and if later their case is overturned and the county officials are charged, they will move the case up from the county to the commandery.

When one person is involved in a lawsuit with one county, his power is insufficient. Therefore the commandery and the county work together. Later, if their case is overturned, the governor will be charged. Therefore, the case is moved up from the commandery to the provincial level.

When one person is involved in a lawsuit with one province, his power is insufficient. Therefore the province and the commandery work together but will be unwilling to settle it. Therefore the litigant must then travel a great distance to the office of the Three Excellencies.[12] If the office of the Excellencies is unable to investigate the case, they might casually extort a sum of "[earnest] money."[13] Then, the indigent person without money, ultimately will not have the means to waste the time fulfilling the required [one-hundred day] waiting period. The powerful and wealthy engage retainers to go for them, and can fulfill a stint of a thousand days, not merely one hundred. Handling cases in this way focuses on helping the powerful and cunning and oppresses the poor and the weak. How can injustice be dealt with in this way?

It is not only in districts and regions that litigation is like this. When military officials try a case, the [plaintiff] also

> begins by being treated unjustly by minor officials, and
> ends with the grave injustice of great officials.

Before the basis of the plaint has been reported, an amnesty is suddenly issued, and [the case] can no longer be tried.

> Upright officers brood on the injustice but cannot obtain redress.
> Cunning officials shield evildoers but do not thoroughly investigate.

This is why commanderies and counties easily bully the people, and why so many under Heaven suffer hunger and poverty.

Setting aside [the topic of] August Heaven's sympathetic resonance, and disastrous visitations that harm grain, [let us] take up for discussion human effort and visible deeds. At present, from the three offices of the [Excellencies] on down to the counties, the areas occupied by non-Chinese peoples, the districts, and the villages, including [the workplaces of] assistant officers and investigators—all of these include departments that manage [the people's] affairs, [and for which] the people must abandon their farming and sericulture to attend to [their cases].

Plaintiffs and litigants as well as those who must respond to officials for official business in a single day waste [the efforts] of ten thousand people.[14] Furthermore, calculating in terms of an individual, if one person has a case, two people must provide assistance. This amounts to three hundred thousand people a day who are disengaged from their occupations. If one uses an average farmer as a standard, then [the impact] is equivalent to three million people suffering starvation.[15] This being the case, how can thieves and villains be pursued and eliminated? How can the Great Peace be pursued and initiated?

Filial Emperor Ming once asked, "Why is no one submitting a petition this morning?" His advisors said, "It's because it's a *fanzhi* [day]."[16] The emperor said, "That the people have abandoned their farming and have traveled a great distance to the imperial palace but are still made to avoid *fanzhi* days, is, in fact, equivalent to robbing them of their time and doing them [a grave] injustice." The emperor then ordered the office of Official Carriages to accept memorials without avoiding *fanzhi* days. Our most enlightened and sage ruler valued the people's time in this way, while officials made light of snatching the people's time in that way. Isn't this what is called

having a ruler but lacking officials,
having a lord but lacking aides,

having a head that is intelligent and perspicacious, but
limbs and arms that are lazy and apathetic?[17]

A passage in the *Book of Odes* says, "The kingdom is verging on extinction. / How is it that you do not consider the state of things?"[18] It laments the three dukes occupying their positions and consuming high salaries, but never being willing to look into the peoples' great suffering.

Confucius hated people who "having not yet obtained something, are anxious about how to get it; and when they get it, their anxiety is lest they should lose it."[19] At present, the [Three] Excellencies and [Nine] Ministers who began serving at the provincial or commandery level and ultimately reached the prime ministership are people whose intelligence and wisdom are not necessarily dim. But it is simply unfortunate that they cravenly put their personal plans first and make the public good secondary. A passage in the *Book of Odes* says, "No one is willing to think of the prevailing disorder; / But who has not parents to suffer from it?"[20] If at present the people labor without rest, how can the grain be produced? "If the people are in want, their prince cannot enjoy the plenty alone."[21] Alas, can we afford to not consider this?

# CHAPTER 19 PREFACE

Surveying the administrative work of officials,
It is contentious lawsuits that occupy them most frequently.
Seeking the source from which these misfortunes arise,
We find it is fraud and deception that generate them.
To eradicate these consequences,
One must stop them at the source.
When the people refrain from fraud,
The world will finally achieve peace.

Thus I have written "Judging Legal Cases," chapter 19.

# 19

## JUDGING LEGAL CASES

The Five Ages were not uniform in their rites.
The Three Dynasties were not uniform in their teachings.[1]

It is not because they capriciously opposed each other, but rather that the world had yielded to change and customs differed. When customs change, the sources of disorder vary. Therefore, when the Three Dynasties pacified the world, all of them introduced change and established [new] laws.

Emperor Gao formulated restrictions in three articles; and
Filial Emperor Wen abrogated the mutilating punishments.[2]

Thus, apart from the prohibitions against murder, assault, and theft and the formulation of a penal code, there were no constants in their leniency or severity. Each followed what was appropriate to the age in an effort to adopt what was necessary to encourage goodness and eliminate evil, and that is all.

Now, the intention behind enacting laws is similar to the impetus for constructing fences and moats to provide protection. One determines the places that beasts repeatedly breach and then increases the depth and thickness [of the protective barriers]. Now,

> though the various forms of treachery are numerous, their causes are few;
> though the various affairs of rulers are complex, their management is uncomplicated.

> Knowing that the causes are few, treachery will be easy to thwart;
> seeing that their management is uncomplicated, governing will be easy to manage.

> If one thwarts the causes, then wickedness and treachery will be stopped;
> if one enacts [necessary] measures, then far and near will be governed.

At present, the legal cases decided in one year, which number in the ten-thousands—and which include

> the litigation of claims and disputes,
> the exposure of assault and robbery,
>
> the rulings of district divisions,
> the rulings of judicial offices—

all come down to one thing in their circumstances. Fundamentally, they all arise from the dishonesty of people and their frequent efforts to swindle each other. Shun charged Long concerning "slanderous speakers and destroyers of right ways who agitate and alarm the people."[3] Thus, from high antiquity people have been troubled by these problems. Therefore, one should first be cautious about one's own "throat and tongue" in order to provide a good example for the common people.[4] Confucius said, "When disorder arises, it is speech that is the stepping-stone leading to it";[5] and "the small man is

> not ashamed of what is not benevolent, and
> not afraid of what is not righteous."[6]

Peering intently,

> ever harboring deceit and deception,
> greedily coveting profits ahead,
> disregarding frugality and shame,
> carelessly [lacuna][7] . . .

in bringing about disastrous permutations, so that every home is affected.

It is not only ordinary people who are like this; people of this ilk are even more prevalent among the enfeoffed nobles, kings, marquises, imperial relatives, and magnates. They borrow money with arrogance and profligacy to indulge in debauched extravagance. They accrue debt in the ten millions but are unwilling to repay their loans. Ordinary people stand at their doors weeping and wailing, but even so, they are bereft of any thoughts of alarm, distress, shame, or sympathy.[8] They frivolously gather with their dissolute drinking companions, passing back their empty [cups] to reach for full ones. Squawking, whining, cursing and cussing, morning till night they are crass and blunt. Indolence and dissipation are the only pastimes that they enjoy.[9] Some attack their creditors, sending them to their deaths. They are no different from bands of thugs who attack, assault, and rob people. Even though they are amnestied or have paid fines, they should no longer be in line for recruitment for regional and central government offices. Yet regional government officials, on the contrary, compete to obtain them. Furthermore, considering anyone who dares to indulge in foolish, vain luxuries and who carries large debt, they are definitely not the ones who will

> save those who are starving and cold and resolve difficulty and distress, or
> rescue those who are poor and destitute and practice ritual and righteousness.

All of them use [their positions to]

> exalt vain luxuries,
> support debauched drunkenness,

and that is all.

The principle of the *Chunqiu* is to punish those who willfully commit offenses and to put to death instigators. Filial Emperor Wen was consummately sparing in action and desirous of employing a virtuous [example].[10] Nevertheless, the Marquis of Heyang, Chen Xin, after being charged with failure to discharge his debts within six months, was imprisoned for six months and then deprived of his territory.[11] Filial Emperor Wu was benevolent and enlightened, but the Marquis of Zhouyang, Tian Pengzu, after being charged with occupying the manor of the Marquis of Zhi and failing to restore it to him, was deprived of his territory.[12] The Marquis of Liyang, Shao Yan, charged with refusal to contribute stallions, was executed and his territory was eliminated.[13] Is it possible that these two emperors, because of their love of money, brought harm to eminent subjects? In fact, they sought to

extirpate the beginnings of deceit and fraud,
enforce the laws of state and family, and
preempt the causes of disaster and disorder

in order to benefit the people. Therefore, one person's conviction and punishment for a crime so that ten thousand families will receive blessings is what the sage ruler enacts with no hesitation. In the *yongping* reign period, territorial lords who accrued debts were immediately punished with seizure [of their territories], dismissal and demotion.[14] After this time no one dared to accrue debts owed to the people, so that the world of its own accord became more frugal and litigious charges naturally dwindled.

Now, among the regional lords and imperial relatives, some are able to control themselves and observe caution in their undertakings.[15] They do not neglect morality or duty; they are restrained, temperate, and attentive to rules. Never having accrued debts,

their persons are as pure as jade, and[16]
their ambitions are as high as clouds.

Some, having already cheated and turned their backs on commoners, memorialize the throne requesting to freeze taxation, hoping that they might to be able to repay their debts. This move would, in fact, oppress and plunder both officials and the people and subvert the emperor.[17] As for this sort of deceit and contempt, there is no greater crime.

The *Classic of Filial Piety* says:

"Exhibit for them virtue and righteousness, and the people will
    rise to put them into practice;
explain to them likes and dislikes, and the people will be made to
    understand prohibitions."[18]

Now, for one who desires

> to change specious falsehoods in order to elevate beneficial influences, and
> to diminish litigious charges in order to lighten officials' workload,

nothing is better than

> modeling and displaying virtuous conduct,
> despising and punishing unseemly acts,
>
> being guided by the laws of Emperors Wen and Wu, and
> being clear about the punishment of deceivers and frauds.

Now, the immorality of marquises, kings, and imperial relatives has progressively become widespread; rogues also continue to proliferate. How can it be said that whenever there is a contentious lawsuit, it is women who have brought it about? Yet this is the opinion that is generally circulated.[19] If all the various roots of disaster are not extirpated at an early point, then some will gradually put forth tendrils, allowing them to create [the situation described above]! Therefore, in essence,

> the reason perspicacious officials are consumed and overwrought, and
> the reason minsters and rulers are distressed and overworked

is fundamentally because everything that is handled in the districts is, for the most part, generated by deceit and deception. Therefore it is said,

> if one recognizes that the sources are few, then corruption will be easy to stop;

if one perceives that the responsibilities are uncomplicated, then government will be easy to manage.

As for the behavior of some women, what is valued is urging them to be chaste. If a woman has already married and shamefully remarries into the X family, the local officials will empathize and thus allow her to remain in the family she has just entered.[20] [This decision] must be due to not understanding how to manage the root cause of disorder, and to not considering what others say about what gives rise to chastity. The chaste woman is not possessed

> of two minds so that she frequently changes; thus we have the ode [that proclaims] "I am not a rock," or
> of immoral behavior so that she elicits worry; thus we praise the sentiment [that states] "I return and inquire."[21]

Once betrothed she does not change—is this not how chastity is preserved and how fathers and elder brothers are put at ease? Their failure to follow these [rules] and the inconsistency in their morals is due to the absence of

> a family without a sense of modesty and shame, and
> a place bereft of sense of purity and devotion.[22]

For people like this, how indeed can they feel shame or regret?

> Contemptuous and disrespectful fathers and elder brothers,
> wanton and dissolute wives and daughters,

fail to consider duties and principles and carelessly neglect constancy and devotion. They borrow [others'] capital to manage living expenses, abscond to manage debts, and finally are driven to the disaster of slashing their bellies, slitting their throats, and destroying their lineages—what place does not have people like this?

The kings of former times, addressing the fact that people's emotions such as joy and anger cannot be stopped, made for them ritual constraints and exalted virtue and deference. For the things people were able to restrain, they established laws and prohibitions and clarified rewards and punishments. At present,

> marketplace sales without mutual cheating, or
> matrimonial arrangements without mutual deception

are not matters beyond the ability of human emotion. Thus, nothing is better than establishing righteousness, setting up laws, and extirpating the sources [of deception]. Initially, though this measure will bring shame to individuals, ultimately it will long benefit ten thousand generations. "Minor offences being punished, the major ones are deterred."[23] This is the way to preserve the common [people] and rescue the obstinately wicked.

Now, as for the essentials of establishing laws—one must cause

> the good person to be encouraged in his virtue and content with this [sort of] governance, and
> the bad person to be pained by his trouble-making and regretful of his actions.

For all cases in which a single daughter has been promised to multiple households, even one who has given birth to ten sons and experienced one hundred amnesties—if she is not allowed even a single chance to return to her home, then this wickedness will be eradicated. Otherwise, shave the heads of the husband and wife and send them one thousand li away to an inhospitable place. Only then can one rectify their hearts and prevent future [lapses]. When wickedness and disorder have been eradicated, then the Great Peace will arise.

Among chaste widows, there are some who

> in sons and daughters are well provided, and
> in wealth and property are amply supplied,

who desire to

> preserve the ritual of one marriage, and
> fulfill the faithfulness of a shared tomb.[24]

They hold fast to principle with firm resolve, remain unchanging in devotion and committed unto death, to the end harboring no thoughts of reneging on their vows. But if they should encounter

> a malevolent uncle, or
> an unrighteous brother,

> some might covet her betrothal gifts,
> some might desire her valuable property, and
> some might appropriate her male children.

Then they will forcibly act as matchmakers and trick women into a marriage, and suddenly strong-arm them to be sent away. Among these women, some

> hang themselves in their rooms, or
> drink poison in the carriage,

ending their lives, destroying their bodies, and orphaning and abandoning their young children. This behavior is equivalent to coercing them to die by suicide. Some second husbands enlist numerous associates, use brutal force to intimidate the woman to get in [the carriage]. They monitor, frog-march, grasp, and restrain them, and only after several days do they ease up. This treatment is nothing short of violently kidnapping women to become wives. Women are weak. Terrorized by a violent group who seize, coerce, and confine them for days, though they may later wish to restore their original intention [of fidelity], they hang themselves or drink poison.[25] [lacunae]

# CHAPTER 20 PREFACE

Considering the Five Thearchs and the Three Kings,
Their excellence or inferiority lay in their predilections.
Since they were desirous of surpassing the [Three] August Ones,
They first had to bring about peace, and
Needed a generation before they could actualize benevolent [government].
This was Confucius's classic [doctrine].
When encountering decadent and evil officials,
Can one avoid using punishments?

Thus I have written "Governing in an Age of Decline," chapter 20.

# 20

# GOVERNING IN AN AGE OF DECLINE

The ones who brought All-Under-Heaven to completion without recourse to a system of regulations were The Three August Ones.[1]

The ones who engraved images of punishments and transformed all within the extremes of the four directions were The Five Thearchs.[2]

The ones who clarified laws and prohibitions and made harmonious all within the Four Seas were the Three Kings.[3]

The place where rewards and punishments are carried out and order is brought to the myriad people is a [well-]governed state.

The place where the ruler establishes laws but his underlings do not carry them out is a disordered state.

The place where officials control the government and the ruler does not restrain them is a perishing state.[4]

Therefore,

> the reason the people are not disordered is because they have officials above them;
> the reason the officers are not depraved is because officials have laws;
> the reason the laws are smoothly carried out is because the state has a ruler;

> the reason the ruler occupies a place of esteem is because he embodies righteousness.
>
> Righteousness is the ruler's governing principle;
> laws are the ruler's commands.

If the Ruler of Men's thoughts are correct when promulgating laws, and if among the noble and base, worthy and worthless, no one will dare to disobey, then the ruler will be situated on high and the people will be governed below. But if the Ruler of Men issues orders and the nobles, officials, and arrogant superiors do not comply with them, then

> the ruler is vulnerable to regicide,
> and the people are vulnerable to disorder.

Laws and commands are the means by which the ruler manages his state. But if the ruler issues commands and they are not followed, this is tantamount to there being no ruler. If the sovereign's commands are not followed, then the commands of the officials will be carried out and the state will be endangered.

Now laws and commands are the bit and reins and the whip and riding crop of the Ruler of Men, while the people are his carriage and horses. If officials abrogate the ruler's laws and prohibitions and carry out their own regulations and commands, then this is a case of "grabbing the ruler's reins and riding crop and driving off on their own." Foolish rulers and benighted authorities are sidelined to the left, while depraved officials who reject the Way grasp the reins on the right. This [overturning of proper hierarchy] is

> why Zou Maxu of Qi dumped the Duke of Hu's [corpse] in the Ju River,[5] and

why Yang Shuzang of Song enabled Hua Yuan's defeat by the
Zheng army,⁶

and no one was able to stop them. Thus,

Chen Heng seized Lord Jian at Xuzhou,⁷ and
Li Dui harmed his lord's father at Shaqiu.⁸

In all of these cases, it was because of long-accumulated factors that they [were able to] seize their rulers' "reins and riding crops."⁹ The "Wenyan" says: "The murder of a ruler by his minister, or of a father by a son, is not due to the events of one morning or of one evening. That which engendered it gradually accumulated through the absence of early detection."¹⁰ For that reason,

functionaries who promulgate laws [on their own authority], and
officials who issue commands [on their own authority],

must be executed.

Critics insist that mutilating punishments and executions are of no use, and that only transformation by virtue will serve [to achieve good government].¹¹ This is not

the argument of those who understand change, or
the words of those who can save the world.

Now,

among the most exalted sages, none surpass Yao and Shun, yet they drove the Four Lads into exile.¹²
Among the greatly virtuous, none surpass Kings Wen and Wu, but they "blazed forth their anger."¹³

A passage in the *Book of Odes* says:

> If my lord directed his anger at [the creators of disorder],
> Disorder would quickly come to an end.
> If my lord directed his approval at [the virtuous],
> Disorder would [also] quickly come to an end.[14]

For this reason, the ruler's pleasure and anger is in fact a means to stopping disorder. Thus, he has [the measures of]

> judicial execution to put a stop to murder, and
> mutilating punishments to suppress cruelty.

Moreover, governing in the present age is like climbing a hill: you must first tread the gentle slopes, and afterward can you scale the summit. Likewise, [the ruler] must

> first set his own state in order, and only then can government [like that of] the Three Kings be put into effect;[15]
> when [the ruler's] Way matches [that of] the Three Kings, only then can the transformative influence of the Five Thearchs be carried out; and
> when [the ruler's] Way matches that of the Five Thearchs, only then can the Way of the Three August Ones be followed.

Moreover,

> laws [formed the decisive criteria of] the government of the Former Kings;
> ordinances represented their personal directives.[16]

> The government of the Former Kings was therefore embraced by the masses of commoners; and

the personal decrees were used for their personal power over others.

If a ruler is sincerely able to promulgate laws and from time to time adjust them, issuing commands and making sure they are carried out, then among the numerous officials and the hundred ministers, none will dare to fail in carrying them out wholeheartedly to the fullest extent.[17] If no one disobeys [the ruler's] personal decrees, then his laws and prohibitions will of a certainty be put into practice. Thus, when

> governmental regulations are invariably followed, and
> legal prohibitions are invariably obeyed,

yet the state is poorly governed, is an impossibility. This is the technique of "now pliant, now rigid,"[18] whereby contemporary [methods] are used to carry out ancient [principles], despised laws become important, and the low [status of the ruler] is made high again.[19]

# CHAPTER 21 PREFACE

Wise rulers are concerned about hardship;
They choose experienced generals,
Provide them with axes, and[1]
Award them with powerful aristocratic ranks.
But in fact many [generals] are ignorant and dimwitted, and
Do not understand the transformations of positional advantage.
In issuing reward and punishments they are unwise.
How can they not be defeated?

Thus I have written "Exhorting Generals," chapter 21.

# 21

## EXHORTING GENERALS

The people of high antiquity were pure, sincere, honest, and simple. Sages of the highest order cared for them, calmly and placidly practicing nonaction. They embodied the Way and practiced virtue. They simplified punishments and were sparing in the use of force. They carried out no killings or executions. Consequently, the people were spontaneously transformed. This was the epitome of virtue.

Later, the people gradually became corrupt and mean-spirited; depraved minds multiplied.[2] Lesser sages followed [those of the highest order]. Observing the people, they established instruction. They instituted punishments and rewards to awe and encourage them. After creating the Five Weapons,[3] they also devised for them laws in order to correct and motivate them. A passage in the *Book of Odes* says:[4]

> Make ready your chariots and horses,
> Your bows and arrows, halberds, and [other] weapons;
> Using watchfulness as your standard,
> Keep at arm's length the *Man*[5] tribes.

Thus it is said: "The time when the military was [first] established is distant indeed."[6] Traversing history from the Five Eras[7] to the present day, there has never been a state that has not relied on virtue to flourish and on the military to be strong.

Nowadays

> ingenious weaponry fills the arsenals;
> the words of Sun[8] and Wu[9] echo in generals' ears.

But generals who try employing them see

> their armies defeated when they advance into battle; and
> their walled cities destroyed when they retreat to a defensive position.

Why is this so? I say:

> the circumstances of our forces and the enemy's are not heard by the ruler above;
> the categories of victory and defeat are not clear in the generals' minds.

The knights and soldiers advance without gaining anything and retreat on their own authority without fear [of punishment]. That is how things are.

Now,

> to drag a heavy load up a slope or to go on an outing of a thousand *li* [in a day] is hard on [an ordinary] horse. But a fine horse will take pleasure in it because [a charioteer like] Wang Liang[10] is worthy of its greatest effort.

> To be in the vanguard of an assault on enemy lines, or to rush to one's death against an implacable foe is hard on [ordinary] people. But a knight of the highest standard will take pleasure in it because an enlightened monarch is worthy of his risking death.

Generally speaking, when a person consents to encounter death or destruction without demurral, if it is not for his own benefit, it is to avert some harm. Regardless [of whether they are] worthy or base, ignorant or wise, everyone is like that. They consider only the difference between benefit or harm [to themselves] and that is all.

> If not for the benefit of a glorious reputation, then it is for the benefit of an ample reward.
> If not to avoid disgrace and dishonor, then it is to avoid disaster and disorder.

Without [considering] these four points,

> a king, however sage, will not be able to make demands on his ministers, and
> loving fathers will not be able to compel their sons.[11]

The enlightened ruler profoundly understands this; therefore he lauds benefits and emphasizes penalties as a form of exchange with those beneath him.[12] [Thus he] makes all

> family members and strangers,
> nobles and hoi polloi,
> the worthy and the base,
> the brilliant and the stupid,

conform to his edicts, and only then will they receive what they want. Thus it is that, on a day when the war drums thunder, and the signal flags and banners all unfurl, the knights all rouse themselves [for battle] and compete to die at the hands of the enemy. How is it that they reject the pursuit of a long life and are happy to die pointlessly? In fact, it is simply that

> righteous knights do it to glorify their reputations, while
> greedy fellows do it to obtain a reward.

Now the number of officials and combatants who suffer defeat, disaster, and death in the execution of their public duties number in the hundreds of thousands. Those on high do not listen to or condole with the sighs and wailing [for] the honored [dead]. Those below moreover do not receive the bounty of generous salaries or reward.

> Principled knights have nothing to encourage them, and
> the common [soldiers] have nothing to look forward to.

This is why people are demoralized, negligent, and unwilling to face death.

Since our troops have been deployed, they have been exposed to hardship [in the war with the Qiang] for five years now. The officials [and generals] in charge of the military number nearly a thousand, and large and small engagements number between scores and hundreds with few achieving victory. Looking into their defeats, one finds that there is no other cause than that

> the generals do not understand the transformations of positional advantage, and
> the knights are not encouraged to die at the hands of the enemy.

The knights' unwillingness to [risk] death, in fact, is due to the generals' incompetence.[13]

> They speak of rewards but do not grant them,
> They speak of punishments but do not inflict them.

The knights who advance are the only ones who suffer the misfortune of death. Those who retreat and take cover all reap the good fortune of staying alive. This is why, at the cusp of combat, they forget about the battle and think only of turning around and fleeing in panic.

Sunzi said: "A general must be wise, humane, respectful, trustworthy, brave, and stern."[14] Therefore,

> being wise, he anticipates the enemy;
> being humane, he has the allegiance of the masses;
> being respectful, he attracts the worthy;
> being trustworthy, he is certain to issue rewards [and punishments];
> being brave, he will increase his soldier's qi,
> being stern, he unifies his commands.

So,

> when the enemy is attacked, he is able to adjust to change;
> when the allegiance of the masses is received, he can ponder his strength for combat;
> when the noble and wise are assembled, clever schemes can be achieved;
> when reward and punishments are certain, the knights will exert their maximum strength;
> when the qi of bravery is increased, the potential of the army will be redoubled;

when his awesome command is unified, the general will be exclusively in charge.

If all six of these qualities are present, he can charge and defeat the fiercest enemy, thus supporting his ruler and bringing tranquility to the people.

Previously, when the Qiang[15] began their rebellion, the [Han] generals and grand marshals, relying on a group of the commanderies and counties,[16] took advantage of their wealth and resources to seize numerous walled cities and occupy advantageous locations. Commanding hundreds of thousands [of soldiers] and leading knights of outstanding valor, they sought to put to death or disperse those who had rebelled and initiated disorder. But when they engaged with the brigands, not only were they unable to capture them, they were repeatedly defeated by them. Then [the Qiang troops] spread like a fog

> joining together in a horizontal alliance,
> sweeping through [the states of] Bing and Liang;
> within, attacking Sili,[17]
> in the east, despoiling Zhao and Wei;
> in the west, ravishing Shu and Han.
>
> Five provinces suffered severe damage, and
> six commanderies were wiped out.

This was not a calamity sent by Heaven; it was simply a failure of command.

Sunzi says, "The commander is the arbiter of people's lives and the lord of the state's security."[18] That is why, in commanderies afflicted with bandits, the prefects and subprefects must not be ignorant of military matters. But today, one sees that among the generals,

> there is not only no anticipation of the enemy's ingenious alliances and shifts, also
> there is no clear faith in [the issuing of] rewards or strict punishments.

The result is that knights and commoners face extreme penury and difficulties.

> Their equipment and weapons are unfamiliar to them, while their generals compassion is not generally guaranteed.

When an emergency suddenly arises, officials impulsively react, endangering their own knights. The knights, because of this, yield to the blandishments of the enemy. In this way, when

> the generals and officials press the resentful to confront the enemy,
> the knights and soldiers will fold their arms and await the bandits.

Now,

> the generals are unable to rally their knights,
> and the knights are unable to use their weapons.

When these two situations arise, it is like being without an army. To be without knights and without weapons, and yet to want to engage in combat, is equivalent to defeat. This outcome is inevitable.[19] Therefore it is said: "Such a defeat is not a calamity sent by Heaven but is the commander's error."

While worthy knights can be found in the world, they are only troubled by the lack of opportunities to take charge and nothing more. Thus, if there is [agricultural] land, then there is a way for the common folk to prosper;

if there are orderly markets, then there is a way for merchants to be drawn in

if there are knights and commoners, then there is a way for the state to be strong;

if there are laws and ordinances, then there is a way for licentious wickedness to be prohibited.

Now,

a state cannot be governed from the outside,
an army cannot be managed from headquarters.

The chiefs and functionaries of the commanderies and districts are fortunate to have at one and the same time decision-making powers over all the things recounted above. But they are incapable of fulfilling imperial mandates [to ensure] the peace and tranquility of the people. They are indeed greedy, extortionate, low-minded, vulgar, and shameless—and nothing more.[20]

Now, when an era has extraordinary persons who go on to achieve extraordinary accomplishments, it is only after extraordinary setbacks that [extraordinary accomplishments will appear.] Thus, when it comes to selecting military chiefs and functionaries, one ought to promote from obscurity[21] men who are clearly superior, martial, generous, talented, enlightened, and [cognizant of] shifting power dynamics. In appointing generals and commanders, one must not recklessly give [excessive] weight to their status, nor give to members of one's family positions of military authority. Doing so can be described as delivering one's state to the enemy.

# CHAPTER 22 PREFACE

The Man and Yi wreaking havoc in China,
Have caused worry in both ancient and current times.
Yao and Shun worried about the people,
And [sent] Gao Yao to suppress the rebels.
King Xuan, in the period of the revival,
[Charged] Nan Zhong to engage at the border.
At present the people [of the borders] die every day,
Why is there a failure to protect them?

Thus I have written "Securing the Frontier," chapter 22.

# 22

## SECURING THE FRONTIER

The governments of enlightened rulers are all-sheltering and universally loving.[1]

They are not partial to the close and intimate;
they are not neglectful of the unfamiliar and distant.

They share with the people the auspicious and the inauspicious, the fortunate and the unfortunate; they empathize with others' feelings of sorrow and joy.[2] They look upon the people as their infants, responding to their misfortune as if [they themselves] were recoiling from a hot surface. Thus, all within the Four Seas are happy and pleased, and everyone is able to make themselves of use to each other.

In the past, the Qiang tribes rebelled, beginning in Liang and Bing, spreading to commands

in the east, where they ravaged Zhao and Wei; and
in the west, where they seized Shu and Han.

Five Provinces[3] were despoiled;
six commanderies were obliterated.

All around for a thousand *li* the wasteland was abandoned and devoid of survivors. Banditry and looting, calamities and destruction [continued] day and night without pause.

> The hundred surnames were wiped out;
> each day and month brought fire and ruin.

Yet the knights of the inner commanderies who did not suffer from these calamities all declared that, for the time being, they would not intervene and await Heaven's own time [for the situation to resolve itself].[4] Can there be any human heart that reasons in that way?

Previously, when the Qiang began to rebel, the dukes, noblemen, councilors, and prefects all wanted to abandon the province of Liang and withdraw to protect the three governorships [near the imperial capital]. The imperial court did not listen to them. Subsequently, the Qiang proceeded to invade [the interior] [lacuna], and the advisors [in favor of abandoning Liang] were greatly disturbed that their ludicrous advice had not been followed.[5] I, with due respect, laugh at them, and their dilemma of "speaking up and regretting it; not speaking up and also regretting it,"[6] is simply the inability to recognize the principle of changing [circumstances]. A territory cannot be without borders;[7] to be without borders is to extinguish the state. Thus, once you lose the province of Liang, the three governorships will become the borders [of the empire];

> once the three governorships are invaded, Hongnong[8] will become the border [of the empire].[9]
> Once Hongnong is invaded, Loyang will become the border region.

Reasoning by analogy, even if one reached the Eastern Sea, that too would become a border. Now if you do not

> intensively increase military preparedness in order to wipe out the enemy, or
>
> select persons of talent [to defend the state's] territorial integrity,

and say that the borders cannot be preserved, and that we will from the outset take the initiative to cede [land] and display our weakness [to the bandit forces], would that not be irrational?[10]

In the past, Yue Yi,[11] marshalling the anxious state of Yan, destroyed mighty Qi, awing all under Heaven.[12] He can truly be called an excellent general. Yet the noble [governor] of Jimo,[13] all alone, preserved his isolated city. Over the course of six years [Jimo] did not fall, and in the end the governor saved his people. Tian Dan[14] lost five thousand soldiers and sent Ji Jie fleeing,[15] recovering more than seventy fortified cities for Qi. One could say that he was excellent in his use of the military. Surrounding [the Qi cities of] Liao and Ju for years on end, [the Yan] forces in the end were unable to seize them. These examples all show that

> one can use great strength to attack great weakness,
> and superior wisdom to counter abysmal stupidity,

but still be unable to prevail. Why? I reply:

> An attacker often has insufficient [force];
> the defender has [strength] to spare.[16]

Previously, all of our commanderies all contained an array of cities with flourishing populations. But

the Qiang barbarians' wisdom was, in fact, not equivalent to that
of a Yue Yi or a Tian Dan;
the distress of our commanderies and districts was not like that of
Liao, Ju, or Jimo.[17]

Instead, all of the officials there were unwilling to shoulder the responsibility of turning their hearts and minds to securing strong defensive measures, and on the contrary, employed their strength plundering their own people, abandoning their granaries and storehouses, and turning their backs on their cities and townships as they fled. Looking at it from this viewpoint, the problem is

not that a city suffers from a lack [of food],
but that the generals can't stomach it.

If you want to repel [foes] and bring tranquility to the people,

focus on employing the virtuous, and
not on one's shrinking territory.

Qi and Wei maintained defensive positions; but their states did not become tranquil by these means.[18]
Ziying[19] chose ceding [territory], but the Qin did not endure by these means.

Emperor Wu [of the Han] drove out the Yi and expanded the boundaries [of the Han Empire] in all directions for thousands of *li*.

In the east he founded Lelang;
in the west he established Dunhuang;

in the south, he extended beyond Jiaozhi;
in the north, he built Shuofang.

Finally settling Nanyue, and
exterminating Dayuan.

Wherever his fearsome army turned,
there were none he failed to obliterate.[20]

Now the marauders encroach on [the territory surrounding] the royal altar-mounds and cannot be stopped.[21] This [tragedy] is nothing more than a self-inflicted wound; it is not due to the error of possessing frontier [territory].

If the lips perish, the teeth get cold;
if the body is wounded, the heart is pained.[22]

These things are necessarily so. Can there be any doubt about it? The superior man perceives the triggers [of events]. How much more is this so for [what] is already obvious?

Previously, frontier troubles were

> as terrifying as the thunder's bolts,
> as brilliant as the sun and moon,

but commentators concealed the facts, saying, "The [border incursions] are nothing more than roving packs of scavenging dogs."[23] "Their understanding was shallow, and they were skilled in making specious arguments that prompted the ruler's indifference."[24] They hoped to induce the court to consider [such] banditry as a minor irritant that did not merit concern. Though the danger had risen to this extent, they still had no desire to rescue [the frontier]. A proverb says:

> As long as a disease doesn't infect your own body, you can say "it's bearable."
> As long as money doesn't flow out of your own house, you can say "spend it."

If the sons and younger brothers of the high nobles had to suffer the depredations of the Qiang so that from morning to night they had to endure their attacks like those endured by the people of the frontier regions, they would vigorously call for chastising the Qiang.

At present, since [the aristocrats] themselves suffer no grief or oppression, they just sit as peacefully as ever. Moreover, they do not understand how to manage preparations for repair, protection, and resistance. Contentedly chatting at leisure, they recline and abandon their Heaven-ordained [responsibilities].[25] When the Qiang, left to themselves, come and go, penetrating deeply [into the realm] and killing many [of our people], only then do [the officials], with all their vulgar mediocrity, go en masse to the imperial palace, where they all mutter the same thing, offer polite apologies, and then withdraw, discussing their lack of results.[26] [But when they are] seated together in the Audience Hall, they are devoid of any sincere expression of concern for their country or pity for common folk. When they turn to face one another with complacent regard, no one is willing to make a corrective counterargument.[27] As the day grows late and time moves on, their deliberations will have resolved nothing, and they adjourn, deferring decisions to some later time. When later developments bring a small [interlude of] security, they tranquilly set aside [the frontier problem] and forget about it. [But] within a week,[28] the enemy will resume their evildoing. Military documents are [then] sent urgently to and fro; plumed dispatches[29] come and go. They became fearful and agitated again, as before. And so it has been, coming and going for nine years.

> If indeed he would turn to good—
> but on the contrary, he proceeds to [greater] evil.[30]

Confusion and chaos! How did things arrive at this extremity? The *Spring and Autumn* derided Zheng's abandoning its troops;[31] then how much more the case for [a state] that throws away its people? If one single person sighs in distress, then the Kingly Way is damaged; how much more so a population of a million calling out, weeping, and moving Heaven's heart?

Furthermore,

> the state is founded on the people,
> and the noble are rooted in the lowly.

Thus, the sage-kings nurtured the people,

> loving them like children,
> worried about them like kinsmen,

> succoring those who were in danger,
> preserving those who were perishing,

> saving them from calamities and distress,
> distancing them from misfortune and disorder.

Thus,

> when [King Wuding of Shang] mounted a punitive expedition against the Guifang,[32] it was not because he was fond of warfare;

> when [King Xuan of Zhou] drove away the Xianyun,[33] it was not because he coveted their territory;

it was to "move the people to cultivate virtue" and to pacify the frontiers.[34] Long ago, the Son of Heaven defended [the state] against the Four Yi,[35] and on their own initiative, the Di and Qiang [tribes] never failed to arrive to pay tribute. Throughout the world, people thought only to pay him homage.[36] Even the reeds along the path relied on [the ruler's] virtue.[37] How much more should this be the case for our people in recent times, who suffer bitterly from misfortune—can they have no salvation?

Generally speaking, that the people respectfully serve their superiors is because they cherish their righteousness and kindness. But

> when [the people] are in pain [and their superiors] show no sense of shame, or
> when [the people] encounter misfortune [and their superiors] show no sense of humanity,

[then the people's] anger, violence, hatred, and antipathy springs from [the superiors'] shamelessness. Now,

> the depredations of the Qiang have been prolonged;
> the injuries and destruction have been numerous;
> the common people have been anxious;
> the grief and misfortune have been profound;

The high-born and the lowly go in circles,[38] and no one can see a time when they might rest. Not once has there been appointed a great general with a unitary command to sweep away the swarming bandits.[39] But the provinces and commanderies instead constantly raise troops one after another without ceasing. Like

> hanging a curtain to block the wind, or
> trenching the sand to stop the flow of a river—

these create no impediment but render one exhausted and nothing more. Now several provinces have called up troops, amounting to more than 100,00 men, all of whom are fed from the pubic granaries, annually amounting to several million bushels.[40] Added to this is the monthly family stipend.[41] While the cost of this personnel is already impossible to sustain, on the other hand, I fear that the cost of sending large armies on brief expeditions is definitely not the correct strategy.

Moreover,

> one who is unsteady can easily be overthrown;
> one who is doubtful can easily be turned around.

Now the bandits have once again occupied our borderlands, but even they do not dare consider [the situation] secure, and should thus easily be dazed and destroyed.[42] As for the common people who have recently left their old lands, their homesickness has not yet abated, and they can easily be roused. In fact, under these circumstances, we should dispatch great generals to kill, punish, press, threaten, rout, terrorize, defeat, and destroy [the Qiang invaders]. But if one is patient and delays for days or months, while people hoard and amass wealth and honors so that each individual thinks only about what happens after things settle down, then they will be hard to rouse. The *Leftover Documents of Zhou* says, "He who would be a sage must act with dispatch."[43] For the same reason, if you are making plans for a defensive war, you had better begin planning early.

# CHAPTER 23 PREFACE

The sentiments of middling people,
Are at odds with the ruler.
They are unable to contemplate the distant future,
And foolishly only consider conditions of the current moment.
They haphazardly cling to their own personal views,
Regarding them as [grand] strategies for the nation.
We ought to examine their words,
To inquire into what they really mean.

Thus I have written "Discussions of the Frontier," chapter 23.

# 23

# DISCUSSIONS OF THE FRONTIER

One who understands the actual nature of bad and good fortune must not be hoodwinked by vacuous discussions;
one who investigates the nature of order and disorder must not be moved by fine words.

For this reason,

[when there are] affairs about which no one expresses doubt, the sage does not deliberate;[1]
where there are frivolous and insubstantial persuasions, the sage does not listen.

Why? Planning does not ignore realities and fall back on disputatious speech. This is why the enlightened ruler first looks exhaustively into the feelings of the people and does not merely commission excellent generals. He makes his own preparations and does not count on enemies [to not attack].[2] Thus,

in his attacks, he will be sure to defeat the foe; or
through his defensive measures, he will be sure to remain whole.

When the Qiang first rebelled,

> their strategy was not yet perfected,
> their coalitions were not yet stable,
> their masses were not yet united,
> and their weapons were not yet prepared.

Some of them took up bamboo poles or [cudgels made from] branches of trees, while others, who were empty-handed, supplemented [the rebel forces]. They were newly formed and disorderly, and they did not yet have any leaders.[3] To crush them would have been easy, but the chiefs of commanderies and prefects were incompetent, cowardly, weak, and did not dare to attack. Thus they allowed the barbarians to gain from their successes and become strong enough to crush provinces and obliterate commanderies.[4] Daily they expanded like a raging fire, bringing ruin and destruction [even] to the capital district,[5] and "extending as far as Guifang."[6] The situation has remained like this for ten years. The common people's suffering harm to this day has not come to an end. But the asinine fools still declare that the time is not yet ripe to come to their aid and that they should await Heaven's own good time. What kind of human beings could entertain reasoning like that?

As a rule,

> the benevolent use their own feelings to empathetically understand others;
> the knowledgeable assess the results of their actions to manage affairs.

Nowadays, the lords and nobles

privately do not feel the pain of the knights and commoners who
    are wiped out, and
publicly do not consider the misfortune of long military service.

They all cling to short-term considerations[7] that avoid what is right in front of them.[8] They casually aver that it is not appropriate to raise troops, and no longer know enough

> to uphold principles established by the [former] emperors and
>     kings, or
> to understand how to bring the crisis to an end.

> The *Book of Changes* says: "It is fitting to guard against
>     harassment."[9]
> The *Book of Odes* glorifies smiting [the barbarians]."[10]

From antiquity onward, there have always been wars; this is in no way a recent phenomenon. The [Zuo] *Tradition* says: "Heaven gives rise to the Five Resources,[11] and the people use all of them. Discarding even one of them will not do. Who can remove weapons? Weapons are the means for intimidating the unruly and for making manifest civil virtues.[12]

> The sages rise by them,
> the disorderly fall by them."[13]

[Lord] Huan of Qi, [Lord] Wen of Jin, and [Lord] Xiang of Song, were Lords of the Lands during an era of decline, but they were burdened with shame that the world was engaged in mutual destruction yet they were unable to save it. How much more is this the case with the ruler of all within the Four Seas, on whom August Heaven has bestowed the mandate?

The grandees of Jin and Chu were officials of [comparatively] small states; even so, they were burdened with shame that they were personally engaged in the encroachment [of other states]. How much more was this so for the Three Dukes, whom the Son of Heaven had made responsible for maintaining the age in good order?

His Honor Liu[14] was benevolent and righteous, extending his beneficence even to the reeds along the road. How much more should it be so for human beings made of flesh and blood, who are the same as us? If one person cries "Alas," the Kingly Way is compromised: How much more so when the people are slaughtered by the hundreds of myriads? A passage in the *Book of Documents* says: "The Son of Heaven is the father and mother of the people."[15] But in the father's and mother's relationship with their children,

> can they sit and watch them being ravaged by bandits and thieves? Can they stand and view them being eaten by dogs and swine?

Leaving aside considerations of benevolence and compassion, let us talk in terms of calculating profit.

> The state takes the people as its foundation;
> the noble take the humble as their root.

Looking back to the very beginning [of time]:

> When the people are endangered but the state remains secure—who benefits?
> When those at the bottom are poor but those on the top remain wealthy—who benefits?[16]

Therefore it is said: "Ruling a state requires managing the resources of the people. If the people are in actual want, how does the ruler manage to be fat?"[17] Now it is through the petty folk that [the ruler] receives Heaven's long-enduring Mandate. I venture to suggest that the sage ruler

> deeply ponder the maladies of the state's foundation, and
> consider extensively the results of disaster or good fortune.

Furthermore,

> things flourish and decay;
> times cycle and shift;
> affairs swirl and recede;
> people evolve and transform.

The wise take into account these signs: Is this not appropriate?

> Meng Ming rectified [his Lord's] error in [the territory] west of the Yellow River.[18]
> Fan Li received recompense at Guxu.[19]

This is how

> a great accomplishment is established in the present generation,
>     and
> a fine reputation is transmitted forever.

Today the borderlands are vexed; every day whole clans suffer the disaster of annihilation. The common people day and night look to the court for salvation, but the lords and high officials feel that it would be too much trouble, and their minions secretly laugh at them. This is what Yanzi[20] meant [when he wrote]: "They

> trivialize filling the silos and granaries, but
> begrudge a cup of boiled grain."[21]

How is [the current situation] different? Nowadays they only know enough to love seeing the registers of their tax collection, but they don't know that what is *not* seen there is that the treatment of the people must be the primary principle. They know that corvee labor is difficult to mobilize, but they don't know that the central states depend on peace in the border regions.

The *Book of Odes* laments:

> some are oblivious to the hue and cry;
> others labor in misery.[22]

Now because the lords and high officials merely take into account that they themselves suffer no injury, they vie to carve off the country's territories and hand them to the enemy. They murder our ruler's people to fatten the Qiang.

> With schemes like this, they cannot be called knowledgeable.
> With officials like this, they cannot be called loyal.

Their abilities and knowledge are insufficient to be allowed to discuss [these matters].

Moreover,

all territory within the four seas is what sage [rulers] pass on to
their sons and grandsons.
The duties of official positions are what the many functionaries
rely on to establish themselves.

The endowment of sons and grandsons is the consideration of the
stability of ten thousand generations.
The accommodation of each person is the [expectation that] each
official gets one term.

Thus,

their instructions routinely are not carried out for very
long, and
their positions cannot be maintained for very long.

This is truly what

the enlightened prince minutely examines, and
what the ruler alone determines.

At present, saying that one does not want to stir the people into a state of vexation is appropriate. If that is the case, preparations ought to be made to defend them. This must be our strategy now:

to ensure that the barbarians will not dare to come, and if
they do come, they will gain nothing from it; and
to ensure that the people will no longer suffer banditry;
but if [bandits] do come, that the [people] will lose
nothing.

But at present, things are not like that. The officials simply begrudge the difficulties posed by the people and make light of the calamity of obliteration and extinction. In this way they are,

> not the masters of others,
> not the commanders of the people;
> not the counsellors of the ruler; and
> not the masters of victory.

Furthermore,

> a discussion is a manifestation of one's vision;
> words are a display of one's mind.
>
> > "They are possessed of the ability,
> > and right it is their movements should indicate it."[23]

A proverb says: "How do you win over someone who is truculent? Nothing is better than making them hear about a situation [themselves]." Now, for all those who say that it is possible to have peace with the frontier still unsecured, we really ought to appoint them and their sons and younger brothers to fill the positions of the Supreme Commander of the Frontier, his chief assistants, and his functionaries. Thereupon the fact and fiction of the situation will finally be settled. Only then will rescuing the frontier be without disaster. When the frontier is without disaster, only then can the Central States achieve tranquility.

# CHAPTER 24 PREFACE

Since the frontier is far from the court,
Their governors arrogate power.
The Masters of Writing do not monitor them,
But believe their duplicitous words.
They order the destruction of commanderies and counties,
And drive the people to move into the interior.
At present, the [border] areas are once again empty and unkempt,
Ensuring that the barbarians will get ideas.

Thus I have written "Populating the Frontier," chapter 24.

# 24

# POPULATING THE FRONTIER

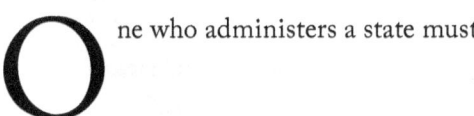

One who administers a state must

    clearly investigate what is true and what is false in close and
        distant [places], and
    foresee and know[1] the wellsprings of bad and good fortune.

Only then will he be able to make full use of his officials' strengths and safeguard and empower his state.

Previously, when the Qiang commenced their rebellion, it arose in its initial stage with incomplete equipment and weapons. Some of the bandits

    grasped bronze mirrors as weaponry,[2] while others
    hefted planks or trays as makeshift shields.

Fearful and in disarray, they were unable to operate as a unit. A fortified city could easily have controlled them,[3] but the commanderies and districts [lacuna] all allowed[4] [the Qiang] to become numerous. It reached a point where the common people were oppressed [by the Qiang] and suffered a violent calamitous misfortune, losing all their goods and property.

The people were embittered and angry,[5] and each of them wanted to take revenge on the enemy. But the generals were all cowardly, deficient, weak, and ineffectual. They did not dare to attack; instead they sat issuing dispatches to deceive the court.

> When in fact a hundred [of our] people were killed, they said it was only one;
> when in fact one barbarian was killed, they said it was one hundred.
> If the barbarians were actually numerous, they said that they were few;
> if they were actually few, they said that they were numerous.

Their skewed, twisted, and crafty wording was primarily an effort to wrest for themselves advantages and profits and not simply

> a grand strategy made out of concern for the nation, or
> an expression of grief over the deaths of the people.

They also

> squandered money and grain,
> exhausted storehouses and granaries,

and furthermore borrowed from the people and forcibly seized their goods. That families with fortunes worth thousands and tens of thousands were stripped until there was nothing left, and that people by the tens of thousands were made destitute and subsequently died, was entirely the result of officials killing them by starvation. The suffering caused by the officials exceeded what arose from encountering the barbarians. Plundering robbers and pillaging barbarians come suddenly and are gone again, and people are not necessarily killed or wounded [by them]. But as for those whom the officials sought out and robbed, no sooner had they turned on their heels than they were smeared on the ground.[6] In some cases their clans were destroyed, their families were extinguished, and they were cut off without descendants. In other cases, orphans, widows, and [young] women were made into other people's slaves and sent far away to be sold, to the point of causing them to be unable to go on living. Such cases were too numerous to count. This sort of [disorder] is what causes Heaven to send down calamities, and what especially disorders yin and yang.[7]

Furthermore, [the importance of]

> dwelling peacefully on one's [native] soil, looking upon leaving as a heavy burden,[8] and
> feeling strongly attached to the graves of one's ancestors,

are matters the worthy and the worthless both agree upon. The people fear relocation more than execution. Execution affects no more than one member of a family, that's all. But [far worse is] suffering the loss of goods and wealth, having land confiscated, and migrating far away, [where they are]

> unfamiliar with practices and conventions, and
> unaccustomed to the water and soil.

> Most will suffer the extinction of their family lines; and
> few are those who will return home.

The Dai [people's] horses gaze northward;
a dying fox heads for its native hills.

The frontier people are cautious and ignorant and especially hate dwelling in the interior [provinces]. Although they know that there is a serious crisis, they still want to maintain their ancestral enterprises and die in their native land.[9] Their sincere wish is not to be driven to the ends of the earth.

The commandery governors, county prefects, and [local] chiefs fear and loathe military affairs. All of them are nonnatives of the area, so the suffering takes no toll on them, and the misfortunes do not involve their families. So they argued for dismantling their commanderies and districts and relocating [people] to the interior.[10] They went as far as to send officials and troops to

> stomp on the people's crops of grain,[11]
> raze their outbuildings and houses,
> level their encampments and stockades, and
> destroy their essential livelihood,

causing violence, theft, dislocation, and plundering. When sending people to the interior [provinces], they abandoned the sick and weak, leaving them to die on the spot.

At the time, the myriad [common] people became angry and aggrieved, weeping tears of blood and crying out aloud in a manner that would sadden ghosts and spirits and arouse the compassion of Heaven's heart. But the petty people, being humble and incapable, were unable go to court on their own [to plead their cases]. They had to rely on officials and their families [for help]. But oppressive officials responded with threats, so they didn't dare resist. The people were thus deprived of their land and bereft of their occupations. They also faced swarms of locusts, droughts, starvation, and exhaustion.

Driven eastward, they became divided and scattered across the prefectures of You, Ji, Yan, Yu, Jing, Yang, Shu, and Han, again encountering hunger and starvation, death and extinction, losing more than half of their cohort.[12] The borderlands in turn became empty and wild, and down to the present day they remain unoccupied. What caused all of these misfortunes to arise was entirely the malfeasance of the functionaries.

Now, land is the basis of the people's livelihood. But in fact, it cannot go for long as wasteland without inciting the ambitions of the enemy. Moreover, when Bian Que[13] treated an illness, he examined blockages and penetrated obstructions.[14]

> What was depleted, he supplemented;
> what was full, he drained.

Thus, the illnesses were cured, and his reputation became illustrious.

> When Yi Yin served as minister to Tang,[15]
>
> he set up [the standards of] "light and heavy" and balanced surplus and shortages,[16]
> he drew down accumulated reserves and distributed them to those in need.

Therefore the Yin[17] ruled [the world] and the [position of] ruler was revered. Jia Yi[18] was pained by [the nation's] suffering [a sort of] paralysis and lameness.[19]

At present, the borderland commanderies each encompass a [radius of] a thousand *li*, and each territory has two counties where the registered households amount to a few hundred. But the commandery governor's jurisdiction, which encompasses [a radius of] ten thousand *li*, is devoid of people. Its excellent fields are abandoned, and no one cultivates or plants them. As for the central provinces and inner commanderies, taking the measure of the land and marking borders, it doesn't amount to half of the area of the borderlands, yet

> its population is in the millions,
> its fields and acreage do not sustain [the people's needs].[20]

People abound but land is limited; there is no way for them to get a foothold. Is this not the same sort of thing as having a paralyzed side, lameness, or ulcerated feet?

> The *Zhou shu*[21] says: "When land is plentiful and people are scarce, no one extracts its resources. This is called 'vacant land.' It can be attacked and subdued.
> When land is scarce and people are numerous, the people are not considered its people. They can be impoverished and exhausted." That is why land and population must be kept in balance.

At the present time, the borderland commanderies have suffered many misfortunes and multiple calls to military service. With one push they enter calamity's door. If one does not benefit them by bringing aid, doing away with harm, and finding a way to encourage them, then after an extended period of time there will be no means to rescue them, and the interior will harbor traitorous intentions. For the Qiang in the west and the bandits in the north, this situation will prompt predatory desires. Truly, that is a big worry.

When one of the many artisans makes a vessel, he reinforces the sides, working on them with redoubled care.[22] How could this be a case of partiality? In fact, it is simply the means by which one strengthens its interior. [Likewise], when the sages of antiquity devised laws, they also took care to augment borderlands. Was it not [in order to] bring security to the central states? Suppose a family is attacked by bandits. They would definitely move the elderly, the young, and the frail to a central area, while the strong, formidable, and bold would defend the exterior.

> Those inside receive support; and
> those outside contend with hardship.

It is like the *qiongqiong* and the *juxu*.[23] Since they trust and support one another, they are able to achieve a peaceful existence.

By imperial mandate the law commands: Every [registered population of] two hundred thousand people, or every one hundred thousand in the border commanderies, may annually nominate one man as "filial and incorruptible."[24] Every group of thirty functionaries was to nominate one deemed "incorruptible."[25] But since the Qiang began their rebellion, the population was reduced, and several times the commandery governor was replaced, so that for ten years they did not manage to make any nominations.

> Those holding office toiled arduously but were not selected;
> the worthy and talented amassed stores [of virtue] but were not recognized.

> The officials had nothing to hope for;
> the farmers had no benefits to seek out.

Therefore, when [people in the central areas] who struggled to plant crops reaped disaster, none were willing to go out to the [frontier].

The [sage-rulers of] antiquity in governing the people, enticed them through profits; they did not coerce them with punishments. The *Yijing* says: "The ancient kings, accordingly, examined the [different] regions [of the kingdom] to observe the [ways of the] people, and to set forth their instructions."[26] For that reason, at the beginning of the *jianwu*-reign period,[27] [the imperial state] took possession of the border commanderies and, even though [their population] amounted to only a few hundred households, ordered that they nominate one "filial and incorruptible" man every year as a way to attract immigrants. At present, under truly expedient circumstances, [the emperor] ought to order that each borderland commandery nominate one "filial" man, that every group of thirty functionaries nominate one "incorruptible" man, and [additionally, establish] that every group of one hundred households can select one "classical scholar." Migrants from the inner commanderies who bring along their wives and children, who are enrolled in the tax registers, and who have been residents for more than five years would also be able to achieve the same nomination privileges as the natives. [The ruler] should also invite migrants to plow the borderlands and import grain;

> those from distant commanderies [who import] a thousand bushels,[28]
> or those from nearby commanderies [who import] two thousand bushels

should be rewarded with the fifth rank of nobility. Those who do not wish to receive noble rank will be rewarded [instead] with twice the value [of grain from] nearby commanderies. In this way, if the gentlefolk and the petty folk both get what is advantageous, then even if one were to order them not to come [to the frontier commanderies], they would be unstoppable. This is the essential method for

>   sharing sorrow and happiness,
>   making corvee and military service equitable,
>   populating the borderland and boundaries, and
>   assuring the safety of the central states.

# CHAPTER 25 PREFACE

Heaven gave birth to spiritual beings;
The sages used them as models.
Milfoil and turtles [facilitate divining by] crack-making and sortilege,
In order to resolve apprehensions and doubt.
The vulgar technicians are shallow and ignorant;
None of them can fathom these arts.
If one aggrandizes himself but is not a worthy,
How is he worth believing?

Thus I have written "Divination Set Forth," chapter 25.

# 25

## DIVINATION SET FORTH

When Heaven and earth opened and divided, there were spirits and people.[1] People and spirits differ in their activities, but their essential qi is connected.

> Actions have elicitations and beckonings;
> destiny includes the "adverse" and the "corresponding."[2]

There are periods of both good and bad fortune; "Heaven is not readily to be relied on."[3] Although sages and worthies investigated these matters, they did not want to presume on their authority. Therefore they devised plastromancy and divination by the milfoil stalk so that the spirits could be consulted.

Confucius said:

> "The virtue of the milfoil is round and spirit-like.
> The virtue of trigrams is squarely exact and wise."[4]

He also said: "When a superior man is about to engage in some activity, he consults with them using words. They receive his order and the answer comes back like an echo's response."[5] This is how Yu the Great obtained Gao Yao and how King Wen obtained his minister Lü Shang.[6] In each case,

> the omen revealed an image; and
> the prognostication plumbed their thoughts,

bringing their good fortune to fruition.

Now,

> when the superior man hears of goodness, he is encouraged, delighted, and progresses [in virtue];[7]
> When he hears of iniquity, he reforms, reflects, and rectifies his failings.

Therefore, he is at peace and enjoys much good fortune.

> When the inferior man hears of goodness [lacuna].[8]
> When he hears of iniquity, he is fearful, fainthearted, and acts recklessly.

Thus, he is wild, impetuous, and has much misfortune. For this reason, for all those who divine by turtle shell or milfoil [stalks], isn't it the case that all

> inquiries about the nature of good or bad fortune, and
> discussions on the cycles of growth and decline,

lead people to cultivate themselves and to be cautious in their actions so that they may be the recipients of good fortune?

Furthermore, in the sage kings' establishment of plastromancy and milfoil divination, they

> did not go against the people in their determination of the auspicious, and
> did not depend on it alone in their judgment of a situation.

Therefore, on the subject of divination, the "Great Plan" says, "Great Concord is what is to be revered."[9] The *Book of Documents* also says, "Availing ourselves of the Great Turtle, we would not dare to see good fortune [in this event]."[10] A passage in the *Book of Odes* says, "Our turtles are weary and will tell us nothing about the plans."[11] From this perspective, we might conclude that the intimations of the milfoil and the turtle [merely] accord with the difficulty or ease of the moment, so that we cannot consider them to be accurate. Or could it be that the world has no more gifted men like the scribe Su, and that those who truly comprehend spiritual matters have become scarce?[12] When it comes to

> the Zhou scribe's milfoil divination for Jingzhong, and
> Zhuangshu's milfoil divination for Muzi,

these examples can be described as divinations that were able to

> inquire into mysteries, trace what was hidden,
> hook things from the deep, and obtain what was distant.[13]

If

> Lord Xian had heeded the words of Scribe Su sooner, or
> if Muzi had paid heed to the warnings of Zhuangshu earlier,

the slanders of Li Ji and the servant Niu could not have insinuated themselves into their midst; nor would they have encountered disasters that destroy kingdoms and endanger men.[14]

The sages

> placed great importance on plastromancy and milfoil divination, even so, when it came to matters for which there was no doubt, they did not consult them.
> [They] had a deep reverence for the sacrificial rites, even so, when it came to heterodox prayers, they did not offer them.

For this reason that it is said: "The sage does not trouble the milfoil and plastron unnecessarily," and that he "respects the spirits and keeps his distance from them."[15] Now, spirits and human beings [embody] different qi and [carry out] different activities. With no impetus to be involved, what do spirits have to do with me? This is why Confucius

> praised King Zhao for not sacrificing to the [Yellow] River, and abhorred Mr. Ji for his quest to Mt. Tai.[16]

Nowadays, ordinary men dally with divination and sacrifice to spirits that are not their own. They are truly deluded.

There is also a fallacious [belief] connecting a person's surname to the Five Notes, establishing a "Five Dwellings" sequence of correspondences [with the Five Phases]. This fabrication of lies is most egregious. In ancient times, there were yin and yang, afterward there were the Five Phases. The Five Thearchs each wielded the energy of [one of] the Five Phases and by this means gave birth to human beings. At a distance of many generations, surnames, personal names, style names, and clan names came into being. Personal names and style names are simply used

> to make distinctions within a large group and to indicate a particular individual, and
> not to signify their association with the Five Notes and determine the "hard" [yang] and "soft." [yin].

Nowadays, when common people cannot trace and document their earliest progenitor, and instead, desire to ascertain their ruling phase through notes and speech. They could not be in greater error.

Now,

> fish live in water and thrive;
> birds nest in trees and brood.

Yet if a person cannot trace his progenitors but finds harmonizing notes acceptable, then

> he may call a bird a fish, but can it survive under water?
> He may call a fish a bird, but can it nest in a tree?

This is an impossibility. Call a colt a calf, but in the end it will become a horse. Thus, as for all surnames associated with notes, they must correspond to [the phase] by which the progenitor of one's clan ruled as king.

> Great Brilliant (Tai Hao) possessed the essence of wood; he received [his charge] from the Year [Sui] and ruled as king.[17] So

his sons and grandsons should all [be associated with] the note *jiao*.

The Divine Husbandman (Shen Nong) possessed the essence of fire. He received [his charge] from the Twinkling Deluder and ruled as king. So his sons and grandsons all ought to be [associated with] the note *zhi*.

The Yellow Emperor (Huang Di) possessed the essence of earth. He received [his charge] from the Suppressor and ruled as king. So his sons and grandsons all should be [associated with] the note *gong*.

The Lesser Brilliance (Shao Hao) possessed the essence of metal. He received [his charge] from Grand White and ruled as king. So his sons and grandsons should all be [associated with] the note *shang*.

Sedate Concern (Zhuan Xu) [possessed] the essence of water. He received [his charge] from the Fire (Star) and ruled as king. So his sons and grandsons should all be [associated with] the note *yu*.

Though names undergo a hundred alterations, the note and phase do not change.

Vulgar artisans also say, "For the dwellings of those with surnames associated with the note *shang* it is auspicious to exit through a west-facing door." This idea is once again void of good sense. In accordance with the Five Phases, one should

> exit, holding to the "prevailing" [direction], and
> enter, settling in the southwest [corner]

to be auspicious and safe.[18] A person with a *shang* surname might enter his house facing the east. But entering the house facing east, on the contrary, allows metal to conquer wood.[19] In such a situation, the quintessential spirits of the [people of that] household will daily be in mutual conflict.[20] The same holds true for each of the Five Phases. It is also held that houses [accord with]

> the sequence of *gong* and *shang*, and
> the direct correspondences to the Year [Star].[21]

If this is true, then by adjusting the number of doors on one's house, can one change the note associated with one's surname and thereby evade an [unfortunate] correspondence? Nowadays:

> In one house, generations of the same surname replace each other. Some have been fortunate and others unlucky.
> In one [official] post, generations of the same surname replace each other. Some have been promoted and others dismissed.

In one palace,

> when King Cheng or King Kang lived there, it flourished daily;
> when King You or King Li lived there, it declined daily.

Viewed from this perspective, that good or bad fortune or flourishing or decline cannot be perceived through examination of a dwelling place is indeed clear.

As for all the various celestial and terrestrial spirits such as the Great Year, Feng Long, Gou Chen, and General Tai Yin—they are, in fact, heavenly officials and are not meant to be served by ordinary people.[22] Heaven has these spirits because they are all entrusted to assist in the completion of the qi of Yin and Yang and to benefit all things—just as the earthly government includes regional commissioners, governors, prefects, and magistrates.

If one moves toward them—why should they be angry?
If one moves away from them—why should they be resentful?

The Way of rulers and that of common people are close, yet it is not fitting that they should fault each other. How much more is this true of spirits who are treated with the highest veneration and whose rules of propriety differ from those of human beings? How can they be faulted?

Furthermore, if one wants to ensure that people avoid ghosts, then this would result in them

> not being able to travel on roads, and
> not being able to live in houses.

This [view] applies to worthy and superior persons who keep their hearts honest and upright and whose quintessential spirit is stable and firm. When it comes to

> worldly vulgarians and inferior persons,
> ignoble concubines and lowly wives,
> shallow rustics and ignorant fools,

after their gradual steeping [in these beliefs] is complete, there have also been numerous instances of their essences becoming scattered and their gall bladders being destroyed.[23] If [people] do not follow the inclinations of their essential sincerity but are compelled by what they fear, this situation will in fact increase their distress and nothing more. How can we make it clear that this is so? What makes a man a man is not

> his height of eight feet, but
> his endowment of quintessential spirit.

Among those who die of fright, it is not illness that has brought it on, and it is not a person's strength that has failed.[24] Rather, in the case of those who never recover, it is because their spiritual essence has left them.

> Meng Ben can approach a fierce tiger and not be afraid.
> An infant will fear an ant and cry out loud.

Perhaps the cognoscenti of our day want to encourage ignorant people who are wasted with illness, demanding of them what they are unable to do. I am once again afraid that they have fallen short of a good [solution].

The root of changing customs and altering conventions, in fact, lay in opening their hearts and rectifying their essential [spirits]. At present, people from birth do not see the correct Way and tarry in the midst of heterodoxy and wild delusion. As for their belief in these things—is difficult to abruptly release them. Only a true king is able to change them.

# CHAPTER 26 PREFACE

The *Book of Changes* mentions historians and spirit mediums,
The *Odes* mentions skillful invocators.
Sages first achieved success [with the people],
Later they expended efforts serving the spirits.
When millions of people rejoice,
Is when the spirits bestow their blessings.
Confucius did not pray,
To show that [good fortune] resides with virtue.

Thus I have written "Spirit Mediums Set Forth," chapter 26.

# 26

## SPIRIT MEDIUMS SET FORTH

In considering people's good or bad fortune,

>behavior is regarded as paramount;
>fate is regarded as decisive.

>Behavior is the substance of the self;
>fate is the determination of Heaven.

>What is in the purview of the self is definitely manageable.
>What is in the purview of Heaven is not fathomable.

The prayers and supplications of shamankas and shamans are indeed helpful. Nevertheless, if virtue is contravened, they will not be effective. The shamankas' and historian's prayers and invocations are, no doubt, the means by which they communicate with ghosts and spirits; but they are helpful in trivial matters and nothing more. When it comes to the great course of fate, there is really nothing they can do. [Their powers] can be compared to a common man's appeal to a higher authority. He can be extricated from the consequences of a minor offense, but he cannot escape [the consequences of] a true crime. Imagine a man in the following [example]: day and night he

> ridicules and disparages the teachings of his lord and father,
> opposes and offends against the restrictions of the sage kings,
> does not control his heart's desires, but
> decides to rectify his faults and [lacuna] reform, and

then casually and abruptly makes multiple appeals for acquittal. It would surely be hopeless. How much better to cultivate oneself, to be careful and timorous and to be without any offense against a superior that requires punishment. This is why Confucius objected to Zilu [praying on his behalf] saying: "My praying has been for a long time."[1] The *Classic of Filial Piety* says: "Thus,

> while parents are alive, comfort them,
> while offering sacrifices, please the spirits."[2]

From this it can be seen that if virtue and righteousness are not disregarded,

> ghosts and spirits will be pleased, and
> fortune and prosperity will be bountiful.

A passage in the *Book of Odes* says:

> "Abundant blessing is sent down,
> Blessing is sent down in large measure;
> Careful and exact is all our deportment;
> We have drunk and we have eaten to the full;
> Our happiness and dignity will be prolonged."[3]

This ode says, when

> a person's virtue and righteousness are fine and bounteous, and when
> the spirits' pleasure and enjoyment is expressed in inebriation and satisfaction

[that person] will receive reciprocal blessings.

> The Lord of Guo beckoned to spirits and death came soon.[4]
> Zhao Ying sacrificed to Heaven and annihilation followed quickly.[5]

This is surely what is meant when it is said:

> "The spirits will not savor his sacrifices, and
> the people will not join in his projects."[6]

Therefore, the Scribe of Lu said: "When a state

> is about to flourish, it listens to the people;
> when it is about to perish, it listens to the spirits."[7]

> King Zhao of Chu refrained from sacrificing to the clouds.[8]
> Lord Jing of Song would not transfer his misfortune.[9]

> Zichan opposed Pi Zao.[10]
> Lord Wen of Zhu ignored a diviner-scribe.[11]

These were all men who examined themselves and knew the Way; they [cultivated] themselves and awaited their destinies. Yan Pingzhong said: "If prayers bring benefits, then curses likewise bring harm."[12]

Ji Liang's admonition of the Marquis of Sui, and Gong Zhiji's persuasion of Lord Yu

are examples of being

> enlightened in the Way of Heaven and man, and conversant with the distinctions between the spiritual and human.[13]

Now, that

> supernatural monstrosities cannot overcome virtue, and depravity cannot harm rectitude

is Heaven's organizing principle.[14] Although there may be exceptions from time to time, the wise nevertheless hold fast to the true path and do not draw near to depraved ghosts. "Depraved ghosts" refers to idle and evil elemental beings. They are not [legitimately] empowered or truly spiritual and numinous. There are such ghosts just as among people there are those who falsify the value of an item in order to create a demand for it. If someone entices them, then they will throng from afar without ceasing, and calamity will be certain. Ghosts and spirits are also like this. Thus, Shen Xu said: "When people are fearful, their qi becomes brilliant and attracts them. When a person has no grievances with others, then these monstrosities will not appear of their own accord."[15] This means that men should not be overly fearful. If they are excessively fearful and needlessly full of dread, they really will summon forth monstrous omens.

Furthermore, just as people have the ranks of nobility, ghosts and spirits have the distinctions of noble and base. As for Heaven, earth, mountains, rivers, the altars of the land and grain, the Five Sacrifices, the hundred officials, ministers and knights who have been of service to the people, these are entities for whom the Son of Heaven and regional lords are charged to offer sacrifices.[16] As for those with whom female and male shamans claim to be in exclusive communications and in whom petty men place their hopes and fears—the seven spirits [known as] the Earth Duke, the Flying Corpse, Bad Luck Bogies, the Lord of the North, Xianju, the Roadthwart, and Direct Correspondences, as well as the people's minor taboos concerning the construction [of buildings]—they are not a source of dread for either Heaven or kings.

In the capitals of former times, people were prohibited from creating various kinds of taboos. But since these taboos and prohibitions were established, auspicious omens have appeared, and their sons and grandsons have prospered, but no more so than in former times. Nevertheless if,

> lords are terrorized by their ministers, and
> superiors frightened of their inferiors,

then this only creates a display of weakness and elicits bullying. I fear this is not the way to bring good fortune upon oneself.

I have read in texts from former times that when the lord of men himself is cultivated and correct, when punishments and rewards are clear, the nation will be well governed, and the people will peaceful. When the people are peaceful and contented, Heaven is pleased and increases [the nation's appointed] time. Therefore, a passage in the *Book of Documents* says: "The king receives Heaven's ever-abiding mandate from the common people."[17] Confucius said:

Those who heaven assists are obedient.
Those who men assist are trustworthy.

To tread the path of trustworthiness, to reflect on obedience, and furthermore, to exalt the worthy—this is how to obtain Heaven's assistance and good fortune in every respect.[18]

This is the most fundamental way to avert evil and disaster and elicit happiness and goodwill.

# CHAPTER 27 PREFACE

The Five Phases and the Eight Trigrams,
Are generated by Yin and Yang.
Their endowment of qi can be meager or voluminous,
And by this means they manifest form.
Heaven displays these images,
But human beings bring them to completion.
If one does not cultivate his behavior,
Good fortune and prosperity will not arrive.

Thus I have written "Physiognomy Set Forth," chapter 27.

# 27

# PHYSIOGNOMY SET FORTH

A passage in the *Book of Odes* says: "Heaven gave birth to the people, they have bodies, they have rules."[1] This is why people's

bodily form, appearance and visage all have semblances and classifications; and
bone structure, nails, and flesh each have divisions and categories

in order to

reveal the course of natural endowments and lifespan, and
illuminate the signs of honor and disgrace.

In one person's body, the qi of the Five Phases and the Eight Trigrams are all present within. Thus, Shi Kuang's comment, "A red complexion portends a short life span; those associated with the phase Fire meet destruction easily.[2] The *Yijing* "Explanations of the Trigrams" says: "The trigram Xun is associated with large sclera."[3] The physiognomic indications of eyes that display white on all four sides [of the iris] indicate a person whose death will be caused by weapons. This phenomenon is similar to the manner in which Metal conquers Wood. The *Yijing* says: "[Bao Xi devised the eight trigrams],

> near at hand, adopting them from his person, and
> from afar, adopting them from things."[4]

"The sage was able to survey all the complex phenomena under the sky, and by drawing comparisons according to form and capacity, represented their material form appropriately."[5] These are things that worthies also examine,

> recording the past to know the future, and
> composing their findings as laws and principles.

Among the methods of anthroscopy,

> some focus on the face,
> some focus on the limbs,
> some focus on the gait, and
> some focus on the voice.

> The face should be broad, symmetrical, smooth, and vibrant.
> The arms and legs should be long, slender, white, and straight.
> The gait should be easy, secure, erect, and grounded.
> The voice should be mild, harmonious, and match [the note] *gong*.[6]

Head, face, hands, feet, figure, and bones should all complement each other. These are the basics.

Now,

> the arrangement of the bones acts as an indicator of prosperity;
> the color of the qi acts as a sign of luck;
> the proportions of the members acts as evidence of age; and
> works of virtue act as a standard for these three.[7]

Heaven's conferral of nature and destiny is decidedly thus.

> Indicators include the clear and the obscure;
> color includes the intense and the faint;
> actions include the stingy and generous, and
> fate includes the past and the future.

Therefore,

> periods of good or bad fortune,
> success or failure in salary or rank

includes no need for [lacuna]. If one is not

> wise and perspicacious, or
> earnest and subtle,

how can one employ these [methods] and hit the mark?

Formerly, the court scribe Shufu passed through the state of Lu. Gongsun Ao heard that he was able to judge a person's physiognomy and presented his two sons to him. Shufu said: "Gu is the one who will feed you; Nan, is the one who will gather up [your remains]. Gu has a prominent lower jaw. He is certain to have descendants in Lu."[8] When Mubo reached old age, Wenbo stayed to take care of him. At his death, Huishu took charge of the mourning.[9] In the end, Lu established Xianzi as ruler and thus carried on the line of Meng.[10]

Considering how

Wangsun Yue read the face of Qiaoru,[11]
Zishang examined Shangchen,[12]
Ziwen feared Yue Jiao,[13]
Shuji detested Shiwo,[14]
Lord Xiang of Shan observed Li of Jin,[15]
Zigong observed Zhu and Lu,
Zangwen heard Yuyue, and
Chen Xian saw Zhang [lacuna],

when worthy people and accomplished servitors observe with good hearts, none will [fail to be] on the mark.[16] When considering

Tang Ju's reading the faces of Cai Ze and Li Dui, and
Xu Fu's reading the faces of Deng Tong and Marquis Tiao,

although the Arbiter of Fate controls rank and prosperity, in their tracing and detailing past actions, they could not err.[17]

Nevertheless, people's bones have [various] configurations, just as

the myriad things have various categories, and
wooden materials have standard applications.

When a clever carpenter accords with these configurations, each piece has something to offer.

Those that are curved are suited to making wheels,
those that are straight are suited to making carriages.
Sandalwood is suited to making wheel spokes, and
elm wood is suited to making hubs.

This is the correct method and standard rule. If [the wood] has certain characteristics but the workman does not take them into account, what will be the result? Thus, all physiognomists are able to estimate the apex of [people's fate], but they are not necessarily able to make them attain it.

> In earth plowed over the course of many years, though it may be fertile, without plowing there will be no harvest.
> For a horse able to run for a thousand *li*, though its bone structure may be sound, without the rider's crop, there will be no reaching the destination.

Now,

> if a goblet is not polished, it cannot become [one of the sacred] vessels;[18]
> if a scholar is not employed, he cannot fulfill [the duties of] his status.

Similarly,

> what Heaven and earth cannot do is ennoble the base; and
> what ghosts and spirits cannot do is impoverish the wealthy.
>
> Some among kings' and dukes' sons and grandsons hold official positions until old age but never achieve prosperity.
> Some among the commoners, criminals, menials, and lowbred inexplicably climb high and attain the highest rank of nobility.

This is a case of receiving a Heaven[-conferred] endowment and destiny and is what must by necessity be so. The *Odes* declares: "Heaven is difficult to rely on."[19]

> The "target" of natural endowments and destiny, and
> the "bull's-eye" of virtuous action

blend together what is achieved and what has been received and cannot be changed.

Essentially,

> osteomancy is considered chief;
> complexion is considered a sign.

The manifestation of the five colors at times reign as "king," and at others, are abrogated.[20] When a wise person sees an auspicious omen, he cultivates his goodness to receive it. If his visage shows worrisome signs, he examines his actions and corrects his failings. The foolish man is perverse and rebellious and does not engage in self-reflection. Though favorable omens appear on his countenance, his good fortune is transformed into disaster. Alas gentlemen, can one dare to be irreverent?

# CHAPTER 28 PREFACE

The *Odes* extols lucky dreams,
Books and annals record many more.
Observing and analyzing actions and events,
The results derived from these divinations are not false.
Good fortune comes from rectitude,
Disaster comes from deficient virtue.
The response of good and bad fortune,
Is dependent on one's actions.

Thus I have written "Dreams Set Forth," chapter 28.

# 28

# DREAMS SET FORTH

Among dreams, there are [those categorized as] "direct," "symbolic," "concentrated essence," "rumination," "personal status," "stimulation," "seasonal," "antithetical," "illness," and "natural endowment."

Formerly, when King Wu's consort, Yi Jiang, conceived Taishu, she dreamed that the Lord on High said to her, "I declare that your son will be [called] Yu, and I shall give him Tang." When he was born, the palm of his hand said "Yu," and it thus became his name. When King Cheng destroyed Tang, he thereupon invested [Yu] with the territory.[1] This is called a "direct" dream.

A passage in the *Book of Odes* says:

The black bear and brown bear,
Are auspicious omens of sons.[2]
The multiheaded snake and serpents,
Are auspicious omens of daughters.[3]

and

There are multitudes and fishes—
Betokening plentiful years.

> There are tortoise-and-snake banners;
> There are falcon banners—
> Betokening the kingdom's burgeoning population.[4]

These are called symbolic dreams.

Confucius lived in an age of disorder. Daily he thought of the Duke of Zhou's virtue, so at night he then dreamt of him. This is called a concentrated essence dream. If people have thoughts about something, then they will dream about them occurring; if they have worries, then they will dream about these matters. These are called dreams of recollection and rumination.

[In the case of a given] situation,

> if an aristocrat dreams of it, then it signifies good luck;
> if a humble person dreams of it, then it signifies bad luck;
> if a superior person dreams of it, then it signifies glory;
> if a petty person dreams of it, then it signifies disgrace.

These are called personal status dreams. Lord Wen of Jin, at the battle of Chengpu, dreamed that the master of Chu bent over him and sucked out his brains. This was truly evil.[5] When he went to war, he was in fact greatly victorious. This is called a dream of culmination and reversal.

> Dreaming when it is dim and rainy makes people feel oppressed and confused.
> Dreaming when it is bright and dry makes people feel disturbed and isolated.
> Dreaming when it is severely cold makes people feel resentful and sorrowful.

Dreaming when it is windy makes people feel they as if they are
 floating and flying.

These are called dreams of stimulating qi.

Spring dreams are of emergence and growth,
summer dreams are of height and brightness,

autumn and winter dreams are of ripening and storage. These are called dreams of seasonal response.

Yin disorders produce dreams of cold;
Yang illnesses produce dreams of heat;
internal illnesses produce dreams of confusion;
external illnesses produce dreams of emergence.[6]

As for dreams of the Hundred Illnesses, some are of scattering, some are of assembling. These are called dreams of insalubrious qi.

As for the disposition of people's hearts, their likes and dislikes are not the same.

Some consider a thing auspicious,
some consider it inauspicious.

One must look into each case individually and always divine in accordance with the individual's inclinations. These are called dreams of natural endowments and temperaments.

Therefore, cases in which what at first [lacuna] discrepancies and shifts . . . [lacuna] . . . this is what is meant by "concentrated essence."[7]

In the day, when one has something on one's mind, and
at night, when one dreams about this matter, and

one moment it appears to be auspicious and one moment it appears to be inauspicious, so that its good or evil import is untrustworthy, this is what is meant by "rumination."

Noble or base, wise or foolish,
male or female, old or young

are what is meant by "personal status."

Wind, rain, chill, and heat are what is meant by "stimulation."
The "reigning" and "assisting" [roles] of the Five Phases

is what is known as "seasonal."[8]

When yin culminates, then there is good fortune;
when yang culminates, then there is bad fortune.

This is what is meant by "antithetical."

Observing what sickens one, and
investigating what one dreams

is what is meant by "illness."

The proclivities and aversions of the heart and temperament are what is meant by "natural endowment." These are the ten major divisions of oneiromancy.[9]

Yet among the categories of those who determine what is auspicious and inauspicious, the majority are antithetical. Why is this the case? Could it be that

people's waking hours are yang, and
people's sleeping state is yin,

so that the functions of yin and yang are reversed? But in fact, this explanation merely addresses ordinary cases. If, for example,

> [one] dreams of something auspicious and considers it a cause for great joy [lacuna],
> which issue forth in one's heart and essence, then it really is auspicious.
> [If] one dreams of something inauspicious and one's thoughts turn to great fear, worry, or sorrow,
> which issue forth in one's heart and essence, then it really is baleful.

That which is known as [lacuna]. . . . The view that "dreams of death and injury occurring in autumn and winter are auspicious" is based on the idea that they accord with the season. Although this is the case, since [these dreams] merely [augur] great harm and nothing more, perhaps it would be better not to dream of them at all.

The major categories of all dream analysis are

> the clear, pure, fresh, and good;
> [lacuna] the appearance of strength and health;
> of bamboo and wood flourishing and beautiful;

of palaces, rooms, vessels, and tools newly made;

> of the square, upright, open, and connected;
> of brilliance, brightness, mildness, and harmony.

All images of ascending heights and moving toward success signify good fortune, happiness, plans completed, and matters accomplished.

All [images]

> of things foul, filthy, rotting, and broken;
> of the withered, desiccated, dark, and obfuscated;
> of the oblique, leaning, opposing, and perverse;
> of the disturbed and disquieted; the tottering and unstable;
> of the closed, obstructed, dark, and gloomy;
> of the loosened, sinking, falling downward

and moving toward decline—all portend [lacuna].

> Strategies planned and not finished,
> issues raised and not realized,

Monstrous, deformed, strange, and abnormal, matters that are loathsome and despicable all portend grief.

> Charts and paintings that are incomplete,
> engravings and inscriptions that are falsified,
> pottery and vessels that are empty

all signify cheating and deception.

Singers, jesters, dancers, and children's games and playthings, all stand for joy and laughter. These are the main divisions.

A dream

> may be very clear but [its augury] will not be fulfilled;
> it may be very obscure yet [its augury] will be realized.

Why is this so? "Basically, it is due to dreams being relayed under conditions of sleepiness, ignorance of analytic terminology, and witless blundering in nomenclature.[10] Therefore, they should also not be relied upon as the sole determinant in deciding matters. When people plan an affair [and] begin to carry it out, there will still be things that cannot accomplished.[11] How much more is this the case for something as confused and disorderly as dreams; can [the augury] indeed be certain? Only in instances in which one is stimulated and pressed by concentrated sincerity and informed by spirits and numinous beings will [the augury] be fulfilled.[12]

For this reason,

> when a superior person has an anomalous dream, it is not simply random; there is indeed a basis for events in it.
> When an inferior person has an anomalous dream, it is not simply nonsense; there is definitely a true portent in it.[13]

Therefore,

> Wu Ding dreamed about obtaining a worthy and got Fu Yue;
> Ershi dreamed about a white tiger and his state was destroyed.[14]

Now, in the case of strange dreams, the majority have a purpose and the minority have no meaning. Now in the dreams of one night, there may be numerous shifts and transformations, and one hundred things arriving and replacing [others], so that the host is unable to thoroughly describe them. The diviner will therefore not be accurate. This is not the fault of the diviner but rather the error of the dreamer. Some recount dreams very thoroughly, yet those who explain them are unable to connect [like] categories when conveying their observations. Thus the good and bad [prognostications] are not fulfilled. This is not due to the misguidance of the manuals but to the error of the interpreter. Thus, the difficulty of divining dreams is that reading its texts is difficult.

Now, in divining a dream, one must

> be attentive to its shifting phenomena;[15]
> examine its portentous fluctuations.[16]

> Within, investigate emotion and intention;
> without, investigate "king" and "minister."[17]

Then,

> the correspondences to the auspicious and baleful,
> the effects of good and evil,

will, for the most part, become evident.

Furthermore, for all people who see an auspicious omen and cultivate their virtue, good fortune will definitely come to fruition. For for all who see an auspicious omen and indulge in licentiousness, their good fortune will transform into bad. For those who see ill-omened manifestations and behave with arrogance and scorn, disaster will definitely come to fruition. Those who see ill-omened manifestations and behave with caution and fear, their bad fortune will be transformed into good.

Thus, when Tai Si had an auspicious dream, King Wen did not dare rejoice in their good fortune. He sacrificed to a multitude of spirits. He divined about it in the Hall of Illumination, and together [with his son Fa], he made obeisance to the auspicious dream.[18] [The king] cultivated and scrutinized [himself], he was cautious and fearful; he heard what was joyful as if it were sorrowful, and therefore was able to bring the good fortune to fruition and possess all under heaven.

The Lord of Guo once in a dream saw Rushou conferring upon him excellent land. Considering the dream lucky, he imprisoned the scribe Yin and forced the whole state to celebrate the dream. Hearing what was [in fact] worrisome, he was joyful. Therefore, he was able to bring to fruition the bad fortune, and his fief was thereby annihilated.[19]

The *Book of Changes* says: "[The hexagrams] cause one to know fear and moreover cast light on worries, calamities, and their causes."[20] For all strange dreams that move the heart, and which involve a person's good or bad fortune or the qi and coloring of their physiognomy, do not inquire into their good or evil [augury]. [Instead], maintain a sense of fear and trepidation, [practice] cultivation and self-scrutiny, and meet them with virtue. Only then will one encounter good fortune and the perpetual blessings of Heaven.

# CHAPTER 29 PREFACE

Arguing contentiously with wild assertions,
Makes it difficult to communicate the Way.
Later [generations] will be doubtful and confused,
And not know what [doctrine] to follow.
Since Gengzi, of earlier times,
There have been those who criticize and cast doubt,
"Indeed, I am not fond of disputing";
But will do so to clarify the truth.

Thus I have written "Explicating Difficulties," chapter 29.

# 29

# EXPLICATING DIFFICULTIES

Gengzi[1] posed a question to the Recluse,[2] saying: "The Way and virtue of Yao and of Shun cannot both be admirable. In fact, aren't they are like the dagger-axe and the buckler in Han Feizi's persuasion?"[3]

The Recluse said: This is a case of not knowing the problem, and therefore not knowing how to reason by analogy. Now,

> a buckler is a "shield"; its nature is to confer advantage;
> a dagger-axe is a "spear"; its nature is to inflict injury.

Thus,

> The dagger-axe is for causing harm,
> the buckler is for protection.

That they cannot both be effective at the same time is determined by their functions.

Now the reason Yao and Shun got along with each other is that they were human beings, not dagger-axes and bucklers. Their Ways were equally humane; they did not harm each other.

> If Shun were a dagger-axe, why was he unable to be as sharp as Yao?[4]
> If Yao were a buckler, why was he unable to be as sturdy as Shun?[5]

The virtue of Yao and Shun can be likened to the way a pair of lamps lights up a dark room. While the first lamp fully illuminates the room, the second makes it much brighter. It is not that the first lamp is dim and the second is bright; instead it shows the good result achieved when the two lamps work together to produce a great brilliance, and what the two sages achieved together to inaugurate [an era of] Great Peace.

Likewise,

> the movements of the [mythical] Peng bird[6] come not from the action of a single feather, and
> the speed of the [legendary] horse Qiyi comes not from the strength of a single leg.

A host [of good qualities] combine to produce limitless effects. The dual excellences of Yao and Shun instantiate this principle.

Boshu[7] said: "My Master, you are wrong. Han Feizi's citing the example of the spear and the shield, which shows that the two cannot both prevail simultaneously, is used to critique the idea that Yao and Shun cannot prevail simultaneously. But to discuss their basic nature in terms of their being humane or rapacious—doesn't this miss the basic meaning of the comparison?"

The Recluse replied: Now as for comparative examples, they arise from [situations where] speaking directly lacks clarity. In such cases, a hypothetical question asking whether a thing is so or is not so clarifies [the discussion]. Whether a thing really has the qualities of "so" and "not so"

> cannot be determined by its superficial appearance;
> it must be based on its intrinsic reality.

Now you propose to make a comparison of [two things] whose natures are [respectively] intrinsic and superficial, but you want to place focus on the nature of the superficial. This [tactic] confuses me. Furthermore, I have heard that to ask a question about yin and get an answer about yang is called "forcing the point." Discussing "west" when I asked about "east," would be what is called an "aggressive tactic." If you want to adhere to your own standard, but later on you change your mind, then you should fastidiously ascertain the facts and not casually perpetrate arbitrary arguments.[8]

Gengzi said: "The Duke of Zhou knew of the evil [intentions of the lords] of Guan and Cai, but he made them serve as ministers of Wugeng,[9] enabling them to act on their poisonous [schemes.] Later, he executed them. How can he not be considered inhumane? If he did not know [about the plot in advance], how can he not be considered lacking in sage [wisdom]? Of these two faults, he must be charged with one of them."

The Recluse replied: A text says that the two princes Guanshu and Caishu relied on Wugeng and Lufu to rebel.[10] Yet it is unclear if [the two princes] were the same [sort of people] as [Wugeng and Lufu], or if they were the opposite. Moreover, Heaven knew of Jie's depravity, but [still allowed him to be] emperor of the Xia, and likewise knew of Djou's depravity, but [still allowed him to be] king of Yin. It allowed the fierce oppression of those two states to cause great harm to ordinary people and to spread their poison and destroy them. Would you also say that these were cases of "being inhumane" or "not knowing"?

Geng

> appointed them without remorse, and
> executed them without pity.

Now in the case of Guan and Cai and the Duke of Zhou, they had

> the family ties of elder and younger brothers, and
> the emotional attachment of flesh and bone.

> It did not take measure of their abilities and then make use of them;
> it did not judge them worthy of the mandate and then appoint them.

Therefore I say that this case is different from Jie and Djou's [relationship with] Heaven."

The Recluse said: Heaven has no favorites.[11] Emperors and rulers who inherit their positions serve Heaven in the same way that they treat their fathers. Kings are considered the "sons [of Heaven]," thus, they serve Heaven in that same way as sons serve fathers. Of the masses bound to the land, not one is not a royal subject. That "any challenge must be met with execution" shows that the ruler's laws are for everyone, without partiality or favor, and that kin and nonkin are regarded [as meriting] the same treatment.[12] The great principle of "obliterate [from consideration] the ties of kinship" emphasizes honoring the ruler's correct principles.[13] That a ruler is established or destroyed is the work of Heaven. The Duke of Zhou's virtue rested upon these principles. Anything beyond the scope of these matters cannot be known.[14]

Qinzi[15] asked the Recluse a question:

> "Plowing and planting are fundamental;
> study and inquiry are secondary.

Lao Dan has a saying: 'A great-spirited man establishes himself in substance; he doesn't entrench himself in adornment.'[16] And Confucius said:

> 'There is plowing—though even in that there is [sometimes] starvation.
> There is learning—though even in that there is [sometimes] emolument.'[17]

I venture to ask, if at present, we encourage everyone to abandon their hoes and plows to join the multitudes who have taken up studying, what would happen?"

The Recluse replied, An excellent question!

> The noble man labors with his mind;
> the petty man labors with his strength.

Thus what Confucius was referring to was only the noble man. Now, as anyone with eyes can see, plowing is the basis of food [production], but using the mind to trace the origin of the Way is the root of both study and plowing.

The *Book of Changes* says:

> "When the Way of Heaven was established, it was called 'yin and yang.'

> When the Way of Earth was established, it was called
> 'pliability and rigidity.'
> When the Way of humankind was established, it was called
> 'humaneness and righteousness.'[18]
> When Heaven reverses[19] the season, there are calamities;[20]
> [When earth reverses the nature of things, there are demons;
> When the people reverse their virtues, there is disorder."

With disorder, demons and calamities arise.[21]

The Recluse said: Alas, do you still not understand this principle? I will tell you. Now in the case of the noble man,

> his worthiness is appropriate to rule a princely state, and
> [his] virtue is appropriate to rule the people.

Only a benevolent and righteous person is appropriate for this position. Thus, [only] a person possessing benevolence and righteousness can be called a noble man. Long ago, Xun Qing had something to say about this:

> "Now humaneness means loving others; one who loves others
> cannot bear their being endangered.
> Righteousness means to gather people together; one who unites
> others cannot bear their facing chaos."[22]

That is why the Noble Man day and night remonstrates with his superiors, speaking boldly without fear or hesitation,

> anxious that his lord [faces] danger and extinction,
> grief-stricken that the people [face] disorder and displacement.

Thus a person who is worthy and noble applies his humane and righteous heart, loving his ruler as if he were his father and mother; and loving the people of his own generation as if they were his children or younger brothers. If parents are about to face the danger of stumbling and falling, or if one's children or younger brothers are about the face the misfortune of sinking and drowning, how could one remain silent? So it is that

> a humane man must be courageous, and
> a virtuous man must be righteous.

Moreover, in a state of total disorder, no one is secure. A passage in the *Book of Odes* says:

> "No one is willing to think of the prevailing disorder,
> [But] who has not parents [to suffer from it]?"[23]

That is to say, when all are imperiled, the anxiety felt for one's parents will be all the deeper. For that reason, the virtuous man or the noble man who feels anxiety for the people, also feels the same on his own behalf. Now, if a thatched roof is completely sodden above, there will be inundation below. When the beams break and the rafters fall, one fears the disaster of being crushed.[24]

Thus, when a great room is on the verge of collapse, those within do not wait for someone to issue orders; they all rush to secure it with props. [In the same way], a benevolent person who protects others without discrimination, at one and the same time protects himself. The *Book of Changes* says: "If the king were [only] intelligent, both he and we might receive the benefit of it."[25] This is why

> [the Woman of] Qishi leaned against a column [of the palace] and groaned,[26] and
> why the Maiden of Chu raised a banner to encourage the king.[27]

As for

> the grace of humanity and kindness, or
> the sentiments of loyalty and affection—
> how can they be repressed?

# CHAPTER 30 PREFACE

In the relations between friends,
Its principles are preserved through the Six Bonds.
It is maintained with awesome decorum;
It [encourages] discussion and instruction on correct principles.
It treasures old agreements,
Whether honored or humble it is unwavering.
At present, the people have been adrift for a long time,
So that none of them have this ability.

Thus I have written "Social Relations," chapter 30.

# 30

## ON SOCIAL RELATIONS

An adage states,

> "In people, we seek the old;
> in vessels, we seek the new."[1]

> Elder and younger brothers across generations may become distant;
> friends and acquaintances across generations may become close.

This is the principle of social relations and the standard sentiment of human beings. But now, it is not so. Many

> think of those who are far off and forget those who are near; or neglect old [acquaintances] and approach the new.

> Some pass through the years and become increasingly distant; some reach midcourse and renounce each other,

> violating the canons and warnings of the sages of former times, and ignoring the oaths and words of long-established importance.[2]

Why is this so? If we take a step back and reflect, it can indeed be understood.

> Situations have regular tendencies;
> patterns have fixed qualities.
>
> When rich and noble, others contend to draw near you; it is a standard tendency in this situation.
> When poor and humble, others contend to abandon you; it is a certainty in the [social] order.

Now,

> in dealings with the rich and noble, above there is the utility of a recommendation, and below there is the advantage of goods and wealth.
> In dealings with the poor and humble, largely there is the expense of [issuing] relief commodities, and to a lesser extent, the disadvantage of [accommodating] borrowers.

Now,

> in the case of an official, though he may combine the evils of Jie or Zhi, if he harnesses a team of four horses and visits gentlemen, the gentlemen will nevertheless consider him honorable and submit to him.[3] How much more is this so if they really have something to gain?
> In the case of an unemployed scholar, though he may possess the worthiness of Yan or Min, if he dresses in coarse cloth and approaches [one's] door, others will nevertheless consider him disreputable and fear he might come again.[4] How much more is this so if they really have something to lose?

Therefore,

> it is easy for the rich and noble to achieve gratification;
> it is difficult for the poor and low-born to achieve satisfaction.

> If you have nice clothes—you're called "extravagant and a climber";
> if you have bad clothes—you're called "destitute and distressed."

> [If you] move slowly—you're labeled "starving and feeble";
> [if you] move quickly—you're labeled "evades responsibility."

> [If you] do not visit superiors—you're labeled "haughty and rude";
> [if you] come repeatedly—you're labeled "looking for food."

> [If you] arrive empty-handed—you're labeled "thoughtless";
> [if you] present a gift—you're labeled "wants a loan."

> [If you] are respectful and unassuming—you're considered worthless;
> [if you're] you're firm and assertive—you're considered unvirtuous.

These are

> the halters and restraints of unemployed scholars; and
> the difficulties and abuses of the poor and lowborn.

Now, occupying a humble and inferior position, one suffers the vexation and sorrow of "The North Gate:"

> in private, bearing the criticism of one's wife and children; and
> in public, bearing the ridicule by high officers.[5]

> One's festive events, not according with ritual;
> one's parting gifts, not extending to all.
>
> Goods and wealth insufficient to please others;
> strength and power insufficient to withstand danger.

If, in a happy and longstanding relationship, there are feelings of fondness, but over a long period of time, there is no interaction, then people will for no reason, and quite naturally, abandon it and become distant. If one is gradually distanced, then

> the more the one who is lowborn blames himself and daily withdraws,
> the more the noble-born person concentrates on his own clique and forgets him.

Now, the lowborn one, subject to gradual distancing, is consigned to a low status, and longs for the noble who, day by day, has forgotten him. This is what is referred to in the ode, "Gu Feng," as the "wife's sorrow and pain" and is the reason Jie Zhitui fled deep into the mountains.[6]

Now,

> with exchanging advantage comes mutual intimacy;
> with exchanging injury comes mutual distance.

This is why

> longstanding promises that are abandoned are inevitably useless;
> and

gradually formed relationships that become intimate are inevitably beneficial.

In the mutual generosity of common people,

> The existence of profit gives rise to intimacy;
> the accumulation of intimacy gives rise to love;
> the accumulation of love gives rise to approval; and
> the accumulation of approval gives rise to regarding them as worthy.

If the emotions deem a person to be worthy, then unwittingly,

> the heart will love him, and
> the mouth will praise him.

> The absence of benefit produces distance;
> the accumulation of distance produces hatred;
> the accumulation of hatred produces disapproval;
> the accumulation of disapproval produces loathing.

If the emotions deem a person loathsome, then, unwittingly,

> the heart will reject him; and
> the mouth will slander him.

Therefore,

> though [the relationships of] the wealthy and noble are new, they tend to become more intimate day by day; and
> though [the relationships of] the poor and lowborn are long-standing, they tend to become more distant day by day.

This is why unemployed scholars cannot compete with those in office. The rulers of this age do not examine what produces friendship, but recklessly believe the words of noble-born ministers. This is why

> pure scholars are alone and concealed in obscurity, and
> cunning powerholders are connected and soar aloft.

Formerly,

> Wei Qi's guests gravitated toward Wu An;
> Chang Ping's underlings moved toward the [Marquis of] Guanjun.[7]

Lian Po's and Honorable Zhai's fortunes moved abruptly from plenty to depletion.[8] Considering the worthiness of these four gentlemen, [in spite of] their acts of kindness during their earlier tenures of high status, if even their followers behaved this way, then how much more would this be so for those born poor and humble? Only officers with the illustrious spirit of exemplars of ages past, and those with righteous determination would not behave this way.

What kindness binds together cannot be undone throughout one's life. What the heart esteems, being lowborn [only] increases that devotion. A passage in the *Book of Odes* says: "The virtuous man, the princely one, / Is uniformly correct in his deportment, / His heart is as if bound to what is correct."[9] Thus,

> it is only after the year grows cold that one comes to know the late shedding of pine and cypress;
> it is only after the world grows perilous that one comes to know the sincerity and devotion of others.[10]

Hou Ying and Yu Rang cast away their bodies in order to repay a kindness.[11]

Zhuan Zhu and Jing Ke laid down their lives in order to realize their utility.[12]

Thus, dying is manageable; arranging one's own death is difficult indeed.[13]

Pang Xun and Bo Diao, in the space of a morning, were arrested but also rewarded for their righteousness.[14] How much more so should this the case for longstanding [friendships]? Thus, Zou Yang discussed this point, saying:

"Jie's dog can be made to bite Yao, and
Zhi's guests can be made to assassinate You."[15]

Surely these are no empty words!

Vulgar scholars, shallow and short-sighted, are anxious about whatever lay before their eyes. If they see that going forward is profitable, then they will be the first to arrive. If they observe that it is of no utility, then they will turn their backs on it. For this reason, those who desire speedy [advancement]

compete to endorse those above them but have no time to receive those below; and

strive to follow those ahead but have no leisure to pity those behind.

For this reason,

Han Anguo was able to give Tian Fen five-hundred measures of cash but was unable to relieve one person in need; and

Zhai Fangjin recommended Chunyu Chang but was unable to promote one scholar.[16]

Now, [Han] Anguo and [Zhai] Fangjin were among the loyal and good of past generations. But if even they were like this, then what of the inferior ministers of a declining age? This is why

> cunning power holders gradually promote their factions, and unemployed scholars become progressively concealed and obscure.

If not an enlightened and sage ruler, then who can bring [this situation] to light and investigate it?

Furthermore, the emergence of kindness and hatred is like the pairing of two people in a relationship. If [the relationship] is mutually agreeable, kindness and affection will be directed toward each other. Extending these feelings to their limit, their quintessential sincerity will radiate toward one another, penetrating the heart and reaching the marrow in an abundance of love and joy, so that it is easy for them to die for each other.[17] For this reason, Master Hou and Yuzi slit their throats without regret.[18]

If [the relationship] is mutually rejected, hearts and emotions will be perverse and intractable. Extending these feelings to their limit, division and hostility will run rampant, [one going to] the extreme east and [one going to] the extreme west, but their hearts are still not content. For this reason, Chen Yu and Zhang Er in old age tried to destroy each other and neither felt regret.[19]

Looking at it from this perspective, in terms of the principle of social relations, feelings are paramount. Not only are friends like this, the relationships of ruler and subject and husband and wife are like this as well. When they are happy, father and son cannot be divided. When they are at odds, the hatred rivals feel toward each other cannot surpass it. For this reason, the sage always takes care over things when they are just beginning in order to manage how they will conclude.

> Wealth and honor are not necessarily valued.
> Poverty and low status are not necessarily disdained.

People's minds admit different preferences; standards of measurement differ by trillions.

> Xu You declined the position of emperor, while
> common people contend for prefectural posts.[20]

> Meng Ke refused an emolument of ten-thousand measures of
>     grain, while
> the small-minded person covets a [position paying] one peck of
>     provisions.[21]

Thus, it is said that quail roam in flocks all day without resting. Haphazardly rising and in flocks halting; they never leaving rushes and grass.

The snow geese fly high; pairs separate and veer off. Covering a thousand [*li*] soaring ten-thousand [*li*], their goal, is the banks of the Pool.[22]

The female and male phoenix soar eighty-thousand feet above, moving to and fro in the great purity, following auspicious winds, drifting, blown about, ascending and descending as they please. Their wishes unfulfilled, melodic and long their cry. With excited calls and spreading wings, they traverse vermillion clouds, approach the Dipper and the pole star, inhaling the bright dews, and for weeks they do not eat, as if their wishes were still unsatisfied.

These three differ in their pursuits; each is content with what they do. This is why

> Boyi gathered ferns and felt no resentment, and
> Chaofu nested in trees of his own accord.[23]

From this it can be seen that the depth of a gentleman's will is indeed difficult to fathom. Among the hundred gentlemen, there has never been a case of one relying on his wealth and nobility to lord it over the poor and humble, claiming that the poor and humble will necessarily submit to him.

A passage in the *Book of Odes* says: "Virtue is as light as a hair, / But few are able to lift it."[24] The world has four things that are very difficult [to do], and no one is able to carry them out.

> The first is called "reciprocity,"
> the second is called "fairness,"
> the third is called "reverence," and
> the fourth is called "steadfastness."

Now

> reciprocity is the root of benevolence;
> fairness is the root of justice;
> reverence is the root of ritual;
> steadfastness is the root of trustworthiness.

Only when the four are established together are the four comportments complete. When the four comportments are completely present, this is called "a true worthy." If

> the four roots are not established,
> the four comportments will be incomplete.

If the four comportments lack even one, this is called a "petty person."

"Reciprocity" refers to a superior person, who when discussing others, regards them in the same way as he considers himself; and when taking action, he considers it in his heart.[25] [Thus]

> the [traits] one lacks should not be used [as the basis] to blame inferiors;
> the [traits] one possesses should not be used [as the basis] to criticize others.[26]

> Feeling one's own fondness for respect, one should greet officers with ceremony,
> Feeling one's own fondness for love, one should approach others with kindness.[27]

> "Wishing oneself to be established, establish others.
> Wishing oneself to be enlarged, enlarge others."[28]

> [If] one approves of another's concern for oneself, then one should first show concern for others;
> [if] one dislikes a person's neglecting one, then one should constantly be concerned for others.

But common conduct is not like that.

> When discussing others, there is no putting oneself in their place.
> When taking action, there is no considering it in one's heart.

> The [traits] one lacks are used [as the basis] to blame inferiors.
> The [traits] one possesses are used [as the basis] to criticize others.

> While lacking in propriety, one criticizes the deference of others.

While lacking in kindness, one criticizes the compassion of others.

If a person is poor and humble, then they are faulted for not being concerned about "me."
If a person is wealthy and noble, then they approve of my not being concerned with others.

If one comports oneself like this, it is indeed difficult to be called benevolent.

One who is called just

within, cherishes a mercy like the turtledove, and
without, maintains a mind like the whetstone and arrow.[29]

Discussion of officers must definitely be fixed on their intent and behavior;
blame and praise must definitely be determined through results and evidence.

Do not follow the vulgar and [echo them] like thunder;
do not rely on reputation and [thereby] deliver judgment.

If virtue is present, don't ridicule poverty or lowliness;
if wickedness is in place, don't fear the rich and noble;

do not flatter superiors or insult inferiors;
do not reject the old and revere the new.

But common conduct is not like this.

Within there is willful partiality toward wife and offspring.
Without there is excessive shielding of acquaintances and friends.

If something can be gained, they [sing] praises;
If something can be resented, they [spread] slander.

Critiques are wide of the mark;
censure and praise lack proof.

[They] duplicitously agree with the noble in order to join their cliques;
[they] duplicitously appropriate the views [of others] in order to join their canine howls.[30]

Serving the wealthy and noble like slaves and servants;
looking upon the poor and humble like hired hands;

one hundred arrive at the gates of power holders;
not one goes to the family who holds no power.

Minds occupied in this way are indeed difficult to call righteous. As for one who is called reverent:

at home he does not dare to be overbearing with his wife and family;
at work he does not dare to be rude to his fellow officers.

He regards the humble in the same way as the noble;
he treats his juniors in the same way as his elders.

He is the first to express courtesy;
he is the last to make comments.

There is no kind intention that he does not reciprocate;
there is no ritual respect that is not returned.[31]

Seeing worthies, he does not place himself above them;
at gatherings, he demurs and yields to others.[32]

In serving, he chooses the toilsome;
at home, he accords with what is humble.
In status, he is satisfied with the lowly;
in nourishment, he is pleased with the meager.

Common people are not like this.

At home they are rude and negligent with wife and children;
outside the home they are dismissive and insulting to their confidantes and friends.

Their intelligence and perspicuity cannot distinguish true and false;
their hearts and intellects cannot distinguish good from bad.

They are foolish but delight in arrogance toward the worthy;
they are young yet enjoy humiliating their elders.

Kind intentions are not repaid;
ritual respect is not reciprocated.

Seeing a worthy, they do not recommend them;
at gatherings, they are incapable of yielding.

In their activities, they are desirous of choosing ease;
at rest, they are desirous of settling in comfort.

For nourishment, they are desirous of expropriating large quantities;
for status, they are set on wrangling for the most honorable.

Seeing people's modesty and yielding, they use it as the basis for laughing at them.
Seeing people's reverence and respect, they use it as the basis for disrespecting them.

They behave this way yet profess themselves to be worthy, able, intelligent, and wise. When comporting themselves like this it is difficult indeed to call them courteous.[33]

That which is called steadfastness, refers to the heart. As for circumspect officers,

their emotions and intentions are concentrated and focused,
their minds and thoughts are distinctive and observant.

They are not driven by the dangerous abyss of vulgarity;
they are not bedazzled by the voices of the majority.

Their intelligence and perspicuity are incomparable;
their steadfast hearts are sincere and profound.[34]
Standing alone they are not afraid;
withdrawn from the world they are without regret.[35]
Their hearts are firm as metal and stone;
Their wills are undaunted by the four seas.[36]

Therefore, by guarding their hearts they complete their trustworthiness.

For the common character, this is not the case.

Within there is no restraint;

without there is no regulation of deportment.
Distorted, prejudicial, treacherous, and perverse,
they seek agreement with the world.
Their mouths have no fixed view,
they are "inconsistent in their virtue," and[37]
"changeable in their conduct."[38]

Managing their conduct like this, it is indeed difficult to call them trustworthy.

Now, as for these four actions,

"They are light as a hair."[39]
They are heavy as a mountain.

The superior person considers them easy,
The small person considers them difficult.

Confucius said: "Is benevolence far off? I desire benevolence and benevolence is here!"[40] But he also said: "Those who know virtue are few."[41] The prejudice and factionalism of the vulgar from ancient times has been like this. It is not, in fact, a feature of the present age. Multitudes of "gentlemen" contend in arrogance and excess. In their greed for pleasure, their contemptuousness and insolence, they are like merchants who "sell at a triple profit to elevate themselves."[42] If they are able to become wealthy and noble, though they accumulate [acts of] cunning and evil, there is competition to praise them, and ultimately they will never incur disapproval. But if they are poor and lowly, though they are reverent and cautious, [lacuna] they will be considered unworthy, and to the end will never be considered acceptable. This is the means by which vulgarization overwhelms and destroys, and how propriety and righteousness erode and disintegrate.

In the world there are three things to be dreaded. What are these three? They are:

feelings being truly indifferent, while words express intimacy;
thoughts being truly disdainful, while writing expresses
    longing;
intentions set on not coming, while outwardly fixing a date.

If they don't trust someone, then they fear they might lose a
    worthy;
if they trust someone, then it could interfere with their plans.

This is what is most detestable about vulgar scholars. For this reason, Confucius hated those whose words exceeded their actions.[43] The *Odes* bewailed "easy and grand words issuing from their mouths / their artful words like reed pipes / and their unblushing faces."[44]

In the vulgar relationships of the current age, while there is still no mutual understanding, there is a desire for depth and stability.

Enfolding [each other] in an embrace and clasping wrists,
laying hands on hearts and swearing oaths,

their casual wishes for mutual aid is simply talk and nothing more. The day they part, having obtained what they want, they abandon and forget each other. Some receive the kindness and goodness of others, at first to navigate a problem. But when they are unable to raise up and promote them [for office], they proceed to revile these acquaintances, bringing up their faults and flaws, openly stating, "I spared no effort. There is nothing that can be done when he himself is simply unacceptable."

A passage in the *Book of Odes* says: "If I had known it would be thus, / it would have been better not to be born."[45] [A relationship] that is at first harmonious but later intractable, and which has a beginning but no conclusion, is not as good as never having the desire [to form a friendship] from the start and staying strong in one's own decisions.

"Our sovereign makes frequent covenants, and disorders are thereby increased."[46] "The great man enters into associations but not cliques";[47] using subtle language to move others, "like a perfectly matching tally,"[48] where, then, is the need for a covenant?

Confucius looked mild and respectful, like one unable to speak. He also "spoke in a straightforward but cautious manner."[49] A scholar is valued for his rhetoric but is disliked for verbosity. Thus it is said: "A balanced mixture of acquired refinement and native substance result in the superior man."[50] Compared to the disloyal, "the resolute, the enduring, the simple, and the slow [still] come closer to benevolence."[51]

Alas! How sad! As for the people of today, with

> words square and actions circuitous;
> mouths upright and hearts twisted;

> their actions and words are contrary;
> their hearts and mouths are opposed.

> If we discuss antiquity, then we know to praise Yi, Qi, Yuan and Yan.[52]

If we speak of the present, then it must concern office, title,
position, and status.

Speaking abstractly, it is known that virtue and righteousness make a worthy. But when offering a recommendation, it is necessarily power and distinction that is foremost.[53] Although a man who is not in office may embody the behavior of a Yan or a Min, and in nature, may possess the qualities of industriousness and humility,

wield the talent of Yi Yin or Lü Shang, and
embrace the Way of relieving the people,

that he will not receive employment in this generation, has indeed already been made clear.[54]

# CHAPTER 31 PREFACE

Only when the ruler has a fine reputation,
When his officers have good names,
And when the two are of the same mind,
Will all they desire be accomplished.[1]
With cherished power and spirit-like techniques,
Not revealing the whole situation to those below,
The state of one's rule will be complete,
And ultimately no one will be able to topple it.[2]

Thus I have written "Enlightenment and Loyalty," chapter 31.

# 31

## ENLIGHTENMENT AND LOYALTY

> Among praiseworthy attributes of those who rule, none is greater than enlightenment;
> among admirable attributes of those who [serve as] ministers, none is finer than loyalty.

These two virtues, from antiquity onward, are what both ruler and minister desire. Yet the fact that

> the enlightened do not appear in unbroken succession, and
> the loyal do not amount to even one in ten thousand,

is not necessarily due to ignorance, inadequacies, or bad reputations. It is simply that what they are seeking is not the correct path. Now,

> enlightenment relies on underlings in order to arise,
> loyalty depends on superiors in order to be fulfilled.

If two people are of the same mind, then their keenness will be sufficient to pierce metal.[3] If they are able to understand this, both of these praiseworthy attributes will both be present. The crucial element resides in

> the enlightened exercise of laws and procedures, and
> the personal control of the levers of power

—nothing more.

> That which is known as "procedure" is making sure underlings do not take unfair advantage [of their positions].
> That which is known as "power" is making sure that positional power does not result in chaos.[4]

> When procedures are truly enlightened, then at a distance of ten thousand *li* or in deepest darkest secrecy, [officials] will not fail to seek the most meticulous [application of procedure].

> When power is truly utilized, then the distant and close, close kin and distant relations, honored and humble, wise and foolish will all offer their allegiance.

The last stage of the House of Zhou was not like this.

> They departed from procedure and abandoned their power.
> They were indolent in their own roles and dependent on others.

Therefore,

> the ducal ministers did not think about loyalty, and the hundred officials did not exert effort;
> the ruler was isolated and hidden above, while the multitudes harbored grievance and chaos below.

Thus, [the dynasty] declined, suffered attacks and occupation so that recovery became impossible.

Now, in the case of emperors and kings,

> their resources are considerable, and
> their authority is great.

> A mere announcement of large reward is sufficient to encourage goodness.
> A mere display of stern authority is able to warn evildoers.

If [the ruler]

> sets forth weighty benefits in order to guide the people, and wields awesome authority in order to motivate them,

then the whole world can be made to

> brave bright blades and not feel resentment, and
> rush into raging fires and not regard it as difficult.

How can one say it is not feasible to bring about order by simply leading them? [The people] are like eagles, which are wild birds, yet hunters tether them, and over the course of a day, are still able to make them attack ferociously without their daring to be indolent. Surely it is not true that one can have servitors yet be unable to make them exert maximal effort!

A passage in the *Book of Odes* says: "In hewing an axe handle, the pattern is not far off."[5] Now, the techniques of spirit illumination are complete in the ruler's person.[6] But if a ruler ignores these [techniques], he will cause his servitors to clamp their mouths shut, bind their tongues, and not dare to speak. This is the reason

> his eyes and ears are blocked, and
> his hearing and vision are unreceptive.

Regulating the power of inferiors is a daily [a duty] that is placed before the ruler. But the ruler abandons it and thereby causes his servitors to become negligent and dilatory and to avoid the court. This is why

> his awesome power does not shine forth and
> his meritorious reputation does not become established.

A passage in the *Book of Odes* says:

> Though my duties are different from yours,
> I am your fellow servant.
> I come to advise with you,
> But you hear me with contemptuous indifference.[7]

Indeed, the feeling of commiseration—all people possess it.[8] For this reason,

> when the ears hear the sound of [people] weeping, there are none who will not feel sad, pained, and brokenhearted on their behalf.
> When the eyes see situations of danger [to people], there are none who will not feel anxious and alarmed on their behalf and rush to save them.[9]

The sense of duty between ruler and minister is great.
The sense of decorum among pedestrians on the street is slight.

Passing by and overhearing [those in distress] or seeing them—

[onlookers] are not merciful or benevolent;
they are not worthies or nobles.

Yet if they behave like this [i.e., rush to save them], then how much more should this be the case of those who face north[10] and enjoy [the ruler's] favor?

For this reason, offering loyalty or helping in times of danger is what both worthy and unworthy people want to do. Their sincere desire to [help] while their actions show the contrary is simply due to their enduring sense that this path is not beneficial and involves harm, and that before their words are shown to be truthful, their persons will face destruction.[11] Surveying cases from ancient times of servitors who, loving their rulers and worrying about their lords, dared to speak out, but whose loyalty and faith did not reach [their lord's ears], and who were interrogated and pressed by his advisors, while those in power overwhelmed and defamed them, treating them as evil, ignorant, and ill-mannered underlings—how could they possibly make their positions clear?

> Filial Emperor Cheng, to his dying day, did not recognize Wang Zhang's upright character;
> Filial Emperor Ai, to his dying day, did not recognize Wang Jia's loyalty.[12]

This is the reason later worthies have

feelings of concern about their rulers and worries about their
> kings, and the
ethos of loyalty, sincerity, correctness, and restraint,

but are nevertheless inclined to hesitate and sigh, observe and inquire when determining a course of action.

"There is a calling crane in the shadows; its young respond to her."[13] "Look at the bird, / seeking its companion's call."[14] In a similar fashion, [if] the lord of the people does not set forth his quintessential sincerity, displaying it before the worthy and loyal, [then] the worthy and loyal will have no means to connect with him. The *Book of Changes* says: "If the king were only enlightened, both he and we might receive the benefit of it."[15] For this reason

> loyal servitors must await an enlightened ruler, and only then will
> > they be able to manifest their fine conduct;
> virtuous officials must have a perceptive ruler, and only then will
> > they be able to make their contributions.

If the ruler is not enlightened, then

> the great ministers will conceal the situation of those beneath
> > them and suppress the loyal, and
> all of the officials will abandon the law and cater to the elite.

Now,

> loyal words are what create peace; not offering them will lead to
> > danger.
> Laws and prohibitions are what create order; not revering them
> > will lead to chaos.

Whether

> loyalty is offered or not, or if
> the law is revered or not—

its control lies with the ruler; it is not something that servitors can accomplish. For this reason, the sage [ruler] seeks [these two] in himself and does not demand [them] from underlings.[16]

For one who serves as ruler, when the procedures of the law are clear, and rewards and punishments are certain, even without any discussion, positional power will produce order by itself. Once positional power is established, the ruler himself will be unable to cause chaos. How much more is this the case for his underlings? Thus,

> when the procedures of the law are unclear, and
> rewards and punishments are uncertain,

though orders are issued throughout the day, the situation will produce chaos by itself. As soon as the situation [shifts to] chaos, the ruler himself will be unable to bring order. How much more is this the case for his underlings?

Thus,

> when power is positional, though the [ruler] may be negligent, chaos will not obtain;
> when power is provisional, even if a great effort is made, it cannot be made orderly.[17]

> That Yao and Shun made themselves reverent and took no overt action, and yet there was bounty, was due to the positional power of order.

That Hu Hai and Wang Mang worked feverishly but their efforts were still insufficient, was due to provisional power.

Therefore, it is said that, the good [ruler] seeks solutions in positional power and does not seek them in other people. Therefore, [when] the enlightened king examines the law and issues orders:

he does not carry out personal agendas and thereby undermine the law;
he does not corrupt orders and thereby defile directives.

Therefore, servitors will

respect his words and uphold his prohibitions,
belabor their minds and fulfill their duties.

This state of affairs comes from legal procedures that are clear and awesome power that is realized.

Now, the use of procedure is the way [of governance]; it is potent, refined, and spirit-like. Speaking about it is inadequate, yet practicing it excels [all other means]. Excelling, it is therefore able to unite [all within] the four seas and illuminate the darkness. The wielding of power is positional. Strong, fierce, and thus formidable, without taking into account nobility or low station, those who wield it are of great consequence. Being of great consequence, they are therefore able to seize the ruler's power and make compliant their generation. Because of this, the discriminating ruler never displays to others his techniques or lends that power to underlings. Confucius said: "[If we get established along with them, we shall find them] unable to weigh occurring events with us."[18] For this reason, the sage is

> visible in his benevolence, and
> secretive in his applications [of power].[19]

Spirit-like, he transforms the people, prompting the people to feel well treated. Only then can he bring about his rule and establishes his merit. When

> his achievements prove efficacious for the people, and
> his good name resounds across generations

only then can

> rulers gain a name for enlightenment and
> servitors achieve reputations for loyalty.

This is what is meant by

> "the rise of the enlightened [ruler] requires underlings, and
> the presence of loyal [servitors] depends on superiors."

When the two are of the same mind, their keenness can pierce metal.

# CHAPTER 32 PREFACE

Human and heavenly feelings are connected;
Qi stimulates mutual resonance.
Good and evil have their corresponding manifestations,
Dissimilar extremes undergo change and transformation.
The sage directs them,
As if steering a boat or a carriage;
Stimulating the vital spirit of the people,
So that no one does not contain excellence.

Thus I have written "Teachings on the Root," chapter 32.

# 32

## TEACHINGS ON THE ROOT

In the age of high antiquity,
during the time of the Great Purity,

primal qi was obscure, dark, and without any sign of form.[1] The myriad essences mixed together, mingled, and were made one. Without intervention, without manipulation, [the primal oneness] remained in this state a long while. Suddenly, it transformed itself.

Clear and turbid separated, becoming Yin and Yang.
Yin and Yang acquired form, producing the two powers.[2]

Heaven and earth mixed and mingled,[3]
the myriad things transformed and purified,

and harmonious qi gave birth to human beings in order to unify and order them.

Thus,

Heaven is rooted in yang,
earth is rooted in yin,

and human beings are rooted in the harmony between them. These three entities differ in function [yet] depend upon each other to become complete. When each accords with its Way, only then will

> harmonious qi arrive and
> the [jade] device and [jade] transept find balance.[4]

> The Way of Heaven is called "bestowal";
> the Way of earth is called "transformation";
> the Way of human beings is called "activity."[5]

Activity is what is known as being moved by and connected to yin and yang and bringing forth the felicitous or anomalous. People's actions being able to move Heaven and earth is just like being

> in a carriage driving a team of horses, or
> beneath the sails rowing a boat.

Though supported and covered, it is still up to me to decide where to go. Confucius said: "In due season, mount the six dragons and drive through the heavens"; and "it is through words and actions that superior persons move heaven and earth; can they afford to be incautious?"[6] From this it can be seen that

> Heaven manifests its signs; and
> human beings complete its deeds.

Hence, a passage in the *Documents* says: "The works of Heaven—it is human beings who carry them out on its behalf."[7] If [lacuna], then one must order one's government to harmonize with heavenly qi in order to bring about its achievements.

Therefore, in the functioning of the Way and its potency, nothing is greater than qi.

> The Way is the root of qi;
> qi is the agent of the Way.[8]

> There must be a root, for only then will qi be produced;
> There must be an agent, for only then will transformations be completed.

For this reason,

> the Way's creation of matter is consummately spiritual and numinous;
> its acts of merit are consummately powerful and great.

> That which makes heaven active;
> that which makes the earth still;
> that which makes the sun bright;
> that which makes the moon luminous;

> the four seasons and the Five Phases,
> the spirits and human beings,
> the infinite variety of things,
> mutations, prodigies, the auspicious and inauspicious;

how could it be that these are not in fact due to qi?

> Turning to its deviations and calamities,

> Heaven's loftiness—qi cracks it;
> earth's vastness—qi moves it;
> a mountain's weight—qi shifts it;

water's flow—qi stops it.

The sun's and moon's divinity—qi eclipses it;
the stars and planets' lodgings—qi topples them.[9]

On some mornings, there is daytime darkness;
on some nights, there is [lacuna].

Great winds send carriages aloft and uproot trees;
accumulated hail becomes ice;[10]

warm springs begin to boil;
*qilin*, dragons, female and male phoenixes,
grubs and locusts—

not one is not produced by qi.

From this it can be seen that qi's [power to] rotate, stimulate, and move is great indeed! [Gradual] changes and [rapid] transformations—what thing is exempt?[11] As for what is changed and what qi moves, it is wondrous.[12] At this time, what true qi contributes is not merely for human beings,

the hundred grains, plants, trees,
birds, beasts, fish, and turtles

all in the embryonic stage of development are nourished by its qi.[13] Sounds enter the ears and thereby stimulate the heart. Men and women hear [lacuna] [them] and by this means contribute essence and spirit.[14] Their substances harmonize and thereby initiate the embryo. The human embryo contains an excellence that completes its body. When it is born, harmony is used to nourish its character. [lacuna] Excellence is contained within,

extending to the four limbs, and
substantiated in blood and arteries.

Thus, its

heart, character, will, thoughts,
ears, eyes, emotions, desires

will all be chaste, incorruptible, and filled with determination to put these virtues into practice. This is how the Five Sovereigns and Three Kings were able to

represent laws by effigy so that the people would not violate them;[15] and
rectify their own virtue so the world by its own accord would be transformed.

For this reason, while laws and commands, punishments and rewards are indeed the methods whereby the people's affairs can be regulated and order elicited, they are insufficient to give rise to the Great Transformation or elicit the Great Peace.[16]

Now, if one desires to

follow the lofty traditions of the Three Kings, or
attain to the consummate achievements of the august sovereigns,

one must first

begin at the beginning and root oneself in the fundamental,
revitalize the Way and elicit harmony;

utilize pure and unadulterated qi to

> bring forth a generous and kindly people,
> banner the standards of luminous virtue and righteousness, and
> create loyal and sincere hearts.

Only then will transformation be praiseworthy and its contributions actualized.

# CHAPTER 33 PREFACE

In the rule of an enlightened king,
Nothing is greater than embodying transformation.
The Way and Moral Potency are the root,
Assisted by benevolence and righteousness.
Mindful that hearts accord with one's rule,
Supervise the people vigorously and extensively.
When all within the four seas are ruled in this way,
How can any decline ensue?

Thus I have written "Transformation Through Virtue," chapter 33.

# 33

# TRANSFORMATION THROUGH VIRTUE

In the governance of the ruler of the people,
nothing is greater than the Way;
   nothing is more magnanimous than virtue;
nothing is more excellent than education; and
nothing is more numinous than transformation.[1]
The Way is the means by which [the people] are supported;
virtue is the means by which they are accommodated;
teaching is the means by which they are educated;
transformation is the means by which they are attracted.[2]

The people have natures, emotions, transformability, and customs.

>Emotion and nature are the root.
>Transformability and customs are the branches.

>Branches grow from the root;
>Actions arise from the heart.

This is why rulers who pacify the world,

give precedence to the root and make the branch secondary, manage their hearts and then govern their actions.

If the heart's essence[3] is upright, then

> treacherous wickedness will have no place to arise, and
> evil thoughts will have no place to reside.

Now, education's alteration of people's hearts is like the government's effect on people's bodies.

> If virtuous government is applied to the people, then many will be robust, good-looking, strong, and long-lived.
> If bad government is applied to the people, then many will be weak, impaired, short-lived, and die of plague.

Thus, the *Book of Documents* praises "completing the full lifespan," and abhors "a disastrous and untimely end."[4]

> When the nation's government is harmful to the enlightened, many people will suffer afflictions of the eye;
> [when its] government is harmful to acuity, many people will suffer afflictions of the ear;
> [when its] government is harmful to farsightedness, many people will suffer untimely deaths.[5]

Now, the body and bones are considered sturdy and strong; nevertheless, they will change in accord with [a nation's] government. How much more is this the case for the potent and subtle qi of the mind and heart that cannot be restored?[6] A passage in the *Book of Odes* says:

In thick patches are those rushes, springing by the wayside;
Let not the cattle and sheep trample them.
Soon they will burst forth; soon they will be completely formed,
With their leaves soft and glossy.[7]

It also says:

The hawk flies up to heaven;
The fishes leap in the deep.
Easy and self-possessed was our prince;
Did he not exert an influence upon people?[8]

Duke Liu's virtue was abundant; his mercy extended to the grass and trees, sheep, oxen, and the six domestic animals.[9] If even these were moved by his virtue, and since his kindness made him unable to bear trampling and treading on living grass, how much more was this so for the people—were there any who were not transformed?

Since the superior person cultivates a joyful and effortless virtue,

extending above to the flying birds, and
reaching down to deep-dwelling fish,

so that there are none who are not delighted and pleased, then how much more so for his officers and the common people? Would there have been any among them who were unkind?

The sages were deeply aware of [these principles]. All of them

practiced self-correction in order to serve as models,
clarified ritual and duty in order to serve as instruction.

They first harmonized virtuous qi in those yet to be born, and afterward inculcated exemplary conduct in [children] capable of laughter.[10]

When people are [still] embryos there is a blending of harmonious [qi] and by this means they become complete.[11] At birth, they are established in upright and correct [conduct] and thereby mature. By this means they will possess

benevolent and dutiful hearts, and
modest and pure aspirations

that adhere to their bones and circulate in their veins, all [present] in the body and complete at birth,

without coarse or foul qi, and
without evil or depraved desires.

Though one might

abandon them beyond the wilds or
cast them into darkness,

to the end they will harbor no act that violates propriety.

Deliver them to some dangerous and forlorn place;
throw them between [weapon] points and blades,

and to the end they will entertain no thought of dishonorable self-preservation. If the people of the entire world behaved in this manner, then where could we find villainous or treacherous people to punish?

> The activities of High Heaven,
> Have neither sound nor smell.
> Take your pattern from King Wen,
> And the myriad regions will repose confidence in you.[12]

This is how the Ji lineage exalted the praiseworthy in the beginning and set aside the use of punishments for a later time.[13]

For this reason, the most sagacious did not

> concentrate on regulating the people's affairs, but
> concentrated on regulating the people's hearts.

Thus it is said: "In hearing litigations, I am like any other person. What is necessary, however, is to cause the people to have no litigations"; and "lead them with virtue; bring them to order with the rites."[14]

> Concentrate on making their natures magnanimous;
> concentrate on making them understand duty.[15]

> If the people are kind and affectionate, then there will be no thought of mutual harm;
> if actions and thoughts are righteous, then there will be no hearts of malice or evil.

Now, circumstances such as these,

> are not due to the prompting of the law; and
> are not due to the enforcement of penalties.

They are, in fact, brought about by teaching and transformation.

The sage deeply reveres virtue and propriety and disdains punishments and chastisements. Hence, Shun first ordered Xie to "reverently set forth the five instructions," and later tasked Gao Yao with the five punishments and the three localities [for punishments].[16] Therefore, all those who established laws did so not

> to spy out people's shortcomings and to punish their transgressions and errors, but rather
> to prevent treachery and wickedness and to avert disaster and failure, and
> to restrict perversity and cruelty and to enter into the true Way.

A passage in the *Book of Odes* says: "The people cling to custom, / They are fond of fine virtue."[17] Thus, the people have hearts in the same way that cultivators have gardens.

> If [gardens] encounter harmonious qi, they will bloom, flourish, and produce fruit;
> If they encounter drought, they will dry, wither, and produce abnormalities.
>
> If the people encounter excellent teachings, then individuals will have genteel hearts.
> [If they] suffer bad government, then people will harbor villainous and rebellious thoughts.

Thus, the good cultivate Heaven's people just as the skilled craftsman makes fermented condiments.

If he begins and ends work according to the right time,
if the coolness and warmth are just right,

then a whole cellar of fermented condiment will be extraordinarily delicious and abundant. If handled by an unskilled craftsman, then a whole cellar of condiment will be a putrid failure and need to be discarded as a loss. Now, the six coordinates[18] are in fact like a cellar, and the black-haired people are like the condiment. Their changes, transformations, words, and deeds reside with the ruler and nothing else.[19]

> If they encounter virtuous officials, then all will embrace loyalty and trustworthiness and proceed with benevolence and magnanimity.
> If they encounter evil officials, then all will embrace wickedness and evil and proceed with vulgarity and unkindness.

> If loyalty and magnanimity accumulate, then Great Peace will ensue;
> if wickedness and unkindness accumulate, then danger and destruction will ensue.

This is why sagacious emperors and enlightened kings all valued transformation by virtue and deplored harsh punishments.

> Virtue is the means by which one cultivates oneself;
> power is the means by which one rules others.

People of the most superior intelligence and those of the most abysmal stupidity are few in number and average people are the most numerous. Average people living the world are like metals smelted in a furnace. They change and transform according to the mold. What the smelting creates—the squareness, roundness, thinness, and thickness—simply follows the constraints of the mold.[20]

Hence,

> the good or evil of an age, and
> the callousness or magnanimity of customs

all rest with the ruler. The most superior sages

> harmonize virtuous qi in order to transform the people's hearts, and
> rectify their demeanor and bearing in order to lead the masses beneath them.

Therefore they are able to make the people of each household worthy of ennoblement. Yao and Shun were such. Next are those who

> embody the Way and the virtue and esteem love and mercy,
> praise education and instruction and revere ritual and yielding.

They are therefore able to make the people to be free of contentious hearts and put aside punishments. Kings Wen and Wu were such. Next are those who

> clarify good and evil and publicize laws and prohibitions,
> regulate reward and punishments and prevent self-interest.

Therefore they are able to make the people flee from treachery and evil and rush toward justice and fairness; and to manage weakness and chaos in order to bring about order and strength.

The revival was able to achieve such results.[21]

If those who govern all under Heaven

> dwell with the profane and give free rein to emotions and desires,
> neglect the affairs of the people and rush toward wine and revelry;
> draw near to wicked youths and distance themselves from worthies and men of talent;
> befriend the calumnious and sycophantic and distance the correct and upright;
> exact heavy taxes to reward those without merit;

and capriciously indulge delight and anger so as to harm the innocent, they will enable

> disorder in the government and thereby corrupt their populace;
> harm themselves and thereby lose their kingdoms.

[Kings] You and Li exemplify this behavior.[22]

Confucius said: "When three walk together there will always be my instructor in their midst. I pick out people's good points and follow them. As for their bad points, I change them in myself."[23] The *Odes* praise those who "look to Yin as a mirror," and "seek for themselves much felicity."[24] Hence, if the lords of this generation can truly make all within the six coordinates and the people of the entire world to

> cherish upright and magnanimous sentiments and be free of shallow and petty hatreds,
> to offer just and upright hearts and be free of treachery and deceitful intent,

then

> the customs of Fu Xi and Shen Nong will once again be seen in this time,[25] and
> unicorns, dragons, and phoenixes will once again gather in the wilds.

# CHAPTER 34 PREFACE

Looking back to remote antiquity,
[We learn of how] the Five Powers began to circulate.
Consulting the *Odes* and the *Documents*,
[We] examine lessons from the past.
[When a dynasty's] qi has been depleted and reached its limit,
The next dynasty will commence.
Though [this theory] is not necessarily correct,
It serves as the basis for traditional views.

Thus I have written "Treatise on the Five Powers," chapter 34.

# 34

# TREATISE ON THE FIVE POWERS

From antiquity, in the days of yore,

Heaven and earth split asunder;
the Three August Ones succeeded each other in their rule.[1]

Each established a title and temple name to represent their reigns. Heaven decreed the five eras, and the first month was adjusted three times.[2] The divinely intelligent [rulers] were conceived by stimulus and born.[3] They arose and came to possess their states, which were lost through neglect and destroyed through accumulated evil. [Yet] the spiritual is numinously refined and the mandate of Heaven has no limit. Some [rulers] the relied on the August Ones [for their status], and some inherited their status through birth.[4] [Events] prior to Tai Hao are very remote indeed.[5] From his time onward, little can be documented. Although [others] gave [these sources] their full attention and concentration, their discussions nevertheless contain errors. Therefore, I compiled these ancient records and have written the "Treatise on the Five Powers."

Across generations, in the accounts of the Three August Ones and the Five Emperors, most consider Fu Xi and Shen Nong to be two of the August Ones. Another one is sometimes referred to as Sui Ren and sometimes referred to as Zhu Rong or Nü Wa. Which are correct and which are incorrect is impossible to know. I have heard that in antiquity there was the Heavenly August One, the Terrestrial August One, and the Human August One, and perhaps that is what is meant by [the Three August Ones], but I am reluctant to elaborate. All of the accounts found in the Five Classics lack authoritative references. Therefore, I must rely on the "Great Preface" of the *Yijing* for what followed Fu Xi and what he bequeathed to later worthies. Although most of it cannot be verified, nevertheless, through a cursory examination, a fraction of it can still be gleaned alongside other efforts to seek the truth.

A giant left footprints upon emerging from Leize.[6] Hua Xu trod on them and gave birth to Fu Xi.[7]

> His salient physical feature was a solar horn.[8]
> He was known in the world as Tai Hao.

His capital was in Chen.[9] His power was that of Wood. He used the dragon as his insignia. Thus, he established dragon officials who were named for dragons.[10] He created the eight trigrams and knotted ropes to make nets for fishing.[11]

Later, his descendant, Di Ku, succeeded Zhuan Xu.[12]

> His salient physical feature was a square cranium.[13]
> His personal appellation was Gao Xin.

His nature was divinely intelligent, his virtuous actions were solemn and reverent. He could calculate when to welcome the sun and send off the moon.[14] He complied with the ordinances of Heaven and was able to determine the rotations of the three regulators (the sun, moon, and stars) to assist the people. He composed the music "Six Blossoms."[15] In his generation there were eight talented men: Bofen, Zhongkan, Shuxian, Jizhong, Bohu, Zhongxiong, Shubao, and Jili. They were

> loyal, reverent, proper, praiseworthy,
> accommodating, kindly, merciful, and harmonious.

All people under Heaven called them the "Eight Exemplars."[16]

His descendant, Jiang Yuan, stepped in a giant's footprint and gave birth to Ji Qi.[17] His salient physical feature was a cleft chin.[18] He served as Yao's Master of Lands.[19] He was also in charge of sowing and planting, assiduously cultivating superior grain.[20] When Yao encountered the flood, ten thousand people were saved by his [efforts]. Therefore, Shun appointed him as "Lord Millet." In the beginning, when Lieshan possessed All under Heaven, his son, called Zhu, was able to cultivate all kinds of grain.[21] Thus, he was put in charge of the altar of grain, and prior to the Xia, was offered sacrifices. With the rise of the Zhou, Qi took his place, and to this day receives sacrifices.

Tai Ren dreamt that she was aroused by a tall person.[22] She gave birth to King Wen. His salient physical feature was his four nipples. He served as the Earl of the West and flourished in Qi.[23] He settled litigation between Yu and Rui and then began his receipt of the mandate.[24] King Wu had fused teeth. He defeated the Yin and put an end to executions. He brought about the Way of Zhou rule. The enfeoffments of those surnamed Ji were numerous: Guan, Cai, Cheng, Huo, Lu, Wei, Mao, Ran, Gao, Yong, Cao, Teng, Bi, Yuan, Feng, Xun, which were all the relatives of King Wen.[25] Yu, Jin, Ying and Han were all the relatives of King Mu.[26] Fan, Jiang, Han, Mao, Zuo, and Ji, were the offspring of the Duke of Zhou. Zhou, Shao, Guo, Wu, Sui, Bin,

Fang, Ang, Xi, Fan, Yang, Hua, Hao, Gong, Mi, Rong, Dan, Guo, Yang, Feng, Guan, Tang, Han, Yang, Gu, Luan, Gan, Xianyu, and Wangshi all belong to the Ji clan.[27]

The head of a numinous dragon emerged from Mount Changyang and stimulated Ren Si. She gave birth to the Red Emperor, Kui Wei.

> His personal name was the Fiery Emperor, and
> his reign name was Shen Nong.

He succeeded Fu Xi. His power is associated with Fire, therefore he made Fire officials and Fire nomenclature. He

> fashioned wood to make the plowshare, and
> bent wood to make the plow handles and hoes.[28]

Midday was the time established for markets, bringing together all the people under Heaven. They made their transactions and left, each acquiring what was appropriate.

[The Red Emperor's] descendant, Qing Du, wedded a dragon and gave birth to Yi Yao, who succeeded Gao Xin.[29] His eyebrows were of eight colors. His reign name was Tang. He created the Da Zhang (Greatly Manifest) music.[30] He initiated the practice of abdicating the throne. When King Wu defeated Yin, he enfeoffed Yao's descendants at Zhu.

Hanshi swallowed a vermillion pearl inscribed with the words: "The Jade Flower will give birth to the Han."[31] A dragon stimulated the lady, and Liu Ji began his rise.[32]

An enormous flash of lightning surrounded the Pivot Star illuminating its field and stimulating Fu Bao.[33] She gave birth to the Yellow Emperor, Xuan Yuan, who replaced the Vermillion Emperor.

He had the face of a dragon, and
his power was the phase Earth.

He used clouds as his insignia. Thus, he created "cloud" officials and cloud nomenclature. He created the Xian Chi music.[34] This period was marked by the beginning of the production of clothing.[35]

Following his reign, Wo Deng saw a large rainbow; she sensed herself being stimulated and gave birth to the Double Splendored Shun of Yu. His eyes had double pupils. He served Yao, and when Yao abdicated the throne, he said, "Oh! You, Shun, the Heaven-determined order of succession now rests in your person. Sincerely hold fast the due mean. If there be distress and want within the four seas, Heaven's largesse will end forever."[36] Thereupon, Shun received the Cultured Ancestor's [i.e., Yao's] resignation. His reign name was You Yu. He created the music, "Nine Shao." He conceded his throne to Yu. When King Wen defeated the Yin, he put Lord Hu in power in Chen and then gave him his eldest daughter, the Grand Lady Ji.[37]

A large star like a rainbow descended upon Huazhu. Nüjie encountered it in a dream and gave birth to the White Emperor, Zhi Qingyang.[38] His reign name was Shao Hao. He assumed the Yellow Emperor's position. His capital was in Qufu. His power was the phase Metal. When he assumed the throne, phoenixes arrived. He therefore used birds as an insignia [for naming his officers]. The phoenixes were regulators of the calendar.

> The Swallows were supervisors of the equinoxes.
> The Shrikes were supervisors of the solstices.
> The Orioles were supervisors of the opening of the seasons.
> The Pheasants were supervisors of the close of seasons.

The Snipes were supervisors of conscripts.
The Ospreys were the supervisors of the military.
The Cuckoos were supervisors of works.
The Falcons were supervisors of corrections.
The Turtle Doves were supervisors of affairs.

These [last] five birds, all of the *jiu* variety, were for gathering [*jiu*] the people. Five types of pheasants were leaders for the five types of artisans; making useful objects, they brought all the people to the same level.[39] This was the beginning of the creation of writing;

> the hundred officials utilized it to rule, and
> the myriad people used it to examine into [their decisions].[40]

[At the time] there were four gifted men called Zhong, Gai, Xiu, and Xi who were talented with metal, wood, and water. Therefore, Zhong served as Gou Mang, Gai served as Rushou, and Xiu and Xi served as Xuanming.[41] They were reverent in acquitting their duties, and for their entire lives did not lose their positions. Thus, they were able to complete [the achievements of] Qiongsang.[42]

Following [Shao Hao's] reign, Xiu Ji saw a shooting star. She sensed herself being stimulated and gave birth to the White Emperor, Wenming of Rong, Yu. His ears had three orifices. He served as Yao's supervisor of works. He oversaw

> the adjustment of water and land,
> the naming of mountains and rivers;[43]
> the demarcation of nine provinces, and
> the administration of the nine tributes.[44]

When his work was complete, he was given a black jade tablet to proclaim his contribution to Heaven. Shun then abdicated the throne, his charge resembling Yao's edict. Yu then ascended the throne. He created the music called Da Xia. His reign name was Xiahou.

[Yu] transmitted his position to his son Qi. Qi's sons Tai Kang and Zhong Kang in turn succeeded him. Their five brothers, all of whom were possessed of beclouded virtue, were unfit for the tasks of rulership. They left and awaited [Tai Kang] north of the Luo River. This place was called Wuguan.[45]

When [Qi's] grandson, Xiang, succeeded to the throne, the Way of Xia began to decline. Thereupon, Archer Yi moved from Chu to Qiongshi, and with the support of the Xia people, took over Xia rule and did away with Xiang.[46] The Lady Min, who was pregnant, escaped through a culvert in the walls and returned to Reng. There she bore Shao Kang, who became director of herdsmen for Reng.[47]

Relying on his archery skills, Yi did not attend to the affairs of the people but indulged in hunting beasts of the plain. He cast off Wuluo, Boyin, Xiong Kun, and Mang Yu and instead employed Han Zhuo.[48] [Han] Zhuo was the slanderous son of the Boming lineage. Boming, Lord Han, hated him and cast him off. Lord Yi took him in, trusted him, gave him assignments, and made him his own chief minister. Han Zhuo

> flattered and seduced those inside the palace,
> offered bounties to those outside it,
>
> fooled and cajoled the people, and
> misled Yi into [leaving to go] hunting.

Having sowed deception, he took Yi's domain and patrimony from him, and those inside and outside all submitted to him. Even then Yi was unrepentant. When he was about to return from the wilds, his own men killed him, boiled him, and gave [his flesh] to his sons to eat. His sons could not bear to eat [his flesh] and died at the Gate of Qiong.[49]

Mi fled to the Youge lineage.[50] [Han] Zhuo took over Yi's wives and concubines and fathered Ao and Yih. Relying on his slanderous wickedness and deceitful treachery, he showed no kindness to the people and sent Ao to employ troops to eliminate the Zhenguan and Zhenxun lineages. He placed Ao in Guo and Yih in Ge.[51] He sent Ao to seek out Shao Kang, who fled to Yu and served there as director of cooks. Si of Yu[52] thereupon married two Yao women to Shao Kang and established him in the settlement Lun, where he controlled one hundred square *li* of land and a population of five hundred military families.[53] He was able

> to extend his virtue, and
> to give his plans a start,

and by these means he gathered in the Xia populace and reinstated their official ranks. Mi, coming from the Youge lineage, collected the last embers of the two domains to extinguish Han Zhuo and establish Shao Kang as ruler.[54] He then

> sent Ru'ai to spy on Ao, and
> sent Lord Zhu to mislead [Ao's younger brother] Xi.

Thus, he extinguished Guo and Ge and restored the traces of Yu, sacrificing to Xia ancestors, served as a correlate of Heaven, erring in none of the old practices.[55] After seventeen generations, Jie lost all under Heaven.

King Wu defeated the Yin and enfeoffed [Yu of Xia's] descendants in Ji, and others were enfeoffed in Zeng. He also enfeoffed the descendants of Shao Hao in Tan.⁵⁶

Ao's ability and strength surpassed one and all. He flaunted his bravery and martial prowess but in the end was destroyed by it. Thus Nangong Gua said: "Yi was skillful at archery, and Ao labored with boats, but neither of them died a natural death."⁵⁷

The Si clan was divided into the lineages of the Xiahou, Youhu, Younan, Zhanxun, Bonou, Xin, Bao, Bi, Ge, Ming, and Zeng—all descendants of Yu.⁵⁸

Twinkling Brilliance, like brilliant white moonlight, stimulated Nüshu in a dark and secluded palace.⁵⁹ She gave birth to the Black Emperor, Zhuanxu. His salient physical feature was his fused ribs.

His personal appellation was Gao Yang;
his reign name was Gong Gong.

He replaced Shao Hao.⁶⁰ His power was the phase Water, and he used water as his insignia. Thus, he created Water officials and Water nomenclature. At the time of Shao Hao's decline, the Nine Li threw morality into chaos. [Gong Gong] then ordered Zhong and Li to bring to order the recalcitrant.⁶¹ He calculated [the course of the] sun and the moon in the east, west, south, and north. He created the music called the Five Blossoms. At the time there were eight talented men: Cangshu, Tuikai, Daoyan, Dalin, Pangjiang, Tingjian, Zhongrong, and Shuda. They were

fair, wise, broad-minded, profound,
clear-sighted, reliable, earnest, and sincere.⁶²

All under Heaven referred to them as the "Harmonious Eight." Gong Gong had a son called Goulong, who was able to pacify the Nine Lands. Therefore, he was called "Lord of the Land." When he died, he became the earth spirit.[63] All under Heaven offer sacrifices to him.

Song Jian swallowed a swallow's egg and gave birth to Xie, who became Yao's Master of Foot Soldiers, and whose duty was to promote loving kindness among the one hundred surnames and adherence to the five categories [of familial affection].[64]

Fu Du saw white vapor penetrating the moon. She was stimulated and gave birth to the Black Emperor, Zi Lü. His salient physical feature was his double elbows. His personal appellation was Tang, and his dynastic name was Yin. He brought about the Great Peace.

Later, in a period of decline, Wu Ding was born.[65] When he ascended the throne, he was silent and did not speak. He contemplated the Way for three years and dreamed that he had obtained a worthy and made him his teacher. Thereupon he ordered that using the likeness from the dream, this person should be sought throughout the Four Quarters[66] in poor and squalid places. When he found Fu Yue, he was at the time serving as a slave working on construction in Fuyan. He elevated him to the rank of grand duke and ordered him to present admonitions day and night. Because he feared that he was negligent and slothful, he decreed:

> Suppose me a weapon of steel; I will use you as a whetstone. Suppose me crossing a great stream; I will use you as a boat with its oars. Suppose me in a year of great drought; I will use you as a copious rain. Open your mind and enrich my mind. (Be) like medicine, which must distress the patient in order to cure his sickness. (Think of me) as one walking barefoot, whose feet are sure

to be wounded, if he does not see the ground.⁶⁷ You will assist me in all things and not abandon me.

Thus, he was able to initiate a revival and was called Gao Zong. When it came to the time of Di Xin and [the Yin] was destroyed, the people referred to [Di Xin] as Djou.

King Wu enfeoffed Weizi in Song and Jizi in Chaoxian.⁶⁸

The Zi clan was divided into the lineages of Yin, Shi, Lai, Song, Le, Xiao, Kongtong, Beiduan, and were all the descendants of Tang.

# CHAPTER 35 PREFACE

The gentleman knows much,
Concerning the words and deeds of former times.
Distinguishing kin groups to discern matters,
Those in antiquity had [the resource of] clan names.
If we broadly examine [lacunae]

Thus I have written "A Record of Lineage and Clan Names,"
    chapter 35.

# 35

# A RECORD OF LINEAGE AND CLAN NAMES

In the past, the sage kings

observed the images of Qian and Kun;[1]
examined the laws of the spiritual and numinous;

sought the duration of the mandate's course,
examined the virtuous acts of the various officers,

and conferred clan names and decreed lineage names[2] to glorify virtuous achievements.[3] Texts say that there were one hundred lineage names related to official posts.[4] The king awarded sons and younger brothers of the feudal lords who had executed their official duties for a thousand generations with clan names based on their occupations—these are what is known as the "hundred clan names." Each of the [hundred] clan names included ten ranks, and thus, from the perspective of the king, were called the "one thousand ranks."

Formerly, Yao

conferred on Xie the clan name Zi;

conferred on Qi the clan name Ji, and
conferred on Yu the clan name Si,

while his lineage name was Youxia. Boyi's clan name was Jiang and his lineage name was Youlü.

Later, throughout the Three Eras, when officials held hereditary posts, they had family names associated with their official positions, and [the names of] their settlements were also used like this.[5] Later, if [families] fell into a decline, they continued to rely on this system of clan names and were unable to change it. Thus, some passed down their original clan names, some used courtesy names, settlement names, and posthumous names.

> Some took names from the names of states,
> some took names from their aristocratic ranks,
> some took names from their official positions,
> some took names from courtesy names,
> some took names from their occupations,
> some took names from their places of residence, and
> some took names from their settlements.[6]

As for the era of the Five Emperors and the Three Kings, there are the "personal appellations."

Wen, Wu, Zhao, Jing, Cheng, Xuan, Dai, and Huan are examples of "posthumous" names. Qi, Lu, Wu, Chu, Qin, Jin, Yan, and Zhao are examples of "state names." Wangshi, Houshi, Wangsun, and Gongsun are examples of "rank names." Sima, Situ, Zhonghang, and Xiajun are examples of "office names." Boyou, Mengsun, Zifu, and Shuzi are examples of "courtesy names." Wushi, Jiangshi, and Taoshi are examples of "occupational names." Dongmen, Ximen, Nangong, Dongguo, and Beiguo are examples of "residential names." Sanniao, Wulu,

Qingniu, and Baima are examples of "settlement names."[7] All of these [are] clan and lineage names. All [of the names] of this sort are too numerous to recount.

The Prince of Wei extinguished Xing; Lord Zhao [of Lu] took a wife of the same surname, and it is said that [in each case, the people involved] descended from a common ancestor.[8] But from ancient times to the present, this [distinction] has not always been observed. The ancient practice of conferring clan names, for the most part, can be used [to distinguish a common ancestor]. But for the remainder, it is difficult [to make the case].

When the house of Zhou began to decline, Wu and Chu usurped the title [of king]. Later, the [rulers of the] seven kingdoms all called themselves king.[9] Thus, the Wang lineage name, the Wangsun lineage name, the Gongsun lineage name, as well as lineage names, posthumous names, and names based on official titles, all existed in each state, so that in the eighteen hundred or so states, posthumous names and official titles numbered in the ten-thousands.[10] Therefore, their earliest ancestors could not have been the same. When it comes to the various branches of the Sun lineage,

> some are of the Wangsun ("King's grandson") branch, and some are of the "various grandson" branches.[11]

Thus, there are

> those who have common ancestors but different surnames,
>    and
> those who have the same name but different ancestors.

There are also confusions and errors, changes and insertions, such as when the wrong name enters the record. Some follow their mother's clan name and some [change their names to] avoid enemies.¹² Some blow the pitchpipe to determine the clan name, though only a sage has this ability.¹³ At present, the people have been scattered for a long time, and few understand notes and pitches. People have always placed importance on correctly determining their ancestors.¹⁴ Therefore, I will provide a brief summary of the most illustrious and await a later scholar's considered additions and corrections to [my survey].

Fu Xi's clan name was Feng, and his descendants were enfeoffed with the four states of Ren, Su, Xuqu, and Zhuanyu. They managed the sacrifices made to Taihao and were also in charge of the sacrifices made to the Eastern Meng [mountains].¹⁵ Duke Xi of Lu's mother, Cheng Feng, was likely a woman of Xuqu. The Ji family wanted to attack Xuqu, but Confucius criticized the plan.¹⁶

Yandi's descendant, Bo Yi, the chief of the four mountains, served Yao by taking charge of ritual propriety. He judged people according to the law and was thus enfeoffed with Lü and Shen. His progeny gave birth to [Jiang] Shang,¹⁷ who served as King Wen's tutor.¹⁸ When the Yin dynasty was defeated, [Jiang Shang] was enfeoffed with Qi. Other [descendants of Yandi] were enfeoffed with Xu and Xiang, others were enfeoffed with Ji, and others were enfeoffed with Shen. The city [of Shen] was in the Yuan district of Nanyang at the foot of Mount Beixu. Thus, a passage in the *Book of Odes* says:

> Full of activity is the chief of Shen,
> And the king would employ him to continue the services,
> With his capital in Xie,
> Where he should be a pattern to the States of the south.¹⁹

Thirty *li* west of Yuan is the city of Lü. Xu was located in Yingchuan. It is equivalent to the present-day Xu county. Rong people bearing the Jiang clan name dwelled between the Yi and Luo Rivers. Lord Hui of Jin moved the [Rong of] Luhun.[20] Zhou, Bo, Gan, Xi, Lu, Yi, and the Guo lineage of Qi, the Gao lineage, the Xiang lineage, the Xi lineage, the Shiqiang lineage, the Dongguo lineage, the Yongmen lineage, the Ziya lineage, the Ziwei lineage, the Zixiang lineage, the Ziyuan lineage, the Ziqian lineage, the Gongqi lineage, the Hangong lineage, the He lineage, and the Lu lineage were all part of the Jiang clan.

Huangdi's sons numbered twenty-five and can be divided into twelve lineages: the Ji, You, Qi, Ji, Teng, Zhen, Ren, Ju, Xi, Ji, Xuan, and Yi.[21] During the Spring and Autumn period, in the state of Jin there was Qi Xi, who promoted his son and recommended his enemy, and because of this he became distinguished for his loyal and honest nature.[22] The Master of Ju was a member of the Ji lineage.[23] During the flourishing of the Xia dynasty, there was a Ren Xi who served as Xia's superintendent of chariots and because of this was enfeoffed with Xue and later transferred to Pi. His progeny, Zhong Hui, resided in Xue and served as Tang's minister of the Left.[24]

The consort of Wang Ji, Tai Ren, and the Xie, Zhang, Chang, Cai, Zhu, Jie, Quan, Bei, Yu, and Kuangda lineages, were all of the Ren clan. A woman of the Jí lineage served as Houji's primary consort and abundantly brought forth the ancestors of Zhou.[25] The Jí lineage was enfeoffed with Yan. There was a lowborn concubine called Jí of Yan. She dreamed that a spirit gave her an orchid and said: "I am Bo Chou; I am you ancestor. With this bloom your state will become fragrant and others will succumb and be enamored."[26] When Lord Wen saw Jí, he gave her an orchid and had her serve him. Jí told him of her dream and said: "I am without merit. If I am fortunate enough to bear a child, no one will believe me. May I use this orchid as proof?" The lord said: "Agreed." She then gave birth to Lord Mu.

As for the branches of the Jí lineage there are the Kan, Yin, Cai, Guang, Lu, Yong, Duan, and Mixu lineages.[27] By the time of the Han, in Hedong there was Zhi Du, and in Runan there was Zhi Junzhang.[28] The pronunciation of their name is the same as that of the Jí of ancient times but it is written differently. Both of these men were famous in their own day.

The reign of Shao Hao began to decline, and the Nine Li tribes threw virtue into disarray. When Zhuan Xu inherited [the realm], he ordered

> Zhong, the Chief of the South, to take charge of Heaven so as to bring the spirits to order, and
> Li, the Chief of Fire, to take charge of earth, so as to bring the people to order.

[Thus] he reinstated the former relations [of the two realms], so that they no longer interfered with each other or held the other in disrespect. This was called 'the cutting of communication between Heaven and earth.[29] Now Li was Zhuan Xu's son, Wu Hui. He was the Governor of Fire under Gao Xin. His unadulterated brilliance illuminated Heaven and brightened the bounties of earth. He shed his luster throughout the four seas, and thus he was called Zhu Rong.[30] Later on, when the Three Miao revived the ways of the Nine Li tribes, Yao raised up the descendants of Zhong and Li, who had not forgotten what had gone before, and once again Xi Bo ruled over them.[31] Thus, the lineage of Zhong and Li for generations brought order to Heaven and earth, divided their various responsibilities, and having spanned the Three Eras, and were enfeoffed with the domain of Cheng.[32] During the reign of the Zhou, they served as King Xuan's grand supervisor of the military. The *Odes* praises them saying, "The King said to the head of the Yin lineage, / 'Give charge to Xiufu, the liege of Cheng.'"³³ When their descendants lost this position, they went to the state of Jin to serve as supervisors of the military. Sima Qian himself claimed to be one of their descendants.³⁴

The grandsons of Zhurong are divided into eight clans: the Ji, Tu, Peng, Jiang, Yun, Cao, Si, and Mi.³⁵ An heir of the Ji clan, Liu Shuan, had a descendant named Dong Fu. He was extremely fond of dragons and was able to find the things they liked to drink and eat. Dragons came to him in large numbers, so he learned to tame them and offered them to Emperor Shun. The emperor bestowed upon him the clan name Dong and the lineage branch-name Huanlong, and enfeoffed him near the Zong River.³⁶ The Zong lineage of Yi and the Shiwei lineage of the Peng clan name were also among those who trained dragons. When Huanlong Peng offered loyal remonstrance, Jie killed him.³⁷ Among all of the sons and grandsons of Zhurong, the branches of the Ji clan name include Kunwu, Ji, Hu, Wen, and Dong.³⁸

The Dong clan Zong lineages of Yi and Huanlong were destroyed by the Xia.³⁹ The Peng clan Pengzu lineages of the Shiwei and Zhuji, were destroyed by the Shang. The Zhou Ren [state] of the Jiang clan was extinguished by the Zhou.⁴⁰

The descendants of the Yun clan were enfeoffed in Yan, Kuai, Lu, and Biyang. [The ruler of] Yan took Zhongren as a wife.⁴¹ He was greedy, stingy, scornful of worthies and slighted the able, and in this way lost his state. Kuai was located between the [Yellow] River and the River Yi. Its lords were arrogant, covetous, and stingy. They reduced the ranks of officials and diminished their emoluments. All of the ministers were demeaned and reduced to submission; superiors and inferiors were at odds with each other. A poet grieved over this turn of events and therefore composed the ode "Gao Qiu" to express his sorrow and grieving, and "Fei Feng" in the hope that the ruler would prioritize education.⁴² Kuai Zhong did not come to his senses, and the Zhong lineage attacked him. Superiors and inferiors were unable to cooperate with each other, prohibitions and punishments were not implemented, and thus, they were destroyed.⁴³ The Master of Lu, Ying'er, married the elder sister of Lord Jing of Jin and made her his wife. Feng Shu, who governed there, killed her. Bozong of Jin was angry and thus attacked and destroyed Lu.⁴⁴ Xun Ying Wuzi attacked and destroyed Biyang.⁴⁵

The Cao clan was enfeoffed in Zhu.⁴⁶ Zhu Yanzi's branch was subdivided and became the "Minor Zhu." They were all destroyed by Chu.

The Mi clan descendant, Xiong Yan, was enfeoffed with Chu under the reign of King Cheng. He was called Yu Xiong, and his courtesy name was Yuzi.⁴⁷ He produced four sons: Bo Shuang, Zhong Xue, Shu Xiong, and Ji Xun. Xun succeeded to the throne and was made Master of Jing. The others were enfeoffed in Kui and Yue. When the Master of Kui did not sacrifice to Zhurong and Yu Xiong, Chu attacked and destroyed them.⁴⁸ This ducal family included the Chu Ji lineage, the Liezong lineage, the Douqiang lineage, the Liangchen lineage, the Qi lineage, the Men lineage, the Hou lineage, the Jirong lineage, the Zhongxiong lineage, the Ziji lineage, the Yang lineage, the Wugou lineage, the Wei lineage, the Shan lineage, the Yang lineage, the Zhao lineage, the Jing lineage, the Yan lineage, the Yingqi lineage, the Lai lineage, the Laixian lineage, the Ji lineage, the Shen lineage, the Diao lineage, the Shen lineage, the He lineage, the Xian lineage, the Jibai lineage, the Wu lineage, the Shenjian lineage, the Yutui lineage, the Gongjian lineage, the Zinan lineage, the Zigeng lineage, the Ziwu lineage, the Zixi lineage, the Wangsun lineage, the Tiangong lineage, the Shujian lineage, the Luyang lineage, the Heigong lineage, [which] are all of the Mi clan.[49]

Chu Ji was Wang Ziao's great-grandson.[50] Fen Mao begat Wei Zhang, Prince Wugou. Chief Minister Sunshu Ao was the son of Wei Zhang. The Supervisor of the Left Army, Shu, was the grandson of [Chu] King Zhuang. The Lord of She, Zhuliang, was third son of the Left Supervisor of the Military, Shu.[51] The Chu grandee, Shen Wuwei, also took Wen as his lineage name.[52]

In the beginning, Djou attacked the Yousu 52.[53] The Yousu lineage gave [Djou] a daughter, Da Ji, and thus destroyed Yin.[54] In the time of King Wu of Zhou, Yousu Fensheng served as Supervisor of Corrections and was enfeoffed in Wen. His descendants include Su Qin of Luoyi.[55]

During the era of the Gaoyang lineage there were eight talented men: Cangshu, Tuikai, Daoyan, Dalin, Pangjiang, Tingjian, Zhongrong, and Shuda. All under Heaven called them the "Eight Joyous Ones."[56] [Gaoyang's] lineage descendants included Gao Yao, who served Shun. Shun said: "Gao Yao, the barbarous tribes disturb our bright great land. There are also robbers, murderers, insurgents, and traitors. You shall serve as the minister [of Crime]."[57] His son, Bo Yi, was able to deal in a discriminating fashion with the hundred things and [thus] was able to assist Shun and Yu.[58] He was also able to tame the birds and beasts. Shun granted him the clan name Ying.[59]

Among [Bo Yi's] descendants there was Zhong Yan, who was born with a bird's body [but who spoke] the language of human beings, and who served as charioteer for Tai Wu.[60] His descendant, Fei Zhong, begat E Lai and Ji Sheng.[61] When King Wu attacked Djou, he also killed E Lai.[62]

Among Ji Sheng's descendants was Zao Fu, who, because of his skillful driving, served King Mu. King Mu wandered to the western sea and forgot to return. Thereupon, Yan of Xu caused disorder. Zao Fu drove [King Mu] a thousand *li* in one day in order to attack him. The king enfeoffed Zao Fu with Zhao city, and because of this he took [Zhao] as his lineage name. His descendants failed to preserve [this fief]. Down to the time of Zhao Su,[63] [they] served as prime ministers of Jin. For eleven generations they held the title of marquis. Five generations later [a descendant] served as King Wu Ling [of Zhao], and five generations after that, Zhao was destroyed. The Gongshu lineage, the Handan lineage, the Ziru lineage, the Yingqi lineage, the Louji lineage, the Lu lineage, and the Yuan lineage were all part of the Ying clan of Zhao.

E Lai's descendants included Feizi, who was skilled at animal husbandry. King Xiao of Zhou enfeoffed him with Qin.[64] After four reigns, King Xuan made [Duke Zhuang of Qin] Grand Master of the Western March, which was a city near the Qin station on the Qian River.[65] Their descendants were numbered among the feudal lords [lacuna]; after [twenty-]five generations they became kings.[66] Six generations later, the First Emperor was born in Handan and was therefore called Zhao Zheng. Additionally, Liang, Ge, Jiang, Huang, Xu, Ju, Liao, Liu, and Ying, were all descendants of Gao Yao. Zhongli, Yunyan, Tuqiu, Xunliang, Xiuyu, Baizhi, Feilian, Miru, Dongguan, Liang, Shi, Bo, Ba, Gongba, Yan, Fu, and Pu are all part of the Ying clan.[67]

Emperor Yao's descendants formed the Gaotang lineage, which later included Liu Lei, who was able to breed dragons. Kongjia gave him the clan name Yulong and appointed him in place of the descendants of Shi Wey.[68] During the Zhou they were the Tangdu lineage. When the Zhou declined, there was Xi Shuzi, who fled the difficulties in Zhou and went to the state of Jin, where he begat Ziyu, who served as an official. Because he brought order to the court, the court was free of disloyal officials. Thus, his lineage name was Shi ["Official"].[69] He served as Minister of Works. Because he was upright in his management of the state, the state was without failures, his lineage name was [also] Sikong, [i.e., "Minister of Works"]. His "sustenance fief" was in Sui, so his lineage name was also Sui.[70]

Shi Wey's grandson, Hui, assisted [Dukes] Wen and Xiang [of Jin] so that there was no conflict among the feudal lords.[71] He was made minister and thereby assisted [Dukes] Cheng and Jing so that the army avoided defeat. He became a commander in Duke Cheng's [central] army and grand tutor, correcting laws and punishments and organizing the canons and statutes. The state was then free of malefactors, and Jin's criminals all fled to Qin.[72] Thereupon the lord of Jin, on [Hui's] behalf, requested from the king a ceremonial cap. The king decreed that Hui of Sui would serve as minster, and because of this [status], he received Fan [as a fief]. At death he was given the posthumous name Wuzi.

Wuzi's son, Wenzi, created a covenant between Jin and Jing (i.e., Chu), enriching the "elder brother and younger brothers" states and making them free of discord. Because of this he was enfeoffed with Xun and Di.

Thus, Emperor Yao's descendants include the Taotang lineage, the Liu lineage, the Yulong lineage, the Tangdu lineage, the Xi lineage, the Shi lineage, the Ji lineage, the Sikong lineage, the Sui lineage, the Fan lineage, the Xun lineage, the Di lineage, the Zhi lineage, the Ji lineage, the Hu lineage, the Qiang lineage, the Rao lineage, the Li lineage, and the Fu lineage.

The Chu Chief Minister Jian asked Wenzi about the virtue of Fan Wuzi.[73] Wenzi responded saying:

That fine man's domestic affairs were well governed, and when he spoke in the domain of Jin, he could exhaust all of the facts without showing any private partiality. His invocators and scribes presented the truth without dishonor. In his domestic affairs there was no distrust, and his invocators and scribes did not make entreaties." Jian returned and recounted [the conversation] to King Kang, saying, "Among spirits or men, there was no cause for complaint. How fitting that that fine man was able to aid five rulers illustriously in their role as hosts to princes."[74]

Thus the Liu lineage, from Tang on down to the time before the Han, possessed virtue that was renowned throughout the world. No one was able to compare to Fan Hui's greatness. This was indeed a case of his self-cultivation establishing the well-being of another. King Wu defeated the Yin and enfeoffed the descendants of Yao at Zhu.

Emperor Shun's clan name was both Yu and Yao. He resided [near the River] Gui. King Wu defeated the Yin and enfeoffed [Shun's descendant], Gui Man, at Chen.[75] This was Duke Hu. The Chenyuan lineage, the Xian lineage, the Yao lineage, the Qing lineage, the Xia lineage, the Zong lineage, the Lai lineage, the Yi lineage, the Situ lineage, and the Sicheng lineage are all part of the Gui clan.[76]

Duke Li's younger son Wan fled to Qi.[77] Duke Huan was pleased with him and made him Head of Artisans and Craftsmen.[78] His sons and grandsons won over the hearts and minds of the people, so he proceeded to seize the rulership and established himself as ruler. This was King Wei [of Qi]. After five generations, [his line] was destroyed.[79] [At this time], the people of Qi began to refer to Chen as Tian.[80] When Han Emperor Gaozu moved all of the [branches of the] Tian lineage to the Land Within the Passes, they were numbered one through eight.⁸¹ Prime Minister Tian Qianqiu, Deputy to the Chancellor Tian Ren, and Tian Xian of Duyang, and Tian Xian of Dang County all derived from Chen. Emperor Wu bestowed upon Qianqiu permission to use a small carriage to enter the palace grounds. Thus, his contemporaries called him the "Carriage" prime minister. As for Wang Mang, he declared himself to be a descendant of Tian An, and based on Tian An's being called Wang Jia, changed his lineage name to Wang.⁸² Wang Mang perpetrated acts of treachery, very much in the manner of Tian An.⁸³ Jingzhong's line included the Pi lineage, the Zhan lineage, the Ju lineage, the Yu lineage, the Xian lineage, the Zi lineage, the Yang lineage, the Wu lineage, the Fang lineage, the Gao lineage, the Mang lineage, and the Qin lineage.⁸⁴

Emperor Yi's eldest son, Wei Zikai, was Djou's elder brother by a concubine.⁸⁵ King Wu enfeoffed him with Song, which is the present-day Suiyang. The Songkong lineage, the Zhuqi lineage, the Ganxian lineage, the Jilaonan lineage, the Juchen lineage, the Jing lineage, the Shifu lineage, the Huangfu lineage, the Hua lineage, the Yu lineage, the Erdong lineage, the Ai lineage, the Sui lineage, the Jiuyi lineage, the Zhongye lineage, the Yuejiao lineage, the Wan lineage, the Huai lineage, the Budi lineage, the Ji lineage, the Niu lineage, the Sicheng lineage, the Wang lineage, the Suo lineage, the Zhi lineage, the Zhao lineage, the Bo lineage, the Youshi lineage, the Sankang lineage, the Renfu lineage, the Yi lineage, the Zheng lineage, the Zheng lineage, the Muyi lineage, the Lin lineage, the Zang lineage, the Hui lineage, the Sha lineage, the Hei lineage, the Weigui lineage, the Ji lineage, the Ju lineage, the Zhuan lineage, the Ji lineage, the Cheng lineage, the Bian lineage, the Rong lineage, the Mai lineage, the Wei lineage, the Huan lineage, the Dai lineage, the Xiang lineage, and the Sima lineage all form part of the Zi clan.⁸⁶

Duke Min's son Fufu He begat Song Fu; Song Fu begat Shizi, Shizi begat Zheng Kaofu, Zheng Kaofu begat Kong Fujia, Kong Fujia begat Mu Jinfu.[87] Mu Jinfu was downgraded to the status of knight.[88] Thus it is said that his line was extinguished in Song. Jinfu begat Qifu, Qifu begat Fangshu, and Fangshu, harried by the Hua lineage, fled to Lu and served as a grandee of Fang.[89] Thus he was called Fangshu. Fangshu begat Boxia, Boxia begat Shuliang He, who served as a grandee in Zou. Thus, he was called Zou Shuhe. He begat Kongzi.[90]

Jin, crown prince of King Ling of Zhou, from his early years possessed abundant virtue.[91] His intelligence was profound and capacious. He was mild, respectful, honest, and quick-witted. When the Gu and Luo Rivers collided and were about to destroy the royal palace, the king wanted to dam them. Crown Prince Jin advised that going against the mind of Heaven was not as good as improving governance.

Duke Ping of Jin sent Shuyu to Zhou. He saw the crown prince and spoke with him, covering five issues but another three were left unresolved.[92] They went back and forth until Shuyu withdrew. He returned and told Duke Ping, "Crown Prince Jin is fifteen years old, and I am unable to communicate with him. I request that you attend to him."

Duke Ping sent Shi Kuang to see Crown Prince Jin.[93] As Crown Prince Jin spoke with Shi Kuang, Shi Kuang was impressed with his virtue and formed a deep bond with him. The prince then asked Shi Kuang, "I have heard that you, grand master, are able to know whether a person's life will be long or short." Shi Kuang responded, saying, "Your complexion is red with white splotches, your voice is shrill and raspy. Your fiery color portends that you will not be long-lived."[94] The prince said, "True. After three years I will ascend to become a guest of God.

You must take care not to speak of this or misfortune will come to you."

After three years the crown prince died. Confucius heard about this and said: "What a pity! This was a case of killing our ruler." The people of the world thought that the prince had predicted the time of his demise. Therefore, they spread the idea of calling him the Immortal Wangzi Qiao. After he became [known as] an immortal, his descendants fled the chaos of Zhou and went to Jin, making a home in Pingyang. Because of this, they took the lineage name Wang. His children and grandchildren delighted in fortifying their natures using the arts of the immortals.

Lu's ducal family includes the Jiao lineage, the Hou lineage, the Zhong lineage, the Zang lineage, the Shi lineage, the Meng lineage, the Zhongsun lineage, the Fu lineage, the Gongshan lineage, the Nangong lineage, the Shusun lineage, the Shuzhong lineage, the Ziwo lineage, the Zishi lineage, the Ji lineage, the Gongzu lineage, the Gongwu lineage, the Gongzhi lineage, the Zigan lineage, the Hua lineage, the Ziyan lineage, the Ziju lineage, the Ziya lineage, the Ziyang lineage, the Dongmen lineage, the Gongxi lineage, the Gongshi lineage, the Shu lineage, the Zijia lineage, the Rong lineage, the Zhan lineage, and the Yi lineage, all of which fall under Lu's Ji clan.

Wei's ducal family includes the Shi lineage, the Shishu lineage, the Sun lineage, the Ning lineage, the Ziqi lineage, the Situ lineage, the Gongwen lineage, the Xigui lineage, the Gongshu lineage, the Gongnan lineage, the Gongshang lineage, the Gongmeng lineage, the Jiangjun lineage, the Ziqiang lineage, the Qiangliang lineage, the Juan lineage, the Huishiya lineage, the Kong lineage, the Zhaoyang lineage, the Tianzhang lineage, the Gu lineage, the Wangsun lineage, the Shigui lineage, the Qiang lineage, the Qiangxian lineage, and the Sui lineage, who all belong to Wei's Ji clan.

Jin's ducal family includes the Xi lineage; a portion of it forms the Lü lineage. Xi Rui also took his settlement name, Ji. His descendants include Lü Qi, whose style name was Jubo. Xi Chou's sustenance fief was in Ku, and his style name was Kuchengshu. Xi Zhi's sustenance fief was in Wen, and his style name was Wenji. Each of them used their fief names as lineage names. The Xi lineage division includes the Zhou lineage and the Qi lineage. Bo Zong, because of his forthright manner, was killed.[95] His son, Zhouli, fled to Chu. Also, because of Xi Wan's forthright and kindly manner, he became the object of Zichang's jealousy and was killed.[96] His son, Pi, fled to Wu and served as grand steward.[97] Taking a warning from his deceased grandfather's actions, who, though correct and upright, still met with disaster, he used flattery and destroyed Wu. All of the Xi lineage divisions, the Youji lineage, the Lü lineage, the Kucheng lineage, the Wen lineage, the Bo lineage, that of the grandson of Marquis Jing, Sun Luanbin, as well as the Fu lineage, the You lineage, the Jia lineage, the Hu lineage, the Yangshe lineage, the Jisu lineage, the Ji lineage, and that of the grandson of Duke Xiang, Sunyan, all are part of Jin's Ji clan.

Marquis Mu of Jin begat Huanshu; Huanshu begat Hann Wan, a grandee who assisted Jin.[98] Ten generations later there was Marquis Wu of Hann. Five generations later there was King Hui of Hann.[99] In another five generations the state of Hann was destroyed. King Xiang's grandson by a concubine, [Hann] Xin, was referred to by ordinary people as Hann Xindu. Emperor Gaozu, because Xin was a royal scion of Hann, made Xin king of Hann; later he was transferred to serve as king of Dai. When he was attacked by the Xiongnu he voluntarily surrendered. The Han sent General Chai to attack him; [the general] beheaded him at Canhe. Xin's wife and children fled to the Xiongnu.[100] In the time of Emperor Jing, Xin's son Tuidang and grandson, Chi, surrendered. The Han appointed Tuidang as the Gonggao Marquis and his son, Chi, was made the Xiangcheng Marquis.[101]

Coming to Hann Yan, during the reign of Emperor Wu he served as a Palace Attendant and was favored like no other. The Andao Marquis, Hann Yue, and the General of the Van, Hann Zeng, were both celebrated in the Han. Their sons and grandsons, depending upon the reigning emperor, were sent to live at Maoling or Duling.[102] There were also the Hanyang and Jincheng Hanns, who were also their descendants. Some of Hann Xin's sons and grandsons remained in Xiongnu territory, where they frequently occupied positions of power and authority as favored servitors.

When it comes to the Liu Marquis, Zhang Liang, he was part of the Ji clan of the ducal family of Hann.[103] When the First Emperor of Qin destroyed Hann, Zhang Liang's younger brother died but had remained unburied. Zhang Liang spent ten million of his family's wealth to avenge Hann. He [tried to] strike the First Emperor at Boliangsha but mistakenly hit a deputy's vehicle instead. The Qin made a furious search for the perpetrator, so Zhang Liang changed his surname to Zhang and hid at Xiapi. There he encountered the immortal Duke Huangshi, who gave him a military text. At the time of the rise of the Duke of Pei, Zhang Liang proceeded to align himself with him.[104] The Duke of Pei ordered him along with Hann Xin to pacify Hann territory and to establish Cheng, the Lord of Hengyang, as the king of Hann, and to establish [Zhang] Liang as Hann's *xindu*. [The rank of] *xindu* was equivalent to the later post of Excellency Over the Masses, that is, *situ*. It is commonly mispronounced. Some say *xindu*, some say *shentu* or *shengtu*.

Nevertheless, all of these words refer to the one post of *situ*. Later writers did not know the origin of the word *xindu* and misconstrued it, thinking that the King of Dai's [i.e., Hann Xin] name was Xindu.[105]

All of Huanshu's descendants, that is, the Youhann lineage, the Yan lineage, the Ying lineage, the Huoyu lineage, the Gongzu lineage, and the Zhang lineage, were descendants of the Ji clan from the state of Hann. Formerly, King Xuan of Zhou also had a Marquis of Hann, whose territory was near Yan. Therefore, a passage in the *Book of Odes* says: "Large is the wall of the city of Hann, / Built by the multitudes of Yan." Their descendants, the Chaoxian, also use the name Hann. After being attacked by Wei Man, they moved to the seacoast.[106]

The Lord of Bi, Gao, shared the clan name of the Zhou [royal line].[107] He was enfeoffed in Bi, and on this basis, made Bi his lineage name. After the Duke of Zhou's death, Gao assumed his official duties.[108] [Later, one of] his descendants lost the position and became a commoner. When Bi Wan served Duke Xian of Jin, in [the duke's] sixteenth year, he ordered Zhao Su to drive forth [in battle] against the Rong. Bi Wan served as his right-hand man, and because he had annihilated Geng and annihilated Wei, he was enfeoffed with Wan, which is equivalent to present-day Hebei County.[109] Wei Ke also had the lineage name Linghu.[110] Nine generations after [Bi] Wan there was Marquis Wen of Wei. Marquis Wen's grandson, Ying, was King Hui of Wei. Five generations later [Wei] was destroyed. The grandson of Bi Yang, Yu Rang, placed himself in service to the Earl of Zhi. The Earl of Zhi treated him as a knight renowned throughout the state. Yu Rang, having received the kindness of one who truly appreciated him, requited the earl of Zhi.[111] All under Heaven commemorated his righteousness. The Wei lineage, the Linghu lineage, the Buyu lineage, the Yedafu lineage, the Boxia lineage, the Weiqiang lineage, and the Yu lineage are all part of the Bi lineage and originate from the Ji clan.

King Li of Zhou's son, [Ji] You, was enfeoffed with Zheng.[112] The descendants of Zheng's Gongshu [Duan] were of the Gongfu lineage.[113] The Xuan lineage, the Si lineage, the Feng lineage, the You lineage, the Guo lineage, the Ran lineage, the Kong lineage, the Yu lineage, the Liang lineage, and the Daji lineage—all ten of these families [honored] the son of Duke Mu of Zheng [as their ancestor].[114] Each one used his courtesy name as his clan name. As for the Boyou lineage, the Mashi lineage, and the Chushi lineage, all of them belong to the Ji clan of Zheng.

Taibo was lord of Wu. Correctly arrayed in flowing ceremonial robes, he implemented the Zhou rituals. When Zhongyong succeeded him, he cut his hair and tattooed his body to adorn his nakedness.[115] When [Zhou] King Wu conquered the Yin, he enfeoffed his descendants in Wu and generously awarded them with North Wu. Ji Zha resided in Yanzhoulai, he was therefore called Yanling Jizi.[116] The younger brother of Helü, King Fugai, fled to Tangxi in Chu. Thus, Tangxi became his lineage name.[117] They all belong to the Ji clan.

Among the grandees of Zheng there was Feng Jianzi. Later, in Hann there was Feng Ting, who served as protector of Shangdang. He placed blame on Zhao and thereby brought about the disaster of Changping in Zhao.[118] In Qin there was the general Feng Jie who was executed alongside Li Si.[119] When the Han arose, there was Feng Tang, who discussed [the position of] generals with Emperor Wen.[120] Later there was Feng Fengshi, who was a man of Shangdang. He reached the rank of general. When his daughter came to serve Emperor Yuan in the rank of Brilliant Companion, he thereupon settled in the capital city.[121] His grandson, Yan, whose courtesy name was Jingtong, was an assiduous scholar and placed great importance on duty.[122] All of the scholars said of him, "For virtue and harmony, there is Feng Jingtong." His written works numbered by the dozens. Filial Emperor Zhang loved and greatly valued his writing.

The Jin grandee, Xun Xi, served Duke Xian. His descendants served as generals in the central army and therefore had the lineage name Zhonghang. Their sustenance fief was in Zhi. Zhi Guo advised the Earl of Zhi but was ignored. He therefore left the Zhonghang lineage and declared before the grand historian that his lineage name would be Fu.[123]

The Jin grandee Sun Boyan supervised archival records.[124] His [lineage] name was therefore Ji ["Records"]. Xin You's two sons oversaw texts with him. Thus, they had the lineage name Dong ["Curator"].[125]

In the *Odes*' celebration of King Xuan, first there was "Zhang Zhong, the filial and friendly," and down to the Spring and Autumn period, in Song there was Zhang Bai.[126] Only Zhang Hou and Zhang Lao of Jin represent truly significant families.[127] Zhang Mengtan served as prime minister to Zhao Jianzi and in that capacity annihilated the Earl of Zhi. He then fled from any reward and tilled land in Mount Fu.[128] Later, there were Zhang Yi and Zhang Chou.[129] Coming to the Han, the Zhang surname proliferated. King of Changshan, Zhang Er, was a man of Liang; Prime Minister Zhang Cang was a man of Yangwu.[130] [There was also] the Marquis of Dongyang, Zhang Xiangru.[131]

Imperial Counsellor Zhang Tang increased the rigor of the statutes and ordinances in order to prevent wrongdoing and to benefit the people. He was also fond of promoting worthy and accomplished scholars and therefore received good fortune and blessings.[132] His son, Anshi, was made General of Chariots and Cavalry and Marquis of Fuping. He was honest, benevolent, frugal, and temperate; cultivated continuity in authority; and delighted in performing secret acts of virtue.[133] By these means his sons and grandsons flourished, and for generations there were worthy descendants. Later the title was changed to the Marquis of Wushi.[134] [Even after] meeting with the chaos of Wang Mang, they enjoyed the benefits of the state without disruption.

The family includes four dukes, world renowned for their loyalty, filial piety, and good works. Previously there was Chancellor Zhang Yu and Imperial Counsellor Zhang Zhong.[135] Later there was Grand Commandant Zhang Pu, a man from Runan, and Grand Tutor Zhang Yu, a man from the kingdom of Zhao.[136] In the capital district and villages, there was not one place where there were no Zhangs. In the Xieyi district of Hedong there is a Zhang City and a West Zhang City. Could it be that the ancestors of the Zhangs of Jin came from this place?

The Yan clan's Shuyong, Shujiu, Shulong, Shugong, Zhilong, Li, Yao, Can, Hui, Liu, Yuan, Fei, and Gaoguo; the Qing clan's Fan, Yin, and Luo; the Man clan's Deng, and You; the Gui clan's Hu, You, and He; the Zhen clan's Hua and Qi; the Ji clan's Qi and Shu; the Yu clan's Shu, Fan, and Tang; the Wei clan's Rao, Rang, and Cha; the Wei clan's Chidi; and the Heng clan's Baidi are all clan names of great antiquity.[137]

In Qi there was Bao Shu, [whose descendants] for generations served as ministers and grandees.[138] In Jin, there was Bao Gui.[139] In the Han dynasty, there was Bao Xuan, whose many years of loyalty and rectitude made him a famous servitor of the Han.[140]

Scholar Li of the Han dynasty was a clerk and his younger brother, Shang, was a general.[141] In present-day Gaoyang the various Li [families] represent a prominent clan.

Formerly there was Zhong Shanfu, whose also held the clan name Fan.[142] His posthumous name was Mu Zhong, and he was enfeoffed in Nanyang.[143] Nanyang is in current-day Henei. Later there was Fan Qingzi.[144]

The Man clan was enfeoffed in Deng, and later used it as a lineage name. In Nanyang's Deng County, north of Shangcai, is the ancient Deng City; and north of new Cai is an ancient Deng city. In the Spring and Autumn era, King Wen of Chu destroyed Deng. In Han times, there was Deng Tong and Deng Guang.[145] In the Later Han, there was Deng Yu of Xinye. Because of his assistance and merit in establishing a new mandate, he was enfeoffed as the marquis of Gaomi.[146] His grandchild, Empress Dowager Deng, was by nature kind, solemn, and enlightened. She restrained and warned her family to refrain from monopolizing power, so that the capital was quiet and peaceful, as if there were no consort families present. She was diligent in her concern for the people; day and night she was never idle. Therefore, though enduring the rebellions by the Qiang people, and floods and food shortages, she managed to restore the country, and to recover peace and plentiful harvests. After the death of Empress Dowager Deng, many disloyal ministers conspired and competed to slander and destroy the Deng family. All under Heaven felt heartache.[147]

The maternal family of Duke Zhao of Lu bore the clan name Gui.[148]

In Han times there was Wei Ao Jimeng.[149]

Heng is in fact a Quanrong name whose ancestral origins can be traced to the Yellow Emperor.[150]

As for the Xu lineage, the Xiao lineage, the Suo lineage, the Changshuo lineage, the Tao lineage, the Fan lineage, the Ji lineage, the Ji lineage, the Fan lineage, and the Tu lineage, all of them are old names of the Yin lineages.[151] When the Han arose, Chancellor of State Xiao He was enfeoffed as the marquis of Zan. He was originally a man of Pei. The Xiao of present-day Changling are his descendants. As for General of the Van Xiao Wangzhi, the Xiao of Donghai and Duling are his descendants.

Imperial Counsellor Fan Yanshou was a man of Xiangyang in Nan commandery. The Fans of Duling and Xinfeng are his descendants.

The Zhou lineage, Shao lineage, Bi lineage, Rong lineage, Shan lineage, Yin lineage, Liu lineage, Fu lineage, Gong lineage, and Chang lineage are all hereditary ducal and ministerial ranks of the Zhou royal house. The Zhou and Shao are male descendants of the Duke of Zhou and the Duke of Shao who inherit the sustenance fiefs of these two dukes and thus act as the king's officials. Thus, the world has had a Duke of Zhou and a Duke of Shao without interruption. Yin was originally an official title. Just as Song has a "grand steward," Chu had a Chief Minister and Deputy of the Left.[152] Yin Jifu was minister to King Xuan. As for his great merit, a passage in the *Book of Odes* says: "The Grand Master Yin, / Is the foundation of our Zhou."[153] Duke Mu of Shan, [Duke] Xiang [of Shan], Duke Qing [of Shan,] and [Duke] Jing [of Shan] represent generations possessed of luminous virtue and talent equaling that of a sage. Thus Shu Xiang praised them by predicting that their line would flourish and prosper.[154]

Kǔcheng is the name of a city. It is located northeast of Yanchi. When later people write the name, some write it as Kucheng. If someone from Qi hears it, they'll write it as Kù. If someone from Dunhuang sees the word, they'll pronounce it Jucheng. Since people who live in Hanyang aren't happy with the words "withered" (*kū*) and "bitter" (*kǔ*), they changed the written form to Guchengshi 古成氏. Tangxi is a name for Xigu in Xiping, Runan. Yu gave his son the courtesy name Qi, that is, the *qi* in the word *qikai* (啓開), "to open." In former times people mistakenly wrote Tangxi 堂谿 with the word *qi* 啓. Later people changed it and thus wrote it as *kai*.[155] As for the ancient [names] Qidiao Kai and Gongye Chang, in previous times when people wrote *diao* 雕, they simplified it to *Zhou* 周; and when they wrote *ye* 冶, they mistakenly wrote *gu* 蠱.[156] Later people also changed it to *gu* 古. Some divided these names to form the Gu, Cheng, Tang, Kai, Gong, Ye, Qi, and Zhou lineages. Some of these lineage names were originally the same but eventually differed. As for dividing, joining, altering, and distinguishing names, there are many examples of this sort. I can only provide this one group of examples—it would be difficult to exhaustively set forth all of them.

The *Book of Changes* says: "The noble man associates with his own kind and makes clear distinctions among things"; "acquires much knowledge of things said and done in the past and so garners his own virtue"; and "accumulates knowledge by studying and becomes discriminating by posing questions."[157] Thus, I have considered in broad outlines the historical records, made selections from the classics and other writings, and relied on records from various localities and available clear-cut accounts in order to make manifest the descendants of worthies and sages to distinguish the founding ancestors of various groups, and to discuss the emergence of lineages and clans. The goal of writing chapters 34 and 35 was to provide reference materials for worthies of future times.

# 36

## POSTFACE

Now, among those born in this age,
Honor is given to those who achieve great deeds.
"The very greatest establish virtue,
Beneath them are those who establish words."[1]
Being useless and untalented,[2]
Lacking the capacity that would enable me to hold office,[3]
I have never even served in the humblest of positions,
And have no way to bring about this sort of contribution.
From the core of my heart I am often possessed by emotion,
And pick up my brush and jot down various compositions.
These words bring together my foolish sentiments,
And simply keep them from being forgotten.
Though the grass and fuel gatherers were obscure and uncultured,
Sages of ancient times still consulted them.
I have made a draft emulating former worthies,
In thirty-six chapters,
In order to transmit the lessons of former times,
The works of Zuo Qiuming, and the Five Classics.[4]
In the transmitted legacy of the sages of former times,
Nothing is greater than their teachings.
Their learning was broad and their memories prodigious;[5]

When in doubt they pondered and inquired.
Their knowledge and insight was thereby formed, and
Their virtue and righteousness was thereby established.
Confucius was fond of study, and
"In his instruction of others he was tireless."[6]

Thus I have written "In Praise of Study," chapter 1.

Generally, officers engaging in study,
Value the root and scorn the branch.
Great men are not flamboyant;
Gentlemen concentrate on substance.
Although ritual propriety facilitates social interactions, and
One must begin by presenting gifts,
Current customs rush toward the inessential,
Which I fear will destroy the practices [of the sage].[7]

Thus I have written "Concentrating on the Root," chapter 2.

People are all endowed with wisdom and virtue;
But they come to grief through the stupefying powers of profit.
To do evil in pursuit of glory,
Is like putting a basin on one's head to view the heavens.
Those who practice benevolence do not become wealthy,
Those who are wealthy are not benevolent.[8]
If [a person] is about to cultivate virtuous behavior,
He must be careful about the basis [of his motivation].

Thus I have written "Suppressing Profit," chapter 3.

The world does not understand how to make appraisals,
Taking into account only [a person's] clan and rank, and[9]

While failing to inquire about his goals and behavior—
His official position and aristocratic title are the only standards.
To be unrighteousness yet wealthy and eminent,
Was what Confucius considered shameful.[10]
[He was] pained by the gradual decline of customs,
And the growing distance from the arts of the sages.

Thus I have written "Appraising Eminence," chapter 4.

Considering what worthies suffer, and
Examining the disasters that jealousy engenders,
[It can be seen that] all envy arises from one's being surpassed by others,
And evolves into deep resentment.
Some focus on fault-finding,
Some fabricate pretexts.
I am pained that my ruler does not examine this point,
But believes slanderous words.

Thus I have written "The Difficulties of the Worthy," chapter 5.

Searching for the origin of enlightenment,
Tracing the emergence of ignorance,
It is resisting good counsel that corrupts,
And how disaster and chaos are formed.
Those holding power,
Uniformly desire to control the ruler,
To thwart and conceal worthy officers,
And thereby monopolize the ruler's power.

Thus I have written "The Enlightened and the Unenlightened," chapter 5.

Looking back upon the former kings,
The ways in which they elicited the Great Peace,
Was to examine achievements for dismissal or advancement,
As written in the Five Classics.
Punishments and reward should reflect the actual case,
And not be based on an empty reputation.
Clearly demonstrate a preference for those with virtuous
    reputations,[11]
And look into [the records of] those promoted [for service at] court.[12]

Thus I have written "Evaluating Merit," chapter 7.

When rulers chose officers,
They all seek the worthy and able.
When officials make recommendations,
They all compete to promote inferior talents.
I detest these craven grifters,
What official business are they capable of managing?
When you purchase medicine and receive a fake,
It's difficult to use it as a cure.

Thus I have written "Thinking About the Worthy," chapter 8.

Examining the fundamental principles of the heavenly and human
    realms,
The interdependence of the three [spheres of Heaven, earth, and
    humankind],
And the triggers for bringing about peace—
These techniques all reside with the ruler.
Esteeming law and selecting worthies,
The state's [stability] derives from him.[13]

If the evil usurp positions,
Then who will there be to keep watch?

Thus I have written "The Fundamentals of Government," chapter 9.

Surveying ancient times to the present,
and events in books and commentaries,
[We see that] rulers all want order, and
Ministers perpetually delight in disorder.
The loyal and the toadies are jumbled together,
Each promoting its own ilk.
[I] am often pained by [the ruler's] failure to perceive [events] clearly,[14]
And by his faith in the words of schemers.

Thus I have written "The Sighs of a Recluse," chapter 10.

Official ranks depend on virtue to flourish;
Virtue values loyalty to stand firm.
This is what the altars of soil and grain rely upon.
Security and danger are bound to these.
If [a person] is not upright, straightforward, or sincere;
Benevolent, kind, gracious or congenial,
Or [if he does not] serve the ruler as if he were Heaven,
Or [if he does not] treat the people as if they were his children,
Then he will be unable to preserve his status,
Or to protect his good name.

Thus I have written "Loyalty and Nobility," chapter 11.

When the kings of former times administered [the nation's] wealth;
They prohibited the people from wrong-doing.[15]

The "Great Plan" expressed concern for the people.[16]
The *Odes* criticized exhausting their resources.[17]
When unscrupulous drifters become numerous,
The essential task of agriculture will decline.
There must be systemic regulation,
But why is there no discussion of this issue?

Thus I have written "On Excessive Luxury," chapter 12.

The accumulation of minute [errors] harms [virtuous] action,
Lust and ease destroy reputations.[18]
Day and night indulging one's desires,
But lacking any expression of remorse.
Deserving but stubbornly resisting advice;
Hearing about virtuous [examples] but not following them:
Minute indulgences invite disgrace,
And in the end ensure disaster.

Thus I have written "Taking Care Over Minutiae," chapter 13.

The enlightened ruler longs for good servitors,
Belaboring his vital energies to find the worthy and intelligent, but
The One Hundred officials are partial and cliquish,
And do not investigate which [talents] are real and which are feigned,
Carelessly elevating those with empty reputations, and
Lavishing false praise on each other.
When they assume office and take on official duties,
They are utterly lacking in contributions or accomplishments.

Thus I have written "Substance and Recommendation," chapter 14.

> Sages sustain the worthy,
> In order assist to the myriad people,[19]
> In the system of the kings of former times,
> All [deemed emoluments] a sufficient substitute for plowing.[20]
> Increasing a rank but lowering the salary,
> Bi Cheng was thereby toppled.[21]
> First increase official's salaries,
> And only then can the Great Peace be realized.[22]

Thus I have written "Ranked Emoluments," chapter 15.

> When the ruler worries, his servitors' must toil—
> This is a common principle of antiquity and present times.
> The ruler is concerned with bringing about peace, so
> His servitors should exhaust their wisdom in this pursuit.
> Steadfast, good, and trustworthy officers,
> All lament numerous amnesties.
> Evil-doers and miscreants in great numbers arise,
> And it is simply because of amnesties.

Thus I have written "On Amnesties," chapter 16.

> When the kings of former times ruled the world,
> They wielded both might and kindness.
> Their rewards were the enfeoffment of nobles,
> Their penalties were the punishments of great severity.
> Only when rewards were substantial and punishments severe,
> Did subjects respect their positions.

> When cultivating the Great Peace,
> One must follow this model.

Thus I have written "The Three Models," chapter 17.

> The people form the foundation of the state,
> Grain is the lifeblood of the people.
> If there is no time to do their daily work,
> How can the grain be plentiful?
> Dukes, ministers, intendants, and officers,
> All draw on the labor of the hundred surnames.[23]
> Their thoughtless appropriation of the people's time,
> Truly makes one protest in fury.

Thus I have written "Using [the People's] Time Sparingly," chapter 18.

> Surveying the administrative work of officials,
> It is contentious lawsuits that occupy them most frequently.
> Seeking the source from which these misfortunes arise,
> We find it is fraud and deception that generate them.
> To eradicate these consequences,
> One must stop them at the source.
> When the people refrain from fraud,
> The world will finally achieve peace.

Thus I have written "Judging Legal Cases," chapter 19.

> Considering the Five Thearchs and the Three Kings,
> Their excellence or inferiority lay in their predilections.[24]
> Since they were desirous of surpassing the [Three] August Ones,[25]
> They first had to bring about peace.

They needed a generation before they could actualize benevolent
  [government]—
This was Confucius's classic [doctrine].[26]
When encountering decadent and evil officials,
Can one avoid using punishments?

Thus I have written "Governing in an Age of Decline," chapter 20.

Sage rulers are concerned about hardship;
They choose experienced generals,
Provide them with axes,[27] and
Award them with powerful aristocratic ranks.
But in fact many [generals] are ignorant and dimwitted, and
Do not understand the transformations of positional advantage.
In issuing rewards and punishments they are unwise.
How can they not be defeated?

Thus I have written "Exhorting Generals," chapter 21.

The Man and Yi wreaking havoc in China,
Is what has caused worry in both ancient and current times.
Yao and Shun worried about the people,
And [sent] Gao Yao to suppress the rebels.[28]
King Xuan, in the period of the revival,
[Charged] Nan Zhong to engage at the border.[29]
At present the people [of the borders] die every day,
Why is there a failure to protect them?

Thus I have written "Securing the Frontiers," chapter 22.

The sentiments of the middling people,
Are at odds with the ruler.

They are unable to contemplate the distant future,
And foolishly only consider conditions of the current moment.[30]
They haphazardly cling to their own personal views,
Regarding them as [grand] strategies for the nation.
We ought to examine their words,
To inquire into what they really mean.

Thus I have written "Discussions of the Frontier," chapter 23.

Since the frontier is far from the court,
Their governors arrogate power.
The Masters of Writing do not monitor them,[31]
But believe their duplicitous words.
They order the destruction of commanderies and counties,
And drive the people to move into the interior.
At present, the [border] areas are once again empty and unkempt,[32]
Ensuring that the barbarians will get ideas.

Thus I have written "Populating the Frontier," chapter 24.

"Heaven gave birth to spiritual beings;
The sages used them as models."[33]
Milfoil and turtles [facilitate divining by] crack-making and sortilege,
In order to resolve apprehensions and doubt.
The vulgar technicians are shallow and ignorant;
None of them can fathom these arts.
If one aggrandizes himself but is not a worthy,
How is he worth believing?

Thus I have written "Divination Set Forth," chapter 25.

The *Book of Changes* mentions historians and spirit mediums,[34]
The *Odes* mentions skillful invocators.[35]
Sages first achieved success [with the people],
Later they expended efforts serving the spirits.[36]
When millions of people rejoice,
Is when the spirits bestow their blessings.[37]
Confucius did not pray,[38]
To show that [good fortune] resides with virtue.

Thus I have written "Spirit Mediums Set Forth," chapter 26.

The Five Phases and the Eight Trigrams,
Are generated by Yin and Yang.
Their endowment of qi can be meager or voluminous,
And by this means they manifest form.
Heaven displays these images,
But human beings bring them to completion.
If one does not cultivate his behavior,
Good fortune and prosperity will not arrive.

Thus I have written "Physiognomy Set Forth," chapter 27.

The *Odes* extols lucky dreams,[39]
Books and annals record many more.
Observing and analyzing actions and events,
The results derived from these divinations are not false.
Good fortune comes from rectitude,
Disaster comes from deficient virtue.
The response of good and bad fortune,
Is dependent on one's actions.

Thus I have written "Dreams Set Forth," chapter 28.

Arguing contentiously with wild assertions,
Makes it difficult to communicate the Way.
Later [generations] will be doubtful and confused,
And not know what [doctrine] to follow.
Since Gengzi, of earlier times,[40]
There have been those who criticize and cast doubt,
"Indeed, I am not fond of disputing";[41]
But will do so to clarify the truth.

Thus I have written "Explicating Difficulties," chapter 29.

In the relations between friends,
Its principles are preserved through the Six Bonds.[42]
It is maintained with awesome decorum;[43]
It [encourages] discussion and instruction on correct principles.[44]
It treasures old agreements,[45]
Whether honored or humble it is unwavering.
At present, the people have been adrift for a long time,[46]
So that none of them have this ability.

Thus I have written "Social Relations," chapter 30.

Only when the ruler has a fine reputation,
When his officers have good names,
And when the two are of the same mind,
Will all they desire be accomplished.[47]
With cherished power and spirit-like techniques,
Not revealing the whole situation to those below,
The state of one's rule will be complete,
And ultimately no one can topple it.[48]

Thus I have written "Enlightenment and Loyalty," chapter 31.

> Human and heavenly feelings are connected;
> Qi stimulates mutual resonance.
> Good and evil have their corresponding manifestations,
> Dissimilar extremes undergo change and transformation.
> The sage directs them,
> As if steering a boat or a carriage;
> Stimulating the vital spirit of the people,
> So that no one does not contain excellence.[49]

Thus I have written, "Teachings on the Root," chapter 32.

> In the rule of an enlightened king,
> Nothing is greater than embodying transformation.[50]
> The Way and Moral Potency are the root,
> Assisted by benevolence and righteousness.[51]
> Mindful that hearts accord with one's rule,
> Supervise the people vigorously and extensively.
> When all within the four seas are ruled in this way,
> How can any decline ensue?

Thus I have written "Transformation Through Virtue," chapter 33.

> Looking back to remote antiquity,
> [We learn of how] the Five Powers began to circulate.
> Consulting the *Odes* and the *Documents*,
> [We] examine lessons from the past.
> [When a dynasty's] qi has been depleted and reached its limit,
> The next dynasty will commence.

Though [this theory] is not necessarily correct,
It serves as the basis for traditional views.

Thus I have written "Treatise on the Five Powers," chapter 34.

The gentleman knows much,
Concerning the words and deeds of former times.
Distinguishing kin groups to discern matters,
Those in antiquity had [the resource of] clan names.
If we broadly examine [lacunae][52]

Thus I have written "A Record of Lineage and Clan Names," chapter 35.

# NOTES

## TRANSLATORS' INTRODUCTION

1. Ma Rong (ca. 89–166 CE), Dou Zhang (d. ca. 144 CE), Zhang Heng (ca. 78–139 CE), and Cui Yuan (ca. 77–142 CE) were four great intellectuals of their time.
2. Emperor He (r. 89–105); Emperor An (r. 107–125).
3. Fan Ye et al., comp. *Hou Hanshu* (Beijing: Zhonghua shuju, 1965), 49:1630. Also, for an excellent study that includes translations of fourteen of Wang Fu's essays, including the five essays included in Wang Fu's *Hou Hanshu* biography, see Margaret J. Pearson, *Wang Fu and the Comments of a Recluse* (Tempe: Center for Asian Studies, Arizona State University, 1989).
4. Huangfu Gui (104–174), a scholar and a general known for quelling the various raids on China made by the non-Chinese Qiang people from 107 to 118 and 140 to 144 CE.
5. *Hou Hanshu* 49:1643. The term 縫掖 *fengye* "large sleeves" comes from a passage of the *Liji*, "Ru Xing" (The conduct of a Confucian), which describes the garb of Confucius.
6. See Etienne Balázs, "La crise sociale et la philosophie politique à la fin des Han," *T'oung Pao* 39 (1950): 83–131; trans. H. M. Wright as "Political Philosophy and Social Crisis at the End of the Han Dynasty," in Etienne Balázs, *Chinese Civilization and Bureaucracy: Variations on a Theme*, ed. Arthur F. Wright (New Haven, CT: Yale University Press, 1964), 226–54; Pearson, *Wang Fu and the Comments of a Recluse*, 26–34;

Ch'en Ch'i-yun, "Confucian, Legalist, and Taoist Thought" in *The Cambridge History of China Volume One: The Ch'in and Han Empires, 221 B.C.–A.D. 220*, ed. Denis Twitchett and Michael Loewe (Cambridge: Cambridge University Press, 1986), 766–807; Rafe de Crespigny, *Northern Frontier: The Policies and Strategy of the Later Han Empire* (Canberra: Australian National University Press, 1984), 90; and Jin Fagen, "Wang Fu shengzu niansui de kaozheng ji *Qianfulun* xieding shijian de tuilun," *Zhongyang yanjiuyuan lishi yuyan yanjiusuo jikan* 40, no. 2 (1969): 781–99.

7. Han Yu's comments can be found in Peng Duo, *Qianfulun jian jiaozheng* (Beijing: Zhonghua shudian, 1985), 482.
8. Balázs, *Chinese Civilization and Bureaucracy*, 199.
9. Ouyang Xiu, *Ouyangxiu quanji* (Shanghai: Guoxue Zhenglishe, 1936), 17.
10. Hsiao Kung-chuan, *A History of Chinese Political Thought*, trans. F. W. Mote, (Princeton, NJ: Princeton University Press, 1979), 1:537.
11. For a concise discussion of these events, see, for example, B. J. Mansvelt Beck, "The Fall of the Han," in *The Cambridge History of China Volume One: The Ch'in and Han Empires, 221 B.C.–A.D. 220*, ed. Denis Twitchett and Michael Loewe (Cambridge: Cambridge University Press, 1986), 317–76.
12. The Five Classics are the *Book of Odes*, the *Book of Documents*, the *Spring and Autumn Annals*, the *Rites*, and the *Book of Changes*. The *Zuozhuan* and the *Guoyu* are dated to ca. 300 BCE.
13. Stephen Durrant, Wai-yee Li, and David Schaberg, trans., *Zuo Tradition: (Zuozhuan): Commentary on the Spring and Autumn Annals*, 3 vols. (Seattle: University of Washington Press, 2016), lxiii–lxiv. For a discussion of political issues at stake circa 57–167 CE, see Denis Twichett and Michael Sloane, eds., *The Cambridge History of China Volume One: The Ch'in and Han Empires, 221 B.C. to A.D. 220* (Cambridge, Cambridge University Press, 1986), 1:291–311.
14. The slightly later *Wenxuan* of Xiao Tong (501–531) includes two dialogues in its selection of *lun*, just as Wang Fu included one dialogue— "Explicating Difficulties"—in his work. Other Han *lun* are comprised of dialogues or represent colloquia such as *Yantielun*. See discussion in Anne Kinney, *The Art of the Han Essay: Wang Fu's Ch'ien-fu lun* (Tempe: Arizona State University, 1990), 31–39.

15. James R. Hightower, "The Wen Hsuan and Genre Theory," *Harvard Journal of Asian Studies* 20 (1957): 513.
16. Huang Hui, ann., *Lunheng jiaoshi*, 4 vols. (Taipei: Taiwan shangwu yinshuguan, 1983, 3:865 [juan 20, part 2, essay no. 61, "Yiwen"]; Alfred Forke, trans., *Lun-Heng*, 2 vols. (1911; reprint edition New York: Paragon Book Gallery, 1962), 2:277–78. The five classics and six arts are variously defined, though generally include the *Odes*, *Book of Documents*, *Rites*, *Book of Changes*, *Spring and Autumn Annals*, and the arts of ritual, music, archery, charioteering, writing, and mathematics.
17. Huang, *Lunheng*, 3:865, [juan 20, part 2, "Yiwen"]; Forke, *Lun-Heng*, 2:277–78.
18. For Yang Xiong, see Ban Gu, *Hanshu* (Beijing: Zhonghua shuju, 1962), 87A.3514; for Huan Tan see *Hou Hanshu*, 28A.955; for Wang Chong see *Hou Hanshu*, 49:629; for Ban Gu see *Hou Hanshu* 40A.1330.
19. *Hou Hanshu*, 3:138.
20. But Michael Schimmelpfennig, in "Tracing the Section and Sentence Commentaries (Zhangju 章句) of the Han Dynasty" [unpublished essay] examines the continued use of this form throughout the Latter Han.
21. See *Hanshu* 87B:3575; David R. Knechtges, ed. and trans., *The Han shu Biography of Yang Xiong (53 B.C.–A.D. 18)* (Tempe: Center for Asian Studies, Arizona State University, 1982), 53.
22. Huang Hui, *Lunheng*, 1112 [juan 27, "Ting Hsien"]; translation based on Forke, *Lun Heng*, 2:145–46.
23. *Qianfulun*, chapter 2, "Attending to the Basics." Following Zhang Jue, *Qianfulun jiaozhu* (Changsha: Yuelu shushe, 2008), 16–26.
24. *Hou Hanshu* 80A–B:2595–2658.
25. See Kinney, *Art of the Han Essay*, 43, 140–148.
26. See Kinney, *Art of the Han Essay*, 43.
27. See note 12 above. It is possible that he had access to the imperial library through his friends, Ma Rong 馬融 and Dou Zhang 竇章, both of whom served as Gentlemen collating Books in the Eastern Hall, where the history of the dynasty was compiled. See, for example, *Hou Hanshu*, 23.822; 60A.1954, 1972; and Pearson, *Wang Fu and the Comments of a Recluse*, 25–26.

28. See Jin Fagen,"Wang Fu shengzu niansui de kaozheng ji *Qianfulun* xieding shijian de tuilun"; Pearson, *Wang Fu and the Comments of a Recluse*, 31–32.
29. For example, the *Analects*, *Xunzi*, *Fayan*, and *Zhonglun* all commence with the topic of study. In an earlier instance, the term 勸學 *quanxue*, "promoting learning," also appears as the trait of a good ruler in *Zuozhuan*, Min 2; Durrant et al., *Zuo Tradition*, 1:247.
30. For example, see chapters 25–28 and 32–34.
31. W. A. C. H. Dobson, *Late Han Chinese* (Toronto: University of Toronto Press, 1964), xix–xx. Dobson describes the two styles that bear some similarity to these conventions: "[Late Han Literary Chinese] is contemporary, keeps abreast of change, and moves perceptibly toward Modern Chinese. Another form [Late Han Classical Chinese] is conservative, deliberately retaining, under the influence of canonical authority, archaic forms and features. . . . Late Han Classical Chinese is not a pure imitation of Archaic Chinese. It is a form in which archaic features give an antique effect. Late Han Literary Chinese avoids these archaisms." Also see William H. Baxter, "Situating the Language of the *Lao-tzu*," in *Lao-tzu and the Tao-te-ching*, ed. Livia Kohn and Michael LaFargue (Albany: State University of New York Press, 1998), 237.
32. Further comments on these two styles can be found in Bernhard Karlgren, "Excursions in Chinese Grammar," *Bulletin of the Museum of Far Eastern Antiquities* 23 (1951): 107–33.
33. On the concept of the Great Peace in Han times, see David Rogacz, "The Idea of Supreme Peace (Taiping) in Premodern Chinese Philosophies of History," *Asian Studies* 26 no. 1 (2022): 401–24.
34. *Shijing*, *Xiao Ya*, "Tian Bao," Mao no. 166, translation based on James Legge, trans., *Chinese Classics*, 5 vols. (Hong Kong: Chinese University of Hong Kong Press, 1970), 4:255–56; and Bernhard Karlgren, *The Book of Odes* (Stockholm: Museum of Far Eastern Antiquities, 1950), "Siao Ya Odes," 34; also Karlgren, *Glosses on the Book of Odes* (Stockholm: Museum of Far Eastern Antiquities, 1964), 109.
35. *Qianfulun* 30, "On Social Relations."
36. Reconstructed phonetics based on Axel Schuessler, *Minimal Old Chinese and Later Han Chinese* (Honolulu: University of Hawai'i Press, 2009).

37. Wang Yunwu and Zhang Yuanqi, eds., *Sibu congkan zhengbian*, 100 vols. (Taibei: Taiwan shangwu yinshuguan, 1979), vol. 18.
38. See Peng Duo, *Qianfulun jian jiaozheng* (Beijing: Zhonghua shuju, 1985), 487. A 1305 edition based on an unspecified earlier edition was printed with the *Baihutong* and *Fengsu tongyi* but was dismissed by Wang Jipei as defective in comparison to that of the *Han Wei Congshu* edition of 1592.
39. Further information on editions can be found in Pearson, *Wang Fu and the Comments of a Recluse*, 173–76.

## CHAPTER I. IN PRAISE OF STUDY

1. See *Xunzi*, chap. 9, "Wangzhi": "Humans possess vital breath, life, and awareness, and add to them a sense of morality and justice. It is for this reason that they are the noblest beings in the world." John Knoblock, *Xunzi: A Translation and Study of the Complete Work*, 3 vols. (Stanford, CA: Stanford University Press, 1988–1994), 2:104.
2. *Lunyu* XVII:23: "The Master said, 'The superior man holds righteousness to be of highest importance'"; James Legge, trans., *The Chinese Classics* (Hong Kong: Chinese University of Hong Kong Press, 1970), 1:329.
3. Huangdi, Zhuan Xu, Di Ku, Yao, and Shun were rulers of the legendary period. Yu is credited with founding the Xia dynasty, Tang established the Shang dynasty, Kings Wen and Wu were the first two rulers of the Zhou, and the Duke of Zhou served as regent to the son of King Wu. Confucius, as the "uncrowned king" also appears in this list. Some scholars believed that Confucius had been a pupil of Lao Dan, the supposed author of the *Laozi*. Hu Chusheng identifies Shu Xiu as Guo Shu, the son of Wang Ji. The divergent and multitudinous accounts of these figures are too numerous to list. A standard overview is provided in Sima Qian, *Shiji*, 10 vols. (Beijing: Zhonghua shuju, 1959), 1–4:1–124; and translated in William H. Nienhauser Jr, trans. and ed., *The Grand Scribe's Records*, 10 vols. (Bloomington: Indiana University Press, 2018–2020), 1:1–61.
4. Compare *Analects* XV:9; Legge, *The Chinese Classics*, 1: 297.
5. Following Wang Jipei's decision to not emend this phrase.

6. *Yijing*, "Da Xu," in Juan Yuan, *Shisanjing zhushu*, 2 vols. (Beijing: Zhonghua shuju, 1979), 1:40 [*juan* 3, p. 28]; James Legge, *The I Ching* (1899; reprint New York: Dover, 1963), 300.
7. The jade arc and jade disc were ceremonial objects. The Xiahou clan possessed a precious stone that was associated with the ducal house of Lu. See *Zuozhuan*, Ding 4; Stephen Durrant, Wai-yee Li, and David Schaberg, trans., *Zuo Tradition* (Zuozhuan): *Commentary on the Spring and Autumn Annals* (Seattle: University of Washington Press, 2016), 3:1749. According to legend, Bian He, also known as He of Chu, found a rock and claimed that it held within a large and valuable piece of jade. When he presented it to the king, the royal lapidary dismissed it as an ordinary stone and had He punished. Later, the stone was opened and He's claim was verified. See *Han Feizi*, in D. C. Lau., ed. *Han Feizi Zhuzi Suoyin* (Hong Kong: The Commercial Press, 2000), 23; translated in W. K. Liao, *The Complete Works of Han Fei Tzu*, 2 vols. (London: Arthur Probsthain 1939), 1:113.
8. The *fu* and *gui* are ritual vessels used to hold food offerings and were made of wood.
9. Chui is mentioned in the *Shangshu* as Shun's minister of works and later came to be known as an ingenious craftsman and master woodworker. See *Shangshu*, "Shun Dian," in Legge, *The Chinese Classics*, 3:45. Also see John S. Major, "Tool Metaphors in the *Huainanzi* and Other Early Texts," in *The Huainanzi and Textual Production in Early China*, ed. Sarah A. Queen and Michael Puett (Leiden: Brill, 2014), 153–98.
10. *Analects* XIV:13; Legge, *The Chinese Classics*, 1:279.
11. *Shijing*, Xiao Ya, "Xiao Yuan," Mao no. 196; Legge, *The Chinese Classics*, 4:322.
12. *Zhou Yi*, "Qian," in *Shisanjing zhushu*, 1:13 [*juan* 1, p. 1]. Translation based on Legge, *The I Ching*, 57.
13. *Analects*: XV:30–31; translation based on Arthur Waley, *Confucianism: The Analects of Confucius* (New York: Harper Collins, 1992), 199.
14. Master of Ji was a loyal servitor of the defeated Shang dynasty. He received the territory of Ji from the newly established Zhou King Wu. The "Six Limitations" are conditions Heaven visits upon people to instill a sense of awe. They are misfortunes that cause early death, sickness, sorrow, poverty, physical deformity, or weakness. See *Shangshu*, "Hong Fan"; Legge, *The Chinese Classics*, 3:343.

15. *Shijing*, *Guo Feng*, "Bei Men," Mao no. 40; Legge, *The Chinese Classics*, 4:65–66. This ode bewails the poet's poverty and fatigue.
16. Dong Zhongshu (ca. 179–104 BCE) was a Confucian philosopher and statesman of the Han dynasty. Jing Junming, better known as Jing Fang (fl. 48 BCE), was a statesman and specialist in the *Yijing*.
17. Reading 養 *yang* as 巷 *xiang*. Ni Kuan (fl. ca. 111 BCE), a specialist in the *Shangshu*, served as imperial counselor. Kuang Heng (fl. ca. 45 BCE), a specialist in the *Odes* and *Rites*, served as chancellor under Han Emperors Yuan and Cheng. See *Hanshu* 58: 2628; 81:3331.
18. Following Wang Jipei's reading of this line.
19. Following Wang Jipei's reading of 逮 *dai* as 違 *wei* and 及 *ji* as 反 *fan*.
20. Zao Fu was a legendary charioteer of the Western Zhou dynasty.
21. Yu Yue argues for reading the text as is: "If a sailor set afloat with a carriage axle, after releasing the moorings, he would sink." He nevertheless does not explain why this unlikely situation would ever occur. No explanation is necessary to understand the parallel example of Zao Fu. Wang Jipei and Zhang Jue read "axle" 軸 *zhu* as 舳 *zhu*, "the stern of a boat," a reasonable interpretation since it is unclear why someone would use the axle of a carriage as a flotation device or how a rope would figure in this scenario. Zhang argues that Wang Fu is using the analogy of a battle ship that uses a line of boats linked with ropes closely following each other (usually written 舳艫 *zhulu*, literally "prow to stern") to do battle. A nautical but nonmilitary example of boats floating prow to stern is mentioned in the description of a tour of inspection made by Emperor Wu, but commentators suggest the phrase is simply a literary way of suggesting a long train of boats. See *Hanshu* 5:196; translated in Homer H. Dubs, trans., *The History of the Former Han Dynasty* (Baltimore: Waverly Press, 1938), 2:95. Zhang suggests that linking the boats would stabilize them, though that is not a likely outcome. Another possible understanding of the passage, reflected in the translation above, is that the sailor (or the sailor in a small boat) is attached to the hawser in order to perform some service—to repair the ship or retrieve something from the water. For naval expeditions in Han times, see Joseph Needham, *Science and Civilization in China* (Cambridge: Cambridge University Press, 1971), 4.3:226.
22. See *Xunzi*, "Quan xue"; Knoblock, *Xunzi*, 1:136.

23. Xi Zhong was a mythical Master of Chariots of the founder of the Xia dynasty. See *Zuozhuan*, Ding 1; Durrant et al., *Zuo Tradition*, 3:1733. Gong Ban, a skilled artisan of the Spring and Autumn period, is mentioned in *Mencius* IV:1; Legge, *The Chinese Classics*, 2:288.
24. *Shijing, Xiao Ya*, "Ju Xia," Mao no. 218; Legge, *The Chinese Classics*, 4:393.
25. *Shijing, Song*, "Jing Zhi," Mao no. 288; Legge, *The Chinese Classics*, 4:322; and Bernhard Karlgren, trans., *The Book of Odes* (Stockholm: Museum of Far Eastern Antiquities, 1950), 249.

## CHAPTER 2. CONCENTRATING ON THE ROOT

1. The sorting of ideas, actions, and physical phenomena into the paired opposite categories of *ben* 本 and *mo* 末 "root" and "branch," and which, by extension also designated further pairings such as primary/secondary, essential/superficial, and essential/inessential, was an important concept in early Chinese philosophy. The terms appear in *Analects* (I:2 XIX:12) and in a wide range of Han sources. For a discussion see John S. Major, *Heaven and Earth in Early Han Thought: Chapters Three, Four, and Five of the* Huainanzi (Albany: State University of New York Press, 1993), 15–22. Wang Fu's inclusion of an entire essay devoted to this concept signals its importance throughout the work.
2. See *Guanzi*, chapter 48, "It is ever so that the way to maintain good order in a state is to be certain, first of all, to make its people prosperous." W. Allyn Rickett, *Guanzi*, 2 vols. (Princeton, NJ: Princeton University Press, 1985), 2:176.
3. See *Analects* XIII:9: The Master observed, "How numerous are the people!" You said, "Since they are thus numerous, what more shall be done for them?" "Enrich them," was the reply. "And when they have been enriched, what more shall be done?" The Master said, "Teach them." James Legge, trans., *The Chinese Classics*, 5 vols. (Hong Kong: Chinese University of Hong Kong Press, 1970), 1:266–67.
4. *Lüshi Chunqiu*, 17/5.2; "Zhidu"; John Knoblock and Jeffrey Reigel, trans., *The Annals of Lü Buwei* (Stanford, CA: Stanford University Press, 2000), 423.

5. Gao You's (ca. 168–212 CE) commentary to *Lüshi Chunqiu*, "Zhi Du," defines 淫學 *yinxue* as 不學正道 *buxue zhengdao*. See Knoblock and Reigel, *The Annals of Lu Buwei*, 423.
6. The phrase translated as "eminent scholar-officials" 列士/烈士 *lieshi*, is also found in the *Xunzi*. See Wang Yunwu, *Sibu congkan zhengbian*, vol. 17, 19:19A [大略 "Da Lüe"], in John Knoblock, trans., *Xunzi: A Translation and Study of the Complete Work* (Stanford, CA: Stanford University Press, 1994), 3:228.
7. The five categories are educational instruction, speech and expression, exemplary officials, filial offspring, and those in the service of others.
8. Compare with *Guanzi*, 立政 *lizheng*; translated in Rickett, *Guanzi*, 1:103.
9. Literally, what is counted *ji* 計 in the nation's financial resources; i.e., the economy.
10. The term *shanggu* 商賈 translated as "trade," according to the *Baihutong* 白虎通, is actually a binome that combines two different kinds of trade: "What does *shanggu* 'trade' mean? *Shang* means 'to estimate'; to estimate the distance, to measure what is enough and what is wanting, to distribute the goods to the four quarters. Therefore we speak of *shang*. *Gu* means 固 *gu* 'to preserve'; to preserve the useful wares, and therewith to await the people's coming to look for what may be of profit to them. The traveling [trade is] called *shang*, the sedentary [trade is] called *gu*." See Tjoe Som Tjan, trans., *Po Hu T'ung: The Comprehensive Discussions in the White Tiger Hall*, 2 vols. (Leiden: Brill, 1949–1952; reprint, Westport, CT: Hyperion Press, 1973), 2:537.
11. The three groups are those engaged in itinerant occupations, craftsmen, and merchants.
12. Reference to those who discuss "matters of emptiness and nothingness" may tacitly refer to Huan Tan's comments on the *Dao De Jing* quoted in the biography of Yang Xiong (53 BCE–18 CE); see *Hanshu* 87B:3585.
13. On the function of "metaphors" *xing* 興, see James J. Y. Liu, *Chinese Theories of Literature* (Chicago: University of Chicago Press, 1979), 109.
14. Following Zhang Jue.
15. See *Liji*, "Nei Ze"; James Legge, trans., *Li Chi*, 2 vols. (New York: University Books, 1967), 1:467; "A filial son, in nourishing his aged, (seeks

to) make their hearts glad, and not to go against their wishes" 樂其心不違其志.

16. The "five" refers to the five groups of learned men categorized as writers who promote empty doctrines, those who compose bombastic works of rhyme-prose and eulogies, officials who concentrate on making connections and cultivating advantageous relationships, officials who neglect family and use lavish funerals to promote an image of filial piety, and sycophantic officials who pervert the cause of justice.

17. The eight include the five listed above and the three groups mentioned in the beginning of the essay: itinerant occupations, craftsmen, and merchants.

18. Following Zhang Jue. There may be a lacuna after the phrase 禍福之所 *huofu zhi suo*; the missing character is likely *zai* 在.

19. This sentence has been emended to read: 此誠治亂之漸 *zhi luan zhi jian*. The term *jian* 漸 refers to the gradual development of a social or political trend, in this case, the spread of nonessential occupations.

## CHAPTER 3. SUPPRESSING PROFIT

1. Wang Xianqian notes missing and disordered graphs in this sentence. Following Zhang Jue's reconstruction.
2. Lacuna reconstructed by Wang Jipei.
3. *Shangshu*, Zhou Shu, "Jiu Gao," 酒誥; James Legge, trans., *The Chinese Classics*, 5 vols. (Hong Kong: Chinese University of Hong Kong Press, 1970), 3:409–10: "'Let not men look only into water; let them look into the glass of other people.' Now that Yin has lost its favoring appointment, ought we not to look much to it as our glass and learn how to secure the repose of our time? '人無於水監，當於民監.'今惟殷墜厥命，我其可不大監撫于時!"
4. *Zuozhuan*, Huan 10; Stephen Durrant, Wai-yee Li, and David Schaberg, trans., *Zuo Tradition* (Zuozhuan)*: Commentary on the Spring and Autumn Annals* (Seattle: University of Washington Press, 2016), 1:111: "The younger brother of the Duke of Yu had possessed a jade. The Duke of Yu asked him for it, but Yu would not offer it. Afterward, the younger brother regretted this and said, 'A Zhou proverb has it that *A*

*common man may be without crime, until cherishing a valuable jade becomes his crime* [italics added to set apart quoted proverb]. What use do I have of this that I should use it to buy harm for myself. What use do I have of this?' So he offered it. The duke also asked for his precious sword, and his younger brother said, 'That one cannot be satisfied. And if he cannot be satisfied, harm will come to me.' Thereupon, he attacked the Duke of Yu, and that is why the Duke of Yu fled to Gongchi."

5. Deng Tong was a male favorite of Han Emperor Wen. The emperor presented him with his own copper mine from which he was able to produce his own coinage. He lost his position and wealth after the death of Emperor Wen. See *Shiji* 125:3191–3193; Burton Watson, trans., *Records of the Grand Historian*, 2 vols. (New York: Columbia University Press, 1961/1993), 2:419–21.

6. See *Shiji* 58:2083–85; Watson, *Records of the Grand Historian*, I:381–84. These two men plotted with the King of Liang to assassinate Yuan Ang in an effort to position the King of Liang as Emperor Jing's successor.

7. King Li reigned ca. 857–842 BCE.

8. *Shijing*, Da Ya, "Sang Rou,"桑柔, Mao no. 257; Legge, *The Chinese Classics*, 4:519–27.

9. *Zuozhuan*, Huan 10; Durrant et al., *Zuo Tradition*, 1:111. See note 4 above.

10. *Zuozhuan*, Ding 13; Durrant et al., *Zuo Tradition*, 3:1813: "The scribe Qiu said, . . . Whoever is wealthy and yet can act as a subject can always be saved from trouble. It is the same whether one is highborn or low. As for your son Gongshu Shu, he is arrogant, and he will fall. Few are the men who are wealthy and yet not arrogant; you are the only such man I have seen. And there has never been a man who was arrogant and yet did not fall. Gongshu Shu will be one of these."

11. *Zuozhuan*, Ai 14; Durrant et al., *Zuo Tradition*, 3:1931—no mention is made of Tui's drinking or his death, though he was in possession of a precious jade that prompted an attack in Wei.

12. See Shanghai Shifan Daxue Guji zhengli xiaozu, *Guoyu* (Shanghai: Guji chubanshe, 1978), "Chuyu," 2.3:572.

13. *Zuozhuan*, Cheng 16; Durrant et al., *Zuo Tradition*, 2:851.

14. Zihan is also known as Yue Xi. See *Zuozhuan*, Xiang 15; Durrant et al., *Zuo Tradition*, 2:1035–36; for Yanzi, see Zhao 3; Durrant et al., *Zuo Tradition*, 3:1351–52.
15. See *Analects* XVI:12. The two were worthies who preferred starving to serving a new regime.
16. See *Shijing*, Xiao Ya, "Bai Ju," 白駒, Mao no. 186; Legge, *Chinese Classics*, 4:299–300. The ode alludes to an officer praised for his purity. For Jie Zhitui, see *Zuozhuan*, Xi 24; Durrant et al., *Zuo Tradition*, 1: 379. He refused any reward after providing great assistance to Chong'er.
17. For Dong Zhongshu (ca. 195–104 BCE) see *Hanshu* 56:2495; see also Sarah A. Queen and John S. Major, trans., *Luxuriant Gems of the Spring and Autumn, Attributed to Dong Zhongshu* (New York: Columbia University Press, 2015), 2–10. Shu Guang (ca. 73–49 BCE), was senior tutor to the future Emperor Yuan who spent the imperial bounty he had received on his elders; *Hanshu* 71:3039.
18. Ji of Cao was a Spring and Autumn era grandee of the state of Cao who advised his lord on the need for interstate civility and later formed friendly relations with Chong'er of Jin. *Guoyu*, "Jin Yu," 4.5. Translation based on Eric Henry, trans., *Conversations of the States* (Seattle: University of Washington Press, forthcoming).
19. Following Peng Duo.
20. "The dragon exceeds the proper limits—there will be occasion for repentance."*Yijing*, "Tuan," on Hexagram 15: "Qian"; James Legge, trans., *The I Ching*, 1899, reprint (New York: Dover, 1963), 226.
21. *Yijing*, Hexagram 1: "Qian"; Legge, *The I Ching*, 58, 226. The individual lines of this hexagram are associated with the movements of a dragon. The sixth line shows it "exceeding its proper limits," and the need for repentance.

## CHAPTER 4. APPRAISING EMINENCE

1. *Chuci* 楚辭, "Shan Gui," 山鬼: "So late in the year, who will glorify me? / with what flowers can I deck myself/who will favor me [歲既晏兮孰華予]?
2. See *Shiji* 3:106; William H. Nienhauser Jr., trans. and ed., *The Grand Scribe's Records*, 10 vols. (Bloomington: Indiana University Press,

2018–2020), 1:50. The Marquis of Chong and E Lai supported Djou, the evil last ruler of the Shang dynasty.
3. *Shiji* 61:2121–27; Nienhauser, *Grand Scribe's Records*, 7:1–6.
4. For Fu Yue see, *Lüshi Chunqiu* 22.5 "Qiu Ren," 求人; John Knoblock and Jeffrey Riegel, trans., *The Annals of Lü Buwei* (Stanford, CA: Stanford University Press, 2004), 579; for Jing Bo and the Duke of Yu, see *Zuozhuan*, Xi 5; Stephen Durrant, Wai-yee Li, and David Schaberg, trans., *Zuo Tradition* (Zuozhuan)*: Commentary on the Spring and Autumn Annals* (Seattle: University of Washington Press, 2016), 1:278.
5. The two kinds of fate controlled by Heaven are wealth and honor. See *Analects* XII:5.
6. *Shijing*, Guo Feng, "Bei Men" 北門, Mao no. 40; James Legge, trans., *The Chinese Classics* (Hong Kong: Chinese University of Hong Kong Press, 1970), 4:65.
7. *Yijing* "Qian" 乾, 上九: 亢龍有悔。 "In the sixth (or topmost line), undivided (we see its subject as) the dragon exceeding the proper limits. There will be occasion for repentance." James Legge, trans., *The I Ching* (1899; reprint New York: Dover, 1963), 58. The "Great Appendix," 1.1 explains how the hexagram "Qian" is lofty and honorable, whereas the hexagram "Kun" is mean. The two have their assigned places based on these distinctions.
8. *Shangshu*, "Yi Ji,"益稷; Legge, *The Chinese Classics*, 3:84. Also see Richard John Lynn, *The Classic of Changes* (New York: Columbia University Press, 1994), 138–39.
9. *Shangshu*, "Yao Dian,"堯典; Legge, *The Chinese Classics*, 3:26.
10. *Zuozhuan*, Zhao, 10, 13, 14; Durrant et al., *Zuo Tradition*, 3:1457, 1503, 1519. As a high minister in the state of Jin 晉 during the reign of Duke Dao 晉悼公 (r. 573–558), Shu Xiang, also called Yangshe Xi 羊舌肸, was appointed tutor of crown prince Biao 彪. His brother, Yangshe Fu 羊舌鮒 (d. 528), was a crooked arbiter of legal cases.
11. Jiyou was a son of Duke Huan of Lu 魯桓公 (r. 712–694 BCE) and the ancestor of the lateral house Jisun 季孫. He served as a high minister to Dukes Min 魯閔公 (r. 662–660 BCE) and Xi 魯僖公 (r. 660–627 BCE) of the state of Lu 魯. Ji You's older brother, Duke Zhuang consulted with Jiyou on naming a successor. Later, Qingfu, a son whom Jiyou had earlier rejected as a successor to Duke Zhuang, murdered

Jiyou's choice of successor, i.e., Ban. See *Zuozhuan*, Zhuang 32; Durrant et al., *Zuo Tradition*, 1:225, after which Duke Min was enthroned.

12. *Zuozhuan*, Xiang 21; Durrant et al., *Zuo Tradition*, 2:1087.
13. *Zuozhuan*, Zhao 20; Durrant, *Zuo Tradition*, 3:1579. This specific quotation does not appear in the *Shangshu*.
14. King Li (r. 878–828 BCE) was a tyrant who was overthrown; King You (r. 781–771 BCE) was held responsible for the fall of the Western Zhou dynasty.
15. Yuan Xian is more commonly known as Zisi 子思. See *Analects* XI:18; Legge, *The Chinese Classics*, 1:243.
16. *Analects* XVIII:10; "The virtuous prince . . . does not seek in one man talents for every employment." Translated in Legge, *The Chinese Classics*, 1: 338.
17. You Yu of the Rong assisted King Mu of Qin in expanding his territory; Meng of the Yue assisted the state of Qi. See *Shiji* 83.2473; Nienhauser, *Grand Scribe's Records*, 7:289.
18. Zhang Yi was a diplomat of the Warring States period noted for his amoral tactics; see *Shiji* 70:2279; Nienhauser, *Grand Scribe's Records*, 7:123. Kang Shu was a younger brother of King Wu of Zhou and a virtuous minister to King Cheng; see *Shiji* 37:1589. Wei Yang is better known as Shang Yang. See *Shiji* 68:2227; translated in Nienhauser, *Grand Scribe's Records*, 7:87–96. His policies enabled Qin to conquer its six rival states and unify China into a centralized state.
19. This phrase is similar to that in *Shijing*, Xiao Ya, "Qing ying" 青蠅 Mao Ode 219; Legge, *The Chinese Classics*, 4:394.
20. Following Zhang Jue.
21. Bian He, also known as He of Chu, found a rock and claimed that it held within a large and valuable piece of jade. When he presented it to the king, the royal lapidary said it was nothing but an ordinary stone and had He punished. Later, the stone was opened and He's claim was verified. The Marquis of Sui is first mentioned in *Chunqiu*, Ai 1; but no mention of the pearl occurs there. The *Mozi* seems to contain one of the earlier references to the pearl; see Yi-Pao Mei, trans., *The Ethical and Political Works of Motse* (London: Arthur Probsthain, 1929), 215–16.
22. *Shijing*, Bei Feng, "Gu Feng" 谷風, Mao no. 35; translated in Legge, *The Chinese Classics*, 4:55.

23. For Chen Ping, see *Shiji* 56:2051; translated in Yang Hsien-yi, *Selections from Records of the Historian* (Beijing: Foreign Language Press, 1979), 253–65; and Burton Watson, trans., *Records of the Grand Historian: Han Dynasty* (New York: Columbia University, 1993), I:117. For Han Xin, see *Shiji* 93:2631; Nienhauser, *Grand Scribe's Records*, 8.1:109.
24. For both men, see *Shiji* 111:2921–28; Nienhauser, *Grand Scribe's Records*, 9.2:311–54. An alternate reading of the phrase 私人 *siren* is "humble individuals" of Pingyang. The "Northern Di" refers to the Xiongnu. Hexi refers to an area in Qinghai and Gansu west of the Yellow River.

## CHAPTER 5. THE DIFFICULTIES OF THE WORTHY

1. For a negative portrayal of Shun, see *Han Feizi* in D. C. Lau, ed. *A Concordance to the Han Feizi*, "Wu Du," 134, translated in W. K. Liao, trans., *The Complete Works of Han Fei Tzu*, 2 vols. (London: Arthur Probsthain, 1939), 2:224. On Wu Zixu, see *Zuozhuan* Ai 11; Stephen Durrant, Wai-yee Li, and David Schaberg, trans., *Zuo Tradition (Zuozhuan): Commentary on the Spring and Autumn Annals* (Seattle: University of Washington Press, 2016), 3:1901–02. The "Wudu" chapter of the *Han Feizi* mentions people of remote antiquity, who strove to be known as moral and virtuous, while those of the "middle age" (中世 *zhong shi*) strove to be wise and resourceful. Next Han Feizi mentions people of the present age. It is unlikely that Wang Fu is here referring to the "middle age" rather than the "present age." We therefore follow Zhang Jue's reconstruction this sentence. See Lau, *A Concordance to the Han Feizi*, 146; translated in Liao, *The Complete Works of Han Fei Tzu*, 2:279.
2. On the Marquis of Qi (r. 484–481 BCE), see *Zuozhuan* Ai 14; Durrant et al., *Zuo Tradition*, 3:1923. The marquis of Qi placed his trust in the man who eventually ousted and killed him. For the Duke of Lu (r. 541–510 BCE), whose misplaced trust forced him into exile, see *Zuozhuan* Zhao 25, 32; Durrant et al., *Zuo Tradition*, 3:1635, 1647. Allusions in the final phrase in this paragraph come from Xiang 31; Durrant et al., *Zuo Tradition*, 3:1289: "Take an example from hunting: if a man is schooled in shooting and driving, he will then be able to capture birds and animals. If he has never ascended a carriage to shoot and drive, then he

will fear that he will be defeated in his purpose, that his carriage will overturn and he will be crushed. How can he spare any time or attention to think of capturing anything?"

3. See *Shiji* 6:255, 258; William H. Nienhauser Jr., trans. and ed., *The Grand Scribe's Records*, 10 vols. (Bloomington: Indiana University Press, 2018–2020), 1:147, 150.

4. Deng Tong's story is found in *Shiji* 125:3192–93. Emperor Wen reigned 179–157 BCE. The crown prince is the future emperor Jing (r. 157–141 BCE).

5. Following Hu Dajun et al., *Wang Fu Qianfulun yizhu* (Lanzhou: Gansu renmin chubanshe, 1991), 43.

6. This statement echoes *Analects* 5.1, 18.1; James Legge, trans., *The Chinese Classics* (Hong Kong: Chinese University of Hong Kong Press, 1970), 1:173, 331. Prince Bigan argued that officials were obliged to criticize their rulers even if it meant death. King Djou justified his execution by saying that he wanted to see if it was true that a sage's heart had seven apertures. Jizi likewise criticized the ruler, but after learning of Bi Gan's fate, he feigned madness and sold himself as a slave. Bo Zong was unsparing in his criticism of his betters; and Xi Wan was an upright official slandered and murdered by rivals. For Bi Gan and Jizi, see *Shiji* 3:107–108; Nienhauser, *Grand Scribe's Records*, 1:51. For Bo Zong, see, *Zuozhuan*, 2 15; Durrant et al., *Zuo Tradition*, 2:823; for Xi Wan, see *Zuozhuan*, Zhao 27; Durrant et al., *Zuo Tradition*, 3:1677.

7. For Fan Ju and Bai Qi, see *Shiji* 79:2401–25; 73:2337; for Dong Zhongshu and Gongsun Hong, see *Shiji* 121:3127–28.

8. For Sun Bin (d. 316 BCE), an alleged descendant of Sunzi, see *Shiji* 65:2162; Nienhauser, *Grand Scribe's Records*, 7:39, where Nienhauser points out that the word *bin* in Sun's name is not a true name but a reference to his amputation. Pang Juan (d. 341 BCE) served in Wei.

9. Han Fei (ca. 280–233 BCE); Li Si (ca. 280–208 BCE). *Shiji* 63:2155; Nienhauser, *Grand Scribe's Records*, 7:2.

10. For Jing Fang (ca. 77–37 BCE) and Emperor Yuan (r. 48–33 BCE), see *Hanshu* 75:3160–67; and Jack Dull, "A Historical Introduction to the Apocryphal (*Ch'an-wei*) Texts of the Han Dynasty" (PhD diss., University of Washington, 1966), 84–89.

11. For Chao Cuo (d. 154 BCE), see *Shiji* 101:2745–48; Nienhauser, *Grand Scribe's Records*, 8.1:343–50. He made the radical decision to reduce the

size of the territories held by feudal lords who had committed crimes. For further description of his policies, see Hsiao Kung-chuan [Xiao Gongchuan], *A History of Chinese Political Thought*, trans. F. W. Mote, vol. 1 (Princeton, NJ: Princeton University Press, 1979), 1:454. Jing Fang believed that natural disasters were an expression of governmental mismanagement. He criticized powerful figures for their administrative failures and on this basis he was accused of treason and executed.

12. Di Yi is also known as Shang Tang 商湯 or Cheng Tang 成湯. His name is recorded on oracle bones as Da Yi (大乙). He led troops against and was imprisoned by Jie, the last evil ruler of the Xia dynasty. See *Shiji* 2:88; 3:93; Nienhauser, *Grand Scribe's Records*, 1:38, 42.
13. See *Shiji* 4:116; Nienhauser, *Grand Scribe's Records*, 1:58.
14. On Confucius becoming a fugitive in Wei, see *Zhuangzi*, "Dao Zhi 盜跖," translated in Richard John Lynn, trans., *Zhuangzi: A New Translation of the Sayings of Master Zhuang as Interpreted by Guo Xiang* (New York: Columbia University Press, 2022), 510.
15. For Shu Xiang (fl. ca. 551 BCE), see *Zuozhuan* Xiang 21, Durrant et al., *Zuo Tradition*, 2:1083; Wang Zhang, see *Hanshu* 76:3238; Qu Yuan (fl. 299 BCE) see *Shiji* 84:2490, in Nienhauser, *Grand Scribe's Records*, 7:301; Jia Yi (ca. 201–169 BCE) *Shiji* 84:2492, in Nienhauser, *Grand Scribe's Records*, 7:302; Zhong Li (fl. 39 CE), see *Hou Hanshu* 41:1406–11; He Chang (fl. 86 CE), see *Hou Hanshu* 43:1480–88; Wang Zhang (d. 24 CE), see *Hanshu* 76; Ping'a was the name of the marquisate of Wang Ren 王仁 (d. 3 CE), see *Hanshu* 98:4029; 99A:4065.
16. *Shijing*, *Xiao Ya*, "Shi Yue Zhi Jiao 十月之交," Mao no. 193; Legge, *The Chinese Classics*, 4:323; and "Yuliu" 菀柳, Mao no. 224 in Legge, *The Chinese Classics*, 4:407.
17. See *Odes, Lu Song*, "You Bi," Mao no. 298; translated in Legge, *Chinese Classics*, 4.614. The ode describes how the ruler and his ministers feasted together after transacting their business.
18. "Sacks tied up" refers to staying hidden or keeping one's mouth shut. See *Yijing*, "Kan" hexagram. See Lynn, *Classic of Changes*, 148.
19. This phrase is likely a version of the saying, "to grab the dust and grasp sounds" 捕風捉影, and refers to forming an opinion of someone based on hearsay.

20. On Bao Jiao, see *Hanshi waizhuan* 1:27, translated in James Robert Hightower, *Han Shih Wai Chuan: Han Ying's Illustrations of the Didactic Application of the* Classic of Songs, (Cambridge, MA: Harvard University Press, 1953), 35; for Xu Yan, see *Shiji* 83:2473, Nienhauser, *Grand Scribe's Records*, 7:289. Both brought about their own deaths in condemnation of the state of the world.
21. The term "manager of beasts" (獸臣司原 *shouchen siyuan*) appears in the "Remonstrance of the Overseer of Hunts" (虞人之箴 *yuren zhi zhen*) found in *Zuozhuan* Xiang 4; Durrant et al., *Zuo Tradition*, 2:919. Echoes of *Shijing*, Mao no. 197, "Xiao Pan," which bewails the effects of slanderers, are also present in this tale. See Legge, *The Chinese Classics*, 4:338.
22. *Shijing Xiao Ya*, "Jie Nan Shan" 節南山; Mao no. 191; Legge, *The Chinese Classics*, 4:310.

## CHAPTER 6. THE ENLIGHTENED AND THE UNENLIGHTENED

1. Following Zhang Jue, *Qianfulun quanyi*, 87nn2–3. Also see *Analects* IX:4, in James Legge, trans., *The Chinese Classics*, 5 vols. (Hong Kong: Chinese University of Hong Kong Press, 1970), 1:217.
2. *Shijing*, *Da Ya*, "Ban 板," Mao no. 25; Legge, *The Chinese Classics*, 4:501.
3. See *Shangshu*, "Shundian" 舜典, in Legge, *The Chinese Classics*, 3:41–42: "He deliberated with the chiefs of the four mountains how to throw open all the doors of communications between the court and the empire, and sought to see with the eyes and hear with the ears of all."
4. See *Shangshu* in Legge, *The Chinese Classics*, 3:23–24, 39–42. Gong Gong and Gun were legendary criminals of high antiquity noted for their disobedience and treachery.
5. The text is corrupt at this point.
6. See *Shiji* 6:269–270; William H. Nienhauser Jr., trans. and ed., *The Grand Scribe's Records*, 10 vols. (Bloomington: Indiana University Press, 2018–2020), 1:157. Zhou Zhang was a general under the rebel king Chen She.
7. Yan Le was the son-in-law of Zhao Gao and prefect of Xianyang; See *Shiji* 6:274; Nienhauser, *Grand Scribe's Records*, 1:161–162.

6. THE ENLIGHTENED AND THE UNENLIGHTENED ⟪ 451

8. Following Zhang Jue. Also see *Zuozhuan*, Xiang 26; Stephen Durrant, Wai-yee Li, and David Schaberg, trans., *Zuo Tradition* (Zuozhuan): *Commentary on the Spring and Autumn Annals* (Seattle: University of Washington Press, 2016), 2:1162.
9. Zhang Lu was originally known as Fan Sui (fl. 266 BCE) but changed his name to preserve his life. Marquis Rang (fl. ca. 271 BCE) was prime minister of Qin. See *Shiji* 79:2402–08; Nienhauser, *Grand Scribe's Records*, 7:233–40.
10. Yuan Si, also known as Yuan Ang (d. ca. 148 BCE), was a palace gentleman under Han Emperor Wen (r. 180–157 BCE). See *Shiji* 101:2737–38; Nienhauser, *Grand Scribe's Records*, 8.1:323–28. Zhou Bo (fl. 179 BCE).
11. The phrase 當塗 *dangtu*, "occupying the road," means "holding official appointments."
12. See *Shiji* 6:271; translated in Nienhauser, *Grand Scribe's Records*, 1:159. The self-designation is *zhen* 朕.
13. The "rotten fish" refers to being beyond salvation.
14. See *Shiji* 6274–275; Nienhauser, *Grand Scribe's Records*, 1:161–62.
15. On Tian Chang, see *Zuozhuan* Ai 14; Durrant et al., *Zuo Tradition*, 3:1925–27. Tian Chang (c. 481 BCE) is also known as Chen Changzi and Chen Heng. For Zhuo Chi see, *Zhanguoce* in SBCK juan 3:48B; translated in James I. Crump, trans., *Chan-kuo ts'e* (rev. ed.) (Ann Arbor: Center for Chinese Studies, University of Michigan, 1996), 108. King Min reigned ca. 300–284 BCE. Xunzi wrote of King Min: "When later generations teach about evil, they must examine his case." See John Knoblock, trans., *Xunzi: A Translation and Study of the Complete Work*, 3 vols. (Stanford, CA: Stanford University Press, 1988–1994), 2:152.
16. See *Shangshu*, "Yi Ji 益稷," in Legge, *The Chinese Classics*, 3: 81.
17. For Xi Wan, see *Zuozhuan*, Zhao 27; Durrant et al., *Zuo Tradition*, 3:1677. For Zichang (a.k.a. Nang Wa), see *Zuozhuan*, Zhao 23; Durrant et al., *Zuo Tradition*, 3:1625. For Qu Yuan, Zijiao, and Zilan, see *Shiji* 84:2484–90; Nienhauser, 7:298–302.
18. Geng Shou and Yan Yan (a.k.a Zhuang Yannian / Yan Yannian), see *Hanshu* 24A:1141; 90:3667; for Chen Tang, Zhi Zhi, and Kuang Heng, see *Hanshu* 70:3007–29.

## CHAPTER 7. EVALUATING MERIT

1. That is, the ruler, whose throne is always aligned so that he faces the auspicious yang direction south and turns his back on the inauspicious yin north.
2. This sentence resembles a passage in *Zuozhuan,* Xiang 27: "賞罰無章何以沮勸?" See Stephen Durrant, Wai-yee Li, and David Schaberg, trans., *Zuo Tradition* (Zuozhuan): *Commentary on the Spring and Autumn Annals* (Seattle: University of Washington Press, 2016), 2:1190–91: "Reward and punishments have no obvious justifications, so how can one deter wrongdoings and encourage good deeds?"
3. In quoting from the *Shujing,* Wang Fu omits the bracketed phrase.
4. *Shangshu,* "Canon of Shun"; James Legge, trans., *The Chinese Classics,* 5 vols. (Hong Kong: Chinese University of Hong Kong Press, 1970), 3:50.
5. Following Wang Jipei's reading of 憲 *xian* as 悉 *xi,* which Yan Shigu defines as 盡 *jin.*
6. Under the Han, the Nine Superintendents were the Superintendent of Ceremonial, the Superintendent of the Palace, the Superintendent of Guards, the Superintendent of Transport, the Superintendent of Trials, the Superintendent of State Visits, the superintendent of the Imperial Clan, the Superintendent of Agriculture, and the superintendent of the Lesser Treasury. See Michael Loewe, "The Structure and Practice of Government," in Denis Twitchett and Michael Loewe, eds., *The Cambridge History of China, Vol. 1, The Ch'in and Han Empires* (Cambridge: Cambridge University Press, 1986), 1:463–90; 491–519.
7. The Three Excellencies (三公) were in theory the highest officials of the imperial government, reporting directly to the emperor. They were the Grand Minister of Finance, the Marshal of State, and the Grand Minister of Works. During the Latter Han, the Grand Ministers of Finance and Works gradually lost power, while the Marshal of State, who functioned as commander-in-chief of the armed forces, remained important. See Twitchett, *Cambridge History of China,* 1492–93.
8. There are two interpretations of the term 王休 *wangxiu.* The first cites the *Shijing, Da Ya,* "Jiang Han," Mao no. 262, in Legge, *The Chinese Classics,* 4:555, reading *xiu* as "excellence/goodness." Thus, the line could read "to create officials who complete the Son of Heaven's fine

virtue." Yu Yue 俞樾 gives a very different reading—"resting and ascending," i.e., "determining those to be removed or promoted," in a usage similar to that found in QFL 27 "Physiognomy," and QFL 28 "Dreams." Yu Yue identifies this term as part of a system in which the Five Phases alternate in various roles—王/旺 *wang* "ascending," 相 *xiang* "assisting," 休 *xiu* "resting," 囚 *qiu* "imprisoned," and 死 *si* "deceased," according to season. See Ban Gu, *Bohutong*, in SBCK, vol. 22, 3:14A, translated in Tjoe Som Tjan, *Po Hu T'ung: The Comprehensive Discussions in the White Tiger Hall*, 2 vols. (Leiden: Brill, 1949–1952; reprint, Westport, CT: Hyperion Press, 1973), 437–38. Peng Duo and Hu Chusheng agree with Yu Yue.

9. Translations of titles in this section follow the "Glossary-Index" in Twitchett, *Cambridge History of China*.
10. In 178 BCE, Emperor requested nominations of men who exhibited these qualities. See Homer H. Dubs, trans., *History of the Former Han Dynasty*, 3 vols. (Baltimore: Waverly Press, 1938–1944), 1:241; *Hanshu* 4:116.
11. See *Han Feizi*, chapter 8: "He lets names define themselves and affairs reach their own settlement [使名自命, 令事自定]. . . . He assigns them tasks according to their ability and lets them settle things for themselves." From Burton Watson, trans., *Han Fei Tzu* (New York, Columbia University Press, 1964), 36.
12. Following Wang Jipei.
13. Following Zhang Jue.
14. Following Zhang Jue.
15. That is, Xia, Shang, and Zhou.
16. The text here reads 戴祀四八 *dai si si ba*—it is unclear what "4 8" (or "48") refers to. Peng Bingcheng and Zhang Jue both say, without explanation, that it means "320," evidently multiplying 4 x 8 x 10, to produce a plausible span of time between the founding of the Han dynasty in 206 BCE and the time when Wang Fu was writing. (See Peng Bingcheng, *Xinyi Qianfulun*, 74n8; and Zhang Jue, *Qianfulun jiaozhu*, 87n11.) Ivan P. Kamenarović says, without citing any authorities, that "4 8" refers to the 48 years between the death of the usurper Wang Mang in 23 CE and the revolt against Emperor Ming in 71, but he does not explain the possible significance of that span of time. Both of these

interpretations rely on an understanding of *daisi* 戴祀 as meaning "a span of years." Zhang cites the *Er ya*, contending that both *dai* and *si* mean "year" in the Chinese of the times of Yao and Shun and in Shang dynasty texts, although no writings survive from "the era of Yao and Shun") and there is no reason to think that Wang Fu is deliberately employing an archaism here. Conceivably, "four eight" could refer to the twelve emperors of the Former Han dynasty, though why they should be enumerated as "four and eight" is also unclear. Reading the binome *daisi* more straightforwardly yields the translation "perform the [imperial] sacrifices." The logic of the passage in which this phrase appears might be understood as follows: "The Han ascended the throne and performed meritorious acts that could be expected to result in an era of Great Peace, but which did not occur because education was not cultivated nor were merits examined." The meritorious conduct alluded to is, as stated, the performance of the [imperial] sacrifices. That still leaves the question of "four eight." We tentatively take "48" as a reasonable estimate of the number of times the sacrifices were performed during the long reign of the Han; (4 x 8 = 32 times is another possibility). Thus we render this passage as "[They] performed the [imperial] sacrifices forty-eight [times?]," putting "times" in brackets and with a question mark to indicate that this is a puzzle that remains unsolved. The timing of imperial sacrifices, the deities worshipped, and the liturgies employed were all hotly contested subjects during the Former Han. For an overview of these debates, see Sarah A. Queen and John S. Major, trans., *Luxuriant Gems of the Spring and Autumn, Attributed to Dong Zhongshu* (New York: Columbia University Press, 2015), 506–10. We thank Christopher Cullen for sharing his insights into this passage.

17. Exemptions from punishments could be purchased.
18. Jing Junming, better known as Jing Fang (fl. 48 BCE), was an *Yijing* specialist and statesman who devised a method of regularly evaluating officials. See *Hanshu* 75:3161–3163.
19. See *Han Feizi* chapter 5: 故群臣陳其言，君以其言授其事，事以責其功。功當其事，事當其言則賞；功不當其事，事不當其言則誅: "Therefore, when a minister utters a word, the ruler should according to the word assign him a task to accomplish, and according to the result of the accomplishment call the task to account. If the result corresponds with the

task and the task with the word, the minister should be rewarded. If the result corresponds not with the task and the task not with the word, he should be censured." Translation from W. K. Liao, trans., *The Complete Works of Han Fei Tzu*, 2 vols. (London: Arthur Probsthain, 1939), vol. 1, 34.
20. *Shangshu*, "Yi Ji," Legge, *The Chinese Classics*, 3:83–84.

## CHAPTER 8. THINKING ABOUT THE WORTHY

1. See *Han Feizi*, chapter 45, "Absurd Encouragements," *Guishi* 詭使; translated in W. K. Liao, trans., *The Complete Works of Han Fei Tzu*, 2 vols. (London: Arthur Probsthain, 1939), 2:230: "Indeed, what the superior values is often contrary to the purpose of government."
2. This is a reference to the Grand Conclusion Cycle (*ji* 紀), a period of 1,520 years, when the solar year, the lunar month, the sexagenary-cycle day, and the diurnal hour, from any arbitrarily chosen index position, theoretically repeats. See John S. Major, *Heaven and Earth in Early Han Thought: Chapters Three, Four, and Five of the* Huainanzi (Albany: State University Press of New York, 1993), 59, 83.
3. The *jie* 節 was a form of official credential. See *Zuozhuan* Wen 8; Stephen Durrant, Wai-yee Li, and David Schaberg, trans., *Zuo Tradition* (Zuozhuan)*: Commentary on the Spring and Autumn Annals* (Seattle: University of Washington Press, 2016), 1:511; *Shiji* 70:2270.
4. The *song* 頌 section of the *Shijing*, i.e., Mao nos. 265–305, consists of hymns or liturgical poems that, as a group, reinforce the Zhou dynasty's claim to legitimacy.
5. *Shijing, Da Ya*, "Reversal," 板 "Ban" Mao no. 254, and "Vast" 蕩 "Dang," Mao no. 255 are stern warnings against royal abuse of power. See James Legge, trans., *The Chinese Classics*, 5 vols. (Hong Kong: Chinese University of Hong Kong Press, 1970), 4:499–510.
6. This sentence is quoted from *Shijing, Da Ya*, "Dang," Mao no. 255, the last stanza. See Legge, *The Chinese Classics,* 4:510. The general sense of this passage is that the past, properly understood, serves as a warning to the present.
7. From ancient times, and to some extent even today, it has been a distinctive feature of Chinese culture that alcoholic drinks were heated before serving, hence the depiction here of "cold drinks" as highly unappetizing.

8. *Laozi* chapter 71.
9. See *Xici*, 2:39; James Legge, trans., *The I Ching* (1899; reprint New York: Dover, 1963), 391–92: "The Master said: 'He who keeps danger in mind is he who will rest safe in his seat; he who keeps ruin in mind is he who will preserve his interests secure; he who sets the danger of disorder before him is he who will maintain the state of order. Therefore the superior man, when resting in safety, does not forget that danger may come; when in a state of security, he does not forget the possibility of ruin; and when all is in a state of order, he does not forget that disorder may come. Thus his person is kept safe, and his state and all his clans can be preserved. This is according to what the *Yi* says, "(Let him say) 'Shall I perish? shall I perish?' (so shall this state be firm, as if) bound to a clump of bushy mulberry trees."
10. A "gentleman of service" refers to the *shi* 士.
11. That is, to live out the lifespan awarded to him by fate.
12. Following Yu Yue, reading the second *yong* 永 as *bao* 保.
13. See *Guoyu*, "Jinyu" 8.17.
14. The Five Classics are the *Odes* (*Shijing*); the *Venerated Documents* (*Shangshu*); the *Changes* (*Zhouyi*); the *Rites* (*Liji*); and the *Spring and Autumn* (*Chunqiu*).
15. "Kindling tools" of various kinds are mentioned in the "Nei Ze" chapter of the *Liji* . See James Legge, trans., *Li Chi* (Oxford University Press, 1879; reprint edition Winberg Chai, 2 vols. New Hyde Park, NY: University Books, 1967), 1:450. Also see Joseph Needham, *Science and Civilisation in China* (Cambridge: Cambridge University Press, 1971), 4.1:87–91. The "bellows stone" is likely the piston used to operate a bellows. See Needham, *Science and Civilisation*, 4:2.1.137–40.
16. The "Six Dragons" is a reference to the first of the sixty-four hexagrams of *The Book of Changes*, *qian* 乾, comprising six yang (unbroken) lines that describe the movements of a dragon. A passage from the Tuan 彖 commentary on hexagram no. 1 is relevant here: (I.4.) "The method of Qian is to change and transform, so that everything obtains its correct nature as appointed (by the mind of Heaven); and (thereafter the conditions of) great harmony are preserved in union. The result is 'what is advantageous, and correct and firm.'" Legge, *The I Ching*, 213. Richard Lynn's translation of this passage brings out more of its

meaning: "The change and transformation of the Dao of Qian in each instance keep the nature and destiny of things correct" (各正性命). Richard John Lynn, trans., *The Classic of Changes: A New Translation of the I Ching as Interpreted by Wang Bi* (New York: Columbia University Press, 2004), 29.

17. "Governing an era" refers back to the theme of *Shijing*, "Dang," Mao no. 255 quoted above. The general sense of this passage is that the past, properly understood, serves as a warning to the present.
18. *Ophiopogon japonicus*.
19. Following Yu Yue's emendation of these lines.
20. These lines resemble but are not identical to a passage in the "Great Plan" (*Hong fan* 洪範) chapter of the *Book of Documents*. That version reads, 人之有能有為使羞其行而邦其昌, which Legge translates as follows: "When men have ability and administrative power, cause them still more to cultivate their conduct, and the prosperity of the country will be promoted." Legge, *The Chinese Classics*, 3.330.
21. Following Zhang Jue. *Yijing*, "Xici," 2:12; Legge, *The I Ching*, 336: "The places of heaven and earth (in the diagrams) having been determined, the sages were able (by means of the Yi) to carry out and complete their ability. (In this way even) the common people were able to share with them in (deciding about) the counsels of men and the counsels of spiritual beings." Lynn, *Classic of Changes*, 94: "Whether consulting with men or consulting with spirits, they allowed the ordinary folk to share in these resources."
22. Commentators explain that *mao tu* 茅土 refers to clumps of earth wrapped in white rushes, bestowed by the ruler on a nobleman as a symbol of a granted fief, which included the right to erect an altar on the fief.
23. Literally, they "ate simple [i.e., consecrated sacrificial] foods and occupied the place of the impersonator of the dead," a highly honored ceremonial status.
24. *Zuozhuan*, Xiang 31; Durrant et al., *Zuo Tradition*, 2:1289. Zichan was a disciple of Confucius; he served as chief minister of the state of Zheng at the end of the fifth century BCE.
25. Following the emendation suggested by Wang Jipei, replacing *e* 惡 with *tian xin* 天心 making it parallel with *xia min* 下民 in the previous line.

26. This is an abbreviated quotation of the above comment made by Zichan in *Zuozhuan*, Xiang 31; Durrant et al., *Zuo Tradition*, 2:1289
27. We follow Peng Bingcheng's emendation of this sentence.
28. Following Zhang Jue and maintaining the character 邑, as representing *shiyi* 食邑, "eating estate," i.e., a district from which one derives sustenance.
29. *Shangshu*, "The Counsels of Gao Yao"; Legge, *The Chinese Classics*, 3:73.
30. This sentence appears to be quoted from a commentary to the *Book of Documents* that is no longer extant.
31. Following Zhang Jue's reading of *de kuang* 德況 as *de ci* 德賜.

## CHAPTER 9. THE FUNDAMENTALS OF GOVERNMENT

1. See "Wen Yan," 文言 in the *Book of Changes*: 坤道其順乎, 承天而時行; "The Dao of Kun consists of compliance: in carrying out Heaven's will, its actions are always timely." From Richard John Lynn, trans., *The Classic of Changes: A New Translation of the* I Ching *as Interpreted by Wang Bi* (New York: Columbia University Press, 2004), 144. Also see James Legge, trans., *The I Ching* (1899; reprint, New York: Dover, 1963), 419.
2. Following Zhang Jue and not emending the text in accordance with Wang Jipei.
3. Following Zhang Jue's reading 惚 *zong* as 愻 *xun*.
4. Following Zhang Jue's reading of 興 *xing* as 喜 *xi*.
5. *Analects* XV:9; in James Legge, trans., *The Chinese Classics*. 5 vols. (Hong Kong: Chinese University of Hong Kong Press, 1970), 297.
6. *Shangshu*, "Lü xing"; Legge, *The Chinese Classics*, 3:601.
7. "Obstruction" *Pi* 否 is Hexagram 12 in the *Yijing* and is associated with the interference of evil people. "Greatness" *Tai* 泰 is Hexagram 11, associated with the ascent of the good. The name of this hexagram is sometimes translated as "Peace." See Lynn, *Classic of Changes*, 205–15.
8. These are mythical figures. Hou Ji ("Lord Millet") is described as the minister of agriculture of sage-king Yao, and also progenitor of the royal house of Zhou. Xie is described as a virtuous minister of Shun,

and as the progenitor of the royal house of Shang. Gao Yao supposedly served as Shun's minister of justice.

9. Huangfu, Kui, and Ju were ministers during the reign of Zhou King You (r. 781–771 BCE); they are blamed here for the disastrous events that brought about the end of the Western Zhou period in 771 BCE.
10. This sentence is quoted without attribution from *Analects* XVII:2. Translated in Legge, *Chinese Classics*, 318.
11. This comment alludes to Li Si (d. 208 BCE) and Zhao Gao; see *Shiji* 6; William H. Nienhauser Jr., ed., *The Grand Scribe's Records*, 10 vols. (Bloomington: Indiana University Press, 2018–2020), 1:127–63.
12. This comment alludes to Liu Bang, founding emperor of the Han dynasty.
13. This comment alludes to Guan Ying (d. ca. 176 BCE) and Fan Kuai (d. ca. 189 BCE), both of whom rose from humble origins to become highly successful military commanders in Liu Bang's rebel army. See *Shiji* 95; Nienhauser, *Grand Scribe's Records*, 8.1:161–201.
14. This comment alludes to Peng Yue (d. ca 196) and Ying Bu (d. 195 BCE). See *Shiji* 90, 91; Nienhauser, *Grand Scribe's Records*, 8.1:35–39; 45–65.
15. The first emperor of the restored Eastern or Latter Han dynasty.
16. The time spans 32 BCE–23 CE.
17. Zhai Yi and Liu Chong were among a small number of officials who vehemently opposed Wang Mang's assumption of the regency on the death of Emperor Ping in 6 CE—the last step before he proclaimed himself emperor. Their effort to overthrow the usurper militarily failed; they were executed and their entire families were exterminated. (Wang Fu exaggerates here: more than just two righteous officials joined the effort to oust Wang Mang.) See *Hanshu* 98:4031–32.
18. *Analects* VIII:13; translated in Legge, *The Chinese Classics*, 1:212.
19. *Shijing, Xiao Ya*, "Bai Ju," Mao no. 186, stanza 4; Legge, *The Chinese Classics*, 4:300. The ode, according to one interpretation, tells of an officer of worth who has left court because his ruler has ignored him. The narrator-persona takes care of the officer's horse and expresses a wish that he stay.
20. *Shijing, Xiao Ya*, "Yu Wu Zheng," Mao no. 194, stanza 5; Legge, *The Chinese Classics*, 4:328.

21. *Yijing*, "Xici," 1.1. See Legge, *I Ching*, 348: "(Affairs; 方 *fang*) are arranged together according to their tendencies, and things are divided according to their classes." Also see Lynn, *Classic of Changes*: "Those with regular tendencies gather according to kind, and things divide up according to group." But also see Zhang Jue, who interprets the word *fang* 方 as *dao* "way," according to the commentary of Kong Yingda 孔穎達 (574–648 CE). See *Shisanjing zhushu*, 1:64A.

22. Qi Xi was a high official of the state of Jin during the early 6th century BCE. Asked to recommend someone for another high position, he nominated the amply qualified Xie Hu, his personal enemy. His reputation for impartiality being thus established, he subsequently was able to recommend his own son. *Zuozhuan*, Xiang 3; Stephen Durrant, Wai-yee Li, and David Schaberg, trans., *Zuo Tradition* (Zuozhuan): *Commentary on the Spring and Autumn Annals* (Seattle: University of Washington Press, 2016), 2:903.

23. The phrase *caiwei* 採薇 "picking ferns," is a reference to the story of Boyi and Shu Qi, worthies of the Shang dynasty noted for their loyalty and purity. They refused to eat the grain of the new dynasty and starved to death trying to forage their own food. See *Shiji* 61:2121; Nienhauser, *Grand Scribe's Records*, 7:1–6. This account also recalls the words of Zou Yang (ca. 168 BCE), a loyal official who was charged by the king of Liang and awaited death. His memorial moved the king and Zou was released. See *Hanshu* 51:2352.

## CHAPTER 10. THE SIGHS OF A RECLUSE

1. The word 此以 *ciyi* in the beginning phrase of this sentence has been emended to 是以 *shiyi*.
2. Wang Jipei notes that a character seems to be missing after the word *dao* 道.
3. Following Zhang Jue glossing 軌 *gui* as 宄 *gui*, which can also be translated as "treason." Also see *Zuozhuan*, Cheng 17; Stephen Durrant, Wai-yee Li, and David Schaberg, trans., *Zuo Tradition* (Zuozhuan): *Commentary on the Spring and Autumn Annals* (Seattle: University of Washington Press, 2016), 2:863.
4. The text literally says *tu gang* 吐剛, "spit out the hard parts." This is an allusion to *Shijing*, *Da Ya*, "Zheng Min," Mao no. 260, which is a song

in praise of the noble minister Zhong Shanfu 仲山甫. The fifth stanza reads, in Legge's translation, "The people have a saying— / 'the soft is devoured, / and the hard is ejected from the mouth.' / But Zhong Shanfu / does not devour the soft / nor eject the powerful. / He does not insult the poor or the widow. / He does not fear the strong or the oppressive." James Legge, trans, *The Chinese Classics*, 5 vols. (Hong Kong: Chinese University of Hong Kong Press, 1970), 4:543–44.

5. Fan Wu 范武, also known as Fan Hui 會, was a grandee of Jin who was given command of the Jin armed forces in 593 BCE. See *Zuozhuan*, Xuan 16.1; Durrant et al., *Zuo Tradition*, 1:685.

6. Hua Yuan 華元 and Yu Shi 魚氏 (also known as Yu Shi 石 and Yu Fu 府) were grandees of the Song who were engaged with other Song lineage heads in complex maneuvers to attain dominance in the Song court. See *Zuozhuan*, Cheng 15; Durrant et al., *Zuo Tradition*, 2:821–23.

7. *Shangshu*, "Hong fan" 洪帆; Legge, *The Chinese Classics*, 3: 337. The passage as quoted here is abbreviated; in full it reads (in Legge's translation), "If you have doubts about any great matter, consult with your own heart; consult with your nobles and officers; consult with the masses of the people; consult the tortoise and milfoil."

8. *Analects* XV:27; Legge, *The Chinese Classics*, 1:302.

9. King Djou is the paradigm of the "bad last ruler" whose sins of omission and commission bring about the end of his dynasty. His name, in proper *pinyin*, is spelled Zhou; we use the unconventional spelling Djou to distinguish him from the Zhou dynasty that succeeded the Shang.

10. Hitherto the king's favorite concubine.

11. Zhao Gao 趙高 (?–207 BCE), despite his humble and possibly criminal background, became a confidential advisor to the King of Qin (later First Emperor of Qin). He was known for his deviousness and ruthlessness. On the death of the First Emperor, he manipulated the succession to his own advantage but later was outmaneuvered and killed.

12. Ershi Huangdi 二世皇帝, "Second Generation Emperor," was the second and last emperor of the Qin dynasty founded by his father—the "First Emperor of Qin."

13. The general meanings of *hao* 好 and *e* 惡 are "good " and "evil." But this passage harkens back to the tale of Daji, where the contrast is between beauty and ugliness.

14. To "deny their physical forms" refers to Zhao Gao's calling a deer a horse.
15. It is not clear what *ci er* 此二, "these two," refers to. Various editors and translators have understood the phrase as referring to "a beautiful woman and a deer," "a horse and a deer," "felonious ministers and jealous concubines," etc. Judging from the context, we believe that Wang Fu is generalizing from the examples of Zhao Gao and Daji, and we translate accordingly.
16. Reading *qun hou* 群后 as *zhu hou* 诸侯.
17. The "Four Disobedient Ones," *Si zi* 四子, namely Gong Gong 共工, Huan Tou 驩兜, San Miao 三苗, and Gun 鯀, are mythical embodiments of disorder. See *Shangshu*, "Shundian," Legge, *The Chinese Classics*, 3:39–40.
18. Wang Jipei suggests that there may be a lacuna before the word 位 *wei*.
19. Reading 逹 as 衰, as suggested by Wang Jipei.
20. See *Dao De Jing*, 57; translated in Lau, *Lao Tzu: Tao De Ching* (Harmondsworth, Middlesex: Penguin, 1979), 118.
21. Jiang Shang 姜尚, also known as Lü Shang 吕尚, was most likely a mythical figure who was said to have lived in the late Shang and early Zhou periods. Despite his uncouth appearance he became a trusted advisor to Zhou King Wen.
22. Di of Xin is King Djou of the Shang dynasty; Zheng is the personal name of Qin Shihuangdi, the First Emperor of Qin.
23. This passage closely follows *Guoyu*, "Zhouyu," 1.3. Eric Henry translates: "That is why, when the Son of Heaven holds court, he has everyone from high ministers to the men-at-arms offer poems; and the blind musicians offer songs, the annalists offer records, the teachers offer criticisms, the blind whose eyes lack pupils offer lyrics, the blind whose eyes retain their pupils offer recitations, and the hundred [blind] declaimers offer speeches of admonition. The common people have their sayings transmitted, the king's attendants cite regulations pertaining to their functions, the king's relations correct the shortcomings of his administration, the blind narrators and the court recorders give instruction, venerable teachers add to this, and only then does the king commence his deliberations. In this way affairs are carried out in such a way that they do not go awry." Eric Henry, trans., *Conversations of the States* (Seattle: University of Washington Press, forthcoming).

24. The "end times" 末世 *moshi* refers to a dynasty hovering on collapse.
25. This passage echoes comments made about Qin law in *Shiji* 8:363: 父老苦秦苛法久矣, 誹謗者族. See William H. Nienhauser Jr., trans. and ed., *The Grand Scribe's Records*. 10 vols. (Bloomington: Indiana University Press, 2018–2020), 2:38.

## CHAPTER II. LOYALTY AND NOBILITY

1. Similar phrasing is used in conjunction with a felicitous divination using the *Yijing* in *Zuozhuan*, Wen 1; Stephen Durrant, Wai-yee Li, and David Schaberg, trans., *Zuo Tradition* (Zuozhuan): *Commentary on the Spring and Autumn Annals* (Seattle: University of Washington Press, 2016), 1:233.
2. See *Laozi* 66.
3. *Shangshu*, "Gao Yao," James Legge, trans., *The Chinese Classics*, 5 vols. (Hong Kong: Chinese University of Hong Kong Press, 1970), 3:73.
4. *Wudai* 五代 refers to the eras of Yao, Shun, and the Xia, Shang, and Zhou dynasties. *Dai* is usually translated as "dynasty," which is not appropriate here; the myths of Yao and Shun are explicitly antidynastic.
5. This incident is recounted in *Shijing*, *Guofeng*, "Po Fu," Mao no. 157; Legge, *The Chinese Classics*, 4:238–39. When King Wu died, he left the kingdom to his young son King Cheng. Acting as regent, the Duke of Zhou administered the kingdom himself, prompting Shang-dynasty partisans as well as the duke's older brother, Guan Shu, to stage revolts. The ode recounts the people's gratitude toward the duke for quelling the revolt.
6. The Duke of Shao, a son of King Wu of Zhou, was highly esteemed for his righteousness. The tale of how people were unwilling to chop down trees associated with him is told in the *Book of Odes*, *Guo Feng*, "Gan Tang," Mao no. 16; Legge, *The Chinese Classics*, 4:26.
7. According to Wang Jipei this sentence and the next one are damaged.
8. Following Zhang Jue.
9. The phrase *benzhi baishi* 本枝百世 is found in the *Book of Odes*, *Da Ya*, "Wen Wang," Mao no. 235; Legge, *The Chinese Classics*, 4:429. It refers to the direct line and collateral branches of descent.
10. Bo Qi 白起 was a Qin general who conquered many cities during Qin's drive to unify the empire. Meng Tian 蒙恬 was also a Qin general who

led several successful campaigns against the Xiongnu on China's northern frontier and supervised the construction of the first Great Wall. Both were forced to commit suicide in the factional struggles that followed the First Emperor's death. Their violent deaths were interpreted as reflecting Heaven's disapproval.

11. Xifu Gong 息夫公 and Dong Xian 董賢 were high officials and imperial favorites during the reign of Han Emperor Ai (7–1 BCE); they are remembered in history as devious flatterers. See *Hanshu* 45:2179; 93: 3733–35.

12. *Yijing*, "Xici," 2; James Legge, trans., *The I Ching* (1899; reprint, New York: Dover, 1963), 392.

13. Literally, "his mirror," i.e., the ability to see things clearly. The phrase comes from *Zuozhuan*, Xi 2; Durrant et al., *Zuo Tradition*, 1:259: "Diviner Yan of Jin said, "Guo will surely perish. The loss of Xiayang did not badly frighten them, and they went on to further exploits. That means Heaven has snatched its mirror from them and increases their affliction. They are certain to underestimate Jin and fail to succor their own people. They will not last through five harvests of grain!" Also see *Guoyu*, "Jinyu," 2.3.

14. Wen Chang 文昌 is a constellation of six stars in Ursa Major and, according to this passage, was the name of a spirit associated with the dispensation of fame and high rank.

15. Si Ming 司命, "Master of Fate," is a constellation of four stars in Ursa Major. It was understood to be a stellar embodiment of a god that dealt out lifespans. The "Nine Songs" section of the *Elegies of Chu* 楚辭 includes two poems titled "The Great Master of Fate" (*da si ming* 大司命) and "The Lesser Master of Fate" (*xiao si ming* 小司命); see Gopal Sukhu, *The Songs of Chu* (New York: Columbia University Press. 2017), 12–15.

16. After the death of Huidi, Empress Dowager Lü Zhi set about having as many men of the Lü clan as possible appointed to high office, challenging the power of the imperial Liu clan. Traditional histories emphasize the exceptional cruelty with which she eliminated her rivals. When she died, in 180 BCE, the entire Lü clan was exterminated by their many enemies.

17. The four kings were Lü Lu 呂祿 and Lü Chan 呂產 (the elder brother and nephew, respectively, of Empress Lü), Lü Tai 呂台, and Lü Tong 呂通.

18. In the early Han period, much of China's territory was divided into kingdoms rather than being ruled directly by the emperor. According to dynastic regulations, all of the kings were supposed to be members of the Liu clan. The appointment of members of the Lü clan as kings was therefore regarded as a serious challenge to imperial authority.
19. They were founders of the Shang and Zhou dynasties, respectively.
20. During the Spring and Autumn period (770–481 BCE), leaders of the large semiautonomous states of the time agreed that one of them would serve as "hegemon" (*ba* 霸), namely, first among equals representing the interests of the Zhou king. The system lasted through the terms of five hegemons but then broke down.
21. The Huo clan was a family of great military leaders. Huo Qubing 霍去病 (ca. 140–117 BCE) led several campaigns against the Xiongnu confederacy that menaced China's northern frontier; he became one of Emperor Wu's favorites. His half-brother Huo Guang 霍光 also held a succession of high offices under Emperor Wu. When the latter died in 87 BCE, he was succeeded by Emperor Zhao, who was only eight years old at the time. Huo Guang seized power and ruled in the emperor's name.
22. When Emperor Zhao died, Huo Guang replaced him with Liu He 劉賀. See *Hanshu* 68:2937–46. For discussion see Anne Behnke Kinney, *Representations of Childhood and Youth in Early China*, (Stanford, CA: Stanford University Press, 2004), 57–60.
23. The Huo clan's domination of the imperial court was continued by Huo Guang's son, Huo Yu 霍禹, his grandsons Huo Shan 山 and Huo Yun 雲, as well as other members of the clan during the reign of another boy ruler, Emperor Xuan. But the clan's wealth and power provoked resentment. On reaching his majority, Emperor Xuan rallied the clan's enemies to overthrow them; all members of the clan were exterminated in 66 BCE, along with large numbers of their allies. See *Hanshu* 68:2948.
24. The Wang clan's long era of influence on the Han imperial family derived in part from the political skills of Wang Zhengjun 王政君, widow of Emperor Yuan and mother of Emperor Cheng (i.e., Empress Dowager). During the reign of Emperor Ai, she held the title of Grand Empress Dowager. When Emperor Ai died childless in 1 BCE, she

and her kinsman, Marshal of State Wang Mang 王莽, installed their hand-picked candidate for the throne: a nine-year-old boy who reigned as Emperor Ping. The Grand Empress Dowager wielded tremendous power in concert with Wang Mang, who strengthened the Wang clan's hold on power by marrying one of his daughters to the boy-emperor. Emperor Ping's death in 6 CE set off a contest for the succession, resolved, not without struggle, by Wang Mang's establishment of the Xin dynasty, bringing the Han dynasty to an end. The Grand Empress Dowager had doubted the wisdom of that move but was forced to support it. She died in 13 CE, aged eighty-four.

25. See *Hanshu* 99A; Homer H. Dubs, *History of the Former Han Dynasty*. 3 vols. (Baltimore: Waverly Press, 1938–1944), 3:219, 233. Emperors sat facing south on all official occasions; for anyone else to adopt this ritual orientation was in effect an act of rebellion.
26. See *Lunyu* IV: 14. Legge, *The Chinese Classics*, 1:16. As quoted here, the second clause is worded slightly differently from the text of the received *Analects*, but the meaning is essentially the same.

## CHAPTER 12. ON EXCESSIVE LUXURY

1. "The fundamental" refers to agriculture and sericulture.
2. *Shijing, Song,* "Yin Wu," Mao no. 305; James Legge, trans., *The Chinese Classics.* 5 vols. (Hong Kong: Chinese University of Hong Kong Press, 1970), 4:646.
3. Nonessential work included the activities of merchants and artisans.
4. For the term 姦宄 *jiangui,* see *Guoyu,* "Jinyu," 6:12: 亂在內為宄, 在外為奸, 御宄以德, 御奸以刑; "Disorders coming from within a state, arise from personal grievances and those that come from without, arise from banditry. Grievances are countered by virtue and banditry by punishment." Translation based on Eric Henry, trans., *Conversations of the States* (Seattle: University of Washington Press, forthcoming).
5. See the *Yijing,* Hexagram 60 節 "Control," "Commentary on the Judgments" 彖 Tuan; James Legge, trans., *The I Ching* (1899; reprint, New York: Dover, 1963), 262.
6. *Shijing, Guo Feng,* "Qi Yue," Mao no. 154; Legge, *The Chinese Classics,* 4:226. The line is not a quotation; Wang Fu here renders the

sense of the poem as a whole. As Legge summarizes, "The Provident arrangements there [in Bin] to secure the constant supply of food and raiment—whatever way was necessary to support and comfort the people."

7. Reigned 620–607 BCE. He was fond of sitting in a high tower shooting crossbow pellets at unsuspecting passersby. See *Zuozhuan*, Xuan 2; Stephen Durrant, Wai-yee Li, and David Schaberg, trans., *Zuo Tradition* (Zuozhuan): *Commentary on the Spring and Autumn Annals* (Seattle: University of Washington Press, 2016), 1:593.

8. There is an implicit comparison here: the duke, who randomly shot people for fun, and the "mindless people" in Wang Fu's own Han period, who roamed about with crossbows to shoot birds but hit others in the face and eyes.

9. The word 簧 *huang* generally refers to a reed used in musical instruments. Peng Bingcheng et al. translate it to mean "whistle." Wang Jipei suggests the word might refer to a transverse flute. Zhang Jue translates 簧 *huang* as 片 *pian* "piece/slice," and notes that since honey was used for medicinal qualities it might have been sold as such in this context. Though as something sweet on a stick, it could also have been a sort of lollipop.

10. *Shijing, Guo Feng*, Mao no. 137, "Dong men zhi fen"; Legge, *The Chinese Classics* 4:206; Bernard Karlgren, trans., *The Book of Odes: Chinese Text, Transcription, and Translation* (Stockholm: Museum of Far Eastern Antiquities, 1950), 88.

11. *Yijing*, Hexagram 37, line 2: "The second line, divided, shows its subject taking nothing on herself but in her central place attending to the preparation of the food." Legge, *The I Ching*, 137.

12. *Shijing, Da Ya*, Mao no. 264, "Zhan ang"; Legge, *The Chinese Classics*, 4:560.

13. Emperor Wen of the Former Han dynasty, r. 179–156 BCE.

14. See *Hanshu* 65:2858; translated in Burton Watson, trans., *Commoner and Courtier in Ancient China: Selections from the History of the Former Han by Pan Ku* (New York: Columbia University Press, 1974), 94.

15. See *Hanshu* 4:134–135; Dubs, *History of the Former Han Dynasty*, 1:272.

16. "Bamboo Tube" and "Damsel's Cloth" were extremely fine fabrics made in Sichuan and Hubei.

17. See Zhao Feng and Wang Le, "Glossary on Textile Terminology," *Journal of the Royal Asiatic Society* (April 2013): 349–87. "Fine plain weave" fabrics were so fine they were said to hold water.
18. Jizi 箕子, a righteous man of the Shang dynasty, remonstrated with King Djou about his excesses, but to no avail.
19. On the correlation of rank and horses, see D. C. Lau, ed., *A Concordance to the Shangshu da zhuan* (Hong Kong: Commercial Press, 1994), 1:4. The *Shangshu da zhuan* 尚書大傳 is one of the earliest known commentaries to the *Shangshu* and is attributed to Fu Sheng 伏勝.
20. *Yijing*, "Xici," 2; Legge, *I Ching*, 385.
21. Lelang was a Han colony in northern Korea; Dunhuang was an important town on the Silk Route.
22. Zhiyang was one of the Baling tomb complexes southwest of Xian in Shaanxi Province.
23. Zeng Xi, also referred to as "Zengzi," was a disciple of Confucius noted for his filial piety.
24. The Duke of Zhou, as regent of the young King Cheng, bore the responsibility of burying kings Wen and Wu.
25. *Yili*, 8, "Pinli" 聘禮, in Seraphin Couvreuer, trans., *Cérémonial* (Paris: Cathasia-France, 1951), 343.
26. *Zuozhuan*, Xuan 2; Durrant et al., *Zuo Tradition*, 1:593. Lord Ling of Jin reigned 629–607 BCE. He was known for his bizarre sense of humor; he was fond of waiting in a high tower to shoot crossbow pellets at unsuspecting passersby.
27. *Zuozhuan*, Cheng 2; Durrant et al., *Zuo Tradition*, 2:725. Duke Wen of Song (r. 610–589 BCE). The two ministers, Hua Yuan and Yue Lü, were criticized by Confucius for not only failing to restrain the duke's extravagant tastes during his lifetime, but also perpetuating the excess in the construction of his tomb.
28. Han Emperor Jing (r. 157–141 BCE). Wei Buhai's fief was confiscated in 143 BCE.
29. Emperor Ming (r. 57–75 CE).
30. The name Sang Min does not appear in any historical source and may be an error for Sangshi 桑氏. Head shaving was a common form of public shaming of criminals in ancient China.

## CHAPTER 13. TAKING CARE OVER MINUTIAE

1. For the word 陂池 *potuo*, reading 池 as 陀 *duo*, meaning "gently sloping" or "eroded."
2. Song Mountain, one of China's five sacred peaks, is located in Henan. "Yellow Springs" is a designation for the underworld.
3. See *Analects* XI:2: "Distinguished for their principles and practices, there were Yan Yuan and Min Ziqian." James Legge, trans., *The Chinese Classics*, 5 vols. (Hong Kong: Chinese University of Hong Kong Press, 1970), 1:237.
4. Zhi refers to the notorious brigand, Robber Zhi; Jie refers to the last ruler of the Xia dynasty, noted for his cruelty.
5. Zhongni is another name for Confucius. Tang was the virtuous founder of the Shang dynasty; Wu was the founder of the Zhou dynasty; Jie was the last ruler of the Xia dynasty; and Djou was the last ruler of the Shang dynasty. A nonstandard spelling of his name (properly Zhou) is used to avoid confusion with the Zhou dynasty.
6. See *Odes, Xiao ya*, "Xiao min," Mao no. 195; Legge, *The Chinese Classics*, 4:333; *Huainanzi*, "Ren jian xun," in D. C. Lau, *Huainanzi zhuzi suoyin* (Hong Kong: Commercial Press, 1992), 18/185/30–18/186/4; translated in John S. Major, Sarah A. Queen, Andrew Seth Meyer, and Harold D. Roth, trans., *The Huainanzi: A Guide to the Theory and Practice of Government in Early Han China* (New York: Columbia University Press, 2010), 721; *Analects* XII:1, I:4; *Shangshu*, "Wu Zi zhi Ge," in Legge, *The Chinese Classics*, 3:158.
7. *Yijing*, "Xici," 2.5 in *Shisanjing zhushu*, 1; *juan* 8:76B; translated in James Legge, trans., *The I Ching* (1899; reprint, New York: Dover, 1963), 391.
8. *Shijing, Xiao Ya*, "Shi Yue Zhi Jiao," Mao no. 193; Legge, *The Chinese Classics*, 4:322. Gui and Yu are mentioned in the ode as contributing to the demise of the Western Zhou dynasty (ca. 771 BCE). The three epochs are the Xia, Shang, and Zhou dynasties. The language here recalls Sima Xiangru's rhapsody "Shanglin Park," i.e., 遂往而不返. See translation in David Knechtges, *Wenxuan, or Selections of Refined Literature. Volume 1. Rhapsodies on Metropolises and Capitals* (Princeton: Princeton University Press, 1982), 1:109.

9. Wang Jipei and Peng Duo both note that there appears to be a character missing at the end of this phrase. Based on rhyme and parallel passages in other texts, Peng Duo supplies the word 象 *xiang*, "image." See parallels in *Hanshu* 21A.985; *Xunzi* 27.78; translated in John Knoblock, trans., *Xunzi: A Translation and Study of the Complete Work*, 3 vols. (Stanford, CA: Stanford University Press, 1988–1994), 3.226.
10. Following Wang Jipei, who renders the phrase 鄂譽鄂譽, 鄂致存亡 [*eyu eyu, e zhi cun wang*] as 鄂鄂譽譽, 以致存亡 [*ee yuyu, yi zhi cun wang*].
11. *Shijing*, Da Ya, "Da ming," Mao no. 236; *Song*, "Min yu xiao zi," Mao no. 286; translation based on Legge, *Chinese Classics*, 4:433, 596.
12. Boyi, a paragon of virtue who lived at the end of the Shang dynasty, starved himself to death rather than switch allegiance to the newly established Zhou dynasty.
13. Wang Mang usurped the Han throne and established the Xin dynasty (7–25 CE).
14. Missing text renders this line unintelligible.
15. Wang Jipei notes that this statement resembles a passage in the *Hanshu* biography of Dong Zhongshu. See *Hanshu* 56:2517.
16. Qing Feng was a wealthy officer at the court of Qi who helped assassinate Lord Zhuang in 548 BCE and then assumed power in Qi until he was expelled in 545 BCE. He fled to Wu, where he was executed by Lord Ling of Chu during an invasion in 538. See *Zuozhuan*, Xiang 28.9; Stephen Durrant, Wai-yee Li, and David Schaberg, trans., *Zuo Tradition* (Zuozhuan): *Commentary on the Spring and Autumn Annals* (Seattle: University of Washington Press, 2016), 2:1219–25. Boyou, also called Liang Xiao (d. 543 BCE), was a notorious drunkard. He headed Zheng's government until he was killed by rivals. See *Zuozhuan*, Xiang 30.10; Durrant et al., *Zuo Tradition*, 2:1261–65.
17. See *Guoyu*, "Jinyu," 8.17, translated by Eric Henry: "When Lord Píng fell ill, Lord Jing of Qin sent Physician He to examine him. After doing so, he came out and said, "Nothing can be done. This is what is termed 'putting males at a distance and drawing close to females.' His infatuation has produced an evil spell. It is due neither to ghosts, nor to his eating, but to infatuation, which has caused his will to weaken. If good ministers do not thrive, Heaven will not aid the state with its decrees. Even if his lordship does not die, he will surely lose the vassal lords." Eric Henry, trans. *Conversations of the States* (Seattle: University of

Washington Press, forthcoming). Lord Ping of Jin died 532 BCE. Also see *Zuozhuan*, Zhao 10.

18. The *Lienüzhuan* includes two accounts of King Zhuang of Chu (r. 613–591 BCE) correcting his faults. See Anne Behnke Kinney, ed., *Exemplary Women of Early China*, (New York: Columbia University Press, 2014), biographies 2.5, 7.9. King Wei of Qi (r. 334–320 BCE) is described as having neglected his rule for the first nine years of his reign. See *Shiji* 46:1888 and *Lienüzhuan* 6.9; Kinney, *Exemplary Women*, 122–23.

19. There are a number of similar accounts recorded in early texts that contrast officers who are offensively blunt but honest with those who are pleasingly deferential but unprincipled. The names and chronologies differ from source to source. The identities of the officers mentioned in this passage seem muddled. According to the *Xinxu*, when King Gong of Chu (r. 590–560 BCE) became ill, he ennobled Guan Su and dismissed Shen Houbo 申侯伯 (rather than Chen Ying). See D. C. Lau, ed., *Xinxu zhuzi suoyin*, (Hong Kong: Shangwu yinshuguan, 1992), 1.6/2/16. Wang Fu's reference to Chen Ying may be an orthographic error for Shen Houbo. The *Lüshi Chunqiu*, 11.5, "Changjian" account is set in the reign of King Wen of Chu (689–677 BCE) and describes Shen Hou as deferential but unprincipled and an officer called Xian Xi who is offensive but truthful. See John Knoblock and Jeffrey Riegel, trans., *The Annals of Lü Buwei* (Stanford, CA: Stanford University Press, 2004), 253. In the reign of King Wei of Qi, Jimo was a worthy man who refused to ingratiate himself with powerful courtiers and was later rewarded with a fief, while the officer E was an unprincipled sycophant and was boiled as a punishment. See *Shiji* 46:1888 and *Lienüzhuan* 6.9; Kinney, *Exemplary Women*, 122–23.

20. A similar statement is found in the *Laozi*, chapter 33.

21. Yanzi or Yan Hui (b. ca. 506 BCE) was the favorite disciple of Confucius. This characterization of Yan Yuan is found in *Yijing*, "Xici zhuan," part 2, chapter 5 in *Shisanjing zhushu*, vol. 1, 8:76C; Legge, *The I Ching*, 393.

22. *Shijing, Xiao ya*, "Tian bao," Mao no. 166; Legge, *The Chinese Classics*, 4:255–56.

23. The five constancies are benevolence, righteousness, propriety, knowledge, and trustworthiness. Quoted passage from *Shijing, Xiao ya*, "Tian bao," Mao no. 166; Legge, *The Chinese Classics*, 4:258.

24. *Shijing, Da ya,* "Zheng min," Mao no. 260; Legge, *The Chinese Classics,* 4:544.
25. *Analects* XII:1.
26. *Shijing, Song,* "Xiao bi," Mao no. 289; Legge, *The Chinese Classics,* 4:544; but compare Ezra Pound, *The Confucian Odes* (New York: New Directions, 1959), 287.
27. *Zuozhuan,* Xiang 23; Durrant et al., *Zuo Tradition,* 2:1115.
28. *Yijing,* "Xici," 1.12. Translation based on Legge, *The I Ching,* 376. Wang Fu's text varies slightly from the standard edition of the *Yijing.*

## CHAPTER 14. SUBSTANCE AND RECOMMENDATION

1. See *Analects* V:27; James Legge, trans., *The Chinese Classics,* 5 vols. (Hong Kong: Chinese University of Hong Kong Press, 1970), 1:183.
2. See Analects XVIII:1; Legge, *The Chinese Classics,* 1:331.The Three Humane Ones (*sanren* 三仁) opposed the corrupt and licentious regime of Djou, last ruler of the Shang dynasty. When their remonstrations went unheeded, Weizi 微子 chose exile, Jizi 箕子 feigned madness, and Bigan 比干 remonstrated until Djou tore out his heart.
3. *See Zuozhuan,* Xiang 29; Stephen Durrant, Wai-yee Li, and David Schaberg, trans., *Zuo Tradition* (Zuozhuan): *Commentary on the Spring and Autumn Annals* (Seattle: University of Washington Press, 2016), 2:1257.
4. Following Hu Dajun, who reads the phrase *yuan cong shi* 掾從事 "senior clerks, assistant officers" as an error for *suiju* 歲舉 "annually recommend."
5. Yan Yuan (also known as Yan Hui), Bu Shang (also known as Zi Xia), and Ran Qiu (also known as Ran You and Bo Niu) were prominent disciples of Confucius.
6. See *Hou Hanshu* 6:261, which notes that natural disasters and the rampages of bandits are in part due to the selection of inappropriate people for public office: 辛卯，詔曰閒者以來，吏政不勤，故災眚屢臻，盜賊多有. 退省所由，皆以選舉不實，官非其人，是以天心未得，人情多怨.
7. The order of the phrases "brings pleasure to one's eyes" and "brings delight to one's heart" are reversed, and the word 面 *mian* is extraneous.

8. Xi Shi and Mao Qiang were beautiful women from the southeastern state of Yue. They were credited with helping to bring about the destruction of the rival state of Wu by distracting its ruler, King Fuchai (r. 495–477 BCE) and leading him to neglect his royal duties. Their names became shorthand for feminine beauty and its dangers.
9. King Xian of Zhou (r. 368–320 BCE). His advisor Su Qin (380–284 BCE) was an advocate of the "Vertical Alliance" of Qi, Chu, Yan, Han, Wei, and Zhao, organized to curb the growing power of the state of Qin. The collapse of the alliance left Qin stronger than ever. See *Shiji* 69:2242, translated in William H. Nienhauser Jr., trans. and ed., *The Grand Scribe's Records*. 10 vols. (Bloomington: Indiana University Press, 2018–2020), 7:97. Following Wang Jipei, the word *shu* 疏, "to keep at a distance," has been added to this sentence.
10. King Kuai of Yan (r. 320–318 BCE) yielded the throne to his chancellor, Zizhi, setting off a struggle for power that destabilized Yan. In 314 BCE, Qi invaded Yan; both Kuai and Zizhi were killed and Yan's power suffered a precipitous decline. See *Shiji* 34:1555–56; Nienhauser, *Grand Scribe's Records*, 5.1:177–78.
11. See *Lüshi chunqiu*, Book 12, "Jie li" 介立; John Knoblock and Jeffrey Riegel, trans., *The Annals of Lü Buwei* (Stanford, CA: Stanford University Press, 2004), 265. This account and other early stories mention worthies who unwittingly eat food that was illegally or unrighteously obtained, and upon learning the source of the food, force themselves to vomit.
12. *Analects* XVIII:10: "The Duke of Zhou said . . . he does not expect one man to be capable of everything." Arthur Waley, trans., *Confucianism: The Analects of Confucius*. Sacred Writings Series. New York: Harper Collins, 1992), 222–23.
13. The identity of the "Four Friends" is uncertain. Some commentators identify them as companions of the Zhou founder King Wen: Da Dian 大颠, Hong Ao 闳夭, San Xuan Sheng 散宜生, and Nangong Di 南宫适; others say that they were companions of Confucius.
14. Reading 駹 *mang* as 尨 *mang*.
15. The translations of this paragraph and the next are based on Zhang Jue's emendation of the text.
16. The text seems damaged at this point.

17. This is a reference to the Warring States period philosopher Gongsun Long, who explored the way language expresses fundamental or superficial properties, taking "hardness" and "whiteness" as examples. His work seems to have been dismissed by intellectuals of that era and beyond as empty wordplay.
18. See similar text in *Yijing*, "Xici," 1.8; James Legge, trans., *The I Ching* (1899; reprint, New York: Dover, 1963), 362; and for the word 兼 *jian*, see *Analects* XI:21.
19. Xiao He, Cao Can, Zhou Bo, and Han Xin were famous supporters of Liu Bang (the future Han Emperor Gaozu) in his struggle to found the Han dynasty. See *Shiji* 53, 54, 57, 92; Burton Watson, trans., *Records of the Grand Historian: Han Dynasty*. 2 vols. (New York: Columbia University Press, 1961–1993). I:91–98, 163–84, 363–80. The implication is that even these greatly skilled generals and high ministers were endowed with a few flaws and not all fine qualities.
20. Wu Han (HHS 18:675–685), Deng Yu (HHS 16:599–607), Liang Tong (HHS 34:1165–70), and Dou Rong (HHS 23:795–808) were allies of Liu Xiu (the future Emperor Guangwu) in his struggle to restore the Han dynasty after the collapse of the Wang Mang interregnum.
21. On the word *kuang* 曠, see *Shangshu*, "Gao Yao Mou," Legge, *The Chinese Classics*, 3:73. The *qilin* was an auspicious composite animal that was believed to appear when sagely government was established.
22. King Zhao of Yan (r. 311–279 BCE). See *Shiji* 43:1558, translated in Nienhauser, *The Grand Scribe's Records*, 5.1:179–80.
23. *Analects* IX:30; Legge, *The Chinese Classics*, 1:226. Legge translates, "It is the want of thought about it. How is it distant?" This quotation suggests that making excuses for failing to live up to one's beliefs is tantamount to an insincere commitment.

## CHAPTER 15. RANKED EMOLUMENTS

1. The *Mencius* 5B.2 claims that specific information concerning the "arrangement of dignities and emoluments" [班爵祿 *banjue lu*] determined by the House of Zhou, "cannot be learned, for the princes, disliking them as injurious to themselves, have all made away with the records of them. Still I have learned the general outline of them."

Translation by James Legge, trans., *The Chinese Classics*, 5 vols. (Hong Kong: Chinese University of Hong Kong Press, 1970), 2:376.
2. See *Yijing*, "Xici," II.12; Richard John Lynn, trans., *The Classic of Changes: A New Translation of the* I Ching *as Interpreted by Wang Bi* (New York: Columbia University Press, 2004), 94.
3. That is, in all directions without limit.
4. *Shijing*, Da Ya, "Huang Yi," Mao no. 241; Legge, *The Chinese Classics*, 4:448–49. Four characters in the QFL version of this ode, found in lines 4, 9, 10, and 12 differ from the Mao *Odes*. Major differences in meaning between the two versions appear only in lines 4 and 9.
5. The three missing characters in this line are supplied in Cheng Rong's 程榮 1592 edition found in the *Han Wei Congshu* 漢魏叢書.
6. In the *Zuozhuan* passage from which this line is quoted, "items" (*wu* 物) refers to "sets of offerings" (*lao* 牢)." According to Zhou ritual regulations, only the Son of Heaven was entitled to twelve sets of offerings. A "set" consisted of a pig, an ox, and a sheep.
7. *Zuozhuan* Ai 7; Stephen Durrant, Wai-yee Li, and David Schaberg, trans., *Zuo Tradition* (Zuozhuan): *Commentary on the Spring and Autumn Annals* (Seattle: University of Washington Press, 2016), 3:1873. QFL slightly diverges from the current text of the *Zuozhuan*.
8. For an example of the ruler plowing the sacred fields, see *Hanshu* 4:117; Homer H. Dubs, *History of the Former Han Dynasty*, 3 vols. (Baltimore: Waverly Press, 1938–1944), 1:242n6. In this account, in the first month of spring Emperor Wen tilled the sacred field to provide millet and grain offerings for the ancestral temple and worship of the god of agriculture.
9. See *Mencius* 5B.2; Legge, *The Chinese Classics*, 2:376.
10. See *Mencius* 5B.2; Legge, *The Chinese Classics*, 2:374. According to Legge, "Head Scholars" were "scholars of the first class attached to the sovereign's immediate government; the 'Attached Meritorious' were representatives of states too small to bear the burden of appearing before the sovereign and were sent into court by the great princes to whom they were attached."
11. Following Zhang Jue in supplying the word 君 *jun* at the beginning of the sentence to complete the four-part structure of 君 "the ruler"; 臣 "ministers"; 吏 "officials"; and 民 "the people."

12. Both quotations focus on measures to promote agriculture. *Shangshu*, "Yao Dian"; Legge, *The Chinese Classics*, 3:18. "Delivering the seasons" refers to securing the correct calendar to promote agriculture. *Shijing*, *Guo feng*, "Qi Yue," Mao no. 154; Legge, *The Chinese Classics*, 4:226. The narrator of the ode describes how he, his wife, and his children take food to the people working in the fields.
13. See *Yijing*, "Hexagram 11"; Lynn, *The Classic of Changes*, 205–06. "Tai" is the name of Hexagram 11. In the commentary on the images, it says, "Heaven and earth perfectly interact: this constitutes the image of Peace.... The ruler, by his tailoring, fulfills the Dao of Heaven and earth and assists Heaven and earth to stay on the right course; in so doing, he assists the people on all sides."
14. The term *jiheng* 璣衡 is an abbreviation of *xuanji yuheng* 璇璣玉衡, a "jade device and jade transept," the name of an astronomical instrument used by the mythical sage-emperor Shun to observe the motions of the heavenly bodies. *Jiheng* can also refer to the bowl and handle of the Northern [Big] Dipper, a celestial counterpart to Shun's instrument. In later times, *xuanji* was a term for an armillary sphere. See Joseph Needham, *Science and Civilisation in China*, vol. 3, "Mathematics and the Sciences of the Heavens and of the Earth" (Cambridge: Cambridge University Press, 1970), 3:334. Also see Legge, *The Chinese Classics*, vol. 3:33; and Dubs, *History of the Former Han Dynasty*, 3:328–29: "The underlying conception was that the sun, the moon, and the planets moved correctly or incorrectly in harmony with the good or evil character of the government, so that Shun, by observing the motion of the stars, was able to determine that his assumption of the throne did or did not please Heaven."
15. As detailed in the "Wang Zhi" chapter of the *Liji*, rulers used the ceremonies of the "drinking entertainment" to nourish and honor the aged. Zhang Jue suggests that the worthy were likewise honored. See James Legge, trans., *Li Chi* (Oxford University Press, 1879; reprint, ed. Winberg Chai, 2 vols. New Hyde Park, NY: University Books, 1967), 1:240. The ode "Crying Deer," is described by Legge as "a festal ode sung at entertainments to the king's ministers and guests from the feudal states." *Shijing*, *Xiao Ya*, "Lu Ming," Mao no. 161; Legge, *The Chinese Classics*, 4:245–47. *Shiji* 12:451 describes the ode as a critique expressing the decline of benevolence and righteousness.

16. *Shijing, Guo Feng*, "Cai Fan," Mao no. 13; Legge, *The Chinese Classics*, 4:22.
17. *Shijing, Guo Feng*, "Shi Shu," Mao no. 113, Legge, *The Chinese Classics*, 4:171–73; also see *Zuozhuan*, Xuan 15 for the initiation of taxation on land.
18. *Shijing, Xiao Ya*, "Da Dong," Mao no. 203; Legge, *The Chinese Classics*, 4:353–56. According to the "Little Preface," the ode is cast in the voice of an officer of the eastern states who complains about the favor shown to the states of the west and the exactions made on them by the government.
19. *Shijing, Xiao Ya*, "Qi Fu," Mao no. 185; Legge, *The Chinese Classics*, 4:298–99. The first character in the ode's title here differs from that found in Mao.
20. *Shijing, Xiao Ya*, "Mian Man," Mao no. 230; Legge, *The Chinese Classics*, 4:418–20.
21. There are various lists of the Five Hegemons of the Spring and Autumn period and often include figures such as Duke Huan of Qi, Duke Wen of Jin, Duke Mu of Qin, Duke Xiang of Song, and King Zhuang of Chu. The six states of the Warring States period were Chu, Qi, Yan, Han, Zhao, and Wei.
22. For an early instance of the concept of the branch lineage, see the account of Lord Zhao of Song in 620 BCE in *Zuozhuan*, Wen 7; see Durrant et al., *Zuo Tradition*, 1:499.
23. Following Zhang Jue's reading of 咸 *xian* as 戾 *li*.
24. *Zuozhuan*, Xiang 21; Durrant et al., *Zuo Tradition*, 2:1079. In this passage, Zang He argues that a ruler who harbors those guilty of wrongdoing encourages crime among the populace.
25. *Shijing, Da Ya*, "Sang Rou," Mao no. 257; Legge, *The Chinese Classics*, 4:526; *Xiao Ya*, "Jiao Gong," Mao no. 224; Legge, *The Chinese Classics*, 4:405.
26. The "Three Excellencies" were the *taiwei* "Grand Commandant"; *situ* "Excellency over the Masses"; and the *sikong* "Excellency of Works." *Shangshu*, "Lü Xing"; Legge, *The Chinese Classics*, 3:610.
27. There is a textual error in this line.
28. See *Mencius* IA.3; Legge, *The Chinese Classics*, 2:131.
29. See *Yijing*, Hexagram 27: "Yi" 頤; Lynn, *The Classic of Changes*, 305.
30. There is a lacuna in this sentence. According to Wang Jipei, this line should read as follows: 国以民為本，君以臣為基，基厚，然後高能可崇也.

## CHAPTER 16. ON AMNESTIES

1. Paul U. Unschuld and Hermann Tessenow, trans., *Huang Di nei jing su wen: An Annotated Translation of Huang Di's Inner Classic*, 2 vols. (Berkeley: University of California Press, 2011), 2:633; chapter 74, "Comprehensive Discourse on the Essentials of the Most Reliable": "In accordance [with the severity of a disease], the composition [of the prescription] should be large or small."
2. Following Zhang Jue.
3. *Zhu* 銖 and *liang* 兩 ("ounce") were denominations of money; twenty-four *zhu* equaled one *liang*. The characteristic coin of the Han dynasty was the *ban liang* 半兩, "half-ounce," and is thus used to mean "a small amount."
4. Following Sun Yirang's emendation of the text. Also see similar text in the *Classic of Filial Piety* (孝經 *Xiaojing*), "Filial Piety of the Common People" (庶人 *Shuren*) in *Shisanjing zhushu*, 2:2549B, [*juan* 3, p. 1].
5. Following Sun Yirang's emendation of this phrase.
6. As described in QFL 13.
7. Following emended text.
8. This statement reflects the theory of sympathetic resonance between Heaven, earth and humankind.
9. See *Han Feizi*, chapter 37, "Nan Er," 難二; Liao, *Han Fei Tzu*, 2:158: "Verily, who spares weeds and reeds, hurts the ears of the rice plants; who tolerates thieves and robbers, injures good citizens."
10. For a definition of *jiangui* 奸宄 (personal grievances and banditry), see *Guoyu*, Jinyu, part 6, item 11: "'I have heard,' Jiao replied, 'that disorders coming from within a state arise from *personal grievances* and those that come from without arise from *banditry*. Grievances are countered by virtue and banditry by punishment. But now you govern in such a way that there is disorder within; this cannot be called the exercise of virtue; to remove a fishbone in the throat, but shrink from confrontation with the strong cannot be called punishment. Virtue and punishment alike unestablished, grievances and banditry have arisen. I am but a frail vessel; I cannot endure to await the outcome.'" [Italics added]. From Eric Henry, trans., *Conversations of the States*. (Seattle: University of Washington Press, forthcoming).
11. *Shangshu*, "Kang Gao"; James Legge, trans., *The Chinese Classics*, 5 vols. (Hong Kong: Chinese University of Hong Kong Press, 1970), 3:393.

12. The five ranks—the Son of Heaven, the Lords of the Lands, the nobles, the grandees, and the knights—are symbolized by distinctive vestments. See *Shangshu*, "Gao Yao Mo," Legge, *The Chinese Classics*, 3:75.
13. The five mutilating punishments were facial tattooing; amputation of the nose; amputation of the feet; castration; and decapitation. See *Shangshu*, "Gao Yao Mo"; Legge, *The Chinese Classics*, 3:74.
14. *Shijing, Da Ya*, "Zhan ang," Mao no. 264; Legge, *The Chinese Classics*, 4:561.
15. See Wang Jipei for a different interpretation.
16. "Qian" 乾 is the name of the first hexagram of the *Yijing* and symbolizes heaven.
17. Following Wang Jipei.
18. The capital of the Eastern Han dynasty.
19. Following Zhang Jue.
20. The "Prefect" was the Prefect of Loyang (the imperial capital); the "Intendant" managed Henan commandery.
21. Di Wulun (d. ca. 86 CE), a high official during the reign of Emperor Zhang of the Latter Han (r. 75–88 CE), was famous for his rectitude.
22. The Three Regulators are the sun, the moon, and the stars. The sun regulates days; the moon, months; and the stars, years.
23. That is, they are not visible to others.
24. The "stars" referred to here are the lunar lodges (*xiu* 宿), namely, the 28 asterisms arrayed along the celestial equator. The phrase *yue zhi cong xing* 月之從星 is quoted from the *Shang shu*: "There are the favorable verifications . . . The course of the moon among the stars will bring wind and rain." See *Shangshu*, "Hong Fan"; Legge, *The Chinese Classics*, 3:342.
25. See *Shang shu*, "Gao Yao Mo." Bernhard Karlgren, trans., *The Book of Documents* (Goteborg: Elanders Boktryckeri Aktiebolag, 1950), 9; *Shisanjing zhushu*, 1:79.
26. The term "law" (法 *fa*) in this context may refer to "penal law." See Miranda Brown and Charles Sanft, "Categories and Legal Reasoning in Early Imperial China: The Meaning of Fa in Recovered Texts," *Oriens Extremus* 50 (2011): 283–306.
27. Emperor Ming reigned between 57 and 75 CE. Jing Province was in present-day Sichuan. The post of "Abundant Talent" was highly

prestigious, though an edict of 76 CE complained of the mediocrity of the nominees. See *Hou Hanshu* 3:133.

28. The "southern commanderies" included parts of present-day Hubei and Sichuan.

29. *Hanshu* 23:1098–99. For terminology and analysis, as well as a translation of the *Hanshu* 23 (Treatise on Penal Law), see A. F. P. Hulsewé, *Remnants of Han Law*, (Leiden: Brill, 1955), 158, 334–35.

30. *Shijing, Xiaoya*, "Qiao Yan," Mao no. 198; Legge, *The Chinese Classics*, 4:341.

31. Wu Han (d. 44 CE) was an early supporter of Emperor Guangwu (r. 25–57). See *Hou Hanshu* 18:684. Emperor Guangwu declared thirteen amnesties during his reign, eleven of which were issued during the lifetime of Wu Han.

32. *Yijing*, "Xici," 1:1; Richard John Lynn, trans., *The Classic of Changes: A New Translation of the* I Ching *as Interpreted by Wang Bi* (New York: Columbia University Press, 2004), 47.

33. For Yu Quan, see *Zuozhuan*, Zhuang 19; Durrant, *Zuo Tradition*, 1:185–86. Chu minister Yu Quan had an argument with his ruler and became so angry that he threatened the ruler with his sword. Yu was so appalled by his own behavior that he subjected himself to the "foot amputation" punishment. For Li Li, see *Shiji* 119:3102–03; Nienhauser, *Grand Scribe's Records*, 10.3:236–237. Li Li was a judge under Duke Wen of Jin (r. 636–628 BCE). He made a mistake in a legal case that resulted in a man's execution. Although the duke was willing to overlook his error, Li fell on his sword and died.

34. *Zuozhuan*, Xuan 16; Stephen Durrant, Wai-yee Li, and David Schaberg, trans., *Zuo Tradition* (Zuozhuan): *Commentary on the Spring and Autumn Annals* (Seattle: University of Washington Press, 2016), 1:687. This quotation is preceded by the following, "When good men are in high offices, then there are none among the people who put their trust in good luck."

35. *Shijing, Daya*, "Min Lao," Mao no. 253; Legge, *The Chinese Classics*, 4:495.

36. *Shijing, Daya*, "Dang," Mao no. 255; Legge, *The Chinese Classics*, 4:507. These are words purportedly spoken by King Wen to the Shang rulers.

37. See, for example, *Zuozhuan*, Xiang 27; Durrant et al., *Zuo Tradition*, 2:1197.
38. See *Shangshu*, "Kang Gao"; Legge, *The Chinese Classics*, 3:388.
39. See *Shangshu*, "Kang Gao"; Legge, *The Chinese Classics*, 3:388.
40. See *Shangshu*, "Shundian"; Legge, *The Chinese Classics*, 3:38–39. The text of the *Shangshu* differs from that of QFL: "He exhibited the statutory punishments . . . [with] money to be received for redeemable offences. Inadvertent offences and those which could be ascribed to misfortune were to be pardoned."
41. Compare with *Zuozhuan*, Zhao 6; Durrant et al., *Zuo Tradition*, 3:1403.
42. See commentary on "Guan" (Viewing), Hexagram 20; Lynn, *The Classic of Changes*, 260; and "Xici," 2:1; Legge, *The I Ching* (1899; reprint, New York: Dover, 1963), 381.

## CHAPTER 17. THE THREE MODELS

1. The "three models" refers to three forms of governing as embodied in the "Three Excellencies" *sangong* 三公, the "marquises" *hou* 侯, and the "chancellors" *xiang* 相. See Rafe de Crespigny, *A Biographical Dictionary of Later Han to Three Kingdoms (23–220 A.D.)* (Leiden: Brill, 2007), 1221–22. See also *Shiji* 57:2077; William H. Nienhauser Jr., trans. and ed., *The Grand Scribe's Records*. 10 vols. (Bloomington: Indiana University Press, 2018–2020), 6:340. For the Han period usage of the term (*yue* 約) sometimes translated as "contract," see Zhang Jianguo, "Shixi Han chu 'Yuefa sanzhang' de falü xiaoli—jian tan *Ernian luling* yu Xiao He de guanxi", in *Faxue yanjiu* (1991): 154–60; Li Junming, "Zhangjiashan Han jian suojian zhiyue xingzheng quan de falü, in *Qin Han shi luncong* 9:271–283; reprint in *Jiandu fazhi lungao* (Guilin: Guangxi shifan daxue chubanshe, 2011), 140–49. Lau and Lüdke suggest that contracts were oral agreements made in front of witnesses and sometimes recorded on written tallies. See Ulrich Lau and Michael Lüdke, *Exemplarische Rechtsfälle vom Beginn der Han-Dynastie: Eine kommentierte Übersetzung des Zouyanshu aus Zhangjiashan/Provinz, Hubei* (Tokyo: Research Institute for Languages and Cultures of Asia and Africa, Tokyo University of Foreign Studies, 2012), 150n796.

2. Emperor Wen enfeoffed the male relatives of Empress Bo (d. 155 BCE). See *Shiji* 49:1971; Nienhauser, *Grand Scribe's Records*, 6:49.
3. For Gongsun Hong's ennoblement, see *Hanshu* 28:2620. This event occurred ca. 128–123 BCE.
4. The Jianwu period was 25–55 CE.
5. According to legend, Ji served both of the mythical rulers, Yao and Shun, managing agriculture, while Xie served Yu by managing the flood. Bo Yi managed ritual, and Gao Yao served Shun as litigator. Bo Yih likely refers to Bo Yi 伯益, another minister who served Shun. The name 禼 xiè, also written both as 禼 and 契, is pronounced as Qi or Xie. Xie was the son of Gao Xin, also known as Di Ku and served Shun regulating the land and waterways. See *Shiji* 1:33–43; Nienhauser, *Grand Scribe's Records*, 1:12–15.
6. King Xuan of Zhou (r. 827/25–782 BCE). See *Shiji* 4:143–45; Nienhauser, *Grand Scribe's Records*, 1:72.
7. *Shijing, Da Ya*, "Song Gao," Mao no. 259; James Legge, trans., *The Chinese Classics*, 5 vols. (Hong Kong: Chinese University of Hong Kong Press, 1970), 4:536. The chief of Shen was a relative of King Xuan of Zhou and served as a defender of the southern border. Xie was the capital of Shen.
8. *Shijing, Da Ya*, "Zheng Min," Mao no. 260; Legge, *The Chinese Classics*, 4:545, celebrates Zhong Shanfu.
9. A *ding* was a bronze vessel (sometimes translated as "cauldron") with three or four legs; it was used for cooking meat in sacrificial rites. See *Yijing*, "Ding," Hexagram no. 50; Richard John Lynn, trans., *The Classic of Changes: A New Translation of the I Ching as Interpreted by Wang Bi* (New York: Columbia University Press, 2004), 455; and James Legge, trans., *The I Ching* (1899; reprint, New York: Dover, 1963), 170.
10. See explication of Cheng Yi and Zhu Xi in Lynn, *Classic of Changes*, 459n14.
11. *Shangshu*, "Shun Dian"; Legge, *Chinese Classics*, 3:50. A number of Han texts also explore the process of examination and degradation. See for example, Tjoe Som Tjan, *Po Hu T'ung: The Comprehensive Discussions in the White Tiger Hall*. 2 vols. (Leiden: Brill, 1949–1952; reprint Westport, CT: Hyperion Press, 1973), 2:504–14. The appointment of the "Three Excellencies" began in 8 BCE. They were the "Grand

Commandant," the "Grand Excellency over the Masses," and the "Grand Excellency of Works." In 51 CE these officials became known as the "Grand Commandant" 太尉, *taiwei*, the "Excellency over the Masses" 司徒 *situ*, and the "Excellency of Works" 司空 *sikong*.

12. Referring to the gift of bells mentioned in Mao 260 cited in note 8 above.
13. *Shangshu*, "Kang Gao"; Legge, *The Chinese Classics*, 3:383: "It was your greatly distinguished father, the king Wen, who was able to illustrate his virtue and be careful in the use of punishments." Also see application of this advice in *Zuozhuan*, Cheng 2; Stephen Durrant, Wai-yee Li, and David Schaberg, trans., *Zuo Tradition* (Zuozhuan): *Commentary on the Spring and Autumn Annals* (Seattle: University of Washington Press, 2016), 2:727.
14. The *Ili*, "Capping of a Great Officer," 士冠禮 states: "A man is permitted to succeed his father as a feudal duke in the expectation that he will imitate his father's worthiness. 繼世以立諸侯，象賢也.
15. See *Bohutong*, 1B:13b–14b "The first thing the King does after his accession to the throne is to give fiefs to the worthy because he is anxious about the pressing needs of the people. Therefore the division of the land into principalities is not for the sake of the Feudal Lords, neither is the institution of administrative offices and bureaus for the sake of the Ministers and great officers. It is all for the benefit of the people." See Tjan, *Po Hu T'ung*, 2:416.
16. See *Bohutong*, 3A:8a–10b; 3A:11a–12b; translated in Tjan, *Po Hu T'ung*, 2:504, 510.
17. *Shijing*, *Wei Feng*, "Fa Tan," Mao no. 112; Legge, *The Chinese Classics*, 4:170 (translation modified).
18. See *Hanshu* 6:187. Dubs explains the situation as follows: "This offering was the means by which the Han emperors took tribute from the nobles of the empire. Nobles were exempt from taxes, but they were required to make an offering proportionate to the size of their estates in order to assist in defraying the expenses of the sacrifices to the imperial ancestors at the time of the offering of the specially fermented liquor in the eighth calendar month. Failure to offer the required amount was punished by dismissal from noble rank or degradation. When Emperor Wu was engaged in military conquests, his nobility

took no part in them; the Emperor became enraged, took advantage of the fact that most of the nobles were lax in paying the full amount, and dismissed half of his nobility." Dubs also suggests the following: "Emperor Wu's reason for making a wholesale purge of his aristocracy in 112 BCE may be found in *Hanshu* 24B:1173, 'The Chancellor of Qi, Bu Shi, memorialized to the Emperor that he and his sons wished to [go and] die [in the expedition against] Nan Yue. The Son of Heaven issued an edict recompensing and promoting him and granting him the rank of Guannei Marquis, forty catties of actual gold, and a thousand *mou* of fields. [This edict] was published [throughout] the empire, but no [one in] the empire responded [by volunteering as Bu Shi had done. Among] the marquises, [who were numbered] by the hundreds, no one sought to go with the armies. When [the time came for] drinking the eighth month liquor, the Privy Treasurer inspected [their offerings of] gold, and marquises were sentenced on account of [the deficiency] in the gold [offered to pay the expenses at the sacrifice of] the eighth month liquor; more than a hundred persons lost their marquisates.' *Hanshu* 17: 638 states that the Lieutenant Chancellor, Zhao Zhou, was sent to prison and committed suicide, because he knew that the marquises had not been paying the full amount as their offerings at the sacrifice of the eighth month liquor. Evidently Emperor Wu became angry at his nobles when they all selfishly refused to volunteer for military service at a time when volunteers were lacking, and cashiered a large proportion of them on the technicality of not having paid their full quota of tribute." Homer H. Dubs, trans., *History of the Former Han Dynasty*, 3 vols. (Baltimore: Waverly Press, 1938–1944), 2:126–128.
19. *Lunyu* XVIII.10; Legge, *The Chinese Classics*, 1:338.
20. *Shijing*, *Xiao Ya*, "Jie Nan Shan," Mao no. 191; Legge, *The Chinese Classics*, 4:313. The next two lines are "I look to the four quarters; / Distress is everywhere; there is nowhere I can drive to." The ode is linked to the plight of the worthy who is unemployed.
21. *Shijing*, *Da Ya*, "Han Yi," and "Jiang Han," Mao nos. 261 and 262; Legge, *The Chinese Classics*, 4:546–55. Marquis of Shao of Han was appointed by King Xuan of Zhou (r. 827–782 BCE), praised for his victories over the Eastern Yi. Marquis Hu of Shao was a protector of King Xuan and served during the Gonghe Regency ca. 841–828 BCE.

22. With a few textual differences, this phrase is largely derived from *Shangshu*, "Kang Wang Zhi Gao"; Legge, *Chinese Classics*, 3:567–68.
23. The character 愚 *yu* in this line is an error.
24. Following Zhang Jue reading 育 *yu* as 盈 *ying*. For 職 *zhi*, see *Shijing*, *Xiao Ya*, "Qiao Yan," Mao no. 198; Legge, *The Chinese Classics*, 4:343.
25. Zhang Jue argues against Wang Jipei's correction of the word 大 *da* as 未 *wei*, citing the sentiment in *Qianfulun* 7, which states: "In former times, the Lords of the Land recommended scholars. If they did so once, they were called 'lovers of virtue.' But for those who failed to recommend scholars [on request from the throne], if they failed once, they were punished by demotion; if they failed twice, they were punished by loss of land. If they failed thrice, they were punished by forfeiting the entirety of their territory and noble rank." In the context of the current essay, because the emperor is not asking nobles to recommend officers, the nobles are no longer in danger of having their territories reduced and are therefore described as 達 *da* "successful" or "prosperous," as in Legge's translation of the word in *Mencius* 7A.9.5; translated in Legge, *The Chinese Classics*, 2:453. On the concept of "independent authority," see Enno Giele, *Imperial Decision-Making and Communication in Early China: A Study of Cai Yong's Duduan* (Wiesbaden: Harrassowitz Verlag, 2006).
26. Following Wang Jipei reading 始 *shi* as *si* 司. The "Royal Regulations" 王制 *wangzhi* refers to the system of sage kings of yore.
27. The figures in this section describe the linear dimensions of an idealized fief.
28. *Yijing*, Hexagram 51,"Quake"; Lynn, *The Classic of Changes*, 460–61, 464n2 . The "Judgement of this hexagram states that "If Quake can startle at one hundred li, one will not lose control over the ladled and fragrant wine." Lynn adds that in antiquity people regarded a hundred li as the standard size of a state. Also see *Bohutong*, 7: "The Enfeoffing of a Feudal Lord," I B.13a; Tjan, *Po Hu T'ung*, 2:415: "The fief of a Feudal Lord does not exceed [a territory of] one hundred li [square], to symbolize the hundred li within which the sound of thunder can be heard."
29. For discussion of the upbringing of Emperor Xuan (r. 91–49 BCE), see Anne Behnke Kinney, *Representations of Children and Youth in Early*

China (Stanford, CA: Stanford University Press, 2004), 78–79; and *Hanshu* 8:74; Dubs, *History of the Former Han Dynasty*, 2:199–203.

30. *Hanshu* 8:74; Dubs, *History of the Former Han Dynasty*, 2:199–203; the quotation appears in *Hanshu* 89:3624. Each official rank was endowed with a fixed amount of grain calculated in the weight measure 石 *shi*, "picul."

31. The *qilin* was a highly auspicious composite mythical beast that only appeared in times of exceptionally good government.

32. *Zuozhuan* Zhao 20; Durrant et al., *Zuo Tradition*, 3:1591 and Legge, *Chinese Classics*, 4:684.

33. *Zuozhuan* Xiang 8; Durrant et al., *Zuo Tradition*, 2:947.

34. This comment echoes a similar passage in chapter 16, where lazy, corrupt, and incompetent officials do not fear punishment because of the frequent granting of amnesties.

35. *Yijing*, Hexagram 21,"Biting Together." The "Judgment" says, "It is by using the force of criminal punishments that one brings about this continuity, and that is what is meant by 'criminal punishment' being 'fitting.'" Lynn, *The Classic of Changes*, 267–68.

36. Wang Cheng 王成 (?– 67 BCE), Huang Ba 黃霸 (d. 51 BCE), Gong Sui 龔遂 (d. 62 BCE), and Shao Xinchen 邵信臣 (fl. 33 BCE) all appear in *Hanshu* 89, "Biographies of Upright Officials."

## CHAPTER 18. USING [THE PEOPLE'S] TIME SPARINGLY

1. *Shangshu*, "Yao Dian"; James Legge, trans., *The Chinese Classics*, 5 vols. (Hong Kong: Chinese University of Hong Kong Press, 1970), 3:18. In Chinese mythology, Xi and He drove the sun chariot in its daily journey across the sky.

2. "The Chinese unit of angular measurement is the *du* 度 ("to measure / pass through"), which is defined as the angular distance traveled by the (mean) sun over the course of one day, such that, depending on the precise value for the solar year, 365 1/4 *du* = 360 degrees." See Daniel Patrick Morgan, "Knowing Heaven: Astronomy, the Calendar, and the Sagecraft of Science in Early Imperial China" (PhD diss., University of Chicago, 2013), 13.

3. See *Hanshu* 11:340. In 5 BCE, Emperor Ai declared, "For the graduations on the clepsydra, [let] 120 [graduations per day] be used as the measure of their size." Yan Shigu remarks, "Previously in the clepsydra, for a day and night together there were 100 graduations [亥]. Now [the Emperor] increased them by twenty." Homer H. Dubs, *History of the Former Han Dynasty*, 3 vols. (Baltimore: Waverly Press, 1938–1944), 3:30–31 and note 5.9. Also see Joseph Needham, *Science and Civilisation in China*, vol. 3, "Mathematics and the Sciences of the Heavens and of the Earth" (Cambridge: Cambridge University Press, 1970), 3:315–20. The Han dynasty inflow clepsydra as equipped with a float surmounted by an indicator rod marked with 100 "notches," indicating the time as the water level in the inflow vessel rose. Wang Fu here is ridiculing the notion that a day could be lengthened by increasing the number of *ke*.
4. *Book of Odes*, *Xiao Ya*, "Si Mu," Mao no. 162; Legge, *The Chinese Classics*, 4:247–49. See Legge's note explaining that according to traditional commentaries, this ode was written not by the officer himself but by others who wished to express sympathy for him and appreciation for his devotion to duty.
5. This statement is a paraphrase of *Lunyu* XIII:9; Legge, *The Chinese Classics*, 1:266.
6. "A lack of days" i.e., a lack of time.
7. *Shangshu*, "Yao Dian"; Legge, *Chinese Classics*, 3:18. As Legge notes, Xi and He were appointed by Yao to "regulate the calendar—a work so necessary for the purpose of agriculture."
8. *Book of Odes*, *Guo Feng*, "Gan Tang Mu," Mao no. 16; Legge, *The Chinese Classics*, 4:26; *Shiji* 34:1550; William H. Nienhauser Jr., trans. and ed., *The Grand Scribe's Records*, 10 vols. (Bloomington: Indiana University Press, 2018–2020), 5.1:171.
9. *Lunyu* XIII:5; translated in Legge, *The Chinese Classics*, 1:265.
10. *Lunyu* XII:13; Legge, *The Chinese Classics*, 1:257.
11. *Zuozhuan*, Zhao 28; Stephen Durrant, Wai-yee Li, and David Schaberg, trans., *Zuo Tradition* (Zuozhuan): *Commentary on the Spring and Autumn Annals* (Seattle: University of Washington Press, 2016), 3:1685.
12. The Three Excellencies, *sangong* 三公, represented the three highest official ranks. They managed all facets of the imperial government.

See Rafe de Crespigny, *Biographical Dictionary of the Later Han to Three Kingdoms (23–220 A.D.)* (Leiden: Brill, 2007), 1231.

13. See A. F. P. Hulsewé, *Remnants of Han Law* (Leiden: Brill, 1955), 72.
14. Following Zhang Jue's reading.
15. See discussion of how many mouths one farmer can feed in *Mencius*, "Wan Zhang," part 2; Legge, *The Chinese Classics*, 2:376; and *Hanshu* 72:3070–3071.
16. A *fanzhi* 反支 day refers to the days in the sexagenary cycle deemed inauspicious. The Yinqueshan 銀雀山 Han Tombs unearthed in 1972 contained 32 strips of bamboo writings that represent sections of a calendar for the year 134 BCE and which include days noted as *fan* 反. Also see *Hou Hanshu* 49:1640n3.
17. The first phrase comes from the *Gongyang zhuan*, Xi, 22; the second may derive from the *Hanshu* biography of Chao Cuo, 晁錯 (d. 154 BCE); *Hanshu* 49:2293, and the third bears similarities to the *Shangshu*, "Gao Yao Mo."
18. *Shijing, Xiao Ya*, "Jie Nan Shan," Mao no. 191; Legge, *The Chinese Classics*, 4:310.
19. *Lunyu* XVII:15; Legge, *The Chinese Classics*, 1:325.
20. *Shijing, Xiao Ya*, "Mian Shui," Mao no. 183; Legge, *The Chinese Classics*, 4:295.
21. *Lunyu* XII:9; Legge, *The Chinese Classics*, 1:325.

## CHAPTER 19. JUDGING LEGAL CASES

1. A similar statement concerning rites and teachings is attributed to Li Si 李斯 in *Shiji* 6:254. The "Five Ages" are variously defined, as Wang Fu acknowledges in QFL 34. Among the various catalogs, he uses the list found in the "Xici" 繫辭 "Great Appendix," part II.2 of the *Yijing*, which refers to the ages of Fu Xi 伏羲, Shen Nong 神農, Huang Di 黃帝, Yao 堯 and Shun 舜. See James Legge, trans., *The I Ching* (1899; reprint, New York: Dover, 1963), 382–83. The "Three Dynasties" refers to the Xia, Shang, and Zhou dynasties.
2. On Emperor Gao's (r. 202–195 BCE) legal code, see *Shiji* 8:362–64; William H. Nienhauser Jr., trans. and ed., *The Grand Scribes Records*, 10 vols. (Bloomington: Indiana University Press, 2018–2020), 2:38: "I

will come to an agreement with you elders that there will be a legal code with only three articles: those who kill a person must die, those who injure a person and steal will be punished according to the offense." This act of 207 BCE is also recorded in *Hanshu* 1A.23; Homer H. Dubs, trans., *The History of the Former Han*, 3 vols. (Baltimore: Waverly Press, 1938–1944), 1:58. Emperor Wen's (r. 180–157 BCE) abrogation of corporal punishments in 167 BCE is cited in the "Treatise on Punishments and Laws" in *Hanshu* 23:1098–1100 and translated in A. F. P. Hulsewé, *Remnants of Han Law* (Leiden: Brill, 1955), 334–35. It is also mentioned in *Shiji* 10:427; and *Hanshu* 4:125, translated in Dubs, *History of the Former Han*, 2:255.

3. According to the "Shundian" chapter of the *Shangshu*, Shun was the second legendary ruler of China's predynastic period. See Legge, *The Chinese Classics*, 3:49.

4. Long 龍 was the Minister of Communication 納言 *nayan*, who, according to the annotations of Kong Anguo 孔安國 (ca. 156–74 BCE) "was the officer of the throat and tongue. Hearing the words of those below, he brought them before the sovereign; receiving the words of the sovereign, he proclaimed them to those below." *Shangshu*, "Shundian," Legge, *The Chinese Classics*, 3:49. The "throat and tongue" officer is also mentioned in *The Book of Odes*, *Da Ya*, Mao no. 260, "Zheng Min" 烝民.

5. See the "Xici" 繫辭 "Great Appendix," of the *Yijing*, part I.8. Legge, trans., *The I Ching*, 363.

6. See the "Xici" of the *Yijing*, part II.5; Legge, trans., *The I Ching*, 391.

7. A similar phrase in found in *Xunzi*, "Contra Twelve Philosophers," 非十二子 "Fei Shier Zi" and the term 規規然 *guiguiran* in the "Gengsang Chu" chapter of *Zhuangzi*, where Lu Deming glosses the term 規規 as "concerned with minutiae." See John Knoblock, trans., *Xunzi: A Translation and Study of the Complete Work*, 3 vols. (Stanford, CA: Stanford University Press, 1988–1994), 1:306n96. The lacuna in this sentence is followed by unintelligible text.

8. The weeping and wailing people are likely those who have lent money or sold items to them.

9. *Shangshu*, 尚書, "Yi Ji" 益稷, "Be not haughty like Zhu of Dan, who found his pleasure only in indolence and dissipation, and pursued a

proud oppressive course. Day and night without ceasing he was thus." Legge, trans., *The Chinese Classics*, 3:84.

10. The implied contrast is, perhaps that he used his virtuous example rather than harsh punishment to govern. Peng Duo and others argue that elements in the phrase 至寡動, 欲任德 are disordered and should read: 至寡欲, 動任德, based on a similar phrases in *Hanshu* 4:135; translated in Dubs, *History of the Former Han*, 1:274: "His sole care was to improve the people by means of his virtue"; 專務以德化民; and *Hanshu* 5:137; translated in Dubs, 1.306, "He restrained his likes and desires"; 滅耆欲. Zhang Jue reads the text as is, i.e., 至寡動, 欲任德, "consummately sparing in action and desirous of employing virtue," understanding the phrase as an expression of Huang-Lao thought. See Zhang Jue, *Qianfulun quanyi*, 1:342n3. Sima Qian notes Emperor Wen's preference for Daoist thought in *Shiji* 23:1160.

11. For Chen Xin, marquis of Heyang, ca 176 BCE, see *Hanshu* 99B:4127.

12. For the marquis of Zhouyang, Tian Pengzu, see *Shiji* 119:1025.

13. See *Hanshu* 16:627.

14. The *yongping* reign period was 58–75 CE.

15. Faulty text reconstructed here.

16. Following Zhang Jue.

17. The difficult term, 封租 *fengzu*, is glossed as "to freeze taxes." The idea here is apparently that by obtaining from the emperor a freeze on the collection of taxes from a lord's populace, the amount of money his people saved would compensate them for the debts the lord owed them for levying more taxes than he was entitled to collect. An example is drawn from *Hou Hanshu* 40:1675–77, in which Liu Chang 劉暢 (d. 98), King of Liang, collected more than his fair share of taxes and ultimately ceded part of his territory to compensate for his crime.

18. See *Xiaojing* 7, "San Cai" 三才. Xiaojing chapter 1; translation from James Legge, trans., *The Sacred Books of China: The Texts of Confucianism in The Sacred Books of the East*, ed. F. Max Müller (Oxford: Clarendon Press, 1899), 3:466–67.

19. These three clauses may be out of sequence. The last clause is also read as follows: "I have also seen recorded in books."

20. Zhang Jue disagrees with Wang Jipei's suggestion to add the word *yi* 乙, the second graph in the series of the celestial stems, after the word

"married" *shi* 適. Adding the word *yi*, the second celestial stem, to indicate the first family renders the usual *jia yi* ordering out of sequence. Nevertheless, Zhang's modern Chinese translation remains agnostic on the point of whether the woman has been ordered to go back to her first husband or to remain with the second. See Jack L. Dull, "Marriage and Divorce in Han China: A Glimpse at 'Pre-Confucian' Society," in *Chinese Family Law and Social Change in Historical Perspective*, ed. David C. Buxbaum (Seattle: University of Washington Press, 1978), 71–73, for examples of local officials' involvement in marriage-related cases. The Qin legal text found at Shuihudi, "Falü dawen," suggests that a woman who absconds from her husband and remarries is to be punished. See, Hulsewé, *Remnants of Ch'in Law*, 167–68 [D145–47]. The Zhangjiashan "Statutes on Abscondence" combine the crimes of bigamy and abscondence. See Robin D. S. Yates and Anthony Barbieri-Low, *Law, State, and Society in Early Imperial China*, 2 vols. (Leiden: Brill 2015), 585; also see 1199–1201, 1207–08. The *Book of Submitted Doubtful Cases*, *Zouyanshu* 奏讞書, part of the cache of texts discovered at Zhangjiashan, judges that "she who marries herself off after her husband is dead and the one who takes her in marriage are both without guilt." See Yates and Barbieri-Low, 1385.

21. *Shijing*, "Bei Feng," "Bo Zhou," Mao no. 26; Legge, *The Chinese Classics*, 4:39, which, according to some interpretations, concerns an unhappy woman who is being pressed to do something against her will and states: "My mind is not a stone / It cannot be rolled about"; and "Zhou Nan," "Ge Tan," Mao no. 2; Legge, *The Chinese Classics*, 4:7, which describes a woman who, after completing her household duties, goes to visit her parents.

22. The phrase 二三其德 *er san qi de*, "inconsistent," is drawn from *Shijing*, Guo Feng, "Meng," Mao no. 58; Legge, *The Chinese Classics*, 4:100.

23. See the "Xici," "Great Appendix," of the *Yijing*, part II.5; Legge, *The I Ching*, 391.

24. The word translated as "marriage" is *jiao* 醮, a nuptial libation rite. See *Liji*, Hun Yi, in *Shisanjing zhushu*, 2:61/452C; translated in Legge, *The Li Chi*, 2:429. Also see *Yili*, Shi Hun Li," in SSJZS, vol.1, 6/ 971B–973A; John Steele, *I-li* (London: Probsthain, 1917), 1:18–41.

25. Text is missing from the end of the essay.

## CHAPTER 20. GOVERNING IN AN AGE OF DECLINE

1. The "Three August Ones" are Sui Ren, Fu Xi, and Shen Nong.
2. The identities of the Five Thearchs vary; one widely used list gives Huangdi (the Yellow Emperor), Zhuanxu, Diku, Yao, and Shun.
3. Yu was the founding king of Xia; Tang was the founding king of Shang; and Wen was the founding king of Zhou.
4. This essay echoes *Guanzi* chapter 15, "Zhong ling 重令" ("On the Importance of Orders"). See W. Allyn Rickett, trans., *Guanzi*, 2 vols. (Princeton, NJ: Princeton University Press, 1985), 1:242–48.
5. Zou Maru, a grandee of Qi, was mistreated by the Duke of Hu. When the opportunity arose, he killed the duke and threw his corpse in the river, thus denying him a proper burial. See *Guoyu*, Chuyu, 2:9.
6. On the eve of battle in 607 BCE, the Song general Hua Yuan refused a request from his charioteer, Yang Zhen (aka Yang Shuzang), for a dish of mutton. The next day, Yang Zhen repaid the insult by driving the chariot into the ranks of Zheng's army. Hua Yuan was captured but managed to escape. See *Zuozhuan*, Xuan 2; Stephen Durrant, Wai-yee Li, and David Schaberg, trans., *Zuo Tradition* (Zuozhuan): *Commentary on the Spring and Autumn Annals* (Seattle: University of Washington Press, 2016), 1:589–591.
7. This act of regicide in 481 BCE was part of an ongoing struggle by the Kan and Chen clans for power in the state of Qi. See *Zuozhuan*, Ai,14; Durrant et al., *Zuo Tradition*, 3:1923–31.
8. Li Dui, also known as Lord Fengyang, as Zhao's commander-in-chief, monopolized power in Zhao. He surrounded the city of Shaqiu as part of a succession dispute in 299 BCE, prompting the starvation of King Wuling of Zhao. See, for example, *Zhanguo ce* in SBCK, vol. 14, 6/15B; translated in James I. Crump, *Chan-kuo ts'e*, rev. ed. (Ann Arbor: Center for Chinese Studies, University of Michigan, 1996), 269; and *Shiji* 43:1803, 1811–16.
9. Following Peng Duo.
10. The "Wenyan" ("Words Explained") is the fourth "Wing" (appendix) of the *Yijing* (*Book of Changes*). James Legge, trans., *The I Ching* (1899; reprint, New York: Dover, 1963), 419–20. Reading 變 *bian* as 辨 *bian*.
11. See similar language in *Zuozhuan*, Zhao 6; Durrant et al., *Zuo Tradition*, 3:1403–1405; and Dong Zhongshu's biography in *Hanshu* 56:2503.

12. The Four Lads (*sizi* 四子), portrayed in early texts as semihuman troublemakers, are Huan Dou 驩兜, Gong Gong 共工, Gun 鯀, and (the chief of the) San Miao 三苗; see *Shujing*, "Shundian," (The canon of Shun), paragraph 12; James Legge, trans., *The Chinese Classics*, 5 vols. (Hong Kong: Chinese University of Hong Kong Press, 1970), 3:39–40.
13. "Blazed forth their anger" is quoted from the *Shijing*, *Da Ya*, "Huang Yi," Mao no. 241. Compare Legge, *The Chinese Classics*, 4:453: "The king rose majestic in his wrath."
14. *Shijing*, *Xiao Ya*, "Qiao Yan," Mao no. 198. Legge, *The Chinese Classics*, 4:341, modified.
15. The Three Kings are the founders of the Xia, Shang, and Zhou. The Five Thearchs are Fuxi, Shennong, Huangdi, Yao, and Shun. The Three August Ones are Tianhuang, Dihuang, and Renhuang. See QFL 34.
16. Also see similar comments in the *Book of Lord Shang* 商君書: "Standards are what the ruler and ministers jointly uphold . . . authority is what the ruler exclusively regulates." From Yuri Pines, trans., *The Book of Lord Shang* (New York: Columbia University Press, 2017), 194. Also see *Lüshi Chunqiu* 呂氏春秋: "The law is what all should conform to." John Knoblock and Jeffrey Riegel, trans., *The Annals of Lü Buwei* (Stanford, CA: Stanford University Press, 2004), 640.
17. "Transmit" refers to transmitting the laws of the former kings. Also see *Han Feizi*, chapter 44, "Shuoyi:" "Law is what the officials take as models. If so, it will not be difficult to make the courtiers get news every day from outside and see the law prevail from the neighbourhood of the court to the state-frontiers." W. K. Liao, *The Complete Works of Han Fei Tzu*, 2 vols. (London: Arthur Probsthain, 1939), 2:217.
18. Confucius, as quoted in *Liji*, "Za ji" (Miscellaneous records): "(Even) Wen and Wu could not keep a bow (in good condition), if it were always drawn and never relaxed; nor did they leave it always relaxed and never drawn. To keep it now strung and now unstrung was the way of Wen and Wu." James Legge, trans., *Li Chi* (Oxford University Press, 1879; reprint, ed. Winberg Chai, 2 vols. New Hyde Park, NY: University Books, 1967), 2:167.
19. Following Wang Jipei; see *Guanzi* 管子, chapter 15, "Zhong Ling" 重令.

## CHAPTER 21. EXHORTING GENERALS

1. The presentation of the axe represents the conferral of the right to kill.
2. Following Peng Duo.
3. Different texts give varying lists of the "five weapons." One version includes the spear, the glaive, the sword, the halberd, and the partisan.
4. This quotation, from *Book of Odes, Da Ya*, "Yi," Mao no. 256, differs from the received text of the *Odes*. See James Legge, trans., *The Chinese Classics*, 5 vols. (Hong Kong: Chinese University of Hong Kong Press, 1970), 4:513.
5. The Man were a non-Sinitic people living beyond China's southern frontier.
6. This quotation comes from comments made by the Song minister Yue Xi. See *Zuozhuan*, Xiang 27; Stephen Durrant, Wai-yee Li, and David Schaberg, trans., *Zuo Tradition* (Zuozhuan): *Commentary on the Spring and Autumn Annals* (Seattle: University of Washington Press, 2016), 3:1203.
7. "Five Eras" 五代 refers to the eras of the "Five Thearchs," i.e., Fu Xi, Shen Nong, Huang Di, Yao, and Shun.
8. Sunzi is the putative author of the military treatise that bears his name.
9. Wu Qi, a native of the state of Wei, was an important military strategist of the Warring States period.
10. Wang Liang, a noble of the Zhou dynasty state of Jin, was famed for his skill at charioteering.
11. *Guanzi* 管子, chapter 64, "Conditions and Circumstances: Explanations:" "The generosity with which the throne treats the people is what makes them keep fighting to the death. Therefore, so long as it treats them generously, the people will respond in the same way. But if it is mean to them, the people will respond with meanness. Therefore, the prince cannot expect his ministers to respond generously to meanness, nor can the father expect it of sons." From W. Allyn Rickett, trans., *Guanzi*, 2 vols. (Princeton, NJ: Princeton University Press, 1985), 1:80.
12. The phrase 以下與市 *yixia yu shi* means something like "to have a transactional relationship with inferiors." See parallel passages in *Han*

Feizi 36, "Criticisms of The Ancients, Series One." Also see item no. 1 in *Shuoyuan*, Book 6: "Repaying Favors": "The relationships of rulers and officers are formed according to the rules of the marketplace. A ruler offers a rank and stipend in order to show hospitable concern for an officer; and the officer does his utmost to repay him. If an officer's merit should exceed all expectation, a ruler will bestow rich reward on him; if a ruler shows surpassing kindness to an officer, then the officer will of necessity die for him to pay his debt of gratitude." From Eric Henry, trans., *Garden of Eloquence* (Seattle: University of Washington Press, 2021), 283.

13. See *Han Feizi*, "Chu jian Qin": "While they all avow their determination to die, in case of emergency, even pulled by naked blades in the front and pushed by axes and anvils from behind, they would run backward and never fight to the death. Not that the gentry and commoners cannot fight to the death, but that their superiors are not capable of making them do so. For rewards are not bestowed as promised; nor are punishments inflicted as announced. Since reward and punishment are of no faith, their gentry and commoners would never fight to the death." W. K. Liao, trans., *The Complete Works of Han Fei Tzu*, 2 vols. (London: Arthur Probsthain, 1939), 1:2–3.

14. *Sunzi*, chapter 1, "Assessments"; Roger Ames, trans., *Sun Tzu: The Art of Warfare*. (New York: Ballantine Books, 1993), 102–03.

15. The Qiang were a pastoral people living in the borderlands of western China. In 107 CE, they rebelled against the Latter Han dynasty and tried to set up their own state; see *Hou Hanshu* 5:207. This rebellion led to several years of instability in that region. This essay was thus written sometime around 111 CE.

16. Reading 群 as 郡. Commanderies were military colonies established in frontier regions to secure the borderlands. The text of this paragraph is corrupt, and the translation is therefore tentative.

17. Sili was a commandery located in the area of present-day Guanzhong in Shaanxi (also known as the Wei River basin) that extended to Loyang in Henan.

18. *Sunzi*, chapter 2 in Ames, *Sun Tzu*, 106, 109. The bracketed words appear in the *Sunzi* but are omitted in QFL.

19. The term 理數 *lishu* represents a principle that is predetermined or fated.
20. Peng Duo notes that the word 陪克 *poke*, "extortionate exactors," is another form of the word 掊克 as found in the ode "Dang" 蕩, Mao no. 255 in the *Book of Odes*, which bewails the oppression wrought by the Western Zhou King Li (r. 857–842 BCE) and his officials: "King Wen said, 'Alas! / Alas! you [sovereign of] Yin-shang, / That you should have such violently oppressive ministers, / That you should have such extortionate exactors, / That you should have them in offices, / That you should have them in the conduct of affairs! / Heaven made them with their insolent dispositions, / But it is you who employ them, and gave them strength.'" Translated by Legge, *The Chinese Classics*, 4:505.
21. The four characters 越取幽奇 *yue qu you qi* have been inserted into this passage from text below, as suggested by Peng Bingcheng 彭丙 in *Xinyi Qianfulun* 新譯潛夫倫, 380n5.

## CHAPTER 22. SECURING THE FRONTIER

1. See a close counterpart passage in *Yantielun* 16, "Territorial Expansion" 地廣 *diguang*: "The Prince is all embracing and all sheltering. There is no place for favoritism in his universal love for all; he confers no extraordinary bounties on those near him, nor does he forget to spread broad his favors to those far away. Translation from Esson M. Gale, trans., *Discourses on Salt and Iron: A Debate on State Control of Commerce and Industry in Ancient China* (Taipei: Ch'eng-wen Publishing Company, 1973), 99. The text is attributed to Huan Kuan 桓寬 (early first century BCE) and is based on his notes from a court discussion organized by Emperor Zhao 漢昭帝 (r. 87–74 BCE) in 81 BCE.
2. The word used here is *shu* 恕, which is generally defined as "reciprocity." See *Analects* XV:23; James Legge, trans., *The Chinese Classics*, 5 vols. (Hong Kong: Chinese University of Hong Kong Press, 1970), 1:301.
3. The five provinces were part of the nine provinces into which China was divided according to the "Yu gong" chapter of the *Shangshu*.
4. The "inner commanderies" are the commanderies located within the empire as distinct from the frontier areas.

5. See biography of Pang Cang 龐參, who, in 111 CE, urged the evacuation of Liang, in *Hou Hanshu* 51:1686–91. See *Hou Hanshu* 58:1866–1867 for the biography of Fang's opponent, Yu Xu 虞詡 (with whom Wang Fu agreed), and whose argument against the evacuation prevailed.
6. Reading *gou* 媾 as *jiang* 講, as in a parallel passage in the *Zhanguoce*, Qin 4.3; James I. Crump, *Chan-Kuo Ts'e*, 2nd ed. rev. (Ann Arbor: Center for Chinese Studies, University of Michigan, 1979), 85–86.
7. Correcting *di wu bian* 地無邊 to read *di buke wu bian* 地不可無邊, as is suggested in Peng Bingcheng's commentary.
8. Hongnong was a commandery in present-day Hubei.
9. See Wicky W. K. Tse, *The Collapse of China's Later Han Dynasty, 25–220 CE The Northwest Borderlands and the Edge of Empire* (New York: Routledge Press, 2018), 98–99; and Rafe de Crespigny, *Fire Over Luoyang: A History of the Later Han Dynasty, 23–220 A.D.* (Leiden: Brill, 2016), 500.
10. *Zhanguoce*, "Book of Zhao," *Sibu congkan* 6:58b; Crump, *Chan-kuo ts'e*, 340–41.
11. Yue Yi 樂毅 (third century BCE) was advisor to the lord of the state of Yan. See his biography in *Shiji* 80:2427–2434; William H. Nienhauser Jr., trans. and ed., *The Grand Scribe's Records*, 10 vols. (Bloomington: Indiana University Press, 2018–2020), 7:255–259.
12. Following Peng Duo, reading 惴 *tuan* 惴 *zhui* as "anxious" or "fearful."
13. Jimo 即墨 was a city in the state of Qi and located in present-day Shandong.
14. Tian Dan 田單 was a Qi general who served as governor of Jimo.
15. Ji Jie 騎刼 was a Yan general and Yue Yi's successor as advisor to the Lord of Yan.
16. This sentence is a near-verbatim quote from the *Sunzi bingfa*, chapter 4. See Roger Ames, *Sun-tzu: The Art of Warfare* (New York: Ballantine Books, 1993), 115 and endnote 133. As Ames points out, the received version of the text (followed here) has 守則有餘, but the Yinqueshan Han slip version of *Sunzi* has 守則不餘.
17. The term 羌虜 *qianglu* is a disparaging name for the Qiang.
18. See Michael Loewe and Edward Shaughnessy, eds., *The Cambridge History of Ancient* China (Cambridge: Cambridge University Press,

1999), 634–37. Wei was defeated by Qi in 353 BCE and 341 BCE, and later, by Qin, ca. 322 BCE.

19. Ziying, the nephew of the First Emperor of Qin, was nominally the third and last ruler of that dynasty and held the title "King of Qin." He reigned for a brief time in 207 BCE.

20. Lelang is in present-day Korea; Dunhuang is in the present-day Gansu Province; Jiaozhi is in the present-day Guangdong Province; Shuofang is in the present-day Autonomous Region of Inner Mongolia; Nanyue is in present-day Vietnam; Dayuan is in the present-day Autonomous Region of Xinjiang.

21. This area represents the imperial capital and surrounding areas.

22. *Zuozhuan* Xi 5; Stephen Durrant, Wai-yee Li, and David Schaberg, trans., *Zuo Tradition* (Zuozhuan): *Commentary on the Spring and Autumn Annals* (Seattle: University of Washington Press, 2016), 1:277: "The Prince of Jin again gained permission to pass through Yu to attack Guo. Gong Zhiqi remonstrated: 'Guo is a buffer for Yu. If Guo perishes, Yu will certainly follow it. Jin cannot be encouraged; aggressors cannot be trifled with. To do this once was too much: how could it be done a second time? The proverb says, *The chariot and its running boards depend upon each other; if the lips perish, the teeth grow cold.*'"

23. Commentators agree that *biao bing* 猋并 is a scribal error for *quan yang* 犬羊. Compare to Shusun Tong's comment in *Shiji* 99:2720: "This is nothing but just a group of robbers who are robbing like mice and stealing like dogs." Translation from Nienhauser, *Grand Scribe's Records*, 8.1:288.

24. A similar phrase is found in the *Gongyangzhuan*, Duke Wen, 12: 惟諓諓善竫言, "shallow and crafty speech."

25. There is a character missing after *tian* 天; following Peng Duo in supplying the missing word as *zhi* 職, "to fulfill responsibilities." See a similar passage *Han Feizi*, chapter 21, "Commentaries on Lao Tzu's Teachings 解老": "Sharpness and brightness, intuition and wisdom, are endowed by heaven. Motion and repose, thinking and worry, are enacted by man. Man by virtue of natural brightness sees, by virtue of natural sharpness hears, [寄於天聰以聽], and thinks and worries owing to natural intelligence." W. K. Liao, trans., *The Complete Works of Han Fei Tzu*, 2 vols. (London: Arthur Probsthain, 1939), 1:180.

26. Reading *zhuang* 狀 as *wu zhuang* 無狀.
27. Reading *zhi* 止 as *zheng* 正, following Wang Jipei.
28. A *xun* 旬 is a period of ten days.
29. A feather attached to a military dispatch indicated that the message was especially urgent.
30. *Shijing, Xiaoya*, Mao no. 194, "Yu wu zheng"; Legge, *The Chinese Classics*, 4:326.
31. *Spring and Autumn Annals*, Duke Min 2; also see Mao preface on ode no. 79, "Qing Ren," translated in Legge, *The Chinese Classics*, 1:131.
32. The Guifang 鬼方 were a hostile ethnic group dwelling beyond China's northeastern frontier.
33. The Xianyun 獫允 were a tribal people supposedly driven out of China by King Xuan in the ninth century BCE.
34. "To move the people to cultivate virtue," is a quotation from the "Xiang" 象 commentary to the *Yijing*, Hexagram no. 18, "Gu," 蠱; Richard John Lynn, trans., *The Classic of Changes: A New Translation of the I Ching as Interpreted by Wang Bi* (New York: Columbia University Press, 2004), 250.
35. The four Yi 四夷, i.e., non-Chinese peoples on all four sides of the Chinese realm.
36. *Odes, Da Ya*, "Wen Wang You Sheng"; Legge, *The Chinese Classics*, 4:463.
37. This passage is an allusion to the title and first line of *Shijing, Da Ya*, Mao no. 246, "Xing wei"; Legge, *The Chinese Classics*, 4:472. One Han interpretation of this ode forwards the idea that a ruler's solicitous concern extends even to grasses and trees and is a measure of his virtue.
38. *Xiang zong* 相從, literally "follow each other," but the implication here is of confusion and futility.
39. *Lu* 虜 usually means "captive" or "slave." Here Wang Fu uses the word as a pejorative term for an enemy. The word 醜 *chou*, according to one set of annotations, means "crowd" 眾 and may reference the ode "Chang Wu" 常武, Mao no. 26; Legge, *The Chinese Classics*, 4:558, which concerns King Xuan's expedition against northern tribes.
40. A Han "bushel" (*hu* 斛) weighed approximately 20 liters.
41. The monthly stipend was paid to the parents of soldiers to compensate them for the loss of their sons' labor.

42. This phrase is quoted from the *Zuozhuan*, Xiang 26; Durrant, et al., *Zuo Tradition*, 2:1179.
43. This sentence is quoted nearly verbatim from the *Yi Zhou shu*, "Zhou zhu jie" 周祝解, "Zhou invocations." See *Sibu beiyao* (Taipei: Zhonghua shuju, 1965), vol. 101, 9:8B.

## CHAPTER 23. DISCUSSIONS OF THE FRONTIER

1. This phrase evokes a passage in *Han Feizi* 30, "Inner Collection of Sayings, First Series: Seven Techniques." See W. K. Liao, *The Complete Works of Han Fei Tzu*, 2 vols. (London: Arthur Probsthain, 1939), 1:288.
2. See *Sunzi Bingfa* 8, "Adapting to the Nine Contingencies:" "Do not depend on the enemy not coming; depend rather on being ready for him. Do not depend on the enemy not attacking; depend rather on having a position that cannot be attacked." Roger Ames, *Sunzi: The Art of Warfare* (New York: Ballantine Books, 1993), 134–36.
3. Following Yu Yue.
4. The translation of the passage beginning with "When the Qiang first rebelled" and ending with "obliterate commanderies" closely follows that of Margaret Scott, "Study of the Qiang" (PhD diss., Cambridge University, 1959), 102.
5. San fu 三輔; the "three chariot-shafts," was an old name for districts near the capital.
6. This phrase, which mentions the *guifang* 鬼方, literally "ghost quarter," comes from *Shijing*, *Da Ya*, "Dang," Mao no. 255; James Legge, trans., *The Chinese Classics*, 5 vols. (Hong Kong: Chinese University of Hong Kong Press, 1970), 1:509. Mao interprets it as meaning "distant quarters." Later, the name is applied to a region beyond China's northern frontier and reflects the belief in traditional Chinese cosmology that the north was a dark, dangerous place associated with death and negativity.
7. The word *yiqie* 一切, "temporary," as used in *Hanshu* 12:249.
8. This sentence is likely missing one character.
9. *Yijing* Hexagram 4: *Meng* 蒙, reading *zhi* 制 as *li* 利; Richard John Lynn, trans., *The Classic of Changes: A New Translation of the I Ching as Interpreted by Wang Bi* (New York: Columbia University Press, 2004), 163.

10. This is a reference to *Shijing, Xiaoya,* Mao no. 177, "Sixth Month," which includes the lines "We smote the Xianyun, and achieved great merit"; Legge, *The Chinese Classics,* 4:281.
11. *Wucai* 五材, later known as *wuxing* 五行, i.e., wood, fire, earth, metal, and water.
12. The term *wende* 文德 appears in the "Commentary on the Images" of "Xiaoxu," the ninth hexagram of the *Yijing,* and is translated by Lynn as "civil virtues." See Lynn, *Classic of Changes,* 192.
13. *Zuozhuan,* Xiang 27; Stephen Durrant, Wai-yee Li, and David Schaberg, trans., *Zuo Tradition* (Zuozhuan): *Commentary on the Spring and Autumn Annals* (Seattle: University of Washington Press, 2016), 2:1203–04.
14. Gongliu 公劉 was an ancient worthy who served as a moral model for the founders of the Zhou dynasty. "Gong" is an honorific used by Zhou historians to refer to their early ancestors and can thus be translated as "His Honor Liu." See *Shiji* 4:112–16; William Nienhauser Jr., trans. and ed., *The Grand Scribe's Records,* 10 vols. (Bloomington: Indiana University Press, 2018–2020), 1:56–57.
15. *Shujing,*"Hongfan" "The Great Plan"; Legge, *The Chinese Classics,* 3:333.
16. The phrase X 者誰也 admits several interpretations. It is here rendered as an interrogative substitute, "for whom." Hu Dajun renders the phrase as posing a choice: "Which is it?"
17. This line is quoted from the *Guoyu,* "Chuyu," 1:5. "To rule a state, please note, is to take to heart the circumstances of the people. If the people are starved to the bone, how can the ruler be plump and well-nourished? 夫君國者, 將民之與處; 民實瘠矣, 君安得肥? Translation based on Eric Henry, trans., *Conversations of the States* (Seattle: University of Washington Press, forthcoming).
18. Meng Ming 孟明 was a general of the state of Qin. See *Zuozhuan,* Xi 32–33; Wen 1– 3; Durrant, *Zuo Tradition,* 1:443, 447, 467, 471, 478. He averted a military disaster by persuading his lord to abandon a planned attack on Zheng after receiving intelligence that Zheng was preparing to resist the attack.
19. Fan Li 范蠡 was a general and military strategist of Yue. He was criticized by King Goujian after Yue was disastrously defeated by Wu in the battle of Kuaiji (494 BCE). Later his advice helped Yue to become rich and powerful enough to avenge the earlier defeat by conquering the state of Wu. Guxu (also written as Gusu) was the capital of Wu.

See *Shiji* 41:1739–46; and *Shiji* 129:3257–58, translated in Burton Watson, trans., *Records of the Grand Historian: Han Dynasty*. 2 vols. (New York: Columbia University Press, 1961), 2:436–38.

20. Yanzi 晏子 was a philosopher who lived near the end of the Warring States period. The sentence quoted here does not appear in the extant version of the work that bears his name, the *Yanzi Chunqiu* (Master Yan's Springs and Autumns). Zhang Jue nevertheless notes similar passages in the transmitted text.
21. The origin of this quotation is unclear.
22. *Shijing, Xiaoya*, Mao no. 205, "Bei Shan"; Legge, *The Chinese Classics*, 4:361, which translates the first line: "Some never hear a sound / And some are cruelly toiled."
23. *Shijing, Xiaoya*, Mao no. 214, "Shang shang zhe hua"; Legge, *The Chinese Classics* 4:385.

## CHAPTER 24. POPULATING THE FRONTIER

1. There is a lacuna after *yu* 預; Hu Chusheng suggests the missing word is 知.
2. Mirrors may have been used to dazzle and blind enemy troops.
3. The three sentences beginning 惶懼攘懷 may be defective. This passage a quoted in the *Taiping yulan* has 邊邊攘攘, 未能制一, 誠易制也, "Vicious, rash, grasping, troublesome, they were incapable of coming together as one; a sincere approach would easily have managed them."
4. Wang Jipei supplies the phrase "did not give a thought to" for the lacuna after *junxian* 郡縣.
5. The passage draws upon the translation of Margaret Scott, "Study of the Ch'iang," (PhD diss., Cambridge University, 1959), 120.
6. This phrase is found in *Shiji* 92.2623— the biography of Han Xin; William H. Nienhauser Jr., trans. and ed., *The Grand Scribe's Records*. 10 vols. (Bloomington: Indiana University Press, 2018–2020), 8.1:90.
7. See similar comments of Zhuang Zhu 莊/嚴助 (ca. 122 BCE) in *Hanshu* 64A:2780.
8. Following Wang Jipei in reading the received text's 夫士重遷 as 安土重遷, as in a passage in the *Hanshu* 10:291.
9. Following Wang Jipei reading 人 *ren* as 大 *da*; though Zhang Jue makes a good argument for reading the text here as is.

10. Reading lacuna after *zheng* 爭 as *huai* 壞.
11. Following Peng Duo reading *fa* 發 as *ba*. 發.
12. See Rafe de Crespigny, *Northern Frontier: The Politics and Strategy of the Late Han Empire* (Canberra: Australian National University, Faculty of Asian Studies Monographs, no. 4, 1984), 91–93, 103, for an account of these events.
13. A semilegendary physician of the mid-Zhou dynasty, ca 500 BCE.
14. According to *Lüshi chunqiu* 20.5, "blockages" can impair the flow of blood, urine, as well as other manifestations of qi. See John Knoblock and Jeffrey Riegel, trans., *The Annals of Lü Buwei* (Stanford, CA: Stanford University Press, 2004), 526–27. Also see Paul U. Unschuld, *Huang Di nei jin su wen: Nature, Knowledge, Imagery in an Ancient Chinese Medical Text* (Berkeley: University of California Press, 2003), 218–22.
15. Tang the Accomplished was a semilegendary founder of the Shang dynasty, ca. 1750 BCE.
16. Text missing; likely the phrase "balanced surplus and shortages."
17. The Shang dynasty is also referred to as the Yin dynasty.
18. A statesman and intellectual of the early Western Han dynasty, second century BCE.
19. See Jia Yi's biography in *Hanshu* 48:2240, where he likens the predations of the Xiongnu in the Western Han to an illness rendering half of the body politic paralyzed and lame.
20. Following Wang Jipei, reading 一全 *yi quan* as 不備 *bu bei*, but also see Zhang Jue, reading the line as 一全 *yi quan* "supplies one-tenth."
21. See *Yi Zhou shu* 逸周書 ("Leftover Documents of Zhou") in *Sibu beiyao*, vol. 101, 3:5 A-B ["Wen Zhuan Jie" 文傳解].
22. Following Zhang Jue, reading *san* 散 as *jing* 敬.
23. The limbs of these mythical beasts were arranged in so that they were required to support one another in order to walk.
24. "Filial and Incorrupt" was the second of the three grades awarded to candidates for service in the imperial bureaucracy. In Wang Fu's time, candidates had to be nominated by someone authorized to do so.
25. The text is corrupt at this point; we follow Yu Yue.
26. *Yijing*, "Images" *Xiang*; Hexagram 20, *Guan* 觀, "Observing"; Legge, *The I Ching* (1899; reprint, New York: Dover, 1963), 292.
27. The *jianwu* 建武 period was from 25 to 55 CE, encompassing most of the reign of emperor Guang Wu.

28. *Hu* 斛 was a measure for grain, conventionally translated as "bushel."

## CHAPTER 25. DIVINATION SET FORTH

1. An early reference to the division of Heaven and earth is found in a fragment of the "Zhong Hou" 中侯, an apocryphal chapter of the *Shangshu* and mentioned in *Guoyu*, "Chuyu," 2:10 in He Zhihua, ed. *Guoyu zhuzi suoyin* (Hong Kong: Shang wu yin shu guan, 1999), 105 The text reads: "King Zhao [of Chu] (r. 515–489 BCE) consulted with Guan Shefu, saying, "What is the meaning of the passage in the *Book of Zhou* according to which Zhong and Li were the ones who caused Heaven and Earth to be cut off from each other? If they had not done so would the people be able to ascend to Heaven?" "That is not what it means," was the response. "In olden times people and spirits did not casually mingle. Those among the people who were of great perception and fixity of purpose . . . the bright spirits did indeed descend. Of these figures, the males were called *xi* and the females *wu*. [Thus] these people were directed to determine the dwelling places and ranks of the spirits, and . . . in this way there were officials in charge of Heaven, Earth, people, spirits, and [sacrificial] objects. . . . People and spirits each had their own spheres of activity; the two realms respected each other and did not mingle." Translated in Eric Henry, *The Conversations of the States* (Seattle: University of Washington Press, forthcoming). Also see Lin, Fu-shih "The Image and Status of Shamans in Ancient China," in *Early Chinese Religion, Part One: Shang to Han*, ed. John Lagerwey and Marc Kalinowski, 2 vols. (Leiden, 2009), 1:397–458.

2. Wang Yi 王逸 (ca. 89–158 CE), comm., *Chuci*, in Hattori Unokichi, *Kanbun Taikei*, 22 vol. (Taipei: Xinwenfeng chubanshe, 1978), 22:7.2 defines "elicitations" and "beckonings" as follows: 招者召也；以手曰招；以言曰召. "'To elicit' means 'to beckon'; to do so using the hand is to elicit; to do so using the voice is to beckon." In the "Quan Xue," 勸學 chapter of the *Xunzi*, the distinction is between beckoning actions and beckoning speech respectively: "Truly, words have the potential to summon disaster and actions have the potential to invite disgrace." See *Xunzi*, chapter 23, translated in John Knoblock, trans.,

*Xunzi: A Translation and Study of the Complete Works*, 3 vols. (Stanford, CA: Stanford University Press, 1988–1994), 1:138. Wang Chong discusses the "adverse" destiny as one in which a person will reap misfortune in spite of good works, while the person of the "according" destiny will reap good fortune in accordance with good works and misfortune in accordance with immoral behavior. See "Ming Yi," in Huang Hui, ann., *Lunheng jiaoshi*, 2 vols, (Taipei: Taiwan shangwu yinshuguan, 1983), 1:49; translated in Alfred Forke, *Lun-Heng*, 2 vols. (1911; reprint ed. New York: Paragon Book Gallery, 1962), 1:138–39. These notions of fate are also discussed in Cho-yun Hsu, "The Concept of Predetermination and Fate in the Han," *Early China* 1, no.1 (Fall 1975): 51–56; and Anne Behnke Kinney, "Predestination and Prognostication in the *Ch'ien-fu lun*," *Journal of Chinese Religions* 19, no. 1 (1991): 27–45.

3. *Shijing, Da Ya*, "Da Ming," Mao no. 236; Legge, *The Chinese Classics*, 4:432.
4. *Yijing*, "Xici," I:11; in *Shisanjing zhushu* I.7.69C; James Legge, trans., *The I Ching*, 371–72, translates the phrase as "Therefore the virtue of the stalks is versatile and spirit-like; that of the diagrams is exact and wise." The term "round" can also indicate the virtue of the stalks as all-encompassing or as an endless cycle.
5. *Yijing*, "Xici," I:10; in *Shisanjing zhushu* 1:7:69A. Also see James Legge, trans., *The I Ching* (1899; reprint, New York: Dover, 1963), 369 and Richard John Lynn, trans., *The Classic of Changes: A New Translation of the* I Ching *as Interpreted by Wang Bi* (New York: Columbia University Press, 2004), 62.
6. For Shun, see *Analects* XII.17.6 in James Legge, trans., *The Chinese Classics*, 5 vols. (Hong Kong: Chinese University of Hong Kong Press, 1970), 1:261. For Lü Shang, see *Shiji* 32:1477–81, translated in William H. Nienhauser Jr., trans. and ed., *The Grand Scribe's Records*, 10 vols. (Bloomington: Indiana University Press, 2018–2020), 5.1:31–46.
7. There is a lacuna after "progresses"; the missing word, according to Peng Bingcheng, is 德 *de*.
8. Zhang Jue suggests that the missing words might be 妒嫉怨誹以傾覆人, from *Xunzi* chapter 3, "Bugou" 不苟: "[If a petty man] has no

ability, he is envious, jealous, resentful, and given to backbiting, so that he subverts and undermines others." Translated in John Knoblock, trans., *Xunzi: A Translation and Study of the Complete Work*, 3 vols. (Stanford, CA: Stanford University Press, 1988–1994), I:175.

9. *Shangshu*, "Hong Fan," Legge, *The Chinese Classics*, 3:337: "If you, the turtle, the milfoil, the nobles and officers, and the common people all consent to a course, this is what is called a great concord."

10. *Shangshu*, see translation in Legge, *The Chinese Classics*, 3:268: This statement, "the wisest men and the great tortoise do not venture to know anything fortunate for it," is said to have been made as a comment on the evils of the Shang dynasty. Wang Fu seems to be using the New Text version of the text, which has 假爾 *jiaer* (availing ourselves) rather than the 格人 *geren* (excellent men) of the Old Text version. The *Liji*, "Quli," part 1, also has the phrase 假爾泰龜 "We depend on thee, O great Tortoise-shell," translated in James Legge, trans., *Li Chi* (Oxford University Press, 1879; reprint, ed. Winberg Chai, 2 vols. New Hyde Park, NY: University Books, 1967), 1:94; see *Shisanjing zhushu*, 1:1251.

11. *Shijing, Xiao Ya*, "Xiao Min," Mao no. 195; Legge, *The Chinese Classics*, 4:331. All three of the divinations cited above show the use of other sources, such as wise counselors, to supplement divinatory responses.

12. Scribe Su is mentioned in *Zuozhuan*, Xi 15.4; Stephen Durrant, Wai-yee Li, and David Schaberg, trans., *Zuo Tradition* (Zuozhuan): *Commentary on the Spring and Autumn Annals* (Seattle: University of Washington Press, 2016), 1:325–27.

13. For Jingzhong, see *Zuozhuan*, Zhuang 22; Durrant et al., *Zuo Tradition*, 1:195–97. This divination was requested by Lord Li of Chen concerning his son, Jingzhong. For Zhuangshu (a.k.a. Shusun Bao), see *Zuozhuan*, Zhao 5, 3:1387–89. This passage describes the divination made for Zhuangshu on the birth of his son Muzi (Shusun Dechen).

14. For Lord Xian of Jin and Li Ji, see *Zuozhuan*, Zhuang 28.2, Xi 4.6, Durrant et al., *Zuo Tradition*, 1:213, 269–71. For the servant Niu, see *Zuozhuan*, Zhao 5; Durrant et al., *Zuo Tradition*, 3:1379–1383. Niu was the illegitimate son of Zhuangshu, who ultimately starved his father to death. Li Ji was a concubine who rose to the position of wife and turned Lord Xian against his own son and original heir to the throne.

15. *Zuozhuan*, Ai 18; Durrant et al., *Zuo Tradition*, 3:1965; also see *Analects* VI:20.
16. *Zuozhuan*, Ai 6; Durrant et al., *Zuo Tradition*, 3:1869; and *Analects* III:6.
17. Tai Hao is also known as Fu Xi 伏羲, "Tamer of Beasts."
18. The southwest corner of the house, referred to as 奧 *ao*, was the coziest place in the house but also where sacrifices to ancestors were offered. See *Analects* III:13.
19. The Phase Metal is associated with the west, and wood is associated with the east. This assertion is in keeping with the "Mutual Conquest" version of the Five Phases, in which each phase is overcome by the next in the series. This was the sequence that applied to the changing of dynasties.
20. "Quintessential spirit" refers to a type of highly refined qi that gives humans their distinctive animate qualities. If a person's quintessential spirit is disturbed, as for example by conflicting correspondences among the Five Phases, that person's life force can be diminished.
21. The "Great Year" (Tai Sui) is a fictious celestial point that moves counter to the orbit of Sui (Jupiter), the "Year Star." The territory of China was divided into twelve sectors, each corresponding to the twelve positions of Jupiter on the ecliptic. Han diviners made auguries based on the activities in various sectors of the sky and the corresponding locations on earth.
22. Feng Long is a rain and thunder deity; Gou Chen is an astral spirit associated with warfare. Little is known about General Tai Yin. He is mentioned in the fourth century CE *Bao Puzi*. See James E. Ware, trans., *Alchemy, Medicine and Religion in China of A.D. 320: The Nei Pian of Ko Hung* (Cambridge, MA: MIT Press, 1966; reprint, New York: Dover, 1981), 285.
23. The concept of "steeping" or "dying" refers to the development of the human personality as it absorbs the moral features encountered in its environment. See Anne Behnke Kinney, *Representations of Childhood and Youth in Early China* (Stanford, CA: Stanford University Press, 2004), 23–24. According to one early theory found in the *Huangdi nei jing su wen*, chapter 8, the gall bladder was the organ from which judgments and decisions originated. See Paul U. Unschuld, *Huang Di nei jing su wen: Nature, Knowledge, and Imagery in an Ancient Chinese Medical Text* (Berkeley: University of California Press, 2003), 135.

24. Following Zhang Jue.

CHAPTER 26. SPIRIT MEDIUMS SET FORTH

1. *Analects* VII:34; James Legge, trans., *The Chinese Classics*, 5 vols. (Hong Kong: Chinese University of Hong Kong Press, 1970), 1:206.
2. *Xiaojing* 8; wording adapted to conform to the flow of the essay. See complete translation in Henry Rosemont Jr. and Roger T. Ames, *The Chinese Classic of Family Reverence: A Philosophical Translation of the Xiaojing* (Honolulu: University of Hawai'i Press, 2009), 109.
3. *Shijing*, Song, "Zhi Jing," Mao no. 274; Legge, *The Chinese Classics*, 4:579.
4. *Zuozhuan*, Zhuang 32; Stephen Durrant, Wai-yee Li, and David Schaberg, trans., *Zuo Tradition* (Zuozhuan): *Commentary on the Spring and Autumn Annals* (Seattle: University of Washington Press, 2016), 1:223. This account expresses the idea that a prosperous domain heeds the people and only one that is about to perish heeds spirits.
5. *Zuozhuan*, Cheng 5; Durrant et al., *Zuo Tradition*, 2:751. In point of fact, the annihilation was that of his clan. Zhao Yingqi was merely exiled.
6. *Zuozhuan*, Zhao 1; Durrant et al., *Zuo Tradition*, 3:1315.
7. *Zuozhuan*, Zhuang 32; Durrant et al., *Zuo Tradition*, 1:223. The Scribe of Lu refers to Zuo Qiuming, the purported author the *Zuozhuan*.
8. *Zuozhuan*, Ai 6; Durrant et al., *Zuo Tradition*, 3:1867.
9. *Lüshi Chunqiu*, chapter 6, part 4; John Knoblock and Jeffrey Riegel, trans. *The Annals of Lü Buwei* (Stanford, CA: Stanford University Press, 2004), 165–66.
10. *Zuozhuan*, Zhao 17; Durrant et al., *Zuo Tradition*, 3:1547–49.
11. *Zuozhuan*, Wen 13; Durrant et al., *Zuo Tradition*, 1:533.
12. *Zuozhuan*, Zhao 20; Durrant et al., *Zuo Tradition*, 3:1581–85.
13. *Zuozhuan*, Huan 6; Durrant, *Zuo Tradition*, 1:97–99; Xi 5, 1:277–79.
14. A similar statement is found in *Shiji* 3.100.
15. A slightly different account of this event appears in the *Zuozhuan*, Zhuang 3; Durrant et al., *Zuo Tradition*, 1:173.
16. The "Five Sacrifices" are variously defined. See *Liji*, "Ji Fa," in *Shisanjing zhushu*, vol. 2, 46.1590; translated in James Legge, trans., *Li Chi* (Oxford University Press, 1879; reprint, ed. Winberg Chai, 2 vols. New

Hyde Park, NY: University Books, 1967), 2:206–07: "A feudal prince, for his state, appointed (five altars for) the five sacrifices—one for the superintendent of the lot; one in the central court, for the admission of light and rain; one at the gates of the city wall; one in the roads leading from the city; one for the discontented ghosts of princes who had died without posterity." Zheng Xuan's note to *Liji*, "Wang Zhi," in *Shisanjing zhushu*, vol. 1, 12:108 defines them as household spirits, i.e., the inner door 戶 *hu*, hearth 灶 *zao*, impluvium (rain catchment system) 霤 *liu*, outer door 門 *men*, and well 井 *jing*.

17. *Shangshu*, "Shao Gao"; Legge, *The Chinese Classics*, 3:432.
18. *Yijing* "Xici" part 1, chapter 12; James Legge, trans., *The I Ching* (1899; reprint, New York: Dover, 1963), 376. The term "obedient" 順 *shun* is construed in the sense of "compliant with moral principles."

## CHAPTER 27. PHYSIOGNOMY SET FORTH

1. *Shijing*, *Da Ya*, "Zheng Min," Mao no. 260; James Legge, trans., *The Chinese Classics* 5 vols. (Hong Kong: Chinese University of Hong Kong Press, 1970), 4:541 and Bernhard Karlgren, trans., *The Book of Odes: Chinese Text, Transcription and Translation* (Stockholm: Museum of Far Eastern Antiquities, 1950), 228.
2. Shi Kuang is a diviner mentioned in the *Zuozhuan*. The exact source of this quotation is unknown but it is similar to a statement made in a conversation between Shi Kuang and the heir apparent Jin found in the *Yi Zhoushu* 逸周書, chapter 64, "Taizi Jin Jie," 太子晉解, in *Sibu beiyao* 四部備要, vol. 101, 9.64.5B, where Shi Kuang states: "Your complexion is red, the color of fire indicates [you] will not live long."
3. *Yijing*, "Shuogua"; James Legge, trans., *The I Ching* (1899; reprint, New York: Dover, 1963), 431.
4. *Yijing*, "Xici," II.2; Legge, *The I Ching*, 382.
5. *Yijing*, "Xici," I.8; Legge, *The I Ching*, 360; and Richard John Lynn, trans., *The Classic of Changes: A New Translation of the* I Ching *as Interpreted by Wang Bi* (New York: Columbia University Press, 2004), 56–57.
6. *Gong* 宮 is the first note in the Chinese pentatonic scale; it represents the standard from which all other notes are derived. See *Huainanzi*

3.29; John S. Major, *Heaven and Earth in Early Han Thought: Chapters Three, Four, and Five of the* Huainanz. (Albany: State University of New York Press, 1993), 134–35.
7. The word *buwei* 部位 generally means "placement" but here indicates "proportion," and refers to the way in which the proportions of a child's body differ from those of an adult.
8. *Zuozhuan*, Wen 1; Stephen Durrant, Wai-yee Li, and David Schaberg, trans., *Zuo Tradition* (Zuozhuan): *Commentary on the Spring and Autumn Annals* (Seattle: University of Washington Press, 2016), 1:461, 541.
9. Mubo is also known as Gongsun Ao; Wenbo, is also known as Gu, and Huishu, is also known as Nan.
10. Meng refers to Meng Xianzi, the son of Wenbo (a.k.a. Gu).
11. *Guoyu*, "Zhouyu," 2.9. "To read," used here to translate *xiang* 相, as in the common English phrase "palm reading."
12. *Zuozhuan*, Wen 1; Durrant et al., *Zuo Tradition*, 1:465.
13. *Zuozhuan*, Xuan 4; Durrant et al., *Zuo Tradition*, 1:611.
14. *Zuozhuan*, Zhao 28; Durrant et al., 3.1687.
15. *Guoyu*, "Zhouyu," 3.1.
16. For Zigong, see *Zuozhuan*, Ding 15; for Zangwen, see *Zuozhuan*, Zhuang 15; the source of the account of Chen Xian is unclear.
17. For Cai Ze see *Shiji* 79; William H. Nienhauser Jr., trans. and ed., *The Grand Scribe's Records*. 11 vols. (Bloomington: Indiana University Press, 2018–2020), 7:246–53; for Deng Tong see *Shiji* 125; Nienhauser, *Grand Scribe's Records*, vol. 11:133–37.
18. This adage alludes a principle that unfinished bronze vessels cannot be placed on the ancestral altar.
19. *Shijing*, *Da Ya*, "Da Ming," Mao no. 236; Legge, *The Chinese Classics*, 4:432; Karlgren, *The Book of Odes*, 188.
20. See *Bohutong*, 9, "Wu Xing," 五行; Tjoe Som Tjan, *Po Hu Tung: The Comprehensive Discussions in the White Tiger Hall*, 2 vols. (Leiden: Brill, 1949–1952; reprint, Westport, CT: Hyperion Press, 1973), 2:439.

## CHAPTER 28. DREAMS SET FORTH

1. *Zuozhuan*, Zhao 1; Stephen Durrant, Wai-yee Li, and David Schaberg, trans., *Zuo Tradition* (Zuozhuan): *Commentary on the Spring and*

*Autumn Annals* (Seattle: University of Washington Press, 2016), 3:1325. King Wu reigned 1049/45–1043 BCE). King Cheng (r. 1043/35–1006 BCE), Taishu's older brother, invested Taishu with Tang, an area west of modern Yicheng County in Shanxi. Taishu's son, Lord Xie 侯燮, changed the name Tang to Jin 晉.

2. *Shijing, Xiao Ya*, "Si Gan," Mao no. 189; James Legge, trans., *The Chinese Classics*, 5 vols. (Hong Kong: Chinese University of Hong Kong Press, 1970), 4:306. On the two different words for "bear," see Shuheng Zhang, "Three Ancient Words for Bear," in *Sino-Platonic Papers* 294 (November 2019): 1–24.

3. *Shijing, Xiao Ya*, "Si Gan," Mao no. 189; Bernhard Karlgren, trans., *The Book of Odes: Chinese Text, Transcription, and Translation*. Stockholm: Museum of Far Eastern Antiquities, 1950), 131. The "Zhaohun" 招䰟 chapter of the *Chuci* describes this snake as having nine heads.

4. *Shijing, Xiao Ya*, "Wu Yang," Mao no. 190; based on Legge, *The Chinese Classics*, 4.309, and Karlgren, *The Book of Odes*, 132.

5. *Zuozhuan*, Xi 28.3; Durrant et al., *Zuo Tradition*, 1:417.

6. Unschuld, *Huang Di neijing su wen: Nature, Knowledge, and Imagery in an Ancient Chinese Medical Text* (Berkeley: University of California Press, 2003), 1:286. See Unschuld's note 56 for similar accounts in other texts.

7. Following Zhang Jue who, in contrast to Peng Bingcheng, notes two rather than one lacuna. Zhang Jue reconstructs this line according to a passage found in the *Meng zhan yi zhi* 夢占逸旨 of Chen Shiyuan 陳士元 (1516–1597 CE) as follows: 故先有所夢，後無差忒者，謂之直. (Thus, cases in which what has at first been dreamt later shows no discrepancies [with what actually occurs], this is called a direct dream). There is also further text missing that describes the "essence" of "dream."

8. See Ban Gu, *Bohutong*, in SBCK, vol. 22, 3:4A; Tjoe Som Tjan, *Po Hu T'ung: The Comprehensive Discussions in the White Tiger Hall*, 2 vols. (Leiden: Brill, 1949–1952; reprint Westport, CT: Hyperion Press, 1973), 2:437. In this system, the Five Phases alternate in various roles of dominance.

9. The current text is missing discussion of "direct" and "symbolic" dreams and thus accounts for only eight categories.

10. Alternately, this line can be translated: "Basically, the dreams that are described are the assertions of the drowsy and ignorant and the descriptions of the witless and blundering."
11. Following Peng Duo's gloss of *cong* 從 as *jiu* 就.
12. See *Lüshi chunqiu*, book 9, 季秋紀, "Almanac for the Third Month of Autumn," essay 5, "On Communication Between Souls," 精通: "所被攻者不樂,非或聞之也,神者先告也。身在于秦,所親愛在於齊,死而志氣不安,精或往來也." John Knoblock and Jeffrey Riegel, trans., *The Annals of Lü Buwei* (Stanford, CA: Stanford University Press, 2004), 219.
13. Following Zhang Jue's interpretation.
14. Wu Ding (r.?–1189 BCE) was a ruler of the Shang dynasty. Ershi, i.e., the Second Generation Emperor (r. 210–207 BCE), was the son and successor of Qin's first emperor (r. 221–210 BCE).
15. The term 變故 *biangu* could also refer to calamitous phenomena.
16. The word *hou* 候 has a wide array of meanings but is here interpreted according to the sense of the following passage from Fang Xuanling 房玄齡 (578–648) et al., comp., Jinshu 晉書, 10 vols. (Beijing: Zhonghua shuju, 1974), 12.2:330: "All floating vapor that covers the heavens so that the sun and moon lose their colors are due to the fluctuations of wind and rain." 凡遊氣蔽天,日月失色,皆是風雨之候也.
17. For "king" and "minister" see above.
18. Tai Si was the consort of Zhou King Wen. See Diwang shiji 帝王世紀 in Li Fang 李昉, ed. *Taiping yulan* 太平御覽, 7 vols. (Tainan: Pingping chubanshe, 1975), 84:3.
19. See *Guoyu*, "Zhou yu" 1.12; "Jinyu," 2.3.; translated in Henry, *Guoyu*, forthcoming. *Zuozhuan*, Zhuang 32; Durrant, *Zuo Tradition*, 1:223.
20. *Yijing*, "Xici zhuan," 2.8; *Shihsanjing zhushu*, 1:90; Legge, *The I Ching*, 399.

## CHAPTER 29. EXPLICATING DIFFICULTIES

1. Gengzi is an imaginary person who serves as interlocutor in this essay.
2. Commentators agree that the Recluse is Wang Fu himself.
3. Here the sense is that the ways of Yao and Shun are mutually opposed to each other. See *Hanfeizi* 40, "Nan shi 難勢," where the mutually exclusive terms are the all-penetrating spear and the impenetrable shield (*maodun* 矛盾); Liao, *Han Fei Tzu*, 2:203–04. In this passage in

## 29. EXPLICATING DIFFICULTIES ☙ 513

the QFL, "dagger-axe and buckler" are essentially synonyms for "spear and shield." The word *fa* 伐 usually means "to mount a punitive expedition"; it is used here in an uncommon but well-attested meaning—a type of shield, here translated as "buckler" (a small shield) to distinguish it from the more common word *dun* 盾 "shield."

4. The text is damaged.
5. The text is damaged.
6. See *Zhuangzi*, "Inner Chapters," in Richard John Lynn, trans., *Zhuangzi: A New Translation of the Sayings of Master Zhuang as Interpreted by Guo Xiang* (New York: Columbia University Press, 2022), 3–18.
7. Wang Xiangqian contends that "Boshu" is an error, and that the interlocutor here should be Gengzi, in a continuation of the previous section.
8. The text is damaged at this point.
9. The lords of Guan and Cai were brothers of the Duke of Zhou. At that time the duke was serving as regent for the future King Cheng. The brothers conspired with Wugeng, a surviving member of the Shang royal family, to rebel against the Duke, who executed them. For another version of this story see *Mencius* 2B9 in James Legge, trans., *The Chinese Classics*, 5 vols. (Hong Kong: Chinese University of Hong Kong Press, 1970), 2:224–25. Also see *Shangshu* "Preface," in Legge, *The Chinese Classics*, 3:10.
10. Lufu 录父 is either the son of Wugeng or part of Wugeng's name. See Mao Tianzhe 毛天哲, "武庚录父"的"录父"是武庚之子," "Wugeng Lufu de 'Lu fu' shi Wu Geng zhi Zi," *Qihe wenhua yanjiu* 淇河文化研究 (2015):10.
11. *Zuozhuan*, Xi 5; Stephen Durrant, Wai-yee Li, and David Schaberg, trans., *Zuo Tradition* (Zuozhuan): *Commentary on the Spring and Autumn Annals* (Seattle: University of Washington Press, 2016), 1:277, which is quoting *Shangshu*, "Cai Zhong Zhi Ming," translated in Legge, *The Chinese Classics*, 3:490.
12. See *Gongyang zhuan*, Zhao 1.
13. *Zuozhuan*, Yin 4; Durrant et al., *Zuo Tradiition*, 1:33.
14. *Yijing*, "Xici," part 2; James Legge, trans., *The I Ching* (1899; reprint, New York: Dover, 1963), 390.
15. "Qinzi" is an unidentified interlocutor and not necessarily a real person.
16. See *Dao De Jing* 38.

17. *Analects* XV.31; Legge, *The Chinese Classics*, 1:303. The passage continues (not quoted in QFL), "The superior man is anxious lest he should not get truth; he is not anxious lest poverty should come upon him."
18. *Yijing*, "Shuo Gua," 2; translated in Legge, *The I Ching*, 422–23.
19. *Fan* 反, "reverse," implies a contravention of the natural order of the Way.
20. The text continues here with two parallel lines and a summary line that have dropped out of the QFL; they are restored here in brackets. Translation is from Durrant et al., *Zuo Tradition*, Xuan 15, 1:681.
21. See similar passage in *Zuozhuan*, Xuan 15; Durrant et al., *Zuo Tradition*, 1:681.
22. The text here is a paraphrase of *Xunzi* 15, "Yi Bing," 議兵; which reads: 彼仁者愛人, 愛人故惡人之害之也, 義者循理, 故惡人之亂之也.
23. *Shijing, Xiao Ya*, "Mian Shui," Mao no. 183; from Legge, *The Chinese Classics*, 4:295.
24. "One fears the disaster of being crushed," meaning "when the state is falling apart." See *Guoyu*, "Lu Yu" 2.7: "Muzi said, 'That I did not draw back from execution was so that I might strengthen our central pillar. I feared that if the pillar was broken, we would be crushed beneath the rafters.'" From Eric Henry, trans, *Conversations of the States* (Seattle: University of Washington Press, forthcoming).
25. *Yijing*, Hexagam 48, line 3; Legge, *The I Ching*, 165.
26. Cishi 次室 (or Qishi 漆室) was a court lady during the reign of Zhou King Mu (r. 956–919 BCE). She was distressed because the king was too old and the heir-apparent was too young, a situation that portended disorder. The story is told in *Lienüzhuan* biography 3.13; translated in Anne Behnke Kinney, trans, and ed., *Exemplary Women of Early China: The* Lienüzhuan *of Liu Xiang* (New York: Columbia University Press, 2014), 60.
27. The unnamed woman of Chu was a court lady during the reign of King Qing Xiang of Chu (298–263 BCE). She raised a banner by the roadside to encourage the indolent king to defend his state. See *Lienüzhuan* biography 6.13; translated in Kinney, *Exemplary Women of Early China*, 130.

## CHAPTER 30. ON SOCIAL RELATIONS

1. *Shangshu*, "Pan Geng," part 1; James Legge, trans., *The Chinese Classics*, 5 vols. (Hong Kong: Chinese University of Hong Kong Press, 1970),

3:225, 229–30. Based on other passages from the "Pan Geng," Legge insists that the meaning is "old families" rather than "old friends."
2. *Analects* XIV:13; Legge, *The Chinese Classics*, 1:280.
3. Jie was the last ruler of the Xia dynasty, and according to legend, precipitated its fall; Zhi was a notoriously brutal bandit of the Spring and Autumn period.
4. Yan Hui was the favorite disciple of Confucius; Min Sun was distinguished by his purity and filial devotion. See *Analects*, Legge, *The Chinese Classics*, 1:113–14.
5. *Shijing, Guo Feng*," Bei Men," Mao no. 40; Legge, *The Chinese Classics*, 4:65–66: "I go out at the north gate, / With my heart full of sorrow. / Straitened am I and poor, / And no one takes knowledge of my distress."
6. *Shijing, Guo Feng*, "Gu Feng," Mao no. 35; Legge, *The Chinese Classics*, 4:55–58. Jie Zhitui remained loyal to Lord Wen of Jin during the latter's years of exile. When Lord Wen returned to Jin, Jie Zhitui refused a reward and joined his mother in seclusion. See *Zuozhuan*, Xi 24; Stephen Durrant, Wai-yee Li, and David Schaberg, trans., *Zuo Tradition (Zuozhuan): Commentary on the Spring and Autumn Annals* (Seattle: University of Washington Press, 2016), 1:379. Also see *Lüshi Chunqiu*, 12.3.1; translated in John Knoblock and Jeffrey Riegel, trans. *The Annals of Lü Buwei*. Stanford, CA: Stanford University Press, 2004), 263–64.
7. Wei Qi is also known as Dou Ying 竇嬰 and Wu An was also called Tian Fen 田蚡. See *Shiji* 107:2843; William H. Nienhauser Jr., trans. and ed., *The Grand Scribe's Records*, 10 vols. (Bloomington: Indiana University Press, 2018–2020), 9.2:146. Wei Qi led an army that quelled a revolt of regional kings against the Han emperor in 154 BCE. He later fell victim to a power struggle within the Dou clan and was executed in 131 BCE. Wu An rose to high office under Dou Ying's sponsorship but later turned against his mentor. The Marquis of Chang Ping is also called Wei Qing 衛青. The Marquis of Guanjun, also called Huo Qubing 霍去病, was Wei Qing's nephew. Both were famous generals known for their successful campaigns against the Xiongnu on the northern frontier. See *Shiji* 111:2938; Nienhauser, *The Grand Scribe's Records*, 9.2:341.
8. Lian Po (fl. 283 BCE) was a great general from the state of Zhao who suffered notable changes in fortune. See *Shiji* 81:2439–49; Nienhauser, *The Grand Scribe's Records*, 7:263–271. Honorable Zhai was also called

Zhai Gong 翟公. He served as Superintendent of Trials from 130 to 127 BCE. While he was in office, his courtyard was always crowded with petitioners, but when he was dismissed no one came to see him. He then posted on his gate a lament for the fickleness of life. See *Shiji* 120: 3113–14; Nienhauser, *The Grand Scribe's Records*, 10.3:260.

9. *Shijing, Cao Feng*, "Shi Jiu," Mao no. 152, translated in Legge, *The Chinese Classics*, 4:222–23.

10. *Analects* IX:27; Legge, *The Chinese Classics*, 1:225.

11. For Hou Ying, see *Shiji* 77:2377–85; Nienhauser, *The Grand Scribe's Records*, 7:215–21. For Yu Rang, see *Shiji* 86:2519–21; Nienhauser, *The Grand Scribe's Records*, 7.2:321–23. Hou Ying was a hermit residing in Wei who advised Wuji, the younger son of King Zhao of Wei (r. 295–277 BCE). Yu Rang disfigured and thus disguised himself to draw close to his enemy and assassinate him.

12. For Zhuan Zhu, *Shiji* 86:2516–2518; Nienhauser, *The Grand Scribe's Records*, 7.2:320–21. Zhuan Zhu was an assassin who devised a complex plot to bring Prince Guang of Wu (r. 514–496 BCE) to the throne. For Jing Ke, see *Shiji* 86:2526–38; Nienhauser, *The Grand Scribe's Records*, 7:325–33. Jing Ke, at the behest of the ruler of Yan, attempted to assassinate the future Qin Shihuangdi in 227 BCE. The attempt failed, and Jing Ke was executed.

13. This sentence is a paraphrase of *Shiji* 81:2451; Nienhauser, *The Grand Scribe's Records*, 7:272, translates the phrase: "it is using one's death to good purpose that is difficult."

14. Both of these figures risked angering their rulers but managed to demonstrate the loyalty of their actions. Pang Xun is tentatively identified as Shu Xu / Tou Xu, a personal attendant of Chong'er, the Marquis of Jin. Shu had charge of the marquis's treasury. When the marquis was forced to flee the state, Shu fled with the treasury but used it to procure the marquis's return. See *Zuozhuan*, Xi 24.1; Durrant et al., *Zuo Tradition*, 1:377. Bo Diao is likely Diao Bo 貂勃, a loyal courtier of King Xiang of Qi. See *Zhanguoce* in *Sibu congkan* 4.56a; James I. Crump, trans., *Chan-kuo ts'e*, 2nd ed. rev. (Ann Arbor: Center for Chinese Studies, University of Michigan, 1979), 210–13.

15. Zou Yang's dates are ca. 206–129 BCE. He served both the King of Wu and the King of Liang. See *Shiji* 83:2475; Nienhauser, *The Grand*

*Scribe's Records*, 7:290. Jie was the last tyrant of the Xia dynasty; Zhi was a famous bandit noted for his cruelty. Xu You was a worthy from the time of the sage ruler Yao noted for his purity.

16. For Han Anguo (fl. 143 BCE) and Tian Fen (d. 131 BCE), see *Shiji* 108:2860; Nienhauser, *The Grand Scribe's Records*, 9.2:290. For Zhai Fangjin (fl. 28 BCE) and Chunyu Zhang, see *Hanshu* 84:3421. Han Anguo 漢安國 (fl. 143 BCE) was a brother of Emperor Jing; he held various high offices and was known for his extravagant lifestyle. Zhai Fangjin (翟方進 fl. 28 BCE) was a Han scholar-official devoted to driving from office persons whom he regarded as unsuitable. He supported the scholar Chunyu Zhang 淳于長 but later turned against him and his associates.

17. On "quintessential sincerity" (*jing cheng* 精誠), see John S. Major, *Heaven and Earth in Early Han Thought: Chapters Three, Four, and Five of the* Huainanzi (Albany: State University of New York Press, 1993), 871: "'Sincerity' denotes complete, uninhibited integration between a person's most basic, spontaneous impulses and his or her expressed words and actions . . . the baseline energy of human consciousness (that is, the *shen*, "spirit") is merged with the Way and partakes of its extreme potency and dynamism. When stimulated by external phenomena, consciousness moves within the mind-body matrix as a wave of qi that culminates in feeling or thought or sound or emotion or some combination of them. . . . In the rare instances . . . an internal response evolves from baseline to full expression totally unimpeded, it produces a moment imbued with extraordinary power. Such sincerity can evoke a response in the minds and bodies of others or paranormal phenomena such as telekinesis."

18. See note on Hou Ying and Yu Rang above.

19. See *Shiji* 89:2571–87; Nienhauser, *The Grand Scribe's Records*, 8:1–25. Chen Yu (d. 204 BCE) was a rebel against the Qin dynasty (221–206 BCE) and close friend of Zhang Er (d. 202), with whom he later rose against the Qin. When Qin attacked the city of Julu, Chen Yu asked for support, but Zhang Er refused. Later, Xiang Yu gave the kingdom of Zhao to Zhang Er, enraging Chen Yu, who attacked and drove him away.

20. Xu You was a legendary recluse who lived in the predynastic era of Emperor Yao (traditionally ca. 2356–2255 BCE).

21. Meng Ke is the philosopher known by his latinized name Mencius. For this incident, see *Mencius* IIB.10.3; Legge, *The Chinese Classics*, 2:226–27. One *zhong* equaled 64 *dou*/pecks; one *sheng* equaled 10 pecks.
22. "Pool" likely refers to the mythological "Pool of Heaven," a constellation mentioned in the "Li Sao." David Hawkes, trans., *Ch'u Tz'u: Songs of the South* (Oxford: Oxford University Press, 1959), 28.
23. Boyi was a legendary worthy who lived at the time of the Shang-Zhou transition. To avoid the disloyalty of eating the food of the new administration, he starved to death. See *Analects* XVI:12. Chaofu was a legendary recluse in the time of Yao. See Huangfu Mi 皇甫謐, (215–282 CE), *Gaoshi zhuan* in *Sibu beiyao*, 104:2A-B.
24. *Shijing, Da Ya*, "Zheng Min," Mao no. 260; Legge, *The Chinese Classics*, 4:544.
25. Following Peng Duo's emendation of this line.
26. On the word 我 *wo*, see W. A. C. H. Dobson, *A Dictionary of the Chinese Particles* (Toronto: University of Toronto Press, 1974), 788.
27. *Mencius* IV.2.28; Legge, *The Chinese Classics*, 2:333.
28. *Lunyu* VI:28; Legge, *The Chinese Classics*, 1:194.
29. *Shijing, Guo Feng*, "Shi Jiu," Mao no. 152; Legge, *The Chinese Classics*, 4:222–23. Legge supplies the following explanatory passage in the *Mao Commentary* (*Maozhuan* 毛傳): "'The dove has a uniform method in feeding her young, giving them their food in the evening in the reverse order in which she had supplied them in the morning.' Equality and justice form the grand allusion of the piece." The second reference is derived from *Xiao Ya*, "Da Dong," Mao no. 203; Legge, *The Chinese Classics*, 4:353. The whetstone is characterized as being level and the arrow as being straight.
30. The "canine howls" are a reference to a passage in the "Jiu Bian" 九辯 of the *Chuci*: "It grieved me to be estranged for no offense of mine,/ And my breast was tormented with bitter pain. / How could I not be downcast and long for my lord/But ninefold are the gates of my lord, / And fierce dogs run out from them and bark." Hawkes, *Ch'u Tz'u: The Songs of the South*, 95.
31. This phrase is based on a passage from the *Yi Zhoushu* 逸周書, "Guanren jie" 官人解; see *Sibu congkan zhengbian*, 14:7.2a.
32. Characters are missing in this line; it is reconstructed based on its negative form in the previous line.

33. Following Peng Duo reading 忠 zhong as 禮 li.
34. Shijing, Guo Feng, "Ding Zhe Fang Zhong," Mao no. 50; Legge, The Chinese Classics, 4:81.
35. Yijing, "Treatise on the Symbolism of the Hexagrams," "Da Guo"; Legge, The I Ching (1899; reprint, New York: Dover, 1963), 302.
36. The "four seas" refers to all territory within the four seas, i.e., the world, and thus meaning "undaunted by the world."
37. Yijing, "Heng"; Legge, The I Ching, 126.
38. Shijing, Guo Feng, "Mang," Mao no. 58; Legge, The Chinese Classics, 4:100.
39. Shijing, Da Ya, "Zheng Min," Mao no. 260; Legge, The Chinese Classics, 4:544.
40. Lunyu VII:29; Legge, The Chinese Classics, 1:204.
41. Lunyu XV:3; Legge, The Chinese Classics, 1:295.
42. Shijing, Da Ya, "Zhan Ang," Mao no. 264; Legge, The Chinese Classics, 4:562. Following the text of the ode, which has the number "three" rather than "one." Following translation in Bernhard Kalgren, trans., The Book of Odes: Chinese Text, Transcription, and Translation (Stockholm: Museum of Far Eastern Antiquities, 1950), 237.
43. Lunyu XIV:29; Legge, The Chinese Classics, 1:28: "The superior man is modest in his speech but exceeds in his actions."
44. Shijing, Xiao Ya, "Qiao Yan," Mao no. 198; Legge, The Chinese Classics, 4:342.
45. Shijing, Xiao Ya, "Tiao Zhi Hua," Mao no. 233; Legge, The Chinese Classics, 4:423.
46. Shijing, Xiao Ya, "Qiao Yan," Mao no. 198; Legge, The Chinese Classics, 4:341
47. Lunyu X:1–2; Legge, The Chinese Classics, 1:227.
48. Xunzi 8, "Ruxiao," John Knoblock, trans., Xunzi: A Translation and Study of the Complete Work, 3 vols. (Stanford, CA: Stanford University Press, 1988–1994), 2:80.
49. Lunyu II:14; Legge, The Chinese Classics, 1:50.
50. Lunyu VI:16; translated in D. C. Lau, Confucius: the Analects (Harmondsworth, Middlesex: Penguin, 1979), 83.
51. Lunyu XIII:27; Legge, The Chinese Classics, 1:274.
52. Boyi and Shu Qi were worthies of the Shang dynasty noted for their loyalty and purity; Yuan Xian, courtesy name Zisi, was a disciple of

Confucius noted for his modesty, incorruptible nature, and willingness to live in poverty; Yan Hui was the favorite disciple of Confucius.

53. The terms *fa* 閥 and *yue* 閱 originally referred to the left and right gates of the mansions of influential families; the phrase can also mean "rank and length of service."

54. Yi Yin, a former slave, assisted the founder of the Shang dynasty. Lü Shang, who feigned madness to escape the service of the last Shang ruler, was later discovered and employed by the founder of the Zhou dynasty.

## CHAPTER 31. ENLIGHTENMENT AND LOYALTY

1. *Yijing*, "Xicizhuan," 2:8; James Legge, trans, *The I Ching* (1899; reprint, New York: Dover, 1963), 362.
2. See *Han Feizi*, "Zhu Dao" translated in W. K. Liao, trans., *The Complete Works of Han Fei Tzu*, 2 vols. (London: Arthur Probsthain, 1939), 31: "The ruler must not reveal his wants. For, if he reveals his wants, the ministers will polish their manners accordingly. The ruler must not reveal his views. For, if he reveals his views, the minsters will display their hues differently."
3. *Yijing*, "Xicizhuan," II:8; translated in Legge, *The I Ching*, 362.
4. For the terms "procedure" *shu* 術 and "positional power" *shi* 勢, see Pines, Yuri. "Worth vs. Power: Han Fei's "Objection to Positional Power" Revisited " *Asiatische Studien—Études Asiatiques* 74, no. 3 (2020): 687–710, https://doi.org/10.1515/asia-2019-0040. Pines states that in the concept of a ruler's positional power (shi 勢), "authority does not derive from his personal qualities. What matters is the power of his position, which allows him to command obedience of his subjects. It is essential therefore that the ruler firmly preserves the right of the final decision in his hands and never relegates it to the underlings."
5. *Shijing, Guo Feng*, "Fa Ke" 伐柯, Mao no. 158; James Legge, trans., *The Chinese Classics*, 5 vols. (Hong Kong: Chinese University of Hong Kong Press, 1970), 4:240.
6. Zhang Jue suggests that the "arts of spirit illumination" refers to the "arts of spiritually illuminated rulership."
7. *Shijing, Da Ya*, "Ban" 板, Mao no. 254; Legge, *The Chinese Classics*, 4:500.

8. *Mencius*, VI.A.6.7; Legge, *The Chinese Classics*, 2: 402.
9. Following Zhang Jue.
10. The ruler sits on his throne facing south and his ministers kneeling before him are facing north.
11. Wang Jipei here cites *Zhuangzi*, "Waiwu," 外物; "What Comes from Without:" "Rulers all wish their ministers to be faithful, but that faithfulness may not secure their confidence; hence Wu Yuan became a wanderer along the Jiang, and Chang Hong died in Shu, where (the people) preserved his blood for three years, when it became changed into green jade. Parents all wish their sons to be filial, but that filial duty may not secure their love; hence Xiaoji had to endure his sorrow, and Zeng Shen his grief." 人主莫不欲其臣之忠, 而忠未必信, 故伍員流於江, 萇弘死於蜀, 藏其血三年, 化而為碧。人親莫不欲其子之孝, 而孝未必愛, 故孝己憂而曾參悲。Translation from James Legge, trans., "The Writings of Chuang Tzu," in *The Texts of Taoism*, part II. (1891; reprint, New York: Dover Publications, 1962), 131.
12. Wang Zhang, critical of Wang Feng's monopoly of power, died in prison in 24 BCE; Wang Jia (d. 2 BCE), an outspoken critic of the Emperor Ai's favorites, also died in prison. See *Hanshu* 86:3488; 76:3238.
13. *Yijing*, Hexagram 61, "Zhongfu." Lynn, *The Classic of Changes*, 524.
14. *Shijing*, Xiao Ya, "Fa Mu" 伐木, Mao no. 165; Legge, *The Chinese Classics*, 4:253.
15. *Yijing*, Hexagram 48, "Jing" 井; Legge, *The I Ching*, 165.
16. See *Analects* XV.20; Legge, *The Chinese Classics*, 1:300; "The Master said, "What the superior man seeks, is in himself. What the mean man seeks, is in others."
17. See *Hanfeizi* 韩非子, "Shinan" 難勢 "A Critique of the Doctrine of Position:" "勢治者, 則不可亂; 而勢亂者, 則不可治也"; "Where there is order by force of circumstance, there can be no chaos; where there is chaos by force of circumstance, there can be no order." Liao, *Han Fei Tzu*, 2:203.
18. QFL erroneously omits the negative *wei* 未 in *Analects* IX.29; Legge, *The Chinese Classics*, 1:226: "unable to weigh occurring events along with us"; 未可與權. Also see E. Bruce Brooks and A. Taeko Brooks, trans, *The Original Analects: Sayings of Confucius and His Successors* (New York: Columbia University Press, 1998), 56. They translate the line as

"cannot [necessarily] be conferred with." Here they further define *quan* as "discretion," the exercise of judgment; the planning level." They also interpret the primary message of this passage as expressing the view that "not all talents operate at the next highest level," and that "one may need to change associates at the chief career transitions: from qualification, to employment, to policy-making 權."

19. *Yijing*, "Xici," I.5; Legge, *The I Ching*, 356.

## CHAPTER 32. TEACHINGS ON THE ROOT

1. The process described here represents an understanding of cosmogony that was widely shared in the Han era and beyond. With some variation of terminology and details, it is found in a number of texts, including *Liezi* chapter 1, translated by A. C. Graham, *The Book of Lieh-tzu: A Classic of the Tao* (New York: Columbia University Press, 1999), 18–20; and *Huainanzi* 3 "Tian Wen Xun" 天文訓; John S. Major, trans., *Heaven and Earth in Early Han Thought: Chapters Three, Four, and Five of the Huainanzi* (Albany: State University of New York Press, 1993), 114–15.
2. Yin is associated with turbid qi, and yang with clear qi. The "two powers" are Heaven and earth.
3. The phrase 壹鬱 *yiyu* has connotations of sexual intercourse. It is similar to 絪縕 *yinyun*, a term found in chapter 5 of the *Yijing*, "Xicizhuan," 2:5 used to designate the comingling of Heaven and earth and its generative power. See translation in Richard John Lynn, trans., *The Classic of Changes: A New Translation of the* I Ching *as Interpreted by Wang Bi* (New York: Columbia University Press, 2004), 85.
4. For the "jade device and jade transept, see chapter 15 notes.
5. "The Way of Heaven Bestows" is the title of chapter 82A of *Chunqiu fanlu*.
6. See *Yijing*, "Qian," in *Shisanjing zhushu* 1:17, 79; and "Xici," 2:1.7; Legge, *The I Ching* (1899; reprint, New York: Dover, 1963), 381.
7. *Shangshu*, "Gao Yao Mou"; Bernhard Karlgren, *Glosses on the Book of Documents* (Stockholm: Museum of Far Eastern Antiquities, 1948), 9; *Shisanjing zhushu*, 1:79.
8. Wang Jipei moved text from chapter 33, "Wu De Zhi," into the present chapter, specifically, the passage beginning with 者道之使也 through 何物不能.

9. Reading 虛 *xu* as 居 *ju*; see Zhang Jue, *Qianfulun quanyi*, 2.574n3.
10. Following Wang Jipei's reading of 憤 *fen* as *ji* 積 and 電 *dian* as 雹 *bao*.
11. Peng Bingcheng, *Qianfulun xinyi*, suggests that the phrase 變化之為 ought to read "變化云為," based on a passage from section 12 of the "Great Appendix" of the *Yijing*: "Therefore, amid the changes and transformations [taking place in Heaven and earth] and the words and deeds of human beings. . . ." See Legge, *The I Ching*, 404.
12. Literally: "As for what is changed, it is wondrous; what is moved by qi," which, according to Zhang Jue, is a transposition of "As for what qi moves and what it changes, it is wondrous." See, Zhang Jue, *Qianfulun quanyi*, 2:575n4.
13. Following Zhang Jue, who amends the original text, which reads 口 *kou*, with 胎 *tai*, See Zhang Jue, *Qianfulun quanyi*, 2:575n5. Since plants do not have mouths, 口 *kou* is likely wrong. Furthermore, the sudden transition from plants to humans seems suspect and more text may be missing here, which Zhang Jue acknowledges in his modern Chinese translation.
14. Modern commentators read 施 *shi* as an intransitive verb, i.e., "contribute it *to* their spirits and qi," even though it is not followed with a preposition. Wang Jipei cites *Zuozhuan*, Zhao 21.1 to bolster this interpretation: "Harmonious sounds enter the ear and are stored in the heart, and when the heart is at ease, there is the pleasure of music." 入于耳而藏于心; Stephen Durrant, Wai-yee Li, and David Schaberg, trans., *Zuo Tradition* (Zuozhuan): *Commentary on the Spring and Autumn Annals* (Seattle: University of Washington Press, 2016), 3:1593. If *shi* is read as a transitive verb, the meaning seems to be that the couple are "contributing" essence and spirit to engender a fetus.
15. On representing the law by effigy, see *Bohutong*, "Wuxing," in Tjoe Som Tjan, *Po Hu T'ung: The Comprehensive Discussions in the White Tiger Hall*. 2 vols. (Leiden: Brill, 1949–1952; reprint, Westport, CT: Hyperion Press, 1973), 2:603–04: "The punishments by effigy employed by the Five Emperors consisted in the representation of the Five Punishments by means of clothing. Those who had committed a crime which should be punished by branding had their heads covered with a cloth." The Five Emperors are the mythological rulers Fuxi, Shennong, Huangdi, Yao, and Shun; the Three Kings are Yu, Tang, and the combined Kings Wen and Wu.

16. For the "Great Transformation 大化, see *Xunzi* 15, "Yi Bing" 議兵, which describes how a virtuous ruler's moral example will transform the entire populace to replicate his own virtuous example. See translation in John Knoblock, trans., *Xunzi: A Translation and Study of the Complete Work*. 3 vols. (Stanford, CA: Stanford University Press, 1988–1994), 2:232.

## CHAPTER 33. TRANSFORMATION THROUGH VIRTUE

1. *Hanshi waizhuan* 5 contains a similar statement: 德也者、包天地之大; "Now as to virtue, it encompasses the magnitude of Heaven and Earth." Translation from James Robert Hightower, *Han Shih Wai Chuan: Han Ying's Illustrations of the Didactic Applications of the Classic of Songs* (Cambridge, MA: Harvard University Press, 1952), 186.
2. See *Lunyu* 16:1.11; James Legge, trans., *The Chinese Classics*, 5 vols. (Hong Kong: Chinese University of Hong Kong Press, 1970), 1:309: "So it is.—Therefore, if remoter people are not submissive, all the influences of civil culture and virtue are to be cultivated to attract them to be so; and when they have been so attracted, they must be made contented and tranquil" [夫如是, 故遠人不服, 則修文德以來之。既來之, 則安之].
3. Peng reads 精 *jing* "essence" as 情 *qing* "feelings."
4. *Shangshu*, "Hong Fan," 洪範, 39–40; Legge, *The Chinese Classics*, 3:343. See a summary of opinions on these terms in Bernhard Karlgren, *Glosses on the Book of Documents* (Stockholm: Museum of Far Eastern Antiquities, 1948), 247.
5. Following Yu Yue's interpretation of this line, reading 傷賢 *shangxian* as 傷睿 *shangrui*.
6. Hu Chusheng, in contrast to other commentators, suggests that in this sentence 不可 *buke* should be read as 可不 *kebu*.
7. *Shijing, Da Ya*, "Xing Wei" 行葦, Mao no. 246; Legge, *The Chinese Classics*, 4:472 (modified). The prince mentioned in this poem is generally considered to be either King Wen of Zhou or his father or grandfather, though a later tradition connects Gong Liu to this ode.
8. *Shijing, Da Ya*, "Han Lu," 旱麓; Mao no. 239; Legge, *The Chinese Classics*, 4:445. This ode is thought to refer to an entertainment given by one of the Zhou kings for his relatives.

9. See *Shijing, Da Ya*, "Gong Liu," 公劉; Mao no. 250; Legge, *The Chinese Classics*, 4:483. As Legge points out, he was not a duke, but his descendants honored him with that title. In the Han, Gong Liu, was identified as an ancient worthy and descendant of Hou Ji who served as a model for the Zhou founders. He is credited with caring for all things, even plants. *Lienüzhuan* 6.3 states: "Have you heard of the conduct of Gong Liu? When sheep and oxen tread on rushes and reeds, he felt sympathy for the common people, and his concern even extended to plants and trees. Would he have countenanced the killing of an innocent person? See Anne Behnke Kinney, *Exemplary Women: The Lienüzhuan of Liu Xiang* (New York: Columbia University Press, 2014), 113.
10. The ability to laugh represents a stage of child development.
11. "Harmonious qi" is the product of the harmonious blending of yin and yang. It is the substance from which all matter emerges.
12. *Shijing, Da Ya*, "Wen Wang," 文王; Mao no. 235; Legge, *The Chinese Classics*, 4:431.
13. The Ji lineage refers to the royal house of Zhou. According to legend, laws were not established until the dynasty's third ruler, King Cheng, assumed the throne.
14. *Analects* XII:13; Legge, *The Chinese Classics*, 1:257; and II:3, 1:146 respectively.
15. Following Peng Duo. Zhang Jue suggests rendering the line "illuminate guidelines and focus on duty."
16. *Shangshu*, "Shun Dian," 舜典; Legge, *The Chinese Classics*, 3:44–45: "[Shun] said, 'Xie, the people continue unfriendly with one another, and do not observe docilely the five orders of relationship. It is yours, as the Minister of Instruction, reverently to set forth the lessons of duty belonging to those five orders. Do so with gentleness . . . Gao Yao. . . . It is yours, as minister of Crime, to employ the five punishments for the treatment of offences, for the infliction of which there are the three appointed places.'"
17. *Shijing, Da Ya*, "Zheng Min," 烝民; Mao no. 260; Legge, *The Chinese Classics*, 4:541. The translation is from Michael Hunter, *The Poetics of Early Chinese Thought: How the* Shijing *Shaped the Chinese Philosophical Tradition* (New York: Columbia University Press, 2021), 51. The two

526 ∽ 33. TRANSFORMATION THROUGH VIRTUE

lines preceding this quotation are: "Heaven birthed the many people; / They have distinctions, they have rules. / The people cling to custom, / They are fond of fine virtue."

18. The "six coordinates" are up-down, left-right, and front-back.
19. This phrase is linked to the phrase 變化云為 *bianhua yunwei*, which appears in the sentence "Therefore amid the changes and transformations (taking place in heaven and earth), and the words and deeds of men, events that are to be fortunate have their happy omens," which is found in *Yijing*, "Xicizhuan," 2.6, Legge, *The I Ching* (1899; reprint, New York: Dover, 1963), 404.
20. A similar statement is found in the biography of Dong Zhongshu (179–104 BCE). See *Hanshu* 56.2501.
21. The "revival" refers to the reign of King Xuan of Zhou (827–782 BCE).
22. King Li (r. 857-842 BCE; and King You (r. 781–771 BCE) were both evil and incompetent rulers who helped prompt the collapse of the Western Zhou.
23. *Analects* VIII:21; Legge, *The Chinese Classics*, 1:202.
24. *Shijing*, *Da Ya*, "Wen Wang," 文王; Mao no. 235; Legge, *The Chinese Classics*, 4:431.
25. Fuxi and Shennong were culture heroes of remote antiquity.

## CHAPTER 34. TREATISE ON THE FIVE POWERS

1. The three "August Ones" are variously identified as Fuxi, Shennong, and Huangdi or the sovereigns of Heaven, earth, and humanity.
2. *Zhengsuo* 正朔 refers to the month in which the lunar year begins upon the succession of a new ruler. See *Liji*, "Da Zhuan," in *Shisanjing zhushu*, 34.16.1506C; James Legge, trans., *Li Chi* (Oxford University Press, 1879; reprint, ed. Winberg Chai, 2 vols. New Hyde Park, NY: University Books, 1967), 2:61; and *Bohu tong*, "San zheng" 三正, 7:5B in SBCK, 22:6B; translated in Tjoe Som Tjan, *Po Hu Tung: The Comprehensive Discussions in the White Tiger Hall*. 2 vols. (Leiden: Brill, 1949–1952; reprint, Westport, CT: Hyperion Press, 1973), 2:549–50.
3. "Stimulus" is the term used to describe the conception of extraordinary figures. Various forms of stimulus are described below.

4. Following Hu Dajun, Li Zhongli, and Li Deqi, trans. and comm., *Wang Fu Qianfu lun yizhu* (Lanzhou: Gansu renmin chubanshe, 1991), Zhang Jue has, "Sometimes succeeding rulers relied on the founding of a state; some relied on their governance and nurturing of the common people."
5. Tai Hao is another name for Fu Xi.
6. Leize was a swamp in the southeast of Pu County in present-day Shandong.
7. Tai Hao (who, according to legend, acceded to the throne 2852 BCE) is Fu Xi's dynastic appellation; he is also known by his personal name Bao Xi 宸羲.
8. The "solar horn" is a bone that juts out of the forehead.
9. Chen was in present-day Huaiyang 淮陽 County in Henan.
10. See *Zuozhuan*, Zhao 17; Stephen Durrant, Wai-yee Li, and David Schaberg, trans., *Zuo Tradition* (Zuozhuan): *Commentary on the Spring and Autumn Annals* (Seattle: University of Washington Press, 2016), 3:1545.
11. See *Yijing*, "Xici," 2; James Legge, trans., *The I Ching* (1899; reprint, New York: Dover, 1963), 382–83.
12. Only the *Qianfulun* identifies Di Ku as the progeny of Fu Xi.
13. Reading *gan* 干 as *dou* 斗, i.e., "Big Dipper." Zhang Jue reads 斗 as alluding to 魁 *kui*, the four stars of the bowl of the Big Dipper that form a square. Here the word 戴 *dai* means "top of the head / calvaria," thus, "square-shaped calvaria."
14. Compare with *Shiji* 1:13; William H. Nienhauser Jr., trans. and ed., *The Grand Scribe's Records*, 10 vols. (Bloomington: Indiana University Press, 2018–2020), 1:5: "He calculated the movements of the sun and moon, welcoming them and speeding their parting."
15. "Six Blossoms" 六英 music is mentioned in *Huainanzi* 淮南子, "Qi Su Xun" 齊俗訓, translated in John S. Major, Sarah A. Queen, Andrew Seth Meyer, and Harold D. Roth, trans., *The Huainanzi: A Guide to the Theory and Practice of Government in Early Han China* (New York: Columbia University Press, 2010), 410; and *Lüshi chunqiu*, "Gu Yue" 古樂; John Knoblock and Jeffrey Riegel, trans. *The Annals of Lü Buwei* (Stanford, CA: Stanford University Press, 2004), 148. Zhang Jue notes that the term refers to a form of music involving six (or more)

instruments. *Bohutong* 白虎通, in *Sibu congkan zhengbian*, 22.2. 8A refers to the music of Di Ku as the "Five Blossoms" *wjing* 五英; translated in Tjan, *Po Hu T'ung*, 2:393. Peng Duo suggests that in the *Qianfulun* passage, 英 *ying* should be read as 茎 *jing* "stalks."

16. See *Zuozhuan*, Wen 17; Durrant et al., *Zuo Tradition*, 1:573. According to the *Zuozhuan* account, these men were descendants of Di Ku.
17. Ji is the royal Zhou clan name. See Edwin G. Pulleyblank, "Ji 姬 and Jiang 姜: The Role of Exogamic Clans in the Organization of the Zhou Polity," *Early China* 25 (2000): 1–27. The personal name, "Qi" refers to the myth of the abandonment of the child also known as Hou Ji 后稷 "Lord Millet."
18. Following Zhang Jue's interpretation of 披頤 *piyi* as "cleft chin." Other annotators read the words as denoting 歧嶷 *qini*, a description of Hou Ji found in *Shijing*, *Da Ya*, "Sheng Min" 生民, Mao no. 245, which Zhu Xi glosses as 峻茂 *junmao* "majestic."
19. On the title *situ* 司徒, see David Keightley, "Public Work in Ancient China: A Study of Forced Labor in the Shang and Western Chou" (PhD diss., Columbia University 1969), 259–80.
20. Lieshan refers to Shennong 神農, also known as Yandi 炎帝. According to *Zuozhuan*, Zhuang 29; Durrant et al., *Zuo Tradition*, 3:1701: "Zhu, a son of the Lieshan lineage, was in charge of the altar of grain and was offered sacrifices until the Xia. Qi of Zhou was also in charge of the altar of grain, and has been sacrificed to has been offered sacrifices since the Shang."
21. Lieshan is another name for Shennong, the "divine husbandman."
22. On Tai Ren, the spouse of Wang Ji 王季 and mother of King Wen, see *Shijing*, *Da Ya*, "Da Ming," 大明, Mao no. 236; James Legge, trans., *The Chinese Classics*, 5 vols. (Hong Kong: Chinese University of Hong Kong Press, 1970), 4:433. The word *gan* 感, "arousal" (which could also be translated as "stimulation"), refers to sexual intercourse. See *Yijing*, "Tuan Zhuan," (Commentary on the Judgments); Richard John Lynn, trans., *The Classic of Changes: A New Translation of the* I Ching *as Interpreted by Wang Bi* (New York: Columbia University Press, 2004), 329.
23. Qi is identified as a place northeast of the West Qi mountains in Shaanxi Province.

24. Yu refers to the state of Yu at the beginning of the Zhou. See *Shiji* 4:117; Nienhauser, *Grand Scribe's Records*, 1:59.
25. The 昭穆 *zhao-mu* system, consisting of two rows of spirit tablets arranged in the ancestral temple, employed alternating terms to denote generations. If a father has the position *zhao*, then his son will be assigned the position *mu*, and the grandson again is given the position *zhao*. See *Liji*," Jitong," *Shisanjing zhushu*, 2:1605B; translated in Legge, *Li Chi*, 2:246.
26. King Mu (r. 956–918 BCE).
27. Reading *lin* 鱗 as *xian* 鮮.
28. The text to the end of this paragraph is drawn from *Yijing*, "Xici," 2; Legge, *The I Ching*, 383.
29. Yi 伊 is Yao's surname. Gaoxin 高辛 was second of the Five Sovereigns of the legendary period, Yao was fourth.
30. *Bohutong* 1:8A describes the music as "Greatly making illustrious the Way of Heaven, Earth and Man"; Tjan, *Po Hu T'ung*, 2:393.
31. Hanshi is the personal name of Liu Bang's mother, while "Jade Flower" seems to represent her avatar or supernatural form. *Shiji* 8:342n5 surveys various theories concerning the surname of Liu Bang's mother. Also see Nienhauser, *Grand Scribe's Records*, 2:2–3n4.
32. Liu Ji is Liu Bang, the founding emperor of the Han dynasty.
33. The "pivot" is the northern celestial pole star and forms part of the "Big Dipper." See John C. Didier, "In and Outside the Square: The Sky and the Power of Belief in Ancient China and the World c. 4500 BC–AD 200," *Sino-Platonic Papers* 192 (September 2009):147–56. The word *ye* in this passage may refer to an astral rather than terrestrial field. See the discussion of the *jiuye*, nine-field, system in David Pankenier, "Applied Field-Allocation Astrology in Zhou China: Duke Wen of Jin and the Battle of Chengpu (632 BC)," *Journal of the American Oriental Society* 119, no. 2 (1999): 266.
34. *Bohutong* 白虎通, 1:8A states that the Yellow Emperor's Xian Chi (咸池) music "was greatly applied (池= 施 *shi*) to all under Heaven and put into practice. Everything (咸 *xian*) that was created by Heaven and was borne by earth received the beneficent application of spiritual power"; Tjan, *Po Hu T'ung*, 2:393.

35. This is not to say that people prior to this time wore no clothing but that the Yellow Emperor devised clothing appropriate for a civilized people and taught the people how to make it.
36. *Lunyu* XX:1; Legge, *The Chinese Classics*, 1:350.
37. See *Zuozhuan*, Xiang 25; translation based on Durrant et al., *Zuo Tradition*, 2:1151.
38. See *Hanshu* 21, part 2, 1012.
39. See *Zuozhuan*, Zhao 17; Durrant et al., *Zuo Tradition*, 3:1545. Wang Fu reproduces the list found in the *Zuozhuan* with minor differences.
40. Following Zhang Jue. Peng Bingcheng and Hu Dajun et al. are vaguer, rendering the phrase: "to increase the understanding of the people."
41. See *Zuozhuan*, Zhao 29; Durrant et al., *Zuo Tradition*, 3:1701. The translators associate each of these posts with one of the Five Phases: Gou Mang, Wood; Gai, Metal; Xiu and Xi, Water.
42. Qiongsang was the dwelling place of Shao Hao.
43. *Shangshu*, "Lü Xing"; Legge, *The Chinese Classics*, 3:595.
44. *Shangshu*, "Yu Gong"; Legge, *The Chinese Classics*, 3:92–127 describes the nine kinds of tribute.
45. See *Shangshu*, "Wu Zi Zhi Ge"; Legge, *The Chinese Classics*, 3:157. This text relates that after Tai Kang had gone on a hunting expedition that lasted more than a hundred days, Qi resisted Tai Kang's return and the five brothers fled with their mother. *Guoyu*, "Chuyu," 1.1, interprets *wuguan* 五觀 as a reference to the five brothers. The *Zhushu jinian* 竹書紀年; Legge, *The Chinese Classics*, 3, "Prolegomena," 118 defines Wuguan as Qi's youngest son. Guan is also interpreted as the name of a place on the Luo River and may signify something like "the Guan Five." See the "Zheng Yi" commentary on *Shiji* 44:1844n1.
46. See *Zuozhuan*, Xiang 4; Durrant et al., *Zuo Tradition*, 2:917.
47. See *Zuozhuan*, Ai 1; Durrant, *Zuo Tradition*, 3:1835. Lady Min was the consort of Xiang.
48. The first four men were virtuous officers. Han Zhuo was a descendant of the ruler of Han, Boming. In high antiquity, Boming had once tried to wrest power from Archer Yi.
49. See *Zuozhuan*, Xiang 4; Durrant et al., *Zuo Tradition*, 2:917.
50. Mi was a minister who served Yi.

51. The QFL seems to have reversed the place names in this sentence. The *Zuozhuan* says: "He placed Ao in Guo and Yi in Ge." See *Zuozhuan*, Xiang 4; Durrant et al., *Zuo Tradition*, 3:917.
52. Si was one of the Yu leaders.
53. *Cheng* 成 was a term for a piece of land comprising 10 square *li* on a side, thus 100 square li; a *lü* 旅 is a brigade of 500 troops.
54. See *Zuozhuan*, Ai 1; Durrant et al.; *Zuo Tradition*, 3:1835. The two Yao women were the daughters of Si of Yu, whose clan name was Yao.
55. *Zuozhuan*, Xiang 4; Durrant et al., *Zuo Tradition*, 2:917, where it is pointed out that the last reference to Yu refers to the legendary controller of floods and not Si of Yu. On the term 配天, see *Liji*, "Jing Jie" 經解: "The son of Heaven forms a ternion with heaven and earth. Hence, in power of his goodness he is their correlate, and his benefits extend at once to all things." 天子者，與天地參。故德配天地，兼利萬物. Legge, *Li Chi*, 2.256. We are grateful to Robert Eno for sharing his understanding of the term 配天.
56. Reading 祁 *qi* as 鄰 *tan*. On the connection of this lineage with Tan, see *Zuozhuan*, Xiang 17; Durrant et al., *Zuo Tradition*, 3:1545.
57. *Lunyu* XIV:6; Legge, *The Chinese Classics*, 1:277; translation based on E. Bruce Brooks and A. Taeko Brooks, trans., *The Original Analects: Sayings of Confucius and His Successors* (New York: Columbia University Press, 1998), 119.
58. According to Zhang Jue, the name Bonou 泊渜 is a mistake for Tongcheng 彤城. See *Shangshu*, "Gu Ming"; Legge, *The Chinese Classics*, 3:545; and *Shiji* 2.89; Nienhauser, *Grand Scribe's Records*, 1:38.
59. "Twinkling Brilliance" 搖光 *yaoguang*, i.e., Eta Ursae Majoris, a star in the constellation of Ursa Major, is the most eastern star in the Big Dipper and one of the brightest stars in the night sky.
60. See *Zuozhuan*, Zhao 29; Durrant et al., *Zuo Tradition*, 3:1701. Here Zhuanxu and Gong Gong are listed as two different people.
61. Following Wang Jipei's addition of *bu* 不 before the word *fu* 服. See *Guoyu*, "Chu Yu," 2: "When affairs began to decline in the time of Shao Hao, the Jiuli tribes threw virtue into disarray. . . . When Zhuan Xu inherited [the realm], he ordered that Zhong, the Chief of the South, take charge of Heaven so as to reduce the spirits to order, and he ordered Li, the Chief of Fire, to take charge of Earth, so as to reduce the people

to order." Translation from Eric Henry, trans., *Conversations of the States* (Seattle: University of Washington Press, forthcoming).
62. The names listed here show minor differences from the list found in *Zuozhuan*, Wen 18; Durrant et al., *Zuo Tradition*, 1:573.
63. *Zuozhuan* Zhao 29; Durrant et al., *Zuo Tradition*, 3:1701. Also see *Guoyu*, "Lu Yu" 1: "When Gonggong Shi was lord over the nine regions, his son Hou Tu was able to pacify the nine provinces, so he is sacrificed to as She, the earth spirit." Translation from Henry, *Conversations of the States*.
64. See *Shiji* 3.91; Nienhauser, *Grand Scribe's Records*, 1:14n151 for a discussion of the title *situ* 司徒, which involves the management of *tu* "foot soldiers," who engaged in military service and public work projects. The five categories of filial affection are the father's sense of duty, the mother's love, the elder brother's friendship, the younger brothers respect, and the child's filial piety.
65. Wu Ding, the earliest known ruler of the Shang, died 1189 BCE.
66. "Throughout the four quarters" refers to the entire realm in all directions.
67. See *Shangshu*, "Shuo Ming"; Legge, *The Chinese Classics*, 3:252.
68. Weizi was the half-brother of Di Xin; Jizi was the uncle of King Djou.

## CHAPTER 35. A RECORD OF LINEAGE AND CLAN NAMES

1. "Qian" and "Kun," both trigrams of the *Yijing*, represent Heaven and earth.
2. Peng Duo and Zhang Jue both argue that many of the characters in QFL 35 that represent names are incorrect. Since their arguments are numerous and lengthy, we will note a number of obvious errors and urge readers to consult Zhang's notes directly for further explication. Also, by Han times, the distinction between the *xing* "clan name" and the *shi* "lineage" name was blurred. See Yan Xia, *Zhongguo zaoqi xing shi zhidu yanjiu* (Tianjin: Tianjin guji chubanshe, 1996). Yuri Pines suggests translating both as "surname," but we will maintain the distinction in the current translation. See Yuri Pines, "Names and Titles in Eastern Zhou Texts," *T'oung Pao* 106 (2020): 714–20.

3. Zhang Jue's text has the word 臣 *chen*, "officials," where Wang Jipei's edition has 后 *hou*, "ruler." Also see *Guoyu*, "Chu Yu," part 2, item 1: 使名姓之後，能知四時之生、犧牲之物、玉帛之類、采服之儀、彝器之量、次主之度、屏攝之位、壇場之所、上下之神、氏姓之出; "[As for] descendants of surname-bearing clans, who were capable of knowing the fruits of the four seasons, the livestock suitable for sacrifice, the varieties of jade and silk brocade, the appropriate types of colored vestments, the capacities of the sacrificial vessels, the hierarchy of worshipped spirits, the positioning of curtains and fans, the locations of sites and grounds, the higher and lower spirits—the names of the respective clans descended therefrom." Translation based on Eric Henry, trans., *Conversations of the States* (Seattle: University of Washington Press, forthcoming).
4. Following Zhang Jue's reading of 民 *min* as 氏 *shi*.
5. The "Three Eras" are the Xia, Shang, and Zhou dynasties.
6. Following Zhang Jue reading 志 *zhi* as 邑 *yi*, "settlement."
7. The name Wulu 五鹿 was derived from the name of a fief Chong Er 重耳 bestowed on Zifan 子犯 (also known as Hu Yan 狐偃). See *Zuozhuan*, Xi 23, 28; Stephen Durrant, Wai-yee Li, and David Schaberg, trans., *Zuo Tradition* (Zuozhuan): *Commentary on the Spring and Autumn Annals* (Seattle: University of Washington Press, 2016), 1:365, 409. However, this passage does not explicitly mention the bestowal of this place on Zifan, also known as Hu Yan 狐偃. Zheng Qiao's 郑樵 text *Tongzhi: Shizu lüe* 通志·氏族略, ca. 1161, provides similar examples.
8. *Zuozhuan*, Xi 25; Ai 12; Durrant et al., *Zuo Tradition*, 1:389, 3.1907.
9. The seven kingdoms were Qin, Chu, Yan, Qi, Wei, Zhao, and Wey.
10. Based on the text of the *Zuozhuan*, Hsu Cho-yun estimates that the number of eastern states was 148, but that figure does not include non-Zhou groups. See Michael Loewe and Edward Shaughnessy, eds., *The Cambridge History of Ancient China* (Cambridge: Cambridge University Press, 1999), 547. Also see the discussion of the "great lineage" and "small lineage system" in Mark Edward Lewis, *Sanctioned Violence in Early China* (Albany: State University of New York, 1990), 33–34: The courts of the feudal lords formed a "small lineage" which was a reduced replica of the "great lineage" of the Zhou king, and the hereditary

officials of these lords formed a "small lineage" which was a reduced replica of the "great lineage" of the feudal state."

11. The "various grandson" branches include the Mengsun, Gongsun, and Shusun.

12. Zhang Jue cites the example of the great-grandson of Xiahou Ying, Xiahou Po. He is said to have changed his surname to that of his wife, the imperial princess Pingyang. See *Hanshu* 41, 2079. Michael Loewe believes that this claim is unsubstantiated. See Michael Loewe, *A Biographical Dictionary of the Qin, Former Han and Xin Periods (221 BC–AD 24)* (Leiden: Brill, 2000), 595.

13. "The *Shangshu* says: '[Yao] appeased and made illustrious the Hundred Clans.' Why are there one hundred clan-names? Anciently the Sages by blowing the musical pitch-pipes fixed the clan-names, and thereby registered the [different kinds of] kindred. Man is born with the Five Constant [Virtues] in him. There are five principal tones: *gong*, *shang*, *jue*, *zhi*, and *yu*, which, combining together five by five, make twenty-five [tones], and further give birth to the four seasons. With the [four] different climates and the [twenty-five] various tones the completion is obtained. Therefore there are one hundred clan-names." See *Bohu tong*, in *Sibu congkan*, 22; "Xingming" 8.7B-8A; translated in Tjoe Som Tjan, *Po Hu Tung: The Comprehensive Discussions in the White Tiger Hall*. 2 vols. (Leiden: Brill, 1949–1952; reprint, Westport, CT: Hyperion Press, 1973), 2:579–80.

14. Following Wang Jipei.

15. See *Zuozhuan*, Xi 21; Durrant et al., *Zuo Tradition*, and 1:351; *Lunyu* XVI.1. These places were all territories in the state of Lu.

16. *Lunyu* XVI.1.

17. *Guoyu*, "Zhengyu," 1: "The Jiang were the descendants of Bo Yi 伯夷. . . . Bo Yi was able to behave in a ritually efficacious way with the spirits and [thus] assist Yao"; translation from Henry, *Conversations of the States*. Also see *Shangshu* in James Legge, trans., *The Chinese Classics*, 5 vols. (Hong Kong: Chinese University of Hong Kong Press, 1970), 3:25 595.

18. See *Shiji* 32.1477–79; translated in William H. Nienhauser Jr., trans. and ed., *The Grand Scribe's Records*, 10 vols. (Bloomington: Indiana University Press, 2018–2020), 5.1, 31–39.

19. *Shijing*, "Da Ya," "Song Gao," 崧高 Mao no. 259; Legge, *The Chinese Classics*, 4: 536. Wang Fu's text differs slightly from Mao; Mao has 謝 xie where Wang Fu has 序 xu.
20. The Luhun were the Rong people bearing the Jiang clan name who dwelled between the Yi and Luo rivers. See *Zuozhuan*, Xi 22; Durrant et al., *Zuo Tradition*, 1:353.
21. Compare to *Guoyu*, "Jinyu," 4, item 9.
22. *Zuozhuan*, Xiang 3; Durrant et al., *Zuo Tradition*, 2:903.
23. *Zuozhuan*, Wen 7; Durrant et al., *Zuo Tradition*, 1:505—here a notice of the marriage between the Lu minister, Meng Mubo and Dai Ji 戴己 of Ju supports this connection.
24. *Zuozhuan*, Ding 1; Durrant et al., *Zuo Tradition*, 3:1733.
25. *Zuozhuan*, Xuan 3; Durrant et al., *Zuo Tradition*, 1:605. Jí 姞 is distinguished from Ji 姬 by the diacritical mark.
26. *Zuozhuan*, Xuan 3; Durrant et al., *Zuo Tradition*, 1:605. The text of the *Zuozhuan* differs slightly: "I am your ancestor. Let this be your child. As the orchid is the most fragrant flower of the domain, people will take him to themselves and love him, just as they do this flower." 余而祖也. 以是為而子, 以蘭有國香, 人服媚之如是,
27. Commentators disagree with some of the names cited by Wang Fu.
28. For Zhi Du, see *Hanshu* 90:3647; for Zhi Junzhang (also called 郅惲 Zhi Yun), see *Hou Hanshu* 29:1023–32.
29. *Guoyu*, "Chuyu," 2.1; translation based on Henry, *Conversations of the States*.
30. *Guoyu*, "Zhengyu," 1; translation based on Henry, *Conversations of the States*.
31. *Guoyu*, "Chuyu," 2.1; translation based on Henry, *Conversations of the States*. The "Three Miao" were an ethnic group that resided in what is present-day southern Henan. In "Xi Bo," Bo is likely an error for He 和.
32. The Three Eras were the Xia, Shang, and Zhou dynasties.
33. *Shijing*, "Da Ya," "Chang Wu" 常武, Mao no. 263; Legge, *The Chinese Classics*, 4:556.
34. Here, Wang Fu's text closely resembles Sima Qian's own account of his ancestry. See *Shiji* 130:3285–86; translated in Burton Watson, trans., *Records of the Grand Historian. Han Dynasty*. 2 vols. New York: Columbia University Press, 1961/1993), 1:42.

35. *Guoyu*, "Zhengyu," 1; has 斟 *zhen* rather than 斯 *si*.
36. *Zuozhuan* Zhao 29; Durrant et al., *Zuo Tradition*, 3:1699.
37. *Hanshi waizhuan* 4.2; James Robert Hightower, *Han Shih Wai Chuan: Han Ying's Illustrations of the Didactic Applications of the Classic of Songs* (Cambridge, MA: Harvard University Press, 1952), 125–26. Here Huanlong is referred to as Guanlong Feng 關龍逢.
38. This list differs from that found in *Guoyu*, "Zhengyu," 1: Kunwu 昆吾, Su 蘇, Gu 顧, 溫, 董. The name Ji 籍 is likely an error for Su 蘇.
39. The QFL has 禿姓 *tuxing* "Tui clan." Zhang Jue persuasively argues that *tui* is an error for 董 *dong*.
40. Following *Guoyu*, "Zhengyu," 1, reading *hui* 會 as *zhou* 舟.
41. See *Guoyu*, "Zhouyu," 2, item 1.
42. *Shijing*, "Guo Feng," "Gao Qiu," 羔裘, Mao no. 146; Legge, *The Chinese Classics*, 4:215–16; *Shijing*, "Guo Feng," "Fei Feng," 匪風, Mao no. 149; Legge, *The Chinese Classics*, 4:218.
43. Zhong was the courtesy name of the lord of Kuai.
44. *Zuozhuan* Xuan 15; Durrant et al., *Zuo Tradition*, 1:679–80.
45. See *Zuozhuan* Xiang 10; Durrant et al., *Zuo Tradition*, 2:968–69. The Master of Biyang's clan name was Yun.
46. See *Shiji* 40.1690; Nienhauser, *Grand Scribe's Records*, 5.1:382–83.
47. See *Shiji* 40.1691; Nienhauser, *Grand Scribe's Records*, 5.1:383.
48. See *Zuozhuan* Xi 26; Durrant et al., *Zuo Tradition*, 1:399.
49. The lineage name Yang 陽 is repeated in this paragraph and may be an error for 揚.
50. See *Shiji* 40:1694; Nienhauser, *Grand Scribe's Records*, 5.1:386. According to the *Shiji*, Juo Ao is Xiong Yi 熊儀 (r. 790–764 BCE). According to Zhang Jue, the relationships as described here are skewed.
51. See *Zuozhuan* Xi 26; Durrant et al., *Zuo Tradition*, 1:399.
52. See *Zuozhuan* Ding 5; Durrant et al., *Zuo Tradition*, 3:1765. Shen Wuwei is also called Shen Zhou. Zhang Jue suggests that he was the progeny of King Wen of Chu (r. 689–677 BCE) and thus took the name Wen as his lineage name.
53. See *Zuozhuan* Xuan 14; Durrant et al., *Zuo Tradition*, 1:673.
54. Text is missing in this sentence. Following Wang Jipei, adding 有 *you* before 伐 *fa*. See parallel text in *Guoyu*, "Jinyu," 1.2. Ji was Da Ji's clan name, Da, Su was her lineage name.

55. Su Qin (380–284 BCE) was a political strategist of the Warring States period. See *Shiji* 69:2241; Nienhauser, *Grand Scribe's Records*, 7:97.
56. See *Zuozhuan* Wen 18; Durrant et al., *Zuo Tradition*, 1:573.
57. See *Shangshu*, "Shun Dian"; Legge, *The Chinese Classics*, 3:44.
58. Reading *xing* 姓 as *wu* 物. See *Guoyu*, "Zhengyu," 1.1; translation based on Henry, *Conversations of the States*.
59. See *Shiji* 5:73; Nienhauser, *Grand Scribe's Records*, 1:87.
60. See *Shiji* 5:174; translated in Nienhauser, *Grand Scribe's Records*, 1:87. Following Zhang Jue in supplying the name Bo Yi.
61. See *Shiji* 5.174; Nienhauser, *Grand Scribe's Records*, 1:88—here he is called Fei Lian 廉.
62. See *Shiji* 5.174; Nienhauser, *Grand Scribe's Records*, 1:88.
63. See *Zuozhuan*, Min 1; trans., Durrant et al., 1.223. Zao Shu (fl. ca. 661 BCE) was an able warrior under Lord Xian of Jin.
64. King Xiao of Zhou reigned from 872 to 866 BCE.
65. Following Peng Duo's reconstruction. See *Shiji* 5.174–78; Nienhauser, *Grand Scribe's Records*, 1:88–90.
66. Zhang Jue theorizes that the missing text is "after 25 generations."
67. Because commentators provide vastly different theories about the accuracy of these names, our translation follows the text in its present condition.
68. See *Zuozhuan*, Zhao 29; Durrant et al., *Zuo Tradition*, 3:1699. We romanize his name 豕韋 as Shi Wey to distinguish him from the other Shi Wei 士蒍 (also called 子輿 Ziyu) mentioned in this passage. *Zuozhuan*, Xiang 24, has the following: "Fan Gai continued, 'Formerly my ancestors from the time before King Shun became the Taotang lineage; under Xia, they became the Yulong lineage; under Shang, the Shiwei lineage; under Zhou, the Tangdu lineage; under Jin, which presides over the covenant of the central domains, the Fan lineage.'" See Durrant et al., *Zuo Tradition*, 2:1125.
69. Reading 李 *li* as 士 *shi*.
70. A "sustenance fief" 食采 *shicai* or 食邑 *shiyi* was a fief awarded to high ministers who could collect taxes from the local populace to support themselves.
71. Shi Wei 士蒍 was the ancestor of the Fan/Shi lineage. His grandson, Fan Hui 范會, also known as Fan Wuzi 范武子, was a grandee of Jin who was given command of the Jin armed forces in 593 BCE.

72. See *Guoyu*, "Jinyu," part 8, item 5.
73. Qu Jian 屈建 (d. 545 BCE) was appointed chief minister in 548 BCE. See *Zuozhuan*, Xiang 25; in Durrant et al., *Zuo Tradition*, 2:1149. Fan Wuzi, also known as Fan Hui, served as minister to Lord Wen of Jin. Wenzi, also known as Zhao Wu 趙武 (died 541 BCE), was the Zhao lineage head.
74. Wang Fu's text differs slightly from the *Zuozhuan* account. *Zuozhuan*, Zhao 20; Durrant et al., *Zuo Tradition*, 3:1583.
75. See *Shiji* 36:1575; Nienhauser, *Grand Scribe's Records*, 5.1:221–22. After King Wu established the Zhou dynasty, he sought descendants of Shun, found Gui Man, and enfeoffed him at Chen. On King Wu's efforts to employ the descendants of the Yellow Emperor, Yao and Shun, see See *Zuozhuan*, Xiang 25; Durrant et al., *Zuo Tradition*, 3:1151.
76. Wang Jipei reads *xian* 咸 (the Xian lineage) as *qian* 鹹.
77. Duke Li of Chen (r. 706–700 BCE).
78. See *Shiji* 36:1578; Nienhauser, *Grand Scribe's Records*, 5.1:225–26.
79. See *Zuozhuan*, Zhuang 22; Durrant et al., *Zuo Tradition*, 1:193–97; *Hanshu* 28.2.1661.
80. The change is related to the phonological similarity between the two names.
81. See *Shiji* 8:386; Nienhauser, *Grand Scribe's Records*, 2:75–76. Diwu Lun (fl. ca. 62 CE) numbered himself as the fifth of these clans to undergo forced migration. See *Hou Hanshu* 41.1395.
82. Tian An was the grandson of the last king of Qi before it was subsumed by the Qin. He was known as Wang Jia 王家, so the family adopted the surname Wang.
83. Tian An is also called (among many other names), Tian Chang or Tian Heng. In 481 BCE he killed the ruler of Qi. See *Zuozhuan*, Ai 14; Durrant et al., *Zuo Tradition*, 3:1931.
84. Jingzhong is the posthumous name of Chen Wan. See *Shiji* 36.1577–78; Nienhauser, *Grand Scribe's Records*, 5.1:24–26.
85. Di Yi was a figure born at the end of the Shang dynasty. He was the son of Tai Ding 太丁 and the father of Wei Ziqi 微子啓 and King Djou of Shang (Di Xin 帝辛). See *Shiji* 3.105; Nienhauser, *Grand Scribe's Records*, 1:49.

86. Wang Jipei reads *han* 韓 as *gan* 幹; Peng Duo argues that the name Jin 近 should be Suo 所; Wang Jipei changes *gui* 歸 to *shi* 師, and suspects *wang* 王 should be *ren* 壬.
87. Lionel M. Jensen, "Wise Man of the Wilds: Fatherlessness, Fertility, and the Mythic Exemplar, Kongzi," *Early China* 70 (1995): 407–47.
88. Fufu He was the son of Duke Min of Song (r. 691–682). Fufu He, after the assassination of Lord Min, declined the throne, which then went to his younger brother, Duke Li. See *Zuozhuan*, Zhao 7; translated in Durrant et al., *Zuo Tradition*, 3:1431.
89. Qifu is also called Zimu Jinfu.
90. See Robert Eno, "The Background of the Kong Family of Lu," *Early China* 28, (2003): 1–41. On the genealogy of Confucius, see Shigeki Kaizuka, *Confucius* (London: George Allen & Unwin, 1956), 49–57.
91. King Ling reigned from 571 to 545 BCE.
92. Duke Ping of Jin reigned from 557 to 532. Shuyu, who is frequently mentioned in the *Zuozhuan*, is also known as Shuxiang 叔向 and Yangshe Xi 羊舌肸.
93. Shi Kuang was a worthy who served Duke Ping of Jin and a diviner mentioned in the *Zuozhuan*. The exact source of this quotation is unknown but it is similar to a conversation between Shi Kuang and the heir apparent Jin found in the *Yi Zhoushu* 逸周書, chapter 64, 太子晉解 "Taizi Jin Jie," 太子晉解, in *Sibu beiyao* 101:9.64.5B, where Shi Kuang states: "Your complexion is red, the color of fire indicates [you] will not live long."
94. Xi Rui (d. ca. 636 BCE) was a grandee of Jin and was also known as Ji Rui 冀芮. See *Zuozhuan* Xi 24; Durrant et al., *Zuo Tradition*, 1:375. Also see *Guoyu*, "Zhouyu" 1.13.
95. See *Zuozhuan* Cheng 15; Durrant et al., *Zuo Tradition*, 2:823.
96. See *Zuozhuan* Zhao 27; Durrant et al., *Zuo Tradition*, 3:1677. Zichang was the chief minister of Chu.
97. See *Zuozhuan* Ding 4; Durrant et al., *Zuo Tradition*, 3:1753.
98. Marquis Mu of Jin (r. ca. 811–785). Huan Shu (fl. ca. 802–731 BCE), was the younger son of Marquis Mu, and the younger brother of Marquis Wen (779–746 BCE). We use the transliteration Hann 韓 to distinguish it from Han 漢. Hann Wan is mentioned in See *Zuozhuan*, Huan 3; Durrant et al., *Zuo Tradition*, 1:85.

99. According to *Shiji* 45.1865, the royal family of Hann began as a junior branch of the Jin's royal family. The founder of the Hann family, Wuzi of Hann, was the uncle of Duke Wu of Jin. Members of the family served as ministers in the state of Jin and were granted Hannyuan (present-day Hanncheng in Shaanxi). Over the course of the Spring and Autumn period, the Hann family gained more influence and power within Jin. In 403 BCE, Jing of Hann, along with Wen of Wei and the Lie of Zhao divided Jin among themselves. Jin's partition marks the end of the Spring and Autumn period and the beginning of the Warring States. Subsequently, Hann was an independent polity.
100. See *Shiji* 93. 2635; Nienhauser, *Grand Scribe's Records*, 8.1:117–18.
101. See *Shiji* 93.2636; Nienhauser, *Grand Scribe's Records*, 8.1:118. Chi is referred to as "Ying" 嬰 in the *Shiji*.
102. Maoling and Duling were sites of imperial tombs where wealthy and powerful families were sent to dwell.
103. Zhang Liang (d. 186 BCE) was a brilliant tactician who provided critical aid to overthrowing the Qin dynasty. See *Shiji* 55; translated in Nienhauser, *Grand Scribe's Records*, 6.3:219–57.
104. "Duke of Pei" was title assumed by Liu Bang after the elders of Pei had put to death the Qin magistrate of Pei and urged Liu Bang to serve instead.
105. *Shijing*, "Da Ya," "Hann Yi," 韓奕, Mao no. 261; translation based on Legge, *The Chinese Classics*, 4:550.
106. Following Wang Jipei's reading of 韓西 *hanxi* as 朝鮮 *chaoxian*. See *Shiji* 11.2985; Watson, *Records of the Grand Historian. Han Dynasty*, 2:258–59.
107. Gao, the Duke of Bi, was the fifteenth son of King Wen of Zhou and a younger brother of King Wu. He therefore bore the Ji clan name.
108. See *Shangshu*; Legge, *The Chinese Classics*, 3:562, 569–76.
109. See *Zuozhuan* Min 1, Durrant, *Zuo Tradition*, 1:233. This incursion occurred in 661 BCE. A chariot crew generally included a driver, an archer stationed on the left, and sometimes, a soldier stationed on the right armed with a spear or dagger-axe.
110. Wei Ke is mentioned in *Zuozhuan*, Xuan 15; Durrant et al., *Zuo Tradition*, 1:682–83. He was noted for having saved a woman from being forced to follow her husband in death.

111. See *Shiji* 8:2519; Nienhauser, *Grand Scribe's Records*, 7:321–22.
112. King Li of Zhou reigned from 857/53 to 840/28 BCE.
113. Following Wang Jipei and reading Gongwen 公文 as Gongfu 公父. Zheng Gongshu 鄭恭叔 is also known as Gongshu Duan 恭叔段. He was the traitorous younger brother of Lord Zhuang of Zheng. Because Lord Zhuang had caused his mother great distress by being breech-born, his mother favored his younger brother, Gongshu Duan, and abetted him in his insurrection. See *Zuozhuan*, Yin 1; translated in Durrant et al., 1:9–13.
114. Duke Mu of Zheng reigned from 627 to 606 BCE. His exploits are mentioned in *Zuozhuan* Xuan 2; Translated in Durrant et al., *Zuo Tradition*, 1:587–91.
115. See *Zuozhuan* Ai 7; Durrant et al., *Zuo Tradition*, 3:1875. Wu Taibo was a member of the Ji clan (姬) of predynastic Zhou and the eldest son of King Tai of Zhou. The King of Zhou chose as his successor his youngest son, Jili. Taibo, along with his younger brother Zhongyong, thus traveled southeast and settled in present-day Jiangsu province. Taibo is said to have founded the state of Wu and was succeeded by Zhongyong. Also see *Shiji* 31:1446; Nienhauser, *Grand Scribe's Records*, 5.1:3.
116. Wang Fu leaps from the founding of the Zhou dynasty to events that occurred around 561 BCE. Ji Zha was the virtuous son of King Shoumeng of Wu (d. 561 BCE). See *Shiji* 31.1449; translated in Nienhauser, *Grand Scribe's Records*, 5.1:5. Yanzhoulai is equivalent to Yanling.
117. Helü (r. 514–496). Fugai tried to seize the throne but then fled to Chu where he was enfeoffed at Fugai by King Zhao of Chu. See *Shiji* 31.1467; Nienhauser, *Grand Scribe's Records*, 5.1:18.
118. In 265, Qin worked to absorb Shangdang's seventeen districts in Hann. Later, when the king of Hann offered to cede the territory, Feng Ting ceded Shangdang to the state of Zhao instead. See *Shiji* 7.2332; Burton Watson, trans., *Records of the Grand Historian: Qin Dynasty* (Hong Kong: Chinese University of Hong Kong, 1993), 122.
119. Feng Jie was the Grand Master of Imperial Scribes. See *Shiji* 6:23, 27–26; Nienhauser, *Grand Scribe's Records*, 1:135, 160.
120. See *Shiji* 102.2757–2761; Nienhauser, *Grand Scribe's Records*, 1:364–67.
121. *Hanshu* 97B:4005.

122. *Hou Hanshu* 28A.962.
123. See *Zhanguoce*, Zhao,1; James I. Crump, trans., *Chan-kuo ts'e*, rev. ed. (Ann Arbor: Center for Chinese Studies, University of Michigan, 1996), 280–81.
124. See *Zuozhuan* Zhao 15; Durrant, et al. *Zuo Tradition*, 3:1527.
125. See *Zuozhuan* Zhao 15; Durrant et al., *Zuo Tradition*, 3:1527.
126. *Shijing*, "Xiao Ya," "Liu Yue," Mao no. 177; Legge, *The Chinese Classics*, 4:284. There are no further clues about Zhang Zhong apart from the traits mentioned in the ode. The suggestion here is that this ode contains the first reference to someone with the name Zhang. The penultimate character in the line is an error, and Wang Jipei regards Zhang Bai as an error for Zhang Gai 張匃, who is mentioned in *Zuozhuan*, Zhao 21.
127. For Zhang Hou, see *Zuozhuan* Cheng 2; Durrant et al., *Zuo Tradition*, 2:717. The translation refers to Zhang Hou by his alternative name, "Xie 解 Zhang." On Zhang Lao, see *Zuozhuan*, Cheng 18; Durrant et al., *Zuo Tradition*, 2:871.
128. See *Zhanguoce*, Qin, items 107, 231; Crump, *Chan-kuo ts'e*, 130, 283–84.
129. For Zhang Yi, ca. 309 BCE, a native of Wei, see *Shiji*. 70; Nienhauser, *Grand Scribe's Records*, 7:123–138. For Zhang Chou, see *Shiji*. 40.1721; Nienhauser, *Grand Scribe's Records*, 5.1:421; and *Zhanguoce*; Crump, *Chan-kuo ts'e*, 156, 382, 403, 498–99.
130. For Zhang Er, see *Shiji* 89:2571; Nienhauser, *Grand Scribe's Records*, 8.1:1; for Zhang Cang, *Shiji*, 96.2675; Nienhauser, *Grand Scribe's Records*, 8.1:205.
131. *Shiji* 103.2764; Nienhauser, *Grand Scribe's Records*, 8.1:374.
132. Zhang Tang was ultimately charged with various crimes and committed suicide. Afterward, Emperor Wu felt regret and promoted Zhang's son. See *Shiji* 122:3144; Watson, *Records of the Grand Historian: Han Dynasty*, "The Biographies of the Harsh Officials," 2:385.
133. Following Wang Jipei's emendation of 矜遂權 *jin sui quan* to *wu yuan quan* 務遠權; Zhang Jue suggests 遠權勢 *yuan quan shi* means "distanced himself from / avoided exerting power."
134. Zhang Jue shows that this enfeoffment was in respect to his descendant, Zhang Chun, ca. 6 BCE.
135. See *Hanshu* 81.3347, 19B.825.

136. See *Hou Hanshu* 45.1528; 44.1496.
137. Commentators suggestions for variant readings are too numerous to list in a note.
138. See *Zuozhuan*, Zhuang 8; Durrant et al., *Zuo Tradition*, 1:155.
139. See *Zuozhuan*, Xuan 12; Durrant et al., *Zuo Tradition*, 1:653.
140. See *Hanshu* 72:3086.
141. "Scholar Li" is Li Yiji 酈食其. See *Shiji* 97.269; Nienhauser, *Grand Scribe's Records*, 8:245.
142. *Shijing*, Da Ya, "Zheng Min," Mao no. 260; Legge, *The Chinese Classics*, 4:541.
143. See *Guoyu*, "Zhouyu" 1.8.
144. See *Zuozhuan*, Zhao 22; Durrant et al, *Zuo Tradition*, 3:1611.
145. See *Shiji* 125.3192; Watson, *Records of the Grand Historian. Han Dynasty*, 2:419. Deng Guang refers to Deng Guanghan. See *Hanshu* 68.2952.
146. See *Hou Hanshu* 16.605.
147. See *Hou Hanshu*, 10A:418–30; and Rafe de Crespigny, *Fire over Luoyang: A History of the Later Han Dynasty 23–220 A.D.* (Leiden: Brill, 2017), 169–219.
148. See *Zuozhuan*, Xiang 31; Durrant et al., *Zuo Tradition*, 2:1277.
149. See *Hou Hanshu* 13.513.
150. The name Duan is considered an error for the name Heng 姮.
151. *Zuozhuan*, Ding 4; Durrant et al., *Zuo Tradition*, 1749. Here Invocator Tuo of Wei mentions the six "houses" of the Yin people (殷民 六族 yinmin liuzu).
152. The word *taishi* "Grand Preceptor" is an error for *taizai* 太宰 "Grand Steward." *Lingyin* and *zuoyin* are translated as Chief Minister and Deputy of the Left respectively.
153. *Shijing*, "Xiao Ya," "Jie Nan Shan," Mao no. 191; Legge, *The Chinese Classics*, 4:309.
154. See *Guoyu*, "Zhouyu" 3.4.
155. In Han times people observed the taboo on Emperor Jing's name—Qi—and wrote *kai* 開 instead.
156. The mistake was based on phonological similarities. See Wang Jipei's note.
157. Lynn, *The Classic of Changes*; 217 [Hexagram 13]; 300 [Hexagram 26]; 133 [Hexagram 26].

## CHAPTER 36. POSTFACE

1. *Zuozhuan*, Xiang 24; Stephen Durrant, Wai-yee Li, and David Schaberg, trans., *Zuo Tradition* (Zuozhuan): *Commentary on the Spring and Autumn Annals* (Seattle: University of Washington Press, 2016), 3:1125. In this passage, "establishing achievements" comes between the two qualities Wang Fu mentions.
2. The word 闒茸 *tarong* denotes "useless minion," or "base/cringing and obsequious/pusillanimous." Sima Qian also used the term; see *Hanshu* 62:2728.
3. Following Wang Jipei reading 先 *xian* as 無 *wu*.
4. The *Zuozhuan* and *Guoyu* are attributed to Zuo Qiuming. The Five Classics are the *Book of Changes, Book of Rites, Book of Odes, Book of Documents,* and the *Spring and Autumn Annals*. An Academician specializing in the *Zuozhuan* was finally appointed in 8 BCE during the reign of Emperor Ping (r. 1 BCE–5 CE), securing its status and prompting the generation of numerous commentaries. See Durrant et al., *Zuo Tradition*, 1:lviii.
5. Reading 識 in the fourth tone.
6. *Lunyu* VII:2; James Legge, trans., *The Chinese Classics*, 5 vols. (Hong Kong: Chinese University of Hong Kong Press, 1970), 1:195.
7. Following Peng Duo.
8. See *Analects* XVII.1; *Mencius* IIIA.3.5; Legge, *The Chinese Classics*, 1:317–18; 2:240.
9. Following Wang Shaolan 王紹蘭 (1760–1835.)
10. *Lunyu* VII:15; Legge, *The Chinese Classics*, 1:200.
11. Following Zhang Jue's reading of 豫 *yu*.
12. Following Zhang Jue. The phrase 揚庭 *yangting* comes from the *Yijing*, Hexagram no. 43, "Kuai" 夬: "the exhibition (of the culprit's guilt) in the royal court." James Legge, trans., *The I Ching* (1899; reprint, New York: Dover, 1963), 151.
13. Compare to *Huainanzi*, "Taizu," 泰族, "The heart is the root of the self; the self is the root of the state"; 身者國之本; John S. Major, Sarah A. Queen, Andrew Seth Meyer, and Harold D. Roth, trans., *The Huainanzi: A Guide to the Theory and Practice of Government in Early Han China* (New York: Columbia University Press, 2010), 825.
14. Following Zhang Jue and leaving the text unemended.

15. *Yijing*, "Xici" 繫辭, the "Great Appendix," 2; Legge, *The I Ching*, 381. The full quotation lists a large population, wealth, instructing the people, and prohibiting wrong-doing as elements that will amass a large population and guard the sage ruler's position.
16. *Shangshu*, "Hong Fan," Legge, *The Chinese Classics*, 3:320–344.
17. *Shijing, Da Ya*, "Ban," Mao no. 254; Legge, *The Chinese Classics*, 4:502.
18. *Zuozhuan*, Xi 23; Durrant et al., *Zuo Tradition*, 1:367. This phrase derives from the advice given by Lord Huan of Qi's daughter, Lady Jiang, to her husband, Chong Er, son of Lord Xian of Jin. Chong Er endured a long period of exile from his realm before finally being installed as ruler of Jin (r. 636–628 BCE). His wife felt that he had become too comfortable in Qi and was gaining a reputation as a slacker rather than returning to Jin to take charge. Lady Jiang's biography appears in *Lienüzhuan* 2.3.
19. See *Yijing*, "Xici" II.12; Richard John Lynn, trans., *The Classic of Changes: A New Translation of the* I Ching *as Interpreted by Wang Bi* (New York: Columbia University Press, 2004), 205–06.
20. The meaning here is that the work done by these officials to help the common people justified taking on administrative rather than agricultural work.
21. See *Yi Zhoushu* 逸周書, "Shiji Jie" 史記解: "Formerly, the head of the Bi Cheng clan forfeited an emolument and increased his official rank. The body of ministers affected poverty and mistreated the common people. Bi Cheng, because of this, perished." 昔有畢程氏, 損祿增爵, 群臣貌匱比而庋民, 畢程氏以亡. The name Bi Cheng Shi means something like "head of the Bi Cheng clan" and was associated with a place called Bi Cheng where King Wen of Zhou trained his troops in Shang times. See Maria Khayutina, "Western 'Capitals' of the Western Zhou Dynasty: Historical Reality and Its Reflections Until the Time of Sima Qian," *Oriens Extremus*, 47 (2008): 25–65.
22. The idea here is, first of all, when rulers employ the worthy, and second, when official salaries are sufficient to allow officials to concentrate on their jobs without being forced to take on other jobs or tempted to take bribes, an era of Great Peace can be realized.
23. This phrase derives from *Shijing, Xiao Ya*, "Jie Nan Shan," Mao no. 191; Legge, *The Chinese Classics*, 4:313.

24. See Tjoe Som Tjan, *Po Hu T'ung: The Comprehensive Discussions in the White Tiger Hall.* 2 vols. (Leiden: Brill, 1949–1952; reprint, Westport, CT: Hyperion Press, 1973), 1:230: "When his spiritual power [harmoniously] combines [that of] Heaven and Earth [the Sovereign] is called 'Thearch' [帝]. When [his spiritual power] is the harmonious combination of consideration for others and sense of the right principles he is called 'King'[王]. [Thus] a distinction is made between abundance and scarcity [of spiritual power]"; 德合天地者稱帝, 仁義合者稱王, 別優劣也. The Five Thearchs are variously defined but generally associated with Huang Di, Zhuanxu, Diku, Yao, and Shun. The Three Huang generally refer to either Sui Ren, Fu Xi, and Shennong or the Divinity of Heaven 天皇, the Divinity of Earth 地皇, and the Divinity of Humankind 人皇. The Three Kings are also variously defined but generally include Yu 禹, Tang 唐, and Kings Wen and Wu of the Zhou dynasty.

25. Sui Ren (an otherwise obscure fire deity), Fuxi (Tamer of Beasts), and Shen Nong (the Divine Farmer) were the culture heroes of remote antiquity.

26. *Lunyu* XIII:12: "The Master said, 'If a truly royal ruler were to arise, it would still require a generation, and then virtue would prevail.'" Legge, *The Chinese Classics,* 1:267.

27. The presentation of the axe represents the conferral of the right to kill.

28. See *Mencius* IIIA.4.7–9; and *Shangshu,* "Shundian," 2.20; translated in Legge, *The Chinese Classics,* 2: 250–52; 3:44–45.

29. See *Shijing, Da Ya,* "Chang Wu," Mao no. 263; Legge, *The Chinese Classics,* 4:555. Strictly speaking, it was not Nan Zhong but one of his descendants who was appointed.

30. Following Zhang Jue.

31. The 臺閣 *taige,* "towers and pavilions," is another term for the officials called "Masters of Writing"; 上書 *shangshu* were powerful officials who "dealt with correspondence and documents relating to senior ministers, the heads of provincial administration, memorials, petitions from common people, and non-Chinese states." See Rafe de Crespigny, *A Biographical Dictionary of Later Han to the Three Kingdoms (23–220 A.D.)* (Leiden: Brill, 2007), 1226.

32. Zhang Jue uses this sentence as partial evidence to date the text to sometime after 141 CE. See *Qianfulun quanyi,* 2:824n5.

33. *Yijing*, "Xici," 1.11; Legge, *The I Ching*, 374; and Lynn, *The Classic of Changes*, 66.
34. *Yijing*, "Xun"; Legge, *The I Ching*, 190.
35. *Shijing*, *Xiao Ya*, "Chu Ci," Mao no. 209; Legge, *The Chinese Classics*, 4:371.
36. According to Zhang Jue, Wang Fu twists the syntax of the following passage from *Zuozhuan* to facilitate a rhyme: 聖王先成 民而後致力於神. See, *Zuozhuan*, Huan 6; Durrant et al., *Zuo Tradition*, 1:97.
37. *Zuozhuan*, Huan 6; Durrant et al., *Zuo Tradition*, 1:97.
38. *Analects* VII:34; Legge, *The Chinese Classics*, 1:206: "Confucius objected to Zilu [praying on his behalf] saying, 'My praying has been for a long time.'"
39. *Shijing*, *Xiao Ya*, "Si Gan," Mao no. 189; Legge, *The Chinese Classics*, 4:305–07.
40. Gengzi is imaginary person who serves as interlocutor in this essay.
41. *Mencius* IIIB.9; translated in Legge, *The Chinese Classics*, 2: 279. This phrase was uttered by Mencius when he was charged with being fond of arguing and responded by saying that it was the nature of the times that made it necessary.
42. See *Bohu tong*, "San Gang Liu Ji," 7.11; Tjan, *Po Hu T'ung*, 2:559: "What are the Three Major Relationships? They are [the relation between] Lord and subject, [the relation between] father and son, and [the relation between] husband and wife. The Six Minor Relationships are [the relation with] father's brothers, [with] elder and younger brothers, [with] one's kinsmen, [with] mother's brothers, [with] teachers and elders, and [with] friends."
43. *Shijing*, *Da Ya*, "Bi Zui," Mao no. 247; Legge, *The Chinese Classics*, 4:477.
44. Hexagram 58 "Dui," 兌 "Commentary on the Images"; Lynn, *The Classic of Change*, 507.
45. *Analects* XIV:13; Legge, *The Chinese Classics*, 1:280.
46. *Analects* XIX:19; Legge, *The Chinese Classics*, 1:345. The term 散 *san*, like the word *qian* 遷, as Legge notes, "is to be understood of the moral state."
47. *Yijing*, "Xicizhuan," 2:8; Legge, *The I Ching*, 362.
48. See *Han Feizi*, "Zhu Dao" translated in W. K. Liao, trans., *The Complete Works of Han Fei Tzu*, 2 vols. (London: Arthur Probsthain, 1939),

31: "The ruler must not reveal his wants. For, if he reveals his wants, the ministers will polish their manners accordingly. The ruler must not reveal his views. For, if he reveals his views, the minsters will display their hues differently."

49. Following Wang Jipei's emending 能 *neng* to 不 *bu*.
50. Rather than imposing morals on the people, when the ruler establishes his own virtue, the people will be transformed through his example. See *Guanzi*, "Junchen," 1; W. Allyn Rickett, trans., *Guanzi*, 2 vols. (Princeton, NJ: Princeton University Press, 1985), 1:405.
51. See *Huainanzi*, "Lanming"; Major et al., *The Huainanzi*, 229.
52. The concluding verses are not extant, though Zhang Jue attempts to devise a reconstruction based on the contents of chapter 35.

# BIBLIOGRAPHY

### EDITIONS AND COMMENTARIES
### (IN CHRONOLOGICAL ORDER)

*Qianfulun* 潛夫論. 10 juan. Facsimile of a Song edition made by Feng Shu 馮舒 (b. 1593). Held by National Library of China.

*Qianfulun* 潛夫論. 10 juan. In Hu Weixin 胡維新 (jinshi 1559), ed. *Liangjing yibian* 兩經遺編. Ming Wanli 10 (1582) printing. Held by National Library of China. See also *Liangjing yibian* 兩經遺編, 12–13. Shanghai: Shangwu yinshuguan.

*Qianfulun* 潛夫論. 10 juan. *Han Wei congshu* 漢魏叢書. Cheng Rong 程榮, ed. 1592.

*Qianfulun* 潛夫論. 10 juan. *Sibu congkan*. Photoreproduction of a Ming facsimile of a Song edition printed by Feng Shu 馮舒. Once held in the Shugu tang 述古堂 of Qian Zeng 錢曾 (1629–1701).

*Qianfulun* 潛夫論. 10 juan. *Guang Han Wei congshu*. He Yunzhong 何允中, ed.

*Qianfulun* 潛夫論. Wang Mo 王謨, ed. 1791.

Wang Jipei 汪繼培 (b. 1775), ed. and comm. *Qianfulun jian* 潛夫論箋. 10 juan. *Huhai lou congshu* 胡海樓叢書 (1817).

*Qianfulun* 潛夫論. 10 juan. *Zishu baijia* 子書百家. Hubei: Chongwen shuju, 1875.

Wang Jipei, comm. Peng Duo 彭鐸 潛夫論箋. Beijing: Zhonghua shuju, 1979.

Wang Jipei, comm. Peng Duo 彭鐸, ed. and punc. *Qianfulun jian jiaozheng* 潛夫論箋校正. Beijing: Zhonghua shuju, 1985; reprint Beijing: Zhonghua shuju, 2010.

Hu Chusheng 胡楚生, ed. and comm. "Qianfulun jiaoshi" 潛夫論校釋. PhD diss., Nanyang daxue Zhongwen yanjiusuo, 1975–1976.

Hu Chusheng 胡楚生, ed. and comm. *Qianfulun jiaoshi* 潛夫論校釋. Taipei: Ding wen shuju, 1979.

*Qianfulun zhuzi suoyin* 潛夫論逐字索引. Hong Kong: Shangwu yinshuguan, 1995.

Zhang Guangbao 張廣保, comm. *Qianfulun: Quanwen zhushi ben* 潛夫論: 全文注釋本. Beijing: Hua Xia chubanshe, 2002.

Zhang Jue 張覺, ed. and comm. *Qianfulun jiaozhu* 潛夫論校注. Changsha: Yuelu shushe, 2008.

Wang Jian 王建, comm. *Qianfulun* 潛夫論. Kaifeng: Henan daxue chubanshe, 2008.

## TRANSLATIONS INTO WESTERN LANGUAGES

Kamenarović, Ivan P. *Wang Fu: Propos d'un erimite (Qianfulun); introduction et traduction du chinois.* Paris: Editions du Cerf, 1992.

Kinney, Anne Behnke. *The Art of the Han Essay: Wang Fu's Ch'ien-fu lun.* Tempe: Center for Asian Studies, Arizona State University, 1992.

Pearson, Margaret J. *Wang Fu and the Comments of a Recluse.* Tempe: Center for Asian Studies, Arizona State University, 1989.

## MODERN CHINESE TRANSLATIONS

Hu Dajun 胡大浚, Li Zhongli 李仲立, and Li Deqi 李德奇, trans. and comm. *Wang Fu Qianfulun yizhu* 王符《潛夫論》譯注. Lanzhou: Gansu renmin chubanshe, 1991.

Peng Bingchen 彭丙成, comm. and trans. *Xin yi Qianfulun* 新譯潛夫論. Taipei: Sanmin shuju, 1998.

Wang Bolin 王柏林, ed. and trans. *Qianfulun duben* 潛夫論讀本. Lanzhou: Gansu renmin chubanshe, 2004.

Wang Ning 王寧, ed. *Pingxi ben baihua Yantielun Qianfulun* 評析本白話鹽鐵論潛夫論. Beijing: Beijing guangbo xueyuan chubanshe, 1992.

Zhang Jue 張覺, comm. and trans. *Qianfulun quanyi* 潛夫論全譯. 2 vols. Guiyang: Guizhou renmin chubanshe, 1999.

## WORKS CITED AND CONSULTED

Ames, Roger. *Sun Tzu: The Art of Warfare*. New York: Ballantine Books, 1993.

Balázs, Etienne. "La crise sociale et la philosophie politique à la fin des Han," *T'oung Pao* 39 (1950): 83–131, trans. H. M. Wright as "Political Philosophy and Social Crisis at the End of the Han Dynasty," in Etienne Balázs, *Chinese Civilization and Bureaucracy: Variations on a Theme*, ed. Arthur F. Wright. New Haven, CT: Yale University Press, 1964.

Barbieri-Low, Anthony J., "Wheeled Vehicles in the Chinese Bronze Age (ca. 2000–741 BCE)," *Sino-Platonic Papers* 99 (February 2000): 1–75.

Baxter, William H. "Situating the Language of the *Lao-tzu*," in *Lao-tzu and the Tao-te-ching*, ed. Livia Kohn and Michael LaFargue, 231–53. Albany: State University of New York Press, 1998.

Beck, B. J. Mansvelt. "The Fall of the Han." In *The Cambridge History of China Volume One: The Ch'in and Han Empires, 221 B.C.–A.D. 220*, ed. Denis Twitchett and Michael Loewe. Cambridge: Cambridge University Press, 1986.

Bielenstein, Hans. *The Bureaucracy of Han Times*. Cambridge: Cambridge University Press, 1980.

———. *Lo-yang in Later Han Times*. Bulletin of the Museum of Far Eastern Antiquities 48 (1976).

———. *The Restoration of the Han Dynasty*. 4 vols. Stockholm: Bulletin of the Museum of Far Eastern Antiquities 21 (1954); 31 (1959); 39 (1967); 51 (1975).

Brooks, E. Bruce, and A. Taeko Brooks, trans. *The Original Analects: Sayings of Confucius and His Successors*. New York: Columbia University Press, 1998.

Brown, Miranda, and Charles Sanft. "Categories and Legal Reasoning in Early Imperial China: The Meaning of 'Fa' in Recovered Tests." *Oriens Extremus* 50 (2011): 283–306.

Ch'en Ch'i-yün. "Confucian, Legalist, and Taoist Thought." In *The Cambridge History of China Volume One: The Ch'in and Han Empires, 221\* B.C. to A.D. 220*, ed. Michael Loewe and Dennis Twitchett. Cambridge: Cambridge University Press, 1986,.

———. *Hsün Yüeh (A.D. 148–209): The Life and Reflections of an Early Medieval Confucian*. Cambridge: Cambridge University Press, 1975.

———. *Hsün Yüeh and the Mind of Late Han China*. Princeton, NJ: Princeton University Press, 1980.

Ch'en Ch'i-yün and Margaret Pearson. "Ch'ien-fu lun." In *Early Chinese Texts: A Bibliographical Guide*, ed. Michael Loewe, 12–15. Berkeley: The Society for the Study of Early China and The Institute of East Asian Studies, University of California, Berkeley, 1993.

Couvreur, Seraphin, trans. *Cérémonial*. Paris: Cathasia-France, 1951.

Crump, James I., trans. *Chan-Kuo Ts'e* (2nd ed. rev.). Ann Arbor: Center for Chinese Studies, University of Michigan, 1979.

de Crespigny, Rafe. *A Biographical Dictionary of Later Han to Three Kingdoms (23–220 A.D.)*. Leiden: Brill, 2007.

———. *Fire Over Luoyang: A History of the Later Han Dynasty, 23–220 A.D.* Leiden: Brill, 2016.

———. *Northern Frontier: The Politics and Strategy of the Late Han Empire*. Canberra: Australian National University, Faculty of Asian Studies Monographs, no. 4, 1984.

Didier, John C. "In and Outside the Square: The Sky and the Power of Belief in Ancient China and the World, ca. 4500 B.C.–AD 200." *Sino-Platonic Papers* (September 2009): 147–56.

Dobson, W. A. C. H. *A Dictionary of the Chinese Particles*. Toronto: University of Toronto Press, 1974.

———. *Late Han Chinese*. Toronto: University of Toronto Press, 1964.

Dubs, Homer H., trans. *History of the Former Han Dynasty*. 3 vols. Baltimore: Waverly Press, 1938–1944.

Dull, Jack L. "A Historical Introduction to the Apocryphal (*Ch'an wei*) Texts of the Han Dynasty." PhD diss., University of Washington, 1966.

———. "Marriage and Divorce in Han China: A Glimpse at 'Pre-Confucian Society.'" In *Chinese Family Law and Social Change in Historical Perspective*, ed. David C. Buxbaum. Seattle: University of Washington Press, 1978.

Durrant, Stephen, Wai-yee Li, and David Schaberg, trans. *Zuo Tradition (Zuozhuan): Commentary on the Spring and Autumn Annals*. 3 vols. Seattle: University of Washington Press, 2016.

Eno, Robert. "The Background of the Kong Family of Lu." *Early China* 28 (2003): 1–41.

Forke, Alfred, trans. *Lun-Heng: Philosophical Essays of Wang Ch'ung*. 2 vols. New York: Paragon Book Gallery, 1962.

Gale, Esson M., trans. *Discourses on Salt and Iron: A Debate on State Control of Commerce and Industry in Ancient China*. Taipei: Ch'eng-wen Publishing Company, 1973.

Gao Xinmin 高新民 and Wang Weixiang 王偉翔. *Qianfu lun shidu* 潛夫論釋讀. Yinchuan: Ningxia renmin chubanshe, 2009.

Giele, Enno. *Imperial Decision-Making and Communication in Early China: A Study of Cai Yong's Duduan*. Wiesbaden: Harrassowitz Verlag, 2006.

Graham, A. C., trans., *The Book of Lieh-tzu: A Classic of the Tao*. New York: Columbia University Press, 1999.

Gu Jiegang 顧頡剛. "Qianfu lun zhong wude xitong," 潛夫論中的五德系統 *Shixue jikan* 史學集刊 3 (1937): 73.

Hawkes, David, trans. *Ch'u Tz'u: Songs of the South*. Oxford: Oxford University Press, 1959.

Henry, Eric, trans. *Conversations of the States*. Seattle: University of Washington Press, forthcoming.

———. *Garden of Eloquence*. Seattle: University of Washington Press, 2021.

Hightower, James Robert. *Han Shih Wai Chuan: Han Ying's Illustrations of the Didactic Applications of the* Classic of Songs. Cambridge, MA: Harvard University Press, 1952.

———. "The Wen Hsuan and Genre Theory." *Harvard Journal of Asian Studies* 20 (1957): 513.

Holzer, Rainer. *Das Ch'ien-fu lun des Wang Fu: Aufsätze und Betrachtungen eines Weltflüchtigen*. Heidelberg: Edition Forum, 1992.

Hsiao Kung-chuan [Xiao Gongchuan]. *A History of Chinese Political Thought*, trans. F. W. Mote. 2 vols. Princeton, NJ: Princeton University Press, 1979.

Hsu, Cho-yun. "The Concept of Predetermination and Fate in the Han," *Early China* 1 (Fall 1975): 51–56.

———. "The Spring and Autumn Period." In *The Cambridge History of Ancient China*, ed. Michael Loewe and Edward L. Shaughnessy, 545–86. Cambridge: Cambridge University Press, 1999.

Huang Hui 黃暉, ann. *Lunheng jiaoshi* 論衡校釋, 4 vols. Taipei: Taiwan shangwu yinshuguan, 1983.

Huang Shengxiong 黃盛. *Wang Fu sixiang yanjiu* 王符思想研究. Taipei: Wenshizhe chubanshe, 1982.

Hulsewé, A. F. P. *Remnants of Ch'in Law*. Leiden: Brill, 1985.

———. *Remnants of Han Law*. Leiden: Brill, 1955.

Hunter, Michael. *The Poetics of Early Chinese Thought: How the* Shijing *Shaped the Chinese Philosophical Tradition*. New York: Columbia University Press, 2021.

Jensen, Lionel M. "Wise Man of the Wilds: Fatherlessness, Fertility, and the Mythic Exemplar, Kongzi." *Early China* 70 (1995): 407–47.

Jin Fagen 金发根. "Wang Fu shengzu niansui de kaozheng ji *Qianfulun* xieding shijian de tuilun" 王符生卒年岁的考证及潜夫论写定时间的推论, *Zhongyang yajiuyuan lishi yuyan yanjiusuo jikan* [Bulletin of the Institute of History and Philology Academia Sinica] 中央研究院历史语言研究所集刊 40, no. 2 (1969): 781–99.

Kanaya Osamu 金谷治, ed. "Gokanmatsu no shisōkatachi— toku ni Ō Fu to Chūchō Tō" 後漢末思想家—特王符仲長統. In *Fukui hakushi shōju kinen Tōyō bunka ronshū* 福井博士頌壽記念東洋文化論集, 287–302. Fukui hakushi shōju kinen ronbunshū kankōkai 福井博士頌壽記念論文集刊行會. Tokyo: Waseda daigaku, 1972.

Karlgren, Bernhard. "Excursions in Chinese Grammar." *Bulletin of the Museum of Far Eastern Antiquities* 23 (1951): 107–33.

Karlgren, Bernhard, trans. *The Book of Documents* (Goteborg: Elanders Boktryckeri Aktiebolag, 1950).

———. *The Book of Odes: Chinese Text, Transcription, and Translation*. Stockholm: Museum of Far Eastern Antiquities, 1950.

———. *Glosses on the Book of Documents*. Stockholm: Museum of Far Eastern Antiquities, 1948.

———. *Glosses on the Book of Odes*. Stockholm: Museum of Far Eastern Antiquities, 1964.

Keightley, David. "Public Works in Ancient China: A Study of Forced Labor in the Shang Dynasty." PhD diss., Columbia University, 1969.

Khayutina, Maria. "Western 'Capitals' of the Western Zhou Dynasty: Historical Reality and Its Reflections Until the Time of Sima Qian." *Oriens Extremus* 47 (2008): 25–65.

Kinney, Anne Behnke. "Predestination and Prognostication in the *Ch'ien-fu lun*." *Journal of Chinese Religions* 19, no. 1 (1991): 27–45.

———. *Representations of Children and Youth in Early China*. Stanford, CA: Stanford University Press, 2004.

Kinney, Anne Behnke, trans. *The Art of the Han Essay: Wang Fu's Ch'ien-fu lun*. Tempe: Center for Asian Studies, Arizona State University, 1992.

Kinney, Anne Behnke, ed. and trans. *Exemplary Women of Early China: The* Lienüzhuan *of Liu Xiang*. New York: Columbia University Press, 2014.

Knechtges, David R., ed. and trans. *The Han shu Biography of Yang Xiong (53 B.C.–A.D. 18)*. Tempe: Center for Asian Studies, Arizona State University, 1982.

——. *Wenxuan, or Selections of Refined Literature. Volume 1. Rhapsodies on Metropolises and Capitals*. Princeton, NJ: Princeton University Press, 1982.

Knoblock, John, trans. *Xunzi: A Translation and Study of the Complete Work*. 3 vols. Stanford, CA: Stanford University Press, 1988–1994.

Knoblock, John, and Jeffrey Riegel, trans. *The Annals of Lü Buwei*. Stanford, CA: Stanford University Press, 2004.

Lau, D. C., ed. *A Concordance to the Shangshu da zhuan*. Hong Kong: Commercial Press, 1994.

——. *Xinxu zhuzi suoyin*. Hong Kong: Shangwu yinshuguan, 1992.

Lau, D. C., trans. *Confucius: The Analects*. Harmondsworth, Middlesex: Penguin, 1979.

——. *Lao Tzu: Tao De Ching*. Harmondsworth, Middlesex: Penguin, 1979.

Lau, Ulrich, and Michael Lüdke. *Exemplarische Rechtsfälle vom Beginn der Han-Dynastie: Eine kommentierte Übersetzung des Zouyanshu aus Zhangjiashan Provinz, Hubei*. Tokyo: Research Institute for Languages and Cultures of Asia and Africa, Tokyo University of Foreign Studies. 2012.

Legge, James, trans. *The Chinese Classics*, 5 vols. Hong Kong: Chinese University of Hong Kong Press, 1970.

——. *The I Ching*. 1899. Reprint, New York: Dover, 1963.

——. *Li Chi*. Oxford, Oxford University Press, 1879. Reprint, ed. Winberg Chai, 2 vols. New Hyde Park, NY: University Books, 1967.

——. *The Sacred Books of China: The Texts of Confucianism in The Sacred Books of the East*, ed. F. Max Müller. Oxford: Clarendon Press, 1899.

——. "The Writings of Chuang Tzu." In *The Texts of Taoism*, part II. 1891. Reprint, New York: Dover Publications, 1962.

Lewis, Mark Edward. *Sanctioned Violence in Early China*. Albany: State University of New York Press, 1990.

Li Junming 李均明. "Zhangjiashan Han jian suojian zhiyue xingzheng quan de falü, 張家山漢簡所見制約行政權的法律. In *Qin Han shi luncong* 秦漢史論叢, 9:271–83. Reprint in Jiandu fazhi lungao 簡牘法制論稿, 140–49. Guilin: Guangxi shifan daxue chubanshe, 2011.

Li Shaohui 李少惠. "Wang Chong yu Wang Fu guanxi fawei" 王充與王符關係發微. *Lanzhou shehui kexue* 6 (1996), 39–41.

Liang Chaowei 梁朝威. "Qianfu lun de zuozhe" 潛夫論的作者.*Qinghua zhoukan* 清華週刊 314 (1924).

Liao, W. K. *The Complete Works of Han Fei Tzu*. 2 vols. London: Arthur Probsthain, 1939.

Lin, Fu-shih. "The Image and Status of Shamans in Ancient China," in *Early Chinese Religion, Part One: Shang to Han*, ed. John Lagerwey and Marc Kalinowski. 2 vols. Leiden: Brill, 2009.

Liu, James J. Y. *Chinese Theories of Literature*. Chicago: Chicago University Press, 1979.

Liu Jihua 劉季華. *Wang Fu yu Qianfu lun* 王符與潛夫論. Taipei: Shiji shuju, 1977.

Liu Shunxun 劉樹勛. "Wang Fu shengzu nian he zhuzuo kao" 王符生卒年和著作考. *Zhongguo zhexueshi yanjiu jikan* 2 (1982): 188–97.

Liu Wenqi 劉文起. *Wang Fu Qianfu lun suo fanying zhi Dong Han qingshi* 王符潛夫論所反映之東漢情勢. Taipei: Wen shi zhe chubanshe, 1995.

Liu Wenying 劉文英. "Guanyu Wang Fu shengping de jige wenti" 關於王符生平的幾個問題. *Lanzhou xuekan* 4 (1990): 55–59.

Liu Wenying. *Wang Fu pingzhuan* 王符評傳. Nanjing: Nanjing daxue chubanshe, 1993.

Liu Yu 刘育. "Lun Wang Fu de xiancai sixiang 論王符的賢才思想." *Xianyang shifan xueyuan xuebao* 咸阳师范学院学报 38, no. 1 (2003): 39–43.

Loewe, Michael. *A Biographical Dictionary of the Qin, Former Han and Xin Periods (221 BC–AD 24)*. Leiden: Brill, 2000.

———. "The Structure and Practice of Government." In *The Cambridge History of China, Vol. 1, The Ch'in and Han Empires*, ed. Denis Twitchett and Michael Loewe. Cambridge: Cambridge University Press, 1986.

Loewe, Michael, and Edward Shaughnessy, eds. *The Cambridge History of Ancient China*. Cambridge: Cambridge University Press, 1999.

Lynn, Richard John, trans. *The Classic of Changes: A New Translation of the I Ching as Interpreted by Wang Bi*. New York: Columbia University Press, 2004.

———. *Zhuangzi: A New Translation of the Sayings of Master Zhuang as Interpreted by Guo Xiang*. New York: Columbia University Press, 2022.

Major, John S. *Heaven and Earth in Early Han Thought: Chapters Three, Four, and Five of the Huainanzi*. Albany: State University of New York Press, 1993.

Major, John S. "Tool Metaphors in the *Huainanzi* and Other Early Texts." In *The* Huainanzi *and Textual Production in Early* China, ed. Sarah A. Queen and Michael Puett, 153–98. Leiden: Brill, 2014.

Major, John S., Sarah A. Queen, Andrew Seth Meyer, and Harold D. Roth, trans. *The Huainanzi: A Guide to the Theory and Practice of Government in Early Han China.* New York: Columbia University Press, 2010.

McLeod, Alexus. *The Philosophical Thought of Wang Chong.* Cham, Switzerland: Palgrave Macmillan, 2018.

———. "Philosophy in Eastern Han Dynasty China (25–220 CE)." *Philosophy Compass* 10, no. 6 (2015): 355–68.

Mei, Yi-Pao, trans. *The Ethical and Political Works of Motse.* London: Arthur Probsthain,1929.

Morgan, Daniel Patrick. "Knowing Heaven: Astronomy, the Calendar, and the Sagecraft of Science in Early Imperial China." PhD diss., University of Chicago, 2013.

Mori Kumao 森熊南. "Ō Fu Sanfu ron zakkō: Kandai no chishikijin" 王符「潛夫論」雜考: 漢代の知識2人. *Okayama daigaku kenkyū shūroku* 52 (1939): 13–21.

Needham, Joseph. *Science and Civilisation in China,* vol. 3, "Mathematics and the Sciences of the Heavens and of the Earth," and vol. 4, "Physics and Physical Technology," Cambridge: Cambridge University Press, 1959/1971).

Nienhauser, William H., Jr., trans. and ed. *The Grand Scribe's Records.* 10 vols. Bloomington: Indiana University Press, 2018–2020.

Ouyang Xiu. *Ouyangxiu quanji.* Shanghai: Guoxue Zhenglishe, 1936.

Pankenier, David. "Applied Field-Allocation Astrology in Zhou China: Duke Wen of Jin and the Battle of Chengpu (632 BC)." *Journal of the American Oriental Society* 119, no. 2 (1999): 266.

Pearson, Margaret J. *Wang Fu and the Comments of a Recluse.* Tempe: Center for Asian Studies, Arizona State University, 1989.

———. "The Worthy Unemployed: A Study of the Political Thought in the Comments of a Recluse (Ch'ien-fu lun) of Wang Fu (fl. A.D. 150)." PhD diss., University of Washington, 1983.

Peng Bingcheng 彭丙成 and Chen Manming 陳滿銘. *Xinyi Qianfulun* 新譯潛伏論. Taipei: Sanmin shuju, 2017.

Pines, Yuri. "Names and Titles in Eastern Zhou Texts." *T'oung Pao* 106 (2020): 714–20.

———. "Worth vs. Power: Han Fei's "Objection to Positional Power" Revisited." *Asiatische Studien—Études Asiatiques* 74, no. 3 (2020): 687–710, https://doi.org/10.1515/asia-2019-0040.

Pines, Yuri, trans. *The Book of Lord Shang*. New York: Columbia University Press, 2017.

Pound, Ezra, trans. *The Confucian Odes*. New York: New Directions, 1959.

Pulleyblank, Edwin G. "Ji 姬 and Jiang 姜: The Role of Exogamic Clans in the Organization of the Zhou Polity." *Early China* 25 (2000): 1–27.

Queen, Sarah A., and John S. Major, trans. *Luxuriant Gems of the Spring and Autumn, Attributed to Dong Zhongshu*. New York: Columbia University Press, 2015.

Rickett, W. Allyn, trans., *Guanzi*. 2 vols. Princeton, NJ: Princeton University Press, 1985.

Rogacz, David. "The Idea of Supreme Peace (*Taiping*) in Premodern Chinese Philosophies of History." *Asian Studies* 26, no.1 (January 2022): 401–24.

Rosemont, Henry, Jr., and Roger T. Ames, trans. *The Chinese Classic of Familial Reverence: A Philosophical Translation of the* Xiao jing. Honolulu, University of Hawai'i Press, 2009.

Schafer, Edward H. *Pacing the Void: T'ang Approaches to the Stars*. Berkeley: University of California Press, 1977.

Schuessler, Axel. *Minimal Old Chinese and Later Han Chinese*. Honolulu: University of Hawai'i Press, 2009.

Scott, Margaret. "Study of the Ch'iang." PhD diss., Cambridge University, 1959.

Shigeki, Kaizuka. *Confucius*. London: George Allen and Unwin, 1956.

Steele, John, trans. *I-Li*. London: Arthur Probsthain, 1917.

Sukhu, Gopal, trans. *The Songs of Chu*. New York: Columbia University Press, 2017.

Tjan, Tjoe Som. *Po Hu T'ung: The Comprehensive Discussions in the White Tiger Hall*. 2 vols. Leiden: Brill, 1949–1952; reprint, Westport, CT: Hyperion Press, 1973.

Tse, Wicky W. K. *The Collapse of China's Later Han Dynasty, 25–220 CE: The Northwest Borderlands and the Edge of Empire*. New York: Routledge Press, 2018.

Twitchett, Denis, and Michael Sloane, eds. *The Cambridge History of China Volume One: The Ch'in and Han Empires, 221* B.C. to A.D. 220.* Cambridge: Cambridge University Press, 1986.

Unschuld, Paul U., *Huang Di nei jing su wen: Nature, Knowledge, and Imagery in an Ancient Chinese Medical Text.* Berkeley: University of California Press, 2003.

Unschuld, Paul U., and Hermann Tessenow, trans. *Huang Di nei jing su wen: An Annotated Translation of Huang Di's Inner Classic.* 2 vols. Berkeley: University of California Press, 2011.

Waley, Arthur, trans. *Confucianism: The Analects of Confucius.* Sacred Writings Series. New York: Harper Collins, 1992.

Wang Bugui 王步貴. *Wang Fu sixiang yanjiu* 王符思想研究. Lanzhou: Gansu renmin chubanshe, 1987.

Wang Yi 王逸 (ca. 89–158 CE), comm. *Chuci.* In Hattori Unokichi, *Kanbun Taiki,* vol. 22. Taipei: Xinwenfeng chubanshe, 1978.

Ware, James E., trans. *Alchemy, Medicine, and Religion in China of A.D. 320: The Nei P'ien of Ko Hung.* Cambridge, MA: MIT Press, 1966. Reprint, New York: Dover, 1981.

Watson, Burton, trans. *Commoner and Courtier in Ancient China: Selection from the History of the Former Han by Pan Ku.* New York: Columbia University Press, 1974.

———. *Han Fei Tzu.* New York, Columbia University Press, 1964.

———. *Records of the Grand Historian. Han Dynasty.* 2 vols. New York: Columbia University Press, 1961/1993.

———. *Records of the Grand Historian. Qin Dynasty.* Hong Kong: Chinese University of Hong Kong, 1993.

Yan Xia 雁俠, *Zhongguo zaoqi xing shi zhidu yanjiu* 中國早期姓氏制度研究. Tianjin: Tianjin guji chubanshe, 1996.

Yang Hsien-yi, trans. *Selections from Records of the Historian.* Beijing: Foreign Languages Press, 1979. 論的著作年代及王符的生卒年推測. *Pingzhun xuekan* 3 (1987): 399–403.

Yates, Robin D. S., and Anthony J. Barbieri-Low. *Law, State, and Society in Early Imperial China.* 2 vols. Leiden: Brill, 2015.

Zhang Jianguo 張建國. "Shixi Han chu 'Yuefa sanzhang' de falu xiaoli— jian tan *Ernian luling* yu Xiao He de guanxi" 試析漢初 "約法三章" 的法律效力——兼談《二年律令》與蕭何的關係. *Faxue yanjiu* 法學研究 (1991): 154–60.

Zhang Qicheng 張其成. *Zhongyi zhexue jichu* 醫哲學基礎. Beijing: Zhongyiyao chubanshe, 2004.

Zhao Feng and Wang Le. "Glossary of Textile Terminology (Based on Documents from Dunhuang and Turfan)." *Journal of the Royal Asiatic Society* (April 2013): 349–87.

Zheng, Shuheng. "Three Ancient Words for Bear." *Sino-Platonic Papers* 294 (November 2019): 1–24.

# INDEX

Ames, Roger, 497n16
*Analects*: on Boyi and Shuqi, 32, 444n15; "By nature we are alike; practice makes us different," 96, 459n10; on Confucius's objection to Zilu praying on his behalf, 429, 547n38; convention of opening a book with an essay on study followed by, 436n29, xxi; a country that has the Way contrasted with a country that doesn't, 99, 459n18; on the Duke of Zhou's refraining from seeking all things in one man, 42, 158, 446n16, 473n12; on enriching the people as a foundation for order in a state, 440n3; on finding outstanding gentlemen of service, 156, 472n1; "If an artisan wishes to perfect his work, he must first sharpen his tools" (XV.9), 95, 458n5; on the impact of kindness in life, 332, 516n10; on leading with virtue and bringing order with the rites, 373, 377, 515n14, 526n23; on making excuses for failing to live up to one's beliefs, 162, 474n23; on plowing and learning, 321, 514n17; *quan* defined as "discretion," 356–57, 521–22n18; on relations between friends, 430, 547nn45–46; on roots (*ben* 本) and branches (*mo* 末), 440n1; on sacrifice made in the southwest corner of the house (奧 *ao*), 507n18; on Shun, 505n6; on the superior man's concerns for the progress of the Way, 8, 438n13; on the superior man's discernment and perceptive capacities, 7, 438n10; on those who are wealthy and not benevolent, 420, 544n8; on violating the canons and warnings of the sages of former times, 327, 515n2; on "What the superior man seeks, is in

*Analects* (*continued*)
himself" (XV.20), 355, 521n16; on why Confucius objected to Zilu praying on his behalf, 290, 508n1; on Yan Yuan and Min (Yan and Min), 147, 469n3

anthroscopy: *buwei* 部位 (proportions) of the body, 299, 510n7; ideal voice compared to *gong* 宮, 298, 509n6

axes: dagger-axes, 317–18, 512n3, 540n109; hewing of an axe handle in the *Book of Odes*, 351; presentation of, 231, 494n1, 546n27; pursuit of the axe and executioner's block, 199

Bao Xi 宓羲. *See* Fu Xi 伏羲 (Tamer of Beasts); Fu Xi 伏羲 (Tamer of Beasts)

Bi Cheng, 163, 425, 545n21

Bian He's (or He of Chu) rough-hewn gem, 6, 43, 438n7, 446n21

Bian Que, 269, 503n13

Bing state: Qiang rebellions in, 238, 243

Biyang, 401, 402, 536n45

Bo Yi (Boyi) (or Bo Yih 伯益, a worthy of the Shang): ferns picked with Shu Qi, 39, 101, 336, 460n23, 518n23; as Shun's minister, 191, 482n5; virtue of, 150, 344, 470n12, 519n52

Bo Zong 伯宗, unsparing criticism of his betters, 52, 410, 448n6

*Bohutong* 白虎通 (*Po Hu T'ung*): on distribution of fiefs to the worthy by a new king, 483n15, 485n28; Five Phases in, 453n8, 511n8; on music, 527–28n15, 529n30, 529n34; on punishments by effigy, 523n15; Thearchs (帝) distinguished from Kings (王), 545n24; on the Three Major Relationships, 547n42

Boming lineage: Boming (Lord Han), 387, 530n48

*Book of Changes. See Yijing* (*Book of Changes*)

*Book of Documents. See Shangshu* (*Book of Documents*)

*Book of Lord Shang* 商君書: on standards for ordinances, 228, 493n16

*Book of Odes* (*Shijing*): on decline of a dynasty related to depletion of *qi*, 431; Jie Zhitui praised in, 32, 330, 444n16, 515n6; lucky dreams extolled in, 429; "The Seventh Month" (instructions on matters great and small), 134–36; "Yu wu zheng" (Mao no. 194), on proceeding to [greater] evil, 249, 499n30; Zhou dynasty's claim to legitimacy reinforced by Song section of (Mao nos. 265–305), 84, 455n4

*Book of Odes* (*Shijing*)—*Mao*: "Bai Ju" 白駒 "White Colt" (Mao no. 186), 32, 99, 444n16, 459n19; "Ban" 板 ("Reversal," Mao no. 254), 61, 83, 352, 450n2, 455n5, 520n7; "Bei Men" (Mao no. 40), 40, 351, 445n6, 515n5; "Bei Men" (Mao no. 40), on poverty and fatigue, 8, 439n15; "Bei Shan" (Mao no. 204), 260, 502n22; "Bi Zui" (Mao no. 247), on relations between friends maintained with decorum, 430, 547n43; "Bo Zhou" (Mao no. 26), on an unhappy woman pressed to do something against her will, 219, 491n21; "Cai Fan" ("Gathering Southernwood") (Mao no. 161), 169, 477n16; "Chang Wu" 常武 (Mao no. 263), 400–401, 535n33; "Chang Wu" 常武 (Mao no. 263), on Nan Zhong, 427, 546n29; "Chang Wu" 常武 (Mao no. 263), on the lack of a unitary command, 251, 499n39; "Chu Ci" (Mao no. 209), on skillful invocators, 429, 547n35; "Da Dong" (communication of Tan's report) (Mao no. 203), 169, 477n18; "Da Ming" 大明 (Mao no. 236), "Heaven is difficult to rely on," 277, 301, 505n3, 510n19; "Da Ming" 大明 (Mao no. 236), on King Wen, 150, 470n11, 528n22; "Dang" ("Vast" 蕩, Mao no. 255), 83, 455nn5–6, 457n17, 480n36, 496n20; "Dang" ("Vast" 蕩, Mao no. 255), on "Considering the gathering of enmities a proof of virtue.," 187, 480n36; "Ding Zhe Fang Zhong" (Mao no. 30), on steadfast hearts, 341, 519n34; "Dong men zhi fen" (Mao no. 137), 134, 467n12; "Fa Ke" (Mao no. 158), 351, 520n5; "Fa Mu" 伐木 (Mao no. 165), on a bird seeking its companion's call, 354 , 521n14; "Fa Tan" (Mao no. 112), 193, 483n17; "Fei Fang" (Mao no. 149), 402; "Gan Tang Mu" (Mao no. 16), on the Earl of Shao, 205, 487n8; "Gao Qiu" (Mao no. 146), 401–2; "Ge Tan" (Mao no. 2), on a woman who visits her parents after completing her household duties, 219, 491n21; "Gong Liu" 公劉 (Mao no. 250), 370–71, 525n9; "Gu Feng" 谷風 (Mao no. 35), 43, 446n22; "Han Lu" (Mao no. 239), 524n8; "Han Yi" 韓奕 (Mao no. 261), on Chaoxian descendant with the name Hann, 412, 540n105; "Han Yi" 韓奕 (Mao no. 261), on the Marquis of Shao of Han, 194–95, 484n21; "Huang Yi" (Mao no. 241), "Blazed forth their anger" quoted in, 227, 493n13; "Huang Yi" (Mao no. 241), on consulting the people and the spirits, 165–66, 475n4; "Jiang Han" (Mao no. 262), 195–96, 484n21; "Jiang Han" (Mao no. 262), on the term the term *wangxiu* 王休, 452n8; "Jiao Gong" (Mao

*Book of Odes* (*Shijing*)—
*Mao* (*continued*)
no. 224), 170, 477n25; "Jie Nan Shan" (Mao no. 191), on a kingdom on the verge of destruction, 58, 209, 450n22, 488n18; "Jie Nan Shan" (Mao no. 191). on drawing on the labor of the hundred surnames, 426, 545n23; "Jie Nan Shan" (Mao no. 191), on Grand Master Yin, 417, 543n153; "Jie Nan Shan" (Mao no. 191), on the labor of the hundred surnames, 436, 545n23; "Jie Nan Shan" (Mao no. 191), on the plight of the worthy who are unemployed, 194, 484n20; "Jing Zhi" (Mao no. 288), 14, 440n25; "Ju Xia" (Mao no. 218), 14, 440n24; "Liu Yue" (or "Sixth Month") (Mao no. 177), on victory over the Xianyun 獫允, 501n10; "Liu Yue" (or "Sixth Month") (Mao no. 177), on Zhang Zhong, 414, 542n126; "Lu Ming" ("Crying Deer") (Mao no. 161), 169, 476n15; "Mang" (Mao no. 58), on those who are "changeable in their conduct," 344, 519n38; "Mian Man" ("Little Oriole") (Mao no. 230), 169, 477n20; "Mian Shui" (Mao no. 183), "No one is willing to think of the prevailing disorder," 210, 323, 488n20, 514n23; "Min Lao" (Mao no. 253), on not giving any indulgence to the wily and obsequious, 187, 480n35; "Po Fu" (Mao no. 147), 463n5; "Qi Fu" ("Minister of War") (Mao no. 185), 169, 477n18; "Qi Yu" (Mao no. 154), on the right person occupying the appropriate position, 168, 477n12; "Qi Yu" (Mao no. 154), on the ruler instructing people in matters great and small, 133, 466–67n6; "Qiao Yan" (Mao no. 198), 185, 228, 257, 343, 344, 480n30, 485n24, 493n14, 501n10, 519n44, 519n46; "Qing Ren" (Mao no. 79), 499n31; "Qing ying" 青蠅 (Mao no. 219), on flattering opportunists, 43, 446n19; "Sang Rou" (Mao no. 257), 31, 170, 443n8, 477n25; "Shang shang zhe hua" (Mao no. 214), "They are possessed of the ability, and right it is their movement should indicate it.," 262, 502n23; "Shi Jiu" (Mao no. 152), 332, 516n9, 518n29; "Shi Shu" ("Big Rats") (Mao no. 113), 169, 477n17; "Shi Yue Zhi Jiao" 十月之交 (Mao no. 193), 54, 449n16; "Shi Yue Zhi Jiao" 十月之交 (Mao no. 193), on Gui and Yu, 149, 469n8; "Si Gan" (Mao no. 189), 305, 511nn2–3; "Si Gan" (Mao no. 189), on luky dreams, 429, 547n39; "Si Mu" (Mao no. 122), 204, 487n4; "Song

Gao" 崧高 (Mao no. 259), on the chief of Shen, 191, 398, 482n7, 535n19; "Tian Bao" (Mao no. 166), xxx–xxiii, 151, 471nn21–22; "Tiao Zhi Hua" (Mao no. 233), 344, 519n45; "Wen Wang" (Mao no. 235), 377, 436n9, 526n24; "Wen Wang" (Mao no. 235), on King Wen as a model, 373, 525n12; "Wen Wang You Sheng," on paying homage to the Son of Heaven, 250, 499n36; "Wu Yang" (Mao no. 190), 305–6, 511n4; "Xiao Min" (Mao no. 195), on plans, 149, 279, 406n11, 469n6; "Xiao Yuan" (Mao no. 196), 7–8, 438n11; "Xing Wei" (Mao no. 246), 370–71, 499n37, 524n7; "Yi" (Mao no. 256), 233, 494n4; "Yin Wu" (Mao no. 305), on the capital of Shang, 131, 466n2; "You Bi" (Mao no. 298), on the feasting of the ruler and his ministers, 54, 449n17; "You Wu Sheng" (Mao no. 194), on dwelling at ease in prosperity, 99, 459n20; "Yuliu" 菀柳 (Mao no. 224), 54, 449n16; "Yu Wu Zheng" (Mao no. 194), on proceeding to [greater] evil, 249, 499n30; "Zhan Ang" (Mao no. 264), 179, 479n14; "Zhan Ang" (Mao no. 264), on merchants who "sell at triple profit to elevate themselves," 342, 519n42; "Zhan Ang" (Mao no. 264), on those who abandon their silk worms and weaving, 134, 467n12; "Zheng Min" (Mao no. 260), on providing a good example for the common people, 215, 489n4; "Zheng Min" (Mao no. 260), on the bodily form, 297, 509n1; "Zheng Min" (Mao no. 260), on virtue, 336, 342, 374, 518n24, 519n39, 525n17; "Zheng Min" (Mao no. 260), praise of Zhong Shanfu, 192, 415, 460–61n4, 543n142; "Zhi Jing" (Mao no. 274), 290, 508n3

Boyou lineage: Boyou identified as a courtesy name, 396; as part of the Ji clan of Zheng, 413

Boyou (or Liang Xiao, d. 543 BCE), 150, 470n16

Bu Shang (Bu, or Zi Xia), 157, 472n5

Cai Ze, 300, 510n17

Cao Can, Liu Bang supported by, 474n19

Chao Cuo, 晁錯 (d. 154 BCE): biography in the *Hanshu*, 488n17; as a confidant of Emperor Jing, 53, 448–49n11

Chen state: Duke Hu (Gui Man), 406, 538n75; Duke Li of Chen (r. 706–700 BCE), 406, 538n77

Chen Heng. *See* Tian Chang (c. 481 BCE, aka Chen Changzi and Chen Heng)

Chen Xin, marquis of Heyang, ca 176 BCE, 216, 490n11

Chong'er (Marquis of Jin), 444n16, 444n18, 517n15
Chu Ji and the Chu Ji lineage, 402, 403
Chu state (1030–223 BCE): banner raised to encourage Qing Xiang of Chu (298–263 BCE), 323, 514n27; identified as one of the six states of the Warring States period, 477n21; King Gong of Chu's (r. 590–560 BCE) ennoblement of Guan Su, 151, 471n19; King Zhao of Chu (r. 515–489 BCE), 280, 291, 504n1, 541n117; King Zhuang of Chu (r. 613–591 BCE), 151, 403, 471n18, 477n21; as one of the seven kingdoms, 397, 533n9. See also *Chuci* (Verses of Chu); King Wen of Chu (r. 689–677 BCE)
*Chuci* (Verses of Chu): on attributes of a superior person, in the "Shan Gui" 山鬼, 39, 444n1; "canine howls" described in the "Jiu Bian" 九辯 chapter of, 339, 518n30; on "elicitations" and "beckonings," 277, 504n2; a nine-headed snake described in the "Zhaohun" chapter of, 511n3
Chui (Cleve Chui), 7, 12–13, 438n9
Chunyu Zhang 淳于長, 334, 517n16
clan names: blurring in the distinction between *xing* "clan name" and the *shi* "lineage" name, 532n2; conferral of the hundred clan names, 281, 395, 533n3; "one thousand ranks" of, 395; as a resource of antiquity, 393, 396, 397. See also Deng clan; Hou clan; Ji clan (姬); Jiang clan; Lü clan; Mi clan; Peng clan; Ren clan; Si clan; Wang clan; Xiahou clan; Zi clan lineages

*Classic of Filial Piety*. See *Xiaojing* (*Classic of Filial Piety*)
Confucius (or Zhongni): on being unrighteous yet wealthy and eminent, 37, 421; as a fugitive in Wei, 54, 449n14; Lao Dan as his teacher, 6, 321, 427n3; on the virtues of Tang and Wu, and of Jie and Dijou, 148, 469n5. See also *Analects*; *Yili* 儀禮 ("Etiquette and Rites")
Cui Yuan 崔瑗 (ca. 77–142 CE), xii, xiii, 433n1

Daji, tale of beauty and ugliness associated with her, 108, 461n13, 462n15
*Dao De Jing*: on the dissipated conduct of gentlemen of service, 111, 462n20; on great-spirited men, 321, 513n16; Huan Tan's comments on it in Yang Xiong's biography in the *Hanshui*, 441n12
Deng clan: Deng Guang, 416, 543n145; Deng Tong, 30, 50–51, 300, 416, 442n5, 448n4, 510n17; Deng Yu of Xinye (marquis of Gaomi), 416, 474n20; Empress Dowager Deng, 416

INDEX ᙇ 567

Deng Guang (Deng Guanghan), 416, 543n145
Dijou. See King Djou of Shang
Di Ku (or Gao Xin 高辛): Eight Exemplars identified as either his contemporaries or descendants, 383, 528n17; his character, features, 382–83, 527nn13–14; identified as one of the Five Thearchs, 384, 437n3, 492n2, 529n29, 546n24; identified as the progeny of Fu Xi in the *Qianfulun*, 382, 527n12; music composed by, 383, 527–28n15; as the second of the Five Sovereigns, 384, 529n29; Zhu Rong as his teacher, 5
Di of Xin (Di Xin 帝辛 of Yin). See King Djou of Shang
Diwu Lun (fl. ca. 62 CE), 538n81
Di Yi 帝乙 (Emperor Yi) (or Shang Tang 商湯 or Cheng Tang 成湯), 124; founding of the Shang dynasty credited to, 437n3, 469n5; imprisonment by Jie of the Xia dynasty, 53, 449n12; lineage of, 407, 538n85; Yi Yin as his assistant, 5, 269, 345, 520n54
Dobson, W. A. C. H., xxii, 436n31
Dong Zhongshu (ca. 179–104 BCE), 9, 34, 52, 439n16, 444n17, 470n15, 492n11
Dou Rong (ally of Liu Xiu), 161, 474n20
Dou Zhang 竇章 (d. ca. 144 CE), 433n1, 435n27, xii, xiii

dragons: dragon officials named for dragons established by Fu Xi, 382, 527n10; "overbearing dragons," 35, 40, 445n7; Six dragons, 87, 456n16
Dubs, Homer H., on Emperor Wu, 483–84n1
Duke Huan of Qi, 406, 477n21
Duke Mu of Shan, 417
Duke Mu of Zheng (r. 627–606 BCE), 413, 541n114
Duke of Zhou: Fan, Jiang, Han, Mao, Zuo, and Ji identified as his offspring, 383; Guan and Cao (his brothers), 319, 320, 513n9; identified as the king's chief helper, 41; lineage of, 417; principles determining his virtue, 320–21; Shu Xiu as his teacher, 6

E Lai, 39, 403, 404, 444–45n2
Emperor Guangwu. See Han dynasty—Eastern Han (25–220 CE)—Emperor Guangwu (Liu Xiu, r. 25–58)
Emperor Ming. See Han dynasty—Eastern Han (25–220 CE)—Emperor Ming (r. 57–75 CE)
Emperor Wen. See Han dynasty—Western Han (206 BCE–7 CE)—Emperor Wen (r. 178–157 BCE)
Emperor Wu. See Han dynasty—Western Han (206 BCE–7 CE)—Emperor Wu (156–87 BCE)

Emperor Xuan. *See* Han dynasty—Western Han (206 BCE–7 CE)—Emperor Xuan (91–49 BCE)

Emperor Zhang. *See* Han dynasty—Eastern Han (25–220 CE)—Emperor Zhang (r. 75–88 CE)

Ershi Huang Di. *See* Qin dynasty—emperors Ershi Huang Di 二世皇帝 (Second Generation Emperor, r. 210–207 BCE)

*Essays of a Recluse* (*Qianfulun* 潛夫論). *See* Wang Jipei 汪繼培 (b. 1775)—*Qianfulun*

exemptions from punishments, 78, 454n17

Fang Xuanling 房玄齡 (578–648), 512n16

Fan Hui (or Fan Wu 范武): Jin armed forces commanded by (593 BCE), 106, 405, 461n5, 537n71; as minister to Lord Wen of Jin, 405–6, 538n73; posthumous name Wuzi, 405

Fan Kuai (d. ca. 189 BCE), a dog butcher, 97, 459n13

Feng Jie, 413

Feng Jingtong (aka Yan), 413–14

Feng Long, 283, 507n22

Feng Ting, 413, 541n118

Five Classics: individual receptivity to the guidance of, xi; Wang Fu's aim to transmit the teachings of, 1, 419, xvii. *See also Book of Odes* (*Shijing*); *Liji* (*Book of Rites*); *Lüshi Chunqiu* 呂氏春秋 (*Spring and Autumn Annals*); *Shangshu* (*Book of Documents*); *Yijing* (*Book of Changes*)

Five Hegemons, 170, 477n21

Five Phases: auspicious directions of dwellings associated with, 282, 507n19; impact on a a person's quintessential spirit, 283, 507n20; the term *wangxiu* 王休 according to, by Yu Yue, 453–54n9

Five Thearchs (or Five Emperors): as exemplars for rulers, 223, 228, 426; Five Eras (*wudai* 五代) of, 118, 463n4; identification of, 523n15; images of punishments engraved by, 225; lists of the identities of, 492n2, 493n15, 494n7, 546n25; personal appellations during the era of, 396–97; punishments by effigy by: 523n15; role in the birth of human beings, 280

Five Weapons, 233, 494n3

Fu Xi 伏羲 (Tamer of Beasts) or Bao Xi 宓羲 or Tai Hao: Bao Xi 宓羲 identified as his personal name, 527n7; birth and character of, 382, 527n8; devising of the eight trigrams by, 298, 509nn4–5; events prior to the time of, 381; identified as one of the Three Huang,

546n24; as king (2852 BCE), 281, 527n7; as one of the Five Emperors, 523n15; as one of the Three August Ones, 381–82, 492n1, 526n1; Tai Hao identified as his name in the world, 382, 507n17, 527n5; in the "Xici" 繫辭 "Great Appendix" of the *Yijing*, 488n1

Fufu He, 408, 539n88

Fu Yue, 39, 311, 390–91

Gao, Lord of Bi, 412, 540n107

Gao You (ca. 168–212 CE)— commentary to *Lüshi Chunqiu*: *yinxue* 淫學, 441n5

Gao Xin 高辛. *See* Di Ku (or Gao Xin 高辛)

Gao Yao: as Shun's minister. *See also Shangshu (Book of Documents)*—"Gao Yao Mo" (Counsels of Gao Yao)

Gengzi, 315, 317, 319, 512n1, 513n7, 547n40

Gong Gong 共工 (legendary criminal): as one of the Four Disobedient Ones (*sizi* 四子), 62, 111, 450n4, 462n17, 493n12; Zhuan Xu (the Black Emperor) distinguished from, 531n60

Gong Liu (Duke Liu), 371, 524n7, 525n9

Gong Liu 公劉 (His Honor Liu), 258, 501n14

Gong Sui 龔遂 (d. 62 BCE), 199, 486n36

Gongsun lineage: identified as a "rank name," 396, 397

Gongsun Ao (or Mubo), 299, 410n9

Gongsun Hong (or Mubo), ennoblement by Emperor Wu (ca. 128–123 BCE), 191, 482n3

Gongsun Long on "hardness" and "whiteness," 160, 474n17

*Gongyangzhuan*, on shallow and crafty speech, 247, 298n24

Gou Chen, 283, 507n22

Grand Conclusion Cycle (ji 紀), 84, 455n2

Great Peace: enriching the people and rectifying learning as the foundation of, 17, 440nn2–3; Wang Fu's theory that harmonious qi can elicit it, xxii

"Great Year" (Tai Sui), 283, 507n21

Guan Ying (d. ca. 176 BCE), a silk merchant valued as military commander under Liu Bang, 97, 459n13

*Guanzi* 管子: concept of 立政 *lizheng*, 441n8; on enriching the people as a foundation for order in a state, 17, 440n2; on the generosity of rulers, 494n11; on governing in an age of decline, 492n4; on the rule of an enlightened king, 431, 548n50

Gun 鯀, as one of the Four Disobedient Ones (*sizi* 四子), 41, 62, 111, 450n4, 462n17, 493n12

*Guoyu* (Conversations of the states): on Shu Xiang, 417, 543n154; Wang Fu's aim to transmit the teachings of, xvii, xxv

*Guoyu* (Conversations of the states)—"Chu Yu" chapter, 531n3, 531n61; on "cutting of communication between Heaven and earth," 400, 535n29; division of Heaven and earth mentioned in, 277, 504n1; on Dou Ziwen of Chu, 277; on managing the resources of the people, 259, 501n17; *wuguan* 五觀 interpreted as a reference to five brothers, 387, 530n45; on the Yao's elevation of the descendants of Zhong and Li, 400, 535n31

*Guoyu* (Conversations of the states)—"Jinyu" chapter: on disorders coming from within a state, 132, 178, 466n4, 478n10; doctors compared to "to rulers of states," 86, 150–51, 456n13, 470–71n17; on heaven withdrawing the ability of the ruler to see clearly, 121, 464n13; on the Huang Di's twenty-five sons divided into twelve lineages, 399, 525n21; on the Lord of Guo's dream of Rushou's conferring land upon him, 313, 512n19

*Guoyu* (Conversations of the states)—"Lu Yu" chapter: on fears of being crushed, 323, 514n24; on Goulong's pacification of the Nine Lands, 390, 532n63

*Guoyu* (Conversations of the states)—"Zhengyu" chapter, on the Jiang, 398, 534n17

*Guoyu* (Conversations of the states)—"Zhouyu" chapter: on inviting artists and and teachers when the Son of Heaven holds court, 113, 462n23; on the Lord of Guo's dream of Rushou's conferral of land upon him, 313, 512n19; on Lord Xiang of Jin's observation of Li of Jin, 300, 510n15, xxv; on reading the face of Qiaoru, 300, 510n11, xxv

Han Anguo 漢安國 (fl. 143 BCE), 333–34, 517n16

Han dynasty—Western Han (206 BCE–7 CE): *ban liang* 半兩 ("half ounce") coin of, 478n3; Bao Xuan as a famous servitor of, 415; gradations of clepsydra during, 203–4, 487n3; imperial sacrifices performed during, 78, 453–54n16; Jianwu period (25–55 CE), 191, 482n4; Scholar Li (Li Yiji 酈食其), 415, 543n141; selection of officials between 32 BCE and 23 CE, 78, 459n16; understanding of cosmogony during, 361, 522n3

Han dynasty—Western Han (206 BCE–7 CE)—Emperor Gaozu (Liu Bang, r. 202–195 BCE): Cao Can as his supporter,

474n19; founding of the Han dynasty, 97, 459n12; humble status of some who contributed to his success, 97; legal code of, 213, 488–89n2; Xiao He as his supporter, 161, 416, 474n19

Han dynasty—Western Han (206 BCE–7 CE)—Emperor (Liu Bang, r. 202–195 BCE): Duke of Pei assumed as his title, 411, 540n104

Han dynasty—Western Han (206 BCE–7 CE)—Emperor Wen (r. 180–157 BCE): abrogation of corporal punishments, 213, 489n2; clothing and frugality of, 136; Deng Tong favored by, 50–51, 442n5, 448n5; enfeoffment of maternal relatives, 191, 482n3; entombment at Zhiyang, 140, 468n22; his virtuous example rather than harsh punishment used to govern, 216, 490n10; norms of, 137, 218; the position of generals discussed with Feng Tang, 413; preference for Daoist thought, 490n10; qualities of men nominated by, 74, 453n10; the sacred field tilled by, 475n8; Yuan Si as a palace gentleman under, 451n10

Han dynasty—Western Han (206 BCE–7 CE)—Emperor Jing (r. 157–141 BCE): Chao Cuo as his confidante, 53; Han Anguo identified as his brother, 517n16; taboo on his name, Qi, 417,

541n155; Wei Buhai's fief confiscated during, 142, 468n28

Han dynasty—Western Han (206 BCE–7 CE)—Emperor Wu (156–87 BCE): the boundaries of the Han expanded by, 246–47; enfeoffment of his prime ministers, 191, 482n2; norms of, 218

Han dynasty—Western Han (206 BCE–7 CE)—Emperor Zhao 漢昭帝 (r. 87–74 BCE) in 81 BCE: death of, 465n22; Huo Guang's ruling in his name, 465n21; *Yantielun* based on his notes, 496n1

Han dynasty—Western Han (206 BCE–7 CE)—Liu He (r. 18 July-14 August 74 BCE), 465n22

Han dynasty—Western Han (206 BCE–7 CE)—Emperor Xuan (91–49 BCE): selection of officials and calculation of their earnings, 197–98, 486n30; upbring of, 197, 485–86n29

Han dynasty—Western Han (206 BCE–7 CE)—Emperor Cheng (r. 33–7 BCE), 98, 353, 465n24

Han dynasty—Western Han (206 BCE–7 CE)—Emperor Ai (r. 7–1 BCE): death of, 465n24; on gradations of clepsydra, 203–4, 487n3; Wang Jia's loyalty not recognized by, 353, 521n12; Xifu Gong 息夫公 and Dong Xian 董賢 as his imperial favorites, 120, 464n11

Han dynasty—Western Han (206 BCE–7 CE)—Emperor Ping (r. 1 BCE–5 CE): death of, 459n17; the status of the *Zuozhuan* secured during his reign, 544n4; Wang Mang's selection of, 466n24

Han dynasty—Western Han (206 BCE–7 CE)—Empress Dowager Wang (Wang Zhengjun), 124, 125, 465–66n24

Han dynasty—Eastern Han (25–220 CE): activities of Wu Han (d. 44 CE), 161, 186, 474n20, 480n31; corruption in Luoyang, the capital of, 180, 479n18; Deng Yu of Xinye's activities during, 161, 416, 474n20; Emperor An (r. 107–125)., 433n2, xii; Emperor He (r. 89–105), 433n2, xii; eunuchs associated with the demise of, xvii; perspective on it, found in the essays in the *Qianfulun*, xvii; Wang Fu identified as one the "Three Worthies" of, xiii–xiv; Yellow Turbans, xv. *See also Hou Hanshu*

Han dynasty—Eastern Han (25–220 CE)—Emperor Guangwu (Liu Xiu, r. 25–57): accession of, xiv; amnesties issued during his reign, 186, 480n31; border commanderies controlled during *jianwu* 建武 period 25 to 55 CE, 272; distaste for *zhangju* 章句 ("commentaries in paragraphs and sentences"), xviii–xix; overthrowing of and punishment of Wang Mang, 98; supporters in his struggle to restore the Han dynasty, 474n20

Han dynasty—Eastern Han (25–220 CE)—Emperor Ming (r. 57–75 CE): the Abundant Talent in charge of the southern commanders, 184–85, 479–80n27, 480n28; accession of, xiv; entombment at Luoyang, 140; the office of Official Carriages ordered to accept memorials on *fanzhi* 反支 days, 209, 488n16; public shaming of the Marquis of Zongyan during his reign, 143, 468n30; revolt against him (71 CE), 453n16

Han dynasty—Eastern Han (25–220 CE)—Emperor Zhang (r. 75–88 CE), xiv–xv; Feng Jingtong's writing valued by, 413–14

Han dynasty—Eastern Han (25–220 CE)—Emperor Xian (r. 189–220 CE), xv

*Han Feizi* and Han Fei (ca. 280–253 BCE): "Chu jian Qin" on unwillingness to risk death, 236–37, 495n12; on laws as a models for officials, in chapter 44 ("Shouyi"), 229,

493n17; on letting names define themselves and affairs reach their own settlement (in chap. 8, "Yangquan"), 74, 453n11; Li Si's killing of Han Fei, 53; on one who cultivates weeds and invasives harms the grain, 178, 478n9; on order and chaos by force of circumstance "Shinan" 難勢, 355, 521n17; portrayal of Shun in the "Wu Du" chapter of, 49, 447n1; on the purpose of government, 83, 455n1; on rulers not revealing their wants, 547–48n49; on tasks and assignments for ministers in chapter 5 (*Zhudao* 主道), 79–80, 454–55n19; Yao and Shun mutually opposed in "Nanshi" 難勢, 317, 512n3; "Zhu Dao" on "The ruler must not reveal his wants," 347, 430, 520n2, 547–48n48

Han state (or Hann state) (403–230 BCE): Boming (Lord Han), 387, 530n48; identified as one of the six states of the Warring States period, 477n21; Qiang rebellions in, 243; royal family of, 410–11, 540n99

Han Xin, 161, 474n19, 502n6

Han Yu, 韓愈 (768–824 CE), Wang Fu described by, xii–xiv

*Hanshi waizhuan*, statement on virtue compared with a statement in the QFL, 369, 524n1

*Hanshu*: biography of Chao Cuo, 晁錯 (d. 154 BCE), 488n17; biography of Dong Zhongshu, 470n15, 492n11; on the calculation of the earnings, for Emperor Xuan's officials, 197, 486n30; on Emperor Gaozu's legal code of, 489n2; on Emperor Wen's abrogation of corporal punishments, 213, 489n2; on Emperor Wen's frugality, 136, 467nn14–15; on Emperor Wen's tilling the sacred field, 475n8; on gradations of clepsydra, 487n3; Huan Tan's comments on the *Dao De Jing* in Yang Xiong's biography, 441n12

Han Zhuo, 387–88, 530n48

harmonious qi: as the blending of yin and yang, 361, 372, 525n11; cultivation of hearts compared with cultivating a garden, 374; Wang Fu's theory that it can elicit Great Peace, 171, 362, xxii

*Hou Hanshu*: biography of Pang Cang 龐參, 497n5; biography of Wang Fu 王符 (ca. 85–162 CE), xii–xiii; on disasters associated with the selection of officials, 157, 472n6; the King of Liang's unfair collection of taxes, 490n17; *lun* as a literary genre employed in, xx–xxi; on the Qiang rebellion (107 CE), 495n15

Hou Ji (or Ji Qi, "Lord Millet"), 96, 192, 383, 458n8, 528nn17–18
Hsiao Kung-chuan [Xiao Gongchuan], xvi
Hsu, Cho-yun, 533n10
*Huainanzi* 淮南子 (ca. 139 BCE): "Lanming," 548n51; literary style of, xxv; on "quintessential sincerity" (*jing cheng* 精誠), 334, 517n17; "Six Blossoms" 六英 music mentioned in, 527n15; "Taizu," 泰族, 544n13; on the Way and Moral Potency as the root, 431, 548n51
Huan Tui, 31, 443n11
Huang Ba 黃霸 (d. 51 BCE), 199, 486n36
*Huang Di nei jing su wen*, on judgements and decisions originating from the gall bladder, 284, 507n23
*Huang Di nei jing su wen*, on prescriptions for treating illness compared with managing a state, 175, 478n1
Huangfu Gui (104–174, General of the Liao), 433n4, xiii
Huangfu (minister during the reign of Zhou King You), 96, 459n9
Huo clan: Huo Guang, 125, 465nn21–22; Huo Shan, 125, 465n23; Huo Yu, 125, 465n23; Huo Yun, 125, 465n23; members of the imperial family exclusively married by, 125

*Ili* ("Capping of a Great Officer" 士冠禮), 483n14

jade. *See* stones and gems
Ji clan (姬): the Dong clan branch of, 401; list of names associated with, 383–84; as one of the eight divisions associated with grandsons of Zhurong, 401; as the royal Zhou clan name, 528n17; use of punishments set aside by, 373, 525n13; Wu Taibo, 413, 541n115; Yao's conferral of the clan name Ji on Qi, 396. *See also* Hou Ji (or Ji Qi, "Lord Millet")
Ji of Cao, 34, 444n18
Ji Sheng (or Fei Lian 廉), 403, 537n61
Jiang clan: as Bo Yi's clan, 396, 398, 534n17; dwelling place of, 399, 535n20; lineages associated with, 399
Jiang Shang 姜尚 (or Lü Shang 呂尚), 6, 398, 462n21
Jin 晉 state: descendants of Bao Gui, 415; Diviner Yan of, 464n13; ducal family of, 410; Duke Dao (r. 573–558), 445n10; Duke Ling of Jin (r. 620–607 BCE), 134, 142, 467nn7–8, 468n26; Duke Ping (or Shuxiang or Yangxhe Xi, r. 557–532), 408, 539nn92–93; Duke Wen of Jin (r. 636–628 BCE), 477n21, 480n33; Lord Ping of Jin (d. 532 BCE),

150–51, 470–71n17; Marquis Mu of Jin (r. ca. 811–785), 410, 539n98; Qi Xi, high official with a reputation for impartiality, 100, 399, 460n22; Sun Boyan, 414, 542nn124–25; Wang Liang famed for his skill at charioteering, 234, 494n10; Wangzi Qiao, crown prince Jin (557–532), 408, 539nn92–93; Xi Rui (or Ji Rui, d. ca. 636 BCE, a prince of Jin), 410, 539n94; Zhang Hou or Xie 解 Zhang, 414, 542n127; Zhang Lao, 414, 542n127. *See also* Fan Hui (or Fan Wu 范武)

Jing Fang (or Jing Junming, fl. 48 BCE), 9, 53, 79, 439n16, 449n11, 454n18

Jingzhong. *See* Tian Jingzhong 田敬仲 (750–? BCE)

Jiyou, 41, 445–46n11

Jizi 箕子, 52, 391, 448n6, 468n18, 472n2, 532n68

Ju (minister during the reign of Zhou King You), 96, 459n9

Kamenarović, Ivan P., 453–54n16

King Cheng of Zhou (r. 1043/35–1006 BCE), 150, 283, 511n1; the Duke of Zhou as his regent, 119, 142, 463n5, 468n24; Kang Shu as his virtuous minister, 43, 446n18; Tang destroyed and Yu invested with territory by, 305;

Xiong Yan (Yu Xiong) enfeoffed with Chu during his reign, 402

King Djou of Shang: identified as Di of Xin (Di Xin 帝辛), 391, 462n22, 538n85; lineage of, 532n68, 538n85; the Marquis of Chong as a supporter, 39, 444–45n2; as the paradigm of the "bad last ruler," 469n5, 108–9, 112, 461n9; Three Humane Ones' opposition to, 472n2

King Kuai of Yan (r. 320–318 BCE), 158, 473n10

King Li of Zhou (857/53 to 840/28 BCE): Ji You identified as his son, 413; tyrannical rule during the Western Zhou, 31, 283, 446n14, 496n20, 526n22, 541n112

King Ling of Zhou (571 to 545 BCE), 408, 539n91

King of Liang: plot to assassinate Yuan Ang, 443n6; Zou Yang's (ca. 206–129 BCE) service to, 333, 460n23, 516n15

King of Liang (Liu Chang, d. 98), unfair collection of taxes by, 490n17

King Wen of Chu (r. 689–677 BCE): Deng destroyed by, 416; the *Lüshi Chunqiu* account set in the reign of, 471n19; Shen Wuwei (Shen Zhou) identified as a progeny of, 536n52

King Wen of Zhou: "Consider the gathering of enmities a proof of virtue" spoken to the Shang rulers, 187, 480n36; the "Four Friends" identified as his companions, 473n13, 53, 524n7, 540n107, 545n21; Jiang Shang as his trusted advisor, 6, 398, 462n21; the prince mentioned in a poem in the *Book of Odes* possibly identified with, 524n7; relatives surnamed Ji, 383, 529n25; Tai Ren identified as his mother, 383, 528n22; Tai Si identified as his consort, 512n18

King Wu of Zhou (1049/45–1043 BCE), 124; founding of the Zhou dynasty, 469n5; Kang Shu identified as his younger brother, 43, 446n18, 511n1; the Master of Ji/Count of Ji as a loyal servant of, 8, 438n14

King Xian of Zhou (r. 368–320 BCE), 158, 473n9

King Xuan of Zhou (827–782 BCE): the lineages of Zhong and Li during the reign of, 400–401; revival during the reign of, 377, 526n21; states received by prime ministers and senior ministers during the time of, 191; victory over the Eastern Yi, 484n21; victory over the Xianyun 獫允, 250, 499n33, 501n10; virtuous officials appointed by, 194–95, 484n21; Yin Jifu as his minister, 191, 417

King You of Zhou: blamed for the fall of the Zhou dynasty, 446n14, 459n9, 526n22; decline of the palace associated with, 283; disasters and portents brought by his assembly of Huangfu, Kui, and Ju, 96; enrichment of, 43

Kuang Heng (fl. ca. 45 BCE), 9, 67, 439n17

Kui (minister during the reign of Zhou King You), 96, 459n9

Lao Dan, 6, 321, 427n3

*Laozi*: on the character of a gentleman entrusted with responsibility, 117–18, 463n2; conquering oneself is called strength, 151, 471n20; illness recognized as an illness, 85

Lau, Ulrich and Michael Lüdke, 481n1

Legge, James: on the term on the term *xiu* 休 as "excellence/ goodness," 453–54n9

Liang Tong (ally of Liu Xiu), 161, 474n20

*Lienüzhuan*, 471n18, 514n26, 525n9, 545n18

*Liji* (*Book of Rites*): Confucius on the "now pliant, now rigid" bow strings of Wen and Wu, 229, 493n18; on the *fengye* 縫掖 "large sleeves" of the garb of Confucius, 433n5, xiii; on the "Five Sacrifices," 293, 508–9n16; the phrase 假爾泰龜 "We

depend on thee, O great Tortoise-shell" in, 279, 506n10
*Liji* (*Book of Rites*)—"Nei Ze" chapter: on filial sons, 23, 441–42n15; on "kindling tools," 87, 456n15
*Liji* (*Book of Rites*)—"Wang Zhi" chapter: on "drinking entertainment" to nourish and honor the aged, 476n15; on faithful ministers, 353, 521n11; household spirits defined in the Zheng Xuan's note to, 509n16
Li Si 李斯 (ca. 280–208 BCE): Han Fei killed by, 53; execution of, 413
Liu Bang. *See* Han dynasty—Western Han (206 BCE–7 CE)—Emperor Gaozu (Liu Bang, r. 202–195 BCE)
Liu lineage: challenged by Empress Dowager Lü, 124, 464n16; Liu He (r. 18 July–14 August 74 BCE), 465n22; selection of the Three Excellencies drawn from members of, 191, 481n1. *See also* emperors of the Han dynasty
Lord Huan of Qi: as a Lord of the Land during an era of decline, 257–58
Lord of Guo, 291, 508n4
Lord Wen of Jin: concubine Jí of Yan in his service, 399; Fan Wuzi (or Fan Hui) as minister to, 405, 538n73; Jie Zhitui's loyalty to, 515n6; as a Lord of the Land during an era of decline, 257–58
Lord Wen of Zhu, 291
Lord Xian of Jin, 279, 506n14, 537n63, 545n18
Lord Zhao of Song, 477n22
Lü clan: Empress Dowager Lü, 124, 464n16; kings in the early Han period as members of, 124, 465n18; Lü Lu, Lü Chan, Lü Tai, and Lü Tong, 124, 464n17
Lu state (1042–249 BCE): ducal family of, 409; Duke Huan of Lu 魯桓公 (r. 712–694 BCE), 445n11; Duke Min 魯閔公 (r. 662–660 BCE), 445n11; Duke of Lu (r. 541–510 BCE), 445n11; Lord Zhao of, 397; Meng Xianzi as the ruler of, 299, 510n10; the Scribe of Lu (Zuo Qiuming, author of the *Zuozhuan*), 291, 508n7; territories of Ren, Su, Xuqu, and Zhuanyu, 398, 534n15
Lufu 彔父, 319, 513n10
*Lunheng* of Wang Chong: on "adverse" destiny and "according" destiny, 505n2; *lun* genre of, xviii, xx; tendency to provide a synopsis of stories, xxv; Wang Chong's contempt for *fu* (rhyme-prose), xix; Wong Chong's distaste for *zhangju* 章句 ("commentaries in paragraphs and sentences"), xviii–xix

*Lunyu*: ii, 519n49; iv, 466n26; vi, 518n28; vii, 420, 519n40, 544n6, 544n11; x, 519n47; xii: on when the people are in want, 220, 488n21; on hearing litigation, 206, 487n10; xiii, 487n5, 487n9, 519n51, 546n26; xiv, 519n43, 531n57; xv, 519n41; xvi, 519n50, 524n2, 534nn15–16; xvii: on anxious people, 209, 488n19; on the reverence for righteousness of the sage, 5, 437n2; xviii, 484n19; xx, 36

*Lüshi Chunqiu* 呂氏春秋 (*Spring and Autumn Annals*): arrangement of chapters of, xxi; on blockages, 269, 503n14; on communication between souls, 311, 512n12; King Wen of Chu's reign (r. 689–677 BCE) as the setting of, 471n19; Shen Hou described in, 471n19; on worthies that force themselves to vomit food they ate illegally, 158, 473n11; Zheng's abandoning its troops derided in, 249

Ma Rong 馬融 (ca. 89–166 CE), 433n1, 435n27, xii, xiii

Marquis of Sui, 43, 292, 446n21

marriage: cases in which a single daughter has been promised to multiple households, 220–21; a homely wife as superior to beauties such as Xi Shi or Mao Qiang, 157, 472n8; local officials' involvement in marriage related cases, 219, 491n20; ritual of one marriage (*jiao* 醮), 221, 490n24; suicide of women whose unrighteous relatives forcibly act as matchmakers, 221–21

*Mencius*: on "arrangement of dignities and emoluments" [班爵祿 *banjue lu*] determined by the House of Zhou, 474–75n1; on the enlightened ruler's concentration of principles and ritual, 477n28; on "Head Scholars," 168, 475n10; phrase uttered by Mencius when he was charged with being fond of arguing, 430, 547n41; on reciprocity, 337, 518n27; on the salaries of ordinary people, 167, 475n9

Mi clan: lineages included in the Mi clan ducal family, 402–3; Xiong Yan enfeoffed under the reign of King Cheng of Zhou, 402

Min Sun, 328, 515n4

Nienhauser, William H.,: on *bin* in the name Sun Bin, 448n8

Nine Superintendents, 73, 452n6

"occupying the road" / "holding official appointments" (*dangtu* 當塗), 64, 100, 451n11

Ouyang Xiu, xv

Pang Juan (d. 341 BCE), 53–54, 448n8
Pang Xun (Shu Xu/ Tou Xu), 333, 517n15
Peng Bingcheng 彭丙成, 453–54n16, 467n9, 496n21, 497n7, 505n7, 511n7, 523n11, 530n40
Peng clan: Pengzu lineages of the Shi Wei and Zhuji destroyd by the Shang, 401
Peng Duo: notes and emendations to Wang Jipei's *Qianfulun jian*, xxviii; the phrase 至寡動, 欲任德 read as 至寡欲, 動任德 with respect to Emperor Wen's virtuous example, 490n10
Peng Yue (d. ca. 196 BCE), a ruffian from Mt Li, 97, 459n14
Pines, Yuri, 520n4, 532n2
Ping'a (marquisate of Wang Ren), 54, 449n15

Qi state (1046–221 BCE): descendants of Bao Shu, 415; destruction of, 245, 497n11; discussion punished and scholars buried by, 50, 448n3; Duke Mu identified as one of the Five Hegemons of the Spring and Autumn period, 477n21; Duke Zhuang 齊莊公 (r. 553–548), 404, 470n16; identified as one of the six states of the Warring States period, 477n21; King Wei of Qi (r. 334–320), 151, 406, 471nn18–19; Li Si's killing of Han Fei in, 53; Marquis of Qi (r. 484–481 BCE), 50, 447–48n2; officer E boiled as punishment by King Wei, 151, 471n19; as one of the seven kingdoms, 397, 533n9; Qing Feng 慶封 (d. 538), 150, 470n16; struggle between the Kan and Chen clans, 492n7; Tian Dan, the governor of Jimo 即墨, 151, 245, 246, 471n19, 497n14; Yue Men, 43, 446n17; Zou Maru of Qi, 226, 492n5

Qiang 羌 people: as one of the Four Yi to pay tribute, 250, 499n35

Qiang 羌 people—rebellions, 244, 248; dating from 107 to 118 and 140 to 144 CE, xiii; Empress Dowager Deng's suppression of, 416

Qifu (or Zimu Jinfu), 408, 539n89

*qilin*, 161, 198, 364, 474n21, 486n31

Qin dynasty (221–206 BCE): Bo Qi 白起 and Meng Tian 蒙恬, 120, 463–67n10; You Yu of Rong, 43, 446n17

Qin dynasty—emperors Qin Shi Huang 秦始皇 (First Emperor, r. 221–210 BCE): birth in Handan as Zhao Zheng (Zheng of Qin), 404; rule via mutilating punishments, 112, 128; Zhao Gao as his confidential advisor, 461n11

Qin dynasty—emperors Ershi Huang Di 二世皇帝 (Second Generation Emperor, r. 210–207 BCE): dream about a white tiger, 311; factional struggles following his death, 463n10; identified as the last emperor of the Qin dynasty, 461n12; isolation from his officials and faith in Zhao Gao (his prime minister), 62, 65–66; Li Si as his imperial grand secretary, 97, 459n11; Zhao Gao as his prime minister, 62, 64–66, 97, 109, 459n11; murder, 109

Qin dynasty—emperors Ziyang, 246, 498n19

Qin Shi Huang. *See* Qin dynasty—emperors Qin Shi Huang 秦始皇 (First Emperor, r. 221–210 BCE)

Qin state (c. 9th century–207 BCE): interest in absorbing districts in Hann, 413, 541n118; King Mu of Qin (r. 956–918/919 BCE), 383, 403–4, 446n17, 514n26; laws against disparagement and calumny, 114, 463n25; as one of the seven kingdoms, 397, 533n9; "Vertical Alliance" of states formed to curb its power, 473n9

Qinze, 321, 513n15

Ran Qiu (Ran, Ran You, or Bo Niu), 157, 472n5

Ren clan, Jí lineage associated with, 399–400, 535n25

San Miao 三苗, 262n17, 493n11

Shang dynasty (c. 1600–1046 BCE): four quarters of. *See also* Bo Yi (Boyi) (or Bo Yih 伯益, worthy of the Shang); Di Yi 帝乙 (Emperor Yi) (or Shang Tang 商湯 or Cheng Tang 成湯); King Djou of Shang; Three Eras

*Shangshu* (*Book of Documents*, or *Shujing*): on blowing pitchpipes to fix the clan names, 398, 534n14; on the decline of a dynasty related to depletion of qi, 431

*Shangshu* (*Book of Documents*)—"Gao Yao Mo" (Counsels of Gao Yao): on the duty of men to act as Heaven's officials, 90, 118, 458n29, 463n3; on the five mutilating punishments, 178, 479n13; on the five ranks, 178, 479n12; on having an intelligent mind and lazy body, 209, 488n17; on human beings who carry out the works of heaven, 362, 522n7; on the word *kuang* 曠, 474n21

*Shangshu* (*Book of Documents*)—"Hong Fan" 洪範 ("Great Plan" chapter): on the Son of Heaven as the father and mother of the people, 258; on the benefits of having men with ability and

administrative power, 88,
457n20; "completing the full
lifespan," 370, 524n5; concern
for the people, 424, 545n16; a
great concord defined in, 279,
506n9; on the great tortoise and
the evils of the Shang dynasty,
279, 506n10; the phrase *yue zhi
cong xing* 月之從星 in, 479n24;
on who one should consult
concerning doubts about a great
matter, 461n7
Shangshu (*Book of Documents*)—"Jiu
Gao" chapter, "Let not men
look only into water; let them
look into the glass of other
people.," 29, 442n3
Shangshu (*Book of Documents*)—
"Kang Gao" chapter, 178, 187,
478n11, 481nn38–39, 483n13
Shangshu (*Book of Documents*)—"Lü
xing" chapter: on achieving
Great Peace, 96, 458n6; on the
naming of mountains and rivers
by Wenming of Rong, 386,
530n43
Shangshu (*Book of Documents*)—"Pan
Geng" chapter, on old friends
and families, 327, 515–16n1
Shangshu (*Book of Documents*)—
"Shao Gao" chapter, 293
Shangshu (*Book of Documents*)—
"Shun Dian" 舜典 chapter: Chui
mentioned in, 438n9; on the
examination and degradation of
the Three Excellencies, 192,

482n11; on the examinations of
merits, 73, 452nn3–4; the Four
Lads (*sizi*) identified in, 493n12;
on Fu Yue and Wu Ding,
390–91, 532n67; on Long 龍 as
the Minister of Communication
納言 *nayan*, 214–15, 489n4; on
money to be received for
redeemable offences, 188, 481n40;
Ni Kuan and Kuang Heng
mentioned in, 9, 439n17; on the
rule of Yao and Shun, 450n3;
Shun identified as the second
legendary ruler of China's
predynastic period, 489n3; Wang
Fu's citation on clan affiliations
that do not appear in it, 41–42,
446n13; Wang Fu's citation on
those who have completed the
accomplishments of Heaven and
earth who do not appear in it,
90, 458n30
Shangshu (*Book of Documents*)—
"Shuo Ming" chapter: on Fu
Yue, 390–91, 532n67
Shangshu (*Book of Documents*)—
"Yao Dian" chapter, 445n9,
476n12, 486n1, 487n7
Shangshu (*Book of Documents*)—"Yi
Ji" chapter, 80, 445n8, 451n16,
455n20, 489–90n9
Shangshu (*Book of Documents*)—"Yu
Gong" chapter: on the
conception of divinely
intelligent rulers, 381, 496n3; on
the five provinces, 496n3

*Shangshu* (*Book of Documents*)—
"Zhong Hou" chapter, the division of Heaven and earth described in, 277, 504n1
Shang (Yin) dynasty (ca. 1600–1046 BCE): Three Humane Ones (*sanren* 三仁) during, 156, 472n2. *See also* Di Yi 帝乙 (Emperor Yi) (or Shang Tang 商湯 or Cheng Tang 成湯); King Djou of Shang
Shao lineage: Duke of Shao, 119, 463n6; identified as hereditary ducal and ministerial ranks of the Zhou royal house, 417
Shao Xinchen 邵信臣 (fl. 33 BCE), 199, 486n36
Shao Yan, marquis of Liyang, 216
Shen Nong 神農 (or Lieshan or Yandi): identified as one of the Three Huang, 546n24; identified as the Red Emperor (Kui Wei), 384; as one of the Five Emperors, 523n15; as one of the Three August Ones, 381–82, 492n1, 526n1; in the "Xici" 繫辭 "Great Appendix" of the *Yijing* on the ages of, 488n1; Zhu identified as his son, 383, 528n20
Shen Wuwei (or Shen Zhou), 403, 536n52
Shi Kuang, a diviner in the *Zuozhuan*, 297, 408, 509n2, 539n93
Shi Wei 士蔿 (or Ziyu 子輿): as the ancestor of the Fan/Shi lineage, 537n71; Pengzu lineages of the

Shiwei, destroyed by the Shang, 401; Xi Shuzi identified as his father, 404–5
Shi Wey, 404, 405, 537n68
*Shiji. See* Sima Qian—*Shiji*
*Shijing. See* Book of Odes (*Shijing*)
Shu Qi (or Qi, worthy of the Shang dynasty), 39, 460n23, 519n52
Shu Xiang (or Yangshe Xi 羊舌肸, fl. ca. 551 BCE), 54, 417, 445n10, 449n15
Shu state: Qiang rebellions in, 243
*Shujing. See Shangshu* (*Book of Documents*, or *Shujing*)
Shun. *See* Yao and Shun
Si clan: the clan name Si conferred on Yu, 396; lineages of, 389; Si of Yu, 388, 531n52, 531n55; Yao's conferral of the clan name Si on Yu, 396
Sima Qian—*Shiji*: on arranging one's one death, 333, 517n13; biography of Han Xin, 474n19, 502n6; on Bo Yi and Shu Qi, 39, 444–45n2; on calculations of the movements of the sun and moon, 382, 527n14; on Emperor Wen's preference for Daoist thought, 490n10; on the five categories of familial affection, 390, 532n64; on Heaven's organizing principle, 292, 508n14; on his ancestry, 401, 535n34; on Kang Shu (ca. 309 BCE), 43, 446n18; on the ode "Cai Fan" ("Crying Deer") (Mao no. 161), 477n15; on Qin

laws against disparagement and calumny, 114, 463n25; robbers compared to dogs by Shusun Tong, 247, 498n23; on the royal family of Hann, 540n99; on the seizure of King Wen of Zhou, 53, 449n13; Three Excellencies identified, 39, 442n2; on the Tian lineage, 538n82; on Wei Yan (or Shang Yang), 43, 446n18; on Yu Rang (Yuzi) and Hou Ying (Master Hou), 333, 334, 516n11; on Zhang Cang, 414, 516n130; on Zhang Chou, 414, 542n129; on Zhang Er (d. 202), 334, 414, 516n119, 542n130; on Zhang Tang, 414–15, 542n132; on Zhang Xiangru (Marquis of Dongyang), 414, 542n131; on Zhang Yi, 414, 542n129; on Zhang Yi (ca. 309 BCE), 43, 414, 446n18, 542n129; on Zhou Zhang's attack on the state of Xi, 62, 450n6; on Zhuan Zhu and Jing Ke, 333, 412, 516n11, 516n12

Six Bonds (and Three Major Relationships), 325, 430, 547n42

Song state (11th cent.–221 BCE): Duke Wen of Song (r. 610–589 BCE), 142, 488n27; Duke Xiong identified as one of the Five Hegemons of the Spring and Autumn period, 477n21; Hua Yuan 華元, 106, 142, 227, 461n6, 468n27, 492n6; Lord Xiang of Song, 257; Yue Lü, 142, 488n27;

Yu Shi 魚氏 (or Yu Fu 魚府 or Yu Fu 魚府), 106, 461n6; Zhang Bai (or Zhang Gai 張匃), 414, 542n126

Spring and Autumn period. *See* Zhou dynasty—Spring and Autumn period (770–479 BCE)

stones and gems: Bian He's rough-hewn gem, 6, 43, 438n7, 446n21; Huan Tui's precious jade, 443n11; jade arc possessed by the Xiahou clan, 6, 438n7; jade device and jade transept, 169, 362, 476n14; the pearl of the Marquis of Sui, 43, 446n21; studying compared with lapidary work, 6, xxvi; vermillion pearl swallowed by Hanshi (Liu Bang's mother), 384, 529n31; when cherishing a jade disc becomes a crime, 30, 442–43n4

Su Qin (380–284 BCE), 158, 403, 473n9, 537n55

Sui Ren, 382, 492n1, 546nn24–25

Sun Bin (d. 316 BCE), 53–54, 448n8

Sunzi, 234, 237, 238, 494n9; advice to a ruler from "Adapting to the Nine Contingencies," 255, 500n2; quote on the force of attackers and defenders from the bamboo slip version of *Sunzi bingfa*, 245, 497n16; Sun Bin (d. 316 BCE) as his alleged descendant, 448n8

Tai Hao. *See* Fu Xi 伏羲 (Tamer of Beasts)
Tai Ren (consort of Wang Ji), 383, 399, 528n22
Tang. *See* Di Yi 帝乙 (Emperor Yi) (or Shang Tang 商湯 or Cheng Tang 成湯)
Tangxi: as the lineage name of King Fugai, 413, 541n117; as a name for Xigu in Xiping, Runan, 417
Three August Ones: All-Under-Heaven brought to completion by, 225, 381; as exemplars for rulers, 223, 228, 426; identification of, 381–82, 492n1, 526n1, 546n24
Three Eras: the Xia, Shang, and Zhou dynasties identified as, 533n5, 535n32
Three Excellencies (*sangong* 三公): examination and degradation of, 192, 482–83n11; harmonizing yin and yang as their comprehensive responsibility, 74; identification of, 39; identified as *taiwei*, *situ*, and *sikong*, 477n26; identified as the highest officials of the imperial government, 452n7; selection from members of the Liu lineage, 191, 481n1
Three Kings: bringing peace as a priority for, 223, 426; as exemplars for rulers, 228, 365; identifications of, 493n15, 523n15, 546n24; laws and prohibitions clarified, 225, 365; personal appellations during the era of, 396–97
Tian Chang (c. 481 BCE, aka Chen Changzi and Chen Heng), 65, 227, 451n15, 492n7
Tian Fen 田蚡 (or Wu An, d. 131 BCE), 332, 333, 515n7, 515n16
Tian Jingzhong 田敬仲 (750–? BCE): Chen Wan 陳完 as his posthumous name, 538n84; lineage of, 407; milfoil divination for, 279, 506n13
Tian Pengzu, marquis of Zhouyang, 216, 490n12

Wang Cheng 王成 (?–67 BCE), 199, 486n36
Wang Chong. *See Lunheng* of Wang Chong
Wang clan: Empress Dowager Wang (Wang Zhengjun), 124, 125, 465–66n24. *See also* Wang Mang 王莽
Wang Fu 王符 (ca. 85–162 CE): biography in the *Hou Hanshu*, xii–xiii; birth in Linjing in Anding commandery, xi–xii; friendship with Cui Yuan (ca. 77–142 CE), 433n1, xii, xiii; friendship with Dou Zhang 竇章 (d. ca. 144 CE), 433n1, 435n27, xii, xiii; friendship with Ma Rong 馬融 (ca. 89–166 CE), 433n1, 435n27, xii, xiii;

friendship with Zhang Heng 張衡 (ca. 78–139 CE), 433n1, xii, xiii; social class of, xvii
Wang Fu 王符 (ca. 85–162 CE)—*Qianfulun* (QFL)—content and organization of: ordering of chapters in, xxi; six broad topics of, xvi–xvii
Wang Fu 王符 (ca. 85–162 CE)—*Qianfulun* (QFL)—editions: notes about the current translation, xxix; textual history of, xxviii–xxix, 437n38; Zhang Jue's edition, xxviii. *See also* Wang Jipei 汪繼培 (b. 1775)—*Qianfulun jian*
Wang Fu 王符 (ca. 85–162 CE)—*Qianfulun* (QFL)—literary style: alternation between semantically patterned prose and contemporary style, xxii, 436n31; essay format of, xvii; four-character phrases, xxii, xxvi; parallel prose, xxii–xxv, xxix
Wang Fu 王符 (ca. 85–162 CE)—*Qianfulun* (QFL)—unusual terms: "dagger-axe and buckler" as synonyms for "spear and shield," 317, 512–12n3
Wang Jia 王嘉 (d. 2 BCE, or Tian An), 353, 407, 521n12, 538n82
Wang Jipei 汪繼培 (b. 1775)—*Qianfulun jian*: notes and emendations, 470n9; Peng Duo's additional notes and emendations (1985), xxviii

Wang Mang 王莽: death of, xiv; as a descendant of Tian An, 407; as prime minister under Grand Empress Dowager Wang, 125, 466n24; provisional power of, 356
Wang Mang 王莽 —Xin "dynasty" (7–25 CE): Guangwu's overthrowing of and punishment of, 98; opposition to him by Zhai Yi and Liu Chong, 98, 459n17; usurpation of the Han throne, 98, 150, 466n24, 470n13, xiv
Wang Shaolan 王紹蘭 (1760–1835), 544n9
Wang Zhang (d. 24 CE), 54, 353, 449n15, 521n12
Warring States period. *See* Zhou dynasty—Warring States period (479–221 BCE)
Wei lineage: ducal family of, 409–10; identified as part of the Bi lineage of the Ji clan, 412–13; Wei Ke, 412, 540n110
Wei state (403–225 BCE): defeat by the Qi (322 BCE), 246, 498n18; defeat by the Qin (322 BCE), 246, 498n18; identified as one of the six states of the Warring States period, 477n21; as one of the seven kingdoms, 397, 533n9; Qiang rebellions in, 243; Wuji identified as the younger son of King Zhao of Wei (r. 295–277 BCE), 516n11; Wu Qi as an important military

Wei state (403–225 BCE) (*continued*)
strategist of, 234, 494n9; Zhang
Yi (ca. 309), 414, 542n129
Weizi 微子, 391, 472n2, 532n68
Western Zhou. *See* Zhou
dynasty—Western Zhou
(1046–771 BCE)
Wey state: as one of the seven
kingdoms, 397, 533n9; princely
men of, 156
White Emperor, Wenming of
Rong (Xiahou as his reign
name): as Yao's supervisor of
works, 386–87, 530n43
Wu state (12th century–473 BCE):
defeat by the state of Yue led by
Fan Li, 259, 501n19; founding by
Wu Taibo, 413, 541n115; Fugai
(or Tangxi), 413, 541n117; Helü
(r. 514–496), 413, 541n117; King
Fuchai (495–477 BCD), 472n8;
Zhongyong as his successor,
413, 541n115
Wu lineage, 402, 407
Wu Ding (r.?–1189 BCE): as the
first ruler of the Shang dynasty,
512n14, 532n65; Fu Yue as his
worthy, 39, 311, 390–91
Wu Han (d. 44 CE), 161, 186,
474n20, 480n31
Wu Taibo, 413, 541n114
Wugeng and Lufu, 319, 513nn9–10
Wulu 五鹿, 397, 533n7

Xi and He, 203, 204, 205, 486n1,
487n7

Xi Rui (or Ji Rui, d. ca. 636 BCE, a
prince of Jin), 410, 539n94
Xi Wan, 52, 67, 448n6
Xi state, Zhou Zhang's attack on,
62, 450n6
Xia dynasty (c. 2070–c. 1600 BCE):
Archer Yi, 387–88, 530nn48–49;
Dong clan lineages destroyed
by, 401; Jie as the last ruler of,
388, 469nn4–5; the mirror of
Yin found in the sovereigns of,
84; Qi (Yu's son) as ruler of, 387,
530n45; Shao Kang as a ruler of,
387, 388, 531n54; Yu's sons Tai
Kang and Zhong Kang. *See also*
Three Eras; Yu 禹 (founder of
the Xia dynasty)
Xiahou clan: jade arc possessed by,
6, 438n7; as a lineage of the Si
clan, 389
Xian lineage, 402, 406, 407, 538n76
Xiao He (supporter of Liu Bang),
161, 416, 474n19
*Xiaojing* (*Classic of Filial Piety*),
290, 508n2; "San Cai" 三才
(chapter 1) on exhibiting virtue
and righteousness, 217, 490n18
Xie (离, or 禼, 契): identified as
Gao Xin's son, 482n5; identified
as Shun's minister, 96, 191, 374,
427, 458–59n8, 482n5, 525n16
*Xinxu*, on King Gong of Chu,
471n19
*Xunzi*, 498n7; convention of
opening a book with an essay
on study followed by, 436n29;

on "elicitations" and "beckonings" in the "Quan Xue" 勸學 chapter of, 277, 504–5n2; on King Min, 451n15; the phrase "eminent scholar-officials" 列士/烈士 lieshi in, 19, 441n6; "Wangzhi" on the nobility of humans, 437n1; "Yi Bing," 322, 514n22, 524n16

Yan Hui (Yan, Yanzi 晏子, or Yan Hui, b. ca. 506 BCE), 32–33, 42, 151, 157, 260, 328, 344, 471n21, 472n5, 502n20, 515n4, 520n52

Yan Le: identified as Zhao Gao's son-in-law, 450n7; ordered by Zhao Gao to kill Ershi Huang Di, 65

Yan Shigu, 452n5, 487n3

Yan state (11th century–222 BCE): clans of, 415; identified as one of the six states of the Warring States period, 477n21; Ji Jie 騎刦 as general of, 245, 497n15; King Zhao of Yan (r. 311–279 BCE), 161, 474n22; as one of the seven kingdoms, 397, 533n9; Yue Yi 樂毅 (third century BCE) as an advisor to the lord of, 246, 497n11

Yang Xiong 揚雄 (53 BCE–18 CE), xix; Huan Tan's comments on the *Dao De Jing* in his biography, 441n12

*Yantielun* of Huan Kuan: on enlightened rulers that are all-sheltering and universally loving, 243, 496n1; Han *lun* represented by, 434n14

Yao and Shun, 84; enlightened rule of, 61, 111; identified as two of the Five Thearchs, 546n24; King Wu's efforts to employ descendants of, 406, 538n75; mutual opposition of, in *Hanfeizi*, 317, 512n3; their success associated with the positional power of order, 344; tranquility brought to their age, 80; as two of the Five Emperors, 523n15; in the "Xici" 繫辭 "Great Appendix" of the *Yijing* on the ages of, 488n1

Yao and Shun—Shun: on accepting criticism from advisors, 66; banishment of, 49; birth of, 385; Bo Yi as his minister, 191, 482n5; Duke Hu (Gui Man) as his descendant, 406, 538n75; Gao Yao as his minister, 96, 191, 241, 374, 403, 427, 459n8, 482n5, 525n16; jade device and jade transept of, 169, 362, 476n14; Ji Hou as his teacher, 5; Long charged with alarming the people, 214–15, 489n4; sagacity and virtue of, 111; Xie as his minister, 96, 191, 241, 374, 403, 427, 459n8, 482n5, 525n16; Zhu of Dan contrasted with him, in the *Shangshu*, 41, 445n8

Yao and Shun—Yao (or Yi Yao, r. traditionally ca. 235–225 BCE): conferral of clan names by, 395–96; elevation of the descendants of Zhong and Li by, 400; Gao Yao as Shun's minister, 278; Hou Ji "Lord Millet" as his minister, 96, 459n8; King Wu's enfeoffment of his descendants, 384; lineages of his descendants, 405; Wenming of Rong as his supervisor of works, 386–87, 530n43; Wu Cheng as his teacher, 5; Xu You as a recluse during his reign, 333, 335, 517n15, 517n20. *See also* Yao and Shun

Yellow Emperor (Huang Di 黃帝): age of in the "Xici" 繫辭 "Great Appendix" of the *Yijing*, 488n1; appropriate clothing devised by, 385, 530n35; Feng Hou as his teacher, 5; his twenty-five sons divided into twelve lineages, 399; identified as one of the Five Thearchs, 546n24; identified as one of the three August Ones, 526n1; as one of the Five Emperors, 523n15; Xian Chi 咸池 music created by, 385, 530n34

Yi Yin, 5, 269, 345, 520n54

*Yijing* (*Book of Changes*): "Da Xu," on how superior persons enhance their virtue, 6, 438n6; the "Great Preface," on Fu Xi, 382; on humaneness and righteousness, 322, 514n18; "Shall I perish? Shall I perish?," 85, 456n9; "Shuo Guo," 321–22; Wenyan ("Words Explained"), 227, 492n10

*Yijing*—hexagrams and trigrams: hexagram 1 (Qian 乾), 35, 179, 395, 438n12, 444n21, 445n7, 456–57n16, 479n16, 522n6, 532n6; hexagram 4 (Meng 蒙), 257, 500n9; hexagram 9 (Xiaoxu 小畜), on intimidating the unruly and making manifest civil virtues, 257, 501n12; hexagram 11 (Tai 泰), 458n7, 476n13; hexagram 12 (Pi 否), 458n7; hexagram 13 (Tong ren 同人), 418, 543n157; hexagram 15 (Qian 謙), 34, 444n20; hexagram 18 (Gu 蠱), on moving people to cultivate virtue, 250, 499n34; hexagram 20 (Guan 觀), 188, 272, 481n42, 503n26; hexagram 21 ("Biting Together" 噬嗑), 199, 486n35; hexagram 26 (Da xu 大畜), 418, 543n157; hexagram 27 (Yi 頤), 171, 477n29; hexagram 28 (Da Guo 大過), on standing alone without regret, 341, 519n35; hexagram 29 (28 坎), on keeping one's mouth shut, 18, 449n18; hexagram 32 (Heng 恆), on those who are "inconsistent in their virtue," 342, 519n37; hexagram 37 (Jia ren 家人), 467n11; hexagram 47 (Kun 困), 35, 395, 445n7, 458n1, 532n1; hexagram 48 (Jing 井), 323, 514n25, 354, 521n15; hexagram 51 ("Quake" 震), 197, 485n28; hexagram 53 (Kuai 夬), 544n12; hexagram 58 (Dui 兌), 547n44; hexagram 60 ("Control" 節), on regulations that bring about order, 133, 466n5; hexagram 61 (Zhongfu 中孚), on a calling crane in the shadows, 354, 521n13; trigram "Xun," 297, 429, 547n34

Yijing—"Xici" 繫辭 "Great Appendix": on the petty person, 149, 469n7; on administering the nation's wealth, 423, 545n15; on affairs (*fang* 方) arranged according to kind, 99, 460n21; on the ages of Fu Xi, Shen Nong, Huang Di, Yao, and Shu, 488n1; on assisting the myriad people, 425, 545n19; on Bao Xi's (Fu Xi's) devising of the eight trigrams, 298, 509nn4–5; on the burial of the dead, 138, 468n20; on consulting the people and the spirits, 165, 475n2; the counsel of the common people, 88, 457n21; on Fu Xi's creation of the eight trigrams, 381, 527n11; on hexagrams Qian and Kun, 445n7; on how to obtain Heaven's assistance and good fortune, 294, 509n18; on matters with regular tendencies gathering according to kind, 186, 480n32; on officers who have a single talent, 161, 474n18, 481n42; on the punishment of major and minor offences, 220, 491n23; on Shen Nong, 384, 529n28; on spiritual beings as models for sages, 428, 547n33; on the success and failure of rulers, 320–21, 513n14; on superior men consulting the spirits, 277–78, 505n5; on the virtue and responsibilities of officials, 120–21, 464n12; the virtue of trigrams described as squarely exact and wise, 277, 505n4; on why the sage is visible in his benevolence, 357, 522n19

Yijing—"Xicizhuan": on fear caused by the hexagrams, 313, 512n20; the phrase 變化云為 *bianhua yunwei* on changes, transformation, words, and deeds, 375, 526n19; references by Wang Fu, 347, 349, 430, 520n1, 520n3, 547n47; *yinyun* 絪縕 used to designate the comingling of Heaven and earth, 361, 522n3

Yili 儀禮 ("Etiquette and Rites"), "Great wealth injures virtue; money obstructs the Rites," 142, 468n25

yin and yang: association with
personal names and style names
before the Five Phases, 280–81;
disordering of, 267; the Five
Phases and the Eight Trigrams
generated by, 295, 429;
harmonious qi as the blending
of, 283, 361, 372, 525n11;
harmonizing of, 73, 93, 95–96,
169; reversing of the functions
of, 309; as the Way of Heaven,
321, 361; yin associated with
turbid qi, and yang associated
with clear qi, 361, 522n2
Yin dynasty. *See* Shang (Yin)
dynasty (ca. 1600–1046 BCE)
Yin Jifu, 191, 417
Ying Bu (d. ca. 195 BCE), a bandit
from the Juye Marsh, 97, 459n14
Yinqueshan 銀雀山 Han Tombs:
*fan* 反 days noted on bamboo
writings from, 488n16; quote
from the bamboo slip version of
*Sunzi*, 497n16
*Yi Zhoushu* 逸周書 ("Leftover
Documents of Zhou"), 509n2,
518n31, 539n93; on "vacant land,"
270
Youge lineage: Minister Mi of, 388,
530n50
Yu 禹 (founder of the Xia dynasty):
founding of the Xia dynasty
credited to, 437n3; Ji's service to,
482n5; King Wu's enfeoffment
of his descendants, 389; Mo Ru
as his teacher, 5; Shao Kang's

restoration of the traces of Yu,
388; Xie's service to, by
managing the flood, 482n5
Yu lineage, 407, 413
Yu state, 383, 529n24; birth of Shun
of Yu, 385
Yu Yue 俞樾: on the term *wangxiu*
王休, 454n8
Yuan Si (aka Yuan Ang, d. ca. 148
BCE), 64, 443n6, 451n10
Yuan Xian (courtesy name Zisi 子
思, or Yuan), 32, 42, 344,
519–20n52
Yue Xi (or Zhihan), 32, 234,
444n14, 494n6
Yue Yi 樂毅 (third century BCE):
as an advisor to the lord of
the state of Yan, 246, 497n11; Ji
Jie 騎刼 as his successor, 245,
497n15

Zeng Xi (or Zengzi), 142, 468n23
Zhai Fangjin (翟方進 fl. 28 BCE),
334, 517n116
Zhai Gong 翟公 (Honarable
Zhai), 332, 515–16n8
Zhang Chou, 414, 542n129
Zhang Heng 張衡 (ca. 78–139 CE),
433n1, xii, xiii
Zhang Hou or Xie 觧 Zhang, 414,
542n127
Zhang Jue: on the phrase *dai si si ba*
戴祀四八, 453–54n16; on the
phrase 至寡動, 欲任德
concerning Emperor Wen's
virtuous example, 490n10; Shen

Wuwei (Shen Zhou) identified as a progeny of King Wen of Chu, 536n52
Zhang Liang (d. 186 BCE), 411, 540n103
*Zhanguoce* 戰國策 (Strategies of the Warring States): on Bo Diao (Diao Bo 貂勃), 333, 516n14; Qin chapter, on speaking up and regretting it, 244, 497n6; Qin chapter, on Zheng Mengtan, 414, 542n128; Zhao chapter, on irrationally ceding land, 245, 497n10; Zhao chapter, on Zhi Guo, 414, 542n123; Zhao chapter, on Zhuo Chi/Zhuo Chui, 65, 451n15
Zhang Zhong, imperial counsellor, 416
Zhao Gao 趙高 (?–207 BCE): as the confidential advisor of Qin Shi Huang, 461n11; Ershi Huang Di gifted with a deer saying it was a horse, 109, 462nn14–15; murdering of Ershi Huang Di, 65, 109; as the prime minister of Ershi Huang Di, 62, 64–66, 97, 109, 459n11; Yan Le identified as his son-in-law, 450n7
Zhao state (403–222 BCE): identified as one of the six states of the Warring States period, 477n21; King Wu Ling of, 404, 492n8; Lian Po (fl. 283 BCE), 332, 515n8; Li Dui (or Lord Fengyang), 227, 300, 492n8; as one of the seven kingdoms, 397, 533n9; Qiang rebellions in, 243; Shangdang ceded to, 413, 541n118

Zhao Su (fl. ca. 661 BCE), 404, 412, 537n63

Zheng state: Duke Mu of Zheng (r. 627–606 BCE), 413, 541n114; Zheng Gongshu (or Gongshu Duan 恭叔段), 413, 541n113; Zichan as a chief minister (at the end of the fifth century BCE), 457

Zhonghang lineage: Zhi Guo as a former member of, 414, 542n123; Zhonghang identified as an "office name," 396

Zhong lineage, 409; Zhong as courtesy name of the lord of Kuai, 402, 536n43

Zhong Shanfu (posthumous name Mu Zhong; clan name Fan): 192, 415, 460–61n4

Zhongxiong and the Zhongxiong lineage, 383, 402

Zhong Zhong: in the *Book of Odes*, "Liu Yue" (Mao no. 177), 414, 542n126

Zhou Bo (f. 179 BCE), 64, 161, 474n19

Zhou dynasty—Western Zhou (1046–771 BCE): Gong Liu 公劉 (His Honor Liu), 258, 501n14; King Xiao of Zhou (r. 872 to 866 BCE), 404, 537n64; King You blamed for its fall, 446n14,

Zhou dynasty—Western Zhou (1046–771 BCE) (continued) 459n9, 526n22; quelling of revolts by the Duke of Zhou, 119, 463n5; Wu as the founder of, 148, 469n5; Zao Fu as a legendary charioteer of, 10, 403–4, 439nn20–21. See also King Li of Zhou; King Wen of Zhou; King You of Zhou; Lu state (1042–249 BCE); Qi state (1046–221 BCE); Three Eras; Wu state

Zhou dynasty—Spring and Autumn period (770–479 BCE): the partitition of Jin marking the end of it, 540n99; system of five hegemons (ba 霸), 124, 465n20

Zhou dynasty—Warring States period (479–221 BCE): maternal relatives relied on during, 88–89; "Vertical Alliance" of states of advocated by Su Qin, 473n9; Zhang Yi (ca. 309 BCE). See also Chu state (1030–223 BCE); Han state (403–230 BCE); Qi state (1046–221 BCE); Wei state (403–225 BCE); Yan state (11th century–222 BCE); Zhao state (403–222 BCE)

Zhou lineage: identified as hereditary ducal and ministerial ranks of the Zhou royal house, 417; Mencius on "arrangement of dignities and emoluments" [班爵祿 banjue lu] determined by the House of Zhou, 474–75n1; ritual regulations, 166, 475n6; the Xi lineage division includes the Zhou lineage and the Qi lineage. See also Duke of Zhou

Zhuangzi, 489n7; "Waiwu," on rulers wishing their ministers to be faithful, 352, 521n11

Zhuan Xu (the Black Emperor): Gao Yang as his personal name, Gong Gong as his reign name, 389; Gong Gong (legendary criminal) distinguished from, 531n60; Lao Peng as his teacher, 5, 437n3, 531–32n61; as one of the Five Thearchs, 492n2, 546n24

Zi clan lineages, 391, 407; Yao's conferral of the clan name Zi on Xie, 396

Zichan, 89, 291, 457n24, 458n26

Zihan (of Yue Xi), 32, 234, 444n14, 494n6

Zizhi, 158, 473n10

Zou Yan (ca. 206–129 BCE), 333, 516n15

Zou Yang (ca. 168 BCE), 333, 460n23, 516n15

Zouyanshu 奏讞書, 491n20

Zuo Qiuming (the Scribe of Lu). See Zuozhuan (or Zuo Tradition) of Zuo Qiuming

Zuozhuan (or Zuo Tradition) of Zuo Qiuming: on Archer Yi, 387, 388, 530n46, 530n49; on the concept of the branch lineage, 477n22; on dragon officials named for dragons, 382, 527n10; on the Duke of Yu and his younger brother, 442–43n4; on the "Eight Exemplars," 383, 528n16; on "establishing achievements," 419, 544n1; examples of being enlightened in the Way of Heaven and man, 292, 508n13; on the five types of pheasants, 386, 530n39; on Gongsun Shu's worship of wealth, 31, 443n11; Gong Zhiqi's comment that if the lips perish the teeth grow cold, 247, 298n22; on harmonious sounds that enter the ear, 364, 523n14; on harsh and lenient governance, 198–99, 486nn32–33; on heaven withdrawing the ability of the ruler to see clearly, 121, 464n13; on Huan Tui, 443n11; its status secured during the reign of Emperor Ping, 544n4; on *jie* 節 a form of official credential, 455n3; on the Jí lineage associated with, 399, 535n25; on Jin grandee Sun Boyan, 414, 542nn124–25; on Lady Min, 387, 530n47; Lord Xian, Li Ji, and Niu, 506n14; physiognomical examinations in, 300, 510nn11–13, xxv; on posts associated with the Five Phases, 386, 530n41; on prosperous domains that listen to the people and those about to perish that heed spirits, 291, 508n4; Scribe Su in, 279, 406n12; on service to Heaven by emperors and rulers, 320, 513n11, 513n13; Shi Kuang, a diviner in, 297, 408, 509n2, 539n93; the term "manager of beasts" in, 450n21; "The sages rise by them, the disorderly fall by them," 257, 501n13; "The spirits will not savor his sacrifices, and the people will not join in his projects.," 291, 508n6; on transformation virtue, 227, 492n11; on unclear distinctions between good and evil, 72, 452n2; Wang Fu's aim to transmit the teachings of, 1, 419, xvii, xxv; Wei Ke mentioned in, 540n110; when "cherishing a jade disc becomes his crime," 30, 442–43n4; on when the majority trust in good luck, 186, 480n34; on why people should not be overly fearful, 292, 508n15; Yan Pinzhong's warning about prayers and curses, 291, 508n12; on Zang He, 89, 477n24; on Zhang Gai 張匄 (Zhang Bai), 414, 542n126; on Zhang Hou, 414, 542n127; on Zhang Lao, 414, 542n127; on Zhao Ying's sacrifices to Heaven, 291, 508n5; on Zhou ritual regulations, 166, 475n6; Zhuan Xu and Gong Gong (legendary criminal) distinguished from each other, 531n60; Zichan quoted in, 89, 477n24

GPSR Authorized Representative: Easy Access System Europe, Mustamäe tee
50, 10621 Tallinn, Estonia, gpsr.requests@easproject.com

www.ingramcontent.com/pod-product-compliance
Lightning Source LLC
Chambersburg PA
CBHW022023290426
44109CB00014B/727